M000223082

The Politics of Secularism in International Relations

Princeton Studies in International History and Politics

SERIES EDITORS

Thomas Christiensen
G. John Ikenberry
Marc Trachtenberg

RECENT TITLES

The Politics of Secularism in International Relations by Elizabeth Shakman Hurd

Social States: China International Institutions by Alastair Iain Johnston

Appeasing Bankers by Jonathan Krishner

Unanswered Threats: Political Constraints on the Balance of Power
by Randall L. Schweller

Producing Security: Multinational Corporations, Globalization,
and the Changing Calculus of Conflict
by Stephen G. Brooks

Driving the Soviets up the Wall: Soviet-East German Relations, 1953–1961
by Hope M. Harrison

Legitimacy and Power Politics: The American and French Revolutions
in International Political Culture
by Mlada Bukovansky

Rhetoric and Reality in Air Warfare: The Evolution of British and
American Ideas about Strategic Bombing, 1914–1945
by Tami Davis Biddle

Revolutions in Sovereignty: How Ideas Shaped Modern International Relations
by Daniel Philpott

After Victory: Institutions, Strategic Restraint, and the Rebuilding of
Order after Major Wars
by G. John Ikenberry

Stay the Hand of Vengeance: The Politics of War Crimes Tribunals
by Gary Jonathan Bass

War and Punishment: The Causes of War Termination and the First World War
by H. E. Goemans

In the Shadow of the Garrison State: America's Anti-Statism and
Its Cold War Grand Strategy
by Aaron L. Friedberg

States and Power in Africa: Comparative Lessons in Authority and Control
by Jeffrey Herbst

The Politics of Secularism in International Relations

Elizabeth Shakman Hurd

PRINCETON UNIVERSITY PRESS

PRINCETON AND OXFORD

Copyright © 2008 by Princeton University Press

Published by Princeton University Press, 41 William Street, Princeton, New Jersey 08540
In the United Kingdom: Princeton University Press, 3 Market Place,
Woodstock, Oxfordshire OX20 1SY

All Rights Reserved

Library of Congress Cataloging-in-Publication Data

Hurd, Elizabeth Shakman, 1970–
the politics of secularism in international relations / Elizabeth Shakman Hurd.
p.   cm. — (Princeton studies in international history and politics)
Includes bibliographical references and index.
ISBN-13: 978-0-691-13007-1 (hardcover : alk. paper)
ISBN-13 (pbk.): 978-0-691-13466-6 (paperback : alk. paper)
1. World politics. 2. Secularism. 3. Religion and politics.
4. Europe—Foreign relations. 5. Middle East—Foreign relations.
6. United States-Foreign relations. I. Title.
D32.H87 2008
327.101 — dc22
2007004038

British Library Cataloging-in-Publication Data is available

This book has been composed in Electra

Printed on acid-free paper. ∞

press.princeton.edu

Printed in the United States of America

10 9 8 7 6 5 4 3

For my parents, Stephen and Susan Shakman

The followers of Qutb speak . . . of enormous human
problems, and they urge one another to death and
murder. But the enemies of these people speak of
what? The political leaders speak of United Nations
resolutions, of unilateralism, of multilateralism, of
weapons inspectors, of coercion and noncoercion. This
is no answer to the terrorists. . . . Who will speak of the
sacred and the secular, of the physical world and the
spiritual world? . . . Philosophers and religious leaders
will have to do this on their own. Are they doing so?
Armies are in motion, but are the philosophers and
religious leaders, the liberal thinkers, likewise in motion?
　　　—Paul Berman, "The Philosopher of Islamic Terror"

The genuine refutation of orthodoxy would require
the proof that the world and human life are perfectly
intelligible without the assumption of a mysterious
God. . . . But to grant that revelation is possible
means to grant that the philosophic account and the
philosophic way of life are not necessarily, not evi-
dently, the true account and the right way of life;
philosophy, the quest for evident and necessary
knowledge, rests itself on an unevident decision . . . ,
just as faith. Hence the antagonism between Spinoza
and Judaism, between belief and unbelief, is ultimately
not theoretical, but moral.
　　　—Leo Strauss, *Liberalism, Ancient and Modern*

Contents

Acknowledgments

MANY PEOPLE, EXPERIENCES, and coincidences have conspired to result in this book. It certainly would not exist were it not for the mind-opening experience of graduate study at Johns Hopkins in the late 1990s. I will always appreciate the good fortune that made it possible for me to work with William Connolly. His formidable intellect, sense of place and purpose in his field and in the world, and his steady and consistent support for this project are deeply appreciated. I am also grateful to Siba Grovogui, first and foremost for his intellectual contributions to my thinking and writing, but also for his sense of comradeship and engaging sense of humor. Earlier, during my time at Yale between 1994 and 1996, Khaled Abou El Fadl, Abbas Amanat, and Gaddis Smith sparked my interest in Islamic law, religion and politics in the Middle East, and U.S. foreign policy, respectively, and I thank them for their excellent courses. I am also deeply grateful to my professor and undergraduate advisor at Wesleyan, Nancy Gallagher, and to another great mentor, Irene Koek at the U.S. Agency for International Development, for encouraging me to pursue the Ph.D.

I owe as much to my current colleagues at Northwestern University, who generously supported my research from start to finish. Both the Political Science Department and the administration at Northwestern ensured that I had the time and energy available to complete this project, and I am appreciative of their support. Among my colleagues, I thank Bonnie Honig for her close reading of my work and her insightful critical contributions at several different stages. For their excellent comments and criticism I am also indebted to my colleagues in international relations: Karen Alter, Risa Brooks, Brian Hanson, Ian Hurd, Michael Loriaux, and Hendrik Spruyt. Each has taken the time to read various drafts and engage with different parts of this project over the past five years.

The Institute for Advanced Studies in Culture (formerly the Center for Religion and Democracy) at the University of Virginia provided me with a postdoctoral fellowship in 2004–5 that made it possible to finish this book. Joseph Davis and Slavica Jakelic offered a particularly warm welcome to Charlottesville at the Postdoctoral Fellows Colloquium in March 2005. I am also grateful to the organizers of the 2003/4 European-American Young Scholars' Institutes Program, José Casanova and Hans Joas, for offering me a fellowship to attend their Summer Institute on Secularization and Religion. My time in Erfurt in the summer of 2003 with scholars working on the vexing questions posed by the secular and the religious deeply informed my thinking on this subject. I want to acknowledge the Institute for Turkish Studies for its support for this project in its early stages with a Dissertation Writing Grant, and the Gifts and Grants Committee of the Alumnae of Northwestern University and the Graduate School at Northwestern for their support in the later stages.

For their time and thought-provoking suggestions at different stages of the project I thank Peter Berger, Linell Cady, José Casanova, Jocelyne Cesari, Roxanne Euben, Haldun Gülalp, Waleed Hazbun, Friedrich Kratochwil, Yosef Lapid, Charles Lipson, Cecelia Lynch, Michael Shapiro, Naoko Shibusawa, Paul Silverstein, and two anonymous reviewers for Princeton University Press. Charles Taylor invited me to sit in on his graduate seminar on secularization at Northwestern in the spring of 2003; it could not have come at a better time. Portions of this book have been presented at the Center for Middle East Studies at the University of Chicago, the Center for the Study of Islam and Democracy, the School of Advanced International Studies at Johns Hopkins, the University of Utah, and ETH Zurich. I appreciate the comments and suggestions received during these meetings. I also want to acknowledge four writers who inspired this book in different ways: Orhan Pamuk (*The White Castle, Snow*), Willa Cather (*Death Comes for the Archbishop*), José Saramago (*The History of the Siege of Lisbon*), and Leila Ahmed (*A Border Passage*). Finally, it has been a pleasure to work with Chuck Myers and the excellent editorial and production staff at Princeton University Press, and I am grateful to have had the opportunity to do so. Thanks to Christopher Swarat and Brian MacDonald for their editorial assistance in the final stages of this project, and to Judith Wilks and Rachel Ricci for help with the translations on the cover..

An earlier version of chapter 2 appeared as "The Political Authority of Secularism in International Relations," *European Journal of International Relations* 10, no. 2 (June 2004): 235–62. Permission to reprint that material here is granted by Sage. An early version of a portion of chapter 3 appeared in "Appropriating Islam: The Islamic Other in the Consolidation of Western Modernity," *Critique: Critical Middle Eastern Studies* 12, no. 1 (Spring 2003). It is also reprinted with permission. Chapter 5 appeared as "Negotiating Europe: The Politics of Religion and the Prospects for Turkish Accession to the EU," *Review of International Studies* 32, no. 3 (July 2006). It is reprinted here with the permission of Cambridge University Press. Portions of chapter 6 appeared in "The International Politics of Secularism: U.S. Foreign Policy and the Islamic Republic of Iran," *Alternatives: Global, Local, Political* 29, no. 2 (March–May 2004). Lynne Rienner Publishers has kindly given permission to use that material here. An extended version of chapter 7 appeared as "Political Islam and Foreign Policy in Europe and the United States, " *Foreign Policy Analysis* 3, no. 4. (October 2007), and I thank Blackwell Publishing and the International Studies Association for permission to reprint the material here. Finally, chapter 8 appeared as "Theorizing Religious Resurgence," *International Politics* 44 (Fall 2007).

I especially want to thank my parents, Steve and Susan Shakman, to whom this book is dedicated, for all they have given me over the years, including the experience of growing up in a home in which religious difference was the norm. Finally, my love and affection for Ian, Alexandra, and Sophie has given life and energy to the process of writing and rewriting this book. I thank Ian for reading it from start to finish and for listening to me work through my ideas, sometimes late at night; and I thank Ally and Sophie for reminding me on a daily basis that lived practices matter just as much as abstract ideas in determining how we relate to each other ethically, politically, and, perhaps, metaphysically.

The Politics of Secularism in International Relations

CHAPTER ONE

Introduction

RELIGION IS A PROBLEM in the field of international relations at two distinct levels. First, in recent years religious fundamentalism and religious difference have emerged as crucial factors in international conflict, national security, and foreign policy. This development has come as a surprise to many scholars and practitioners. Much contemporary foreign policy, especially in the United States, is being quickly rewritten to account for this change. Second, the power of this religious resurgence in world politics does not fit into existing categories of thought in academic international relations. Conventional understandings of international relations, focused on material capabilities and strategic interaction, exclude from the start the possibility that religion could be a fundamental organizing force in the international system.

This book argues that these two problems are facets of a single underlying phenomenon: the unquestioned acceptance of the secularist division between religion and politics. Standard privatization and differentiation accounts of religion and politics need to be reexamined. Secularism needs to be analyzed as a form of political authority in its own right, and its consequences evaluated for international relations. This is the objective of this book. My central motivating question is how, why, and in what ways does secular political authority form part of the foundation of contemporary international relations theory and practice, and what are the political consequences of this authority in international relations? I argue, first, that the secularist division between religion and politics is not fixed but rather socially and historically constructed; second, that the failure to recognize this explains why students of international relations have been unable to properly recognize the power of religion in world politics; and, finally, that overcoming this problem allows a better understanding of crucial empirical puzzles in international relations, including the conflict between the United States and Iran, controversy over the enlargement of the European Union to include Turkey, the rise of political Islam, and the broader religious resurgence both in the United States and elsewhere.

This argument makes four contributions to international relations theory. First, secularism is an example of what Barnett and Duvall describe as "productive power" in international relations, defined as "the socially diffuse production of subjectivity in systems of meaning and signification."[1] Secularism is a form of productive power that "inheres in structures and discourses that are not possessed or controlled by any single actor."[2] The issue, then, is not the attitude of individual social scientists toward religion and politics (though this is also an interesting subject) but the "ideological conditions that give point and force to the theoretical apparatuses employed to describe and objectify" the secular and the religious.[3] These theoretical apparatuses are identified in this book as laicism and Judeo-Christian secularism. These traditions of secularism are collective dispositions that shape modern sensibilities, habits, and beliefs regarding the secular and the religious. Secular theory and practice are given equal footing here in accordance with MacIntyre's argument that "there ought not to be two histories, one of political and moral action and one of political and moral theorizing, because there were not two pasts, one populated only by actions, the other only by theories. Every action is the bearer and expression of more or less theory-laden beliefs and concepts; every piece of theorizing and every expression of belief is a political and moral action."[4]

Second, this book examines the connections between secularist tradition and contemporary forms of nationalism. As Anthony Marx has argued, "despite denials and formal commitments to liberal secularism, the glue of religious exclusion as a basis for domestic national unity has still not been fully abandoned."[5] Taking Marx's argument about religious exclusion and national unity as a starting point, I shift the focus from religion and toward the ways in which modern forms of secularism have been consolidated both through and against religion as bases of unity and identity in ways that are often exclusionary. Like Asad, I am interested in "how certain practices, concepts, and sensibilities have helped to organize, in different places and different times, political arrangements called secularism"[6] and how these arrangements inflect modern forms of national identification.

Third, this book challenges the separation of the domestic and international spheres by illustrating how individual states and suprastate actors construct their interests and identities. As Wæver suggests, "it seems that constructivism has for contingent reasons started out working mostly at the systemic level," and there is a need to consider the "benefits of the opposite direction."[7] In his critique of Wendt's exclusive focus on systemic-level factors, Ringmar argues that "a theory of the construction of identities and interests is radically incomplete as long as it views individuals and collective entities only from the perspective of the system."[8] Referring to the work of Lynch and Barnett, Saideman describes "the power of constructivist theorizing when domestic politics is made a central part of the story."[9] This focus on the domestic angle counters a tendency in international relations theory, identified by Hall in his study of the systemic consequences of national collective identity, to "relegate domestic-societal interaction, sources of conflict, or societal cohesiveness (such as ethnic, religious, or other domestic sources) to the status of epiphenomena."[10] Situated at the interface of domestic and international politics, this book contributes to the attempt to redress this structural and systemic bias in international relations theory by demonstrating how shared interests, identities, and understandings involving religion and politics developed at the domestic and regional levels become influential at the systemic level.[11] To paraphrase Hall, my objective is to "uncover the consequences of [secularist] collective identity . . . in the modern era within a framework that results in a useful correction to an existing body of theoretical literature."[12] In the process, I explore the cultural and normative foundations of modern international relations.

Fourth, this book presents an alternative to the assumption that religion is a private affair. This assumption is common in realist, liberal, and most constructivist international relations theory. Conventional wisdom has it that between 1517 and the Peace of Westphalia in 1648 religion mattered in European politics. Since Westphalia, however, religion has been largely privatized. The idea behind this "Westphalian presumption" is that religion had to be marginalized, privatized, or overcome by a cosmopolitan ethic to secure international order.[13] One result of this presumption is that in most accounts of international relations "religion is thus essentially peripheral, and reflection on international politics is pursued as if it concerned an autonomous space that is not fundamentally disturbed by its presence."[14] I argue that authoritative forms of secularism that dominate modern politics are themselves contingent social constructions influenced by both so-called secular and religious assumptions about ethics, metaphysics, and politics. From this perspective, not only is religion on its way back into international relations—it never really departed. The conventional understanding that religion was fully privatized in 1648 appears as another dimension of what Teschke has described as the "myth of 1648."[15] As Taylor argues, "the origin point of modern Western secularism was the Wars of Religion; or rather, the search in battle-fatigue and horror for a way out of them. The need was felt for a ground of coexistence for *Christians* of different confessional persuasions."[16] If Westphalia signaled *both* a dramatic break from the past *and* "a consolidation and codification of a new conception of political authority"[17] that was secular and also deeply Christian, then perhaps contemporary international relations is witnessing the gradual emergence of a series of post-Westphalian, postsecular conceptions of religiopolitical authority. These developments, combined with the Christian dimensions of the original Westphalian settlement, make it difficult to subsume international relations into realist and liberal frameworks that operate on the assumption that religion is irrelevant to state behavior.[18] In some ways, we are back to Europe in 1517. In other ways, we never left.

STRUCTURE OF THE BOOK

The politics of secularism has gone virtually unacknowledged in political science. The consensus surrounding secularism in the social sciences has been "such that not only did the theory remain uncontested but apparently it was not even necessary to test it, since everybody took it for granted."[19] As Keddie suggests, "questions of control and of power . . . all too rarely enter the discussions of secularism."[20] In international relations and foreign policy, the politics of secularism have been sidelined, as Brooks observes:

> Our foreign policy elites . . . go for months ignoring the force of religion; then, when confronted with something inescapably religious, such as the Iranian revolution or the Taliban, they begin talking of religious zealotry and fanaticism, which suddenly explains everything. After a few days of shaking their heads over the fanatics, they revert to their usual secular analyses. We do not yet have, and sorely need, a mode of analysis that attempts to merge the spiritual and the material.[21]

To approach secularism as a discursive tradition and form of political authority is neither to justify it nor to argue for what Mahmood describes as "some irreducible essentialism or cultural relativism."[22] It is instead "to take a necessary step toward explaining the force that a discourse commands."[23] As Chatterjee argues, "the task is to trace in their mutually conditioned historicities the specific forms that have appeared, on the one hand, in the domain defined by the hegemonic project of [secular] modernity, and on the other, in the numerous fragmented resistances to that normalizing project."[24] This also involves an attempt to forge "the link between collective identities and the institutional forms of collective action derived from those identities."[25]

This book is structured around three sets of arguments that develop and illustrate my overarching claim that the traditions of secularism described here are an important source of political authority in international relations. Chapters 2 and 3 discuss the constitution of these forms of secularist authority and their relationship to religion. While on the one hand secularism emerged out of and remains indebted to both the Enlightenment critique of religion and Judeo-Christian tradition (chapter 2), on the other hand it has been constituted and reproduced through opposition to particular representations of Islam (chapter 3). Chapter 4 introduces domestic Turkish and Iranian renegotiations of the secular. Chapters 5 and 6 demonstrate how secularism contributes to political outcomes in international relations between the West and the Middle East. Understanding relations between Europe, the United States, and the countries of the Middle East and North Africa requires accounting not only for the geopolitical and material circumstances of the states involved but also for the social and cultural context within which international politics unfolds. This context is shaped by the politics of secularism. Chapters 7 and 8 describe the implications of my argument for attempts to theorize political Islam and religious resurgence.

Chapters 2 and 3 introduce the history and politics of the secularist traditions described in this book, their relationship to religion, and their implications for international relations theory and practice. Chapter 2 describes the history of secularism and its relation to both the Enlightenment critique of religion and Judeo-Christian tradition. I argue that two trajectories of secularism, or two strategies for managing the relationship between religion and politics, are influential in international relations: laicism and Judeo-Christian secularism. The former refers to a separationist narrative in which religion is expelled from politics, and the latter to a more accommodationist narrative in which Judeo-Christian tradition is the unique basis of secular democracy. These forms of secularism are discursive traditions.[26] They each defend some form of the separation of church and state but in different ways and with different justifications and different political effects. Both aspire to what Casanova refers to as the "core and central thesis of the theory of secularization": the functional differentiation of the secular and the religious spheres.[27] Laicism, however, also adopts two corollaries to this differentiation argument, advocating the privatization and, in some cases, the decline or elimination of religious belief and practice altogether.[28] These two varieties of secularism take us some distance toward understanding the assumptions about religion and politics that underlie theory and practice in international relations. They help to explain the practices and lived traditions that are associated with contemporary forms of secularism. As LeVine and Salvatore argue, "the most dynamic core of a tradition resides . . . not in codified procedures or established institutions, but rather in the anthropologically and sociologically more complex level of the 'living tradition,' which overlaps more institutionally grounded levels yet is nurtured by social practice."[29]

With its origins in the French term *laïcité*,[30] the objective of laicism is to create a neutral public space in which religious belief, practices, and institutions have lost their political significance, fallen below the threshold of political contestation, or been pushed into the private sphere. The mixing of religion and politics is regarded as irrational and dangerous. For modernization to take hold, religion must be separated from politics.[31] In order to democratize, it is essential to secularize. Either a country is prodemocracy, pro-Western, and secular, or it is religious, tribal, and theocratic. Laicism adopts and expresses a pretense of neutrality regarding the assumption that a fixed and final separation between religion and politics is both possible and desirable. This makes it difficult for those who have been shaped by and draw upon this tradition to see the limitations of their own conceptions of religion and politics. In other words, laicism presents itself as having risen above the messy debate over religion and politics, standing over and outside the melee in a neutral space of its own creation. The politics of laicism is more complex than is suggested by this alleged resolution.

The second tradition of secularism that is influential in the international relations literature emphasizes the role of Christianity, and more recently Judeo-Christianity, as the foundation for secular public order and democratic political institutions. Unlike laicism, what I call Judeo-Christian secularism does not attempt to expel religion, or at least Judeo-Christianity, from public life. It does not present the religious-secular divide as a clean, essentialized, and bifurcated relationship, as in laicism. This form of secularism therefore seems counterintuitive, at least at first. It corresponds only in part with Berger's authoritative definition of secularization as "the process by which sectors of society and culture are removed from the domination of religious institutions and symbols."[32] For in this second trajectory of secularism, Euro-American secular public life is securely grounded in a larger Christian, and later Judeo-Christian, civilization. This is a Tocquevillian approach to secularism in which "Christianity does not need to be invoked that often because it is already inscribed in the prediscursive dispositions and cultural instincts of the civilization."[33] Judeo-Christian dispositions and cultural instincts are perceived to have culminated in and contributed to the unique Western achievement of the separation of church and state. In this tradition, "separation of church and state functions to soften sectarian divisions between Christian sects while retaining the civilizational hegemony of Christianity in a larger sense."[34] Although sectors of Western society and culture have been partially removed from the domination of religious institutions and symbols à la Berger, political order in the West remains firmly grounded in a common set of core values with their roots in Latin Christendom.

Secularism, in its Judeo-Christian trajectory, is one of these core values. It is part of a Christian, later Judeo-Christian, theopolitical inheritance that constitutes the "common ground" upon which Western democracy rests. The West, Samuel Huntington argues, displays a unique dualism between God and Caesar, church and state that is essential for democracy to flourish. Secular government must be firmly embedded in the Judeo-Christian faith for democracy to survive. The West's religious heritage bolsters democracy by offering a set of common assumptions within which politics can be conducted. Religious tradition is a source of political cohesion and moral sustenance; citizens who share religious sensibilities and enter into democratic deliberation will produce something approaching a moral consensus.[35] The "West" is defined by its secular *and* Judeo-Christian political culture and tradition. They go together. This is Judeo-Christian secularism.

The tradition of Judeo-Christian secularism is mobilized in many contexts, but perhaps its most significant effect in international relations is to fuel the conviction that non-Western civilizations and in particular Islamic civilization lack the tools to differentiate between religion and politics. In this view secularism is seen as a unique Western achievement. In international relations, the presumption that secular order is uniquely suited to a particular geographical region (the West) and a particular set of people (Europeans and their descendants) reinforces religious divisions and encourages their adoption as the basis of exclusive forms of political community.

Chapter 3 continues the analysis of the history and politics of secularism but shifts the focus to the relation between secularism and representations of Islam. If the traditions of secularism identified in chapter 2 are deeply intertwined with both Enlightenment values and Judeo-Christianity, they have a different yet equally important relationship to Islam. More than any other single religious or political tradition, Islam represents the "nonsecular" in European and American political discourse. This is because secularist traditions, and the European and American national identities and practices with which they are affiliated and in which they are embedded, have been constructed through opposition to Islam. A laicist and Judeo-Christian secular West has been consolidated in part through opposition to representations of an antimodern, anti-Christian, and theocratic Islamic Middle East. Opposition to the concept of Islam is built into secular political authority and embedded within the national identities with which it is associated and through which it is expressed. This means that negative associations of Islam not only run deep in the Euro-American secular traditions described in this book but help to constitute them. By bringing together the literature on the construction of laicism in nineteenth-century France and early American representations of Islam, I clarify how these representations of Islam contributed to the consolidation of Euro-American forms of secularism and the identification of French and American national identities as laicist and Judeo-Christian secularist, respectively.

Chapter 4 bridges the conceptual and historical arguments of chapters 2 and 3 with the more applied arguments of chapters 5 and 6. Its primary objective is to introduce domestic Turkish and Iranian renegotiations of the secular. Woven into these historical accounts are examples of how the epistemological and evaluative stances described in the preceding chapters as laicism and Judeo-Christian secularism operate in practice to condition Western responses to religiopolitical developments in Turkey and Iran. Developments in these countries do not fall easily into categories available to Western observers for understanding religion and politics. I argue that the attempt to remake the public realm in Turkey and Iran is not a threat to the foundation of modern politics but a modern contestation of authoritative practices of secularism authorized and regulated by state authorities since the founding of the modern Turkish Republic by Atatürk in 1923 and the rise of Reza Shah in Iran in 1925. It *is* modern politics.

The historiographical accounts presented in chapter 4 are also part of a broader historical and political context that is referred to but not described in chapters 5 and 6. Chapter 4 therefore also serves as an important preface to these chapters, which focus on the political consequences of secularist authority in European and American representations of and relations with Turkey and Iran. I argue that a comprehensive understanding of relations between the West and the Middle East requires an understanding not only of material forces, hard-wired state interests, and structural constraints but also the politics of secularism. Attempts to explain relations between Europe, the United

States, and the Islamic Middle East and North Africa through recourse to fixed and objectively given state interests, the characteristics of individual leaders, bureaucratic politics, the international system, or other traditional explanatory variables are important but insufficient. I reformulate the questions brought to the analysis of these international relationships by arguing that secularist authority is a productive part of the cultural sensibilities and normative foundation of contemporary international relations that contributes in crucial ways to political outcomes in relations between states and between states and suprastate entities such as the European Union (EU).

The cases developed in chapters 5 and 6 demonstrate how the analytics developed in this book "travel," to use Price and Reus-Smit's terminology.[36] As Bukovansky suggests, "the interpretive method does not lend itself to a formal, systematic demonstration of the causal impact of culture."[37] These two chapters are what she would describe as "plausibility probes" that suggest "the way in which ideas about [secularism] shaped the political positions taken by strategic actors."[38] Chapter 5 argues that prevailing explanations of European resistance to Turkish accession that rely upon the assumption that opposition is based exclusively upon support for a "Christian Europe" miss a crucial part of the story concerning the cultural and religious basis of this resistance. Cultural and religious opposition to Turkey's accession is not only about defending the idea of a Christian Europe; the prospect of Turkish accession has stirred up a more fundamental controversy about European identity and the politics of religion within Europe itself. Turkey has turned toward a different trajectory of secularism that conforms to neither Kemalism (a Turkish version of laicism) nor the two prevailing trajectories of secularism described in this book: laicism and Judeo-Christian secularism. This new tradition of secularism threatens not only the Kemalist establishment in Turkey but European secularists as well. As a result, Turkey's potential accession to the EU has propelled the controversial ontological questions of what it means to be secular and European into the public spotlight. There is a sense of urgency in Europe that the religion-and-politics question and its relationship to an ever-evolving European identity be resolved before Turkey is admitted to the EU. The Turkish case is therefore controversial in cultural and religious terms not only because it involves the potential accession of a Muslim-majority country to an arguably, at least historically, Christian Europe, though this is important, but also and more fundamentally because it brings up long-dormant dilemmas *internal* to Europe regarding how religion and politics relate to each other. Turkey's candidacy destabilizes the European secular social imaginary.[39] It involves unfinished business in the social fabric of the core EU members, including what it means to be secular (both in Europe and in Turkey) and how religion, including but not limited to Islam, should relate to European public life.

This cultural sticking point is what the debate over Turkish accession is really about, and it is for this reason that it is culturally—in addition to economically and politically—so contentious. Even if economic and political obstacles to Turkish accession are lifted, even if Turkey is deemed to be in unambiguous conformity with the so-called Copenhagen criteria, this argument suggests that European opposition to Turkish membership will persist. This is due to nagging discord within Europe concerning how religion relates to European identity and institutions, and whether alternative trajectories of secularism such as the current Turkish one that moves *away* from European-inspired Kemalism toward a different variety of secularism can ever be considered fully European. This story is more complex than the assertion that European cultural and religiously based opposition to Turkey is due to the defense of the concept of a Christian Europe. It also explains why many European secularists have expressed misgivings about and, in some cases, opposition to Turkish accession despite their discomfort with the idea of a Christian Europe.

Chapter 6 also illustrates how collective traditions regarding religion and politics developed primarily at the domestic level become influential at the systemic level. A comprehensive understanding of American-Iranian relations requires considering not only fixed and pregiven strategic and material interests but also the cultural, historical, and social traditions and relations through which these interests take shape and are expressed. Laicism and Judeo-Christian secularism provide the conceptual apparatus and cultural backdrop through which American opposition to Iran has been consolidated and legitimized. They form the cultural and religious foundation of modern American relations with Iran. Laicism has been the prevailing secularist narrative in American discourse on Iran since the revolution of 1978–79. On the one hand, and according to this account, the revolution was unacceptable because it imported religion into public life, compromising the most basic tenet of laicism. On the other hand, and following Judeo-Christian secularist assumptions, distinctions between religious and political authority are not only historically absent from Iran, but unthinkable due to the nature of Islam itself. According to this second account, the revolution confirmed the existence of "natural" linkages between Islam and theocracy in contrast to alleged natural linkages between Christianity and democracy.

These two varieties of secularist tradition worked together to fuel powerful American condemnations of the revolution and the representation of revolutionary Iran as a threat not only to American national interests but also to the foundations of American national identity itself. From 1979 onward, to stand for a secular (laicist, Judeo-Christian, or both) and democratic United States was to oppose an Islamic (theocratic, tyrannical) Iran. The process of representing Islam specifically (the power of which is illustrated in chapter 3) and Iranians more generally as a threat helped to solidify American notions of secular democracy, freedom, and righteousness in opposition to Iranian theo-

cracy, tyranny, and falsehood. This opposition helps to explain the fervor with
which the American government and many citizens have opposed postrevolutionary Iran. This opposition is a function not only of powerful American
geopolitical interests in the Middle East; it is part of an attempt to define and
instantiate American national identity and American collective subjectivity as
secular, Judeo-Christian, and democratic.

The third and final section of the book is about the implications of my
argument for international relations theory. Many attempts to theorize
religion in international relations add a concern for religious beliefs, actors,
and institutions into the already existing literature on sovereignty, security,
global governance, conflict resolution, human rights, intercivilizational dialogue, and the role of transnational actors. I take a different approach. I investigate the extent to which secularist traditions concerning what religion is and
how it relates to politics determine the kinds of questions deemed worth asking
about religion and international politics and the kinds of answers one expects
to find.[40] Secularism is part of the cultural and normative basis of international
relations theory. The traditions of secularism described in this book are part
of the ontological and epistemological foundation of the discipline. Chapters
2 and 3 identify and critique these secularist habits, tropes, and discursive
regularities. Chapters 4, 5, and 6 illustrate their effects upon the historiography of the Middle East and relations between the United States, Europe,
Turkey, and Iran. Chapters 7 and 8 use that critique to identify new political
possibilities that are obfuscated by secularist practice, habit, and scientific
pretension.[41] By failing to conform to the categories available to international
relations theorists for understanding religion and politics, both political Islam
and religious resurgence offer an opportunity to revisit the epistemological
foundations of the discipline and to begin to articulate these possibilities.

The relationship between secularist representations of political Islam and
international relations is the subject of chapter 7. There are two principal
secularist evaluative stances on political Islam in the international relations
field, corresponding to the two trajectories of secularism described in chapter
2. Laicism represents political Islam as an unnatural infringement of religion
upon would-be secular public life in Muslim societies. It is conceived as a
threat to democratic laicist public order, and support for any public role for
Islam is seen as a throwback to premodern times. Judeo-Christian secularism
represents political Islam as a normal commingling of religion and politics
that stands in sharp distinction to the uniquely Western separation of religion
and state. Political Islam is thus a natural consequence of fixed differences
between incommensurable civilizations. Building on Euben's account of the
effects of Western rationalism upon the study of Islamic fundamentalism, I
argue that secularist accounts of political Islam "conceal their 'mechanisms
of production' within claims of objectivity resulting in images which say less
about what [political Islam] 'really is' than about the ways in which [secularist]

assumptions derived from Western history and experiences . . . produce our understandings of [it]."[42]

Both traditions of secularism described in this book lead to understandings of political Islam as the refusal to acknowledge the privileged status of the private sphere and the transgression of Western secular categories of public and private. The result is that in contemporary international relations theory and practice political Islam appears almost exclusively in a transgressive or regressive capacity. It is perceived as a threat to the privileged status of the private sphere and the first step on the road to theocracy. This transgression is often linked rhetorically to the alleged Muslim proclivity for terrorism and totalitarianism, both of which also refuse to honor the privileged status of the private sphere.[43] The result is that Muslim negotiations of public and private, sacred and secular, often appear as unnatural or even nonexistent. This also explains why political Christianity and political Judaism, which also present significant challenges to the secularist public-private distinction, are generally received more warmly and less fearfully than political Islam. This is because the forms of secularism that predominate today in Europe and the United States emerged out of Latin Christendom and remain indebted to European religious traditions. Islamic traditions, on the other hand, have a different history of negotiating this divide. Several of these diverse Islamic traditions are described in chapter 6.

To make this argument is not to deny that there are forms of Islam, such as Al-Qaeda and the Taliban, which are transgressive and even regressive by almost any standard of judgment. The point is that not *all* forms of what is categorized by secularist authority as political Islam pose a threat that can be met with either the imposition of secularization from outside or the exclusion of particular nonsecular Islamic-majority states from international society. Accompanying secularist representations of political Islam is the insistence that secular democratic states work to ensure that Muslim-majority states either follow a laicist trajectory, in which secular modernization and those who support it are favored over rivals who support some kind of public role for Islam, or face increasing isolation from the international community as religious backwaters. Political Islam is seen as a failed attempt at modernization or a reversion to premodern social order, and thus as poorly equipped to contribute to the public life of Muslim-majority societies. In a laicist framework, these shortcomings are not irremediable but can be alleviated through the importation of Western-style democracy and the secularization of society. This leads to development and foreign assistance programs that seek to privatize religion in order to promote democratization. In a Judeo-Christian secularist framework, the Islamic refusal to acknowledge the special status of the private sphere confirms the difference of Islamic civilization. Incommensurable worldviews and incompatible social and political practices lead to an insurmountable divide between civilizations. Political options are limited to tense coexistence, war, or (perhaps) conversion.

Chapter 8 examines the notion of religious resurgence. Neither a passing aberration on the road to modernization nor a confirmation of insurmountable cultural and religious difference in world politics, as most conventional accounts have it, religious resurgence occurs whenever authoritative secularist settlements of the relationship between religion and politics are challenged. The resurgence is a manifestation of the attempt to refashion the secular, in which the terms of the debate involving religion and politics, presumed to have been resolved long ago, are disputed once again. Religious resurgence is evidence of a controversy over how metaphysics and politics relate to each other and to the state that calls into question fundamental received definitions of the secular. Secularist epistemological commitments stand in the way of effectively theorizing the breadth, diversity, and significance of this resurgence and thwart effective political responses to it. If what is identified as religious resurgence is a political contestation of the fundamental contours and content of the secular, then this contest signals the disruption of preexisting standards of what religion is and how it relates to politics. The resurgence of religion is evidence of a live and ongoing controversy over the relationship between the sacred, the profane, and the political that cuts through and calls into question the definition of and boundaries between mundane and metaphysical, secular and sacred. Religious resurgence therefore must be understood not through Western categories of the sacred and secular, but as a process through which these basic ontologies of political and religious order are being renegotiated and ultimately refashioned.[44]

International relations theory has struggled with religion because it has failed to consider the politics involved in the designation and enforcement of particular conceptualizations of the secular. It has not come to terms with secularism as a contested social construct. Confusion results from the fact that the religious and the political, the sacred and the secular, are presumed to be stable categories aligned with familiar modern liberal divisions between public and private. This assumption about the stability and normativity of these categories is unsustainable given the varieties of secularism that exist in the world today and the evidence of ongoing change and contestation surrounding the secular. Secularist authority plays a constitutive role within modern politics, including modern international politics.

The argument developed in this book is premised upon an understanding of secularism and its history and politics, as well as a set of methods and assumptions about the study of world politics. The remainder of this introductory chapter provides background to the concept of secularism and an account of my sources and methods.

BACKGROUND TO A CONCEPT

Secularism refers to a public settlement of the relationship between politics and religion. The secular refers to the epistemic space carved out by the ideas and practices associated with such settlements. Secularization is the historical process through which these settlements become authoritative, legitimated, and embedded in and through individuals, the law, state institutions, and other social relationships.

The notion of the *saeculum* emerged in the thirteenth century in reference to a binary opposition within Christianity. Priests who withdrew from the world (*saeculum*) formed the religious clergy, while those who lived in the world formed the secular clergy.[45] The term "secular" was used in English, often with negative connotations, to distinguish clergy living in the wider world from those in monastic seclusion. In a second transformation, and by the sixteenth century, the term began to shed its affiliation with Godlessness and the profane; Keane notes that in this era "the word 'secular' was flung into motion and used to describe a world thought to be in motion. In this case, to 'secularise' meant to make someone or something secular—converting from ecclesiastical to civil use or possession."[46] By the end of the Thirty Years' War, secularization referred to the transfer of church properties to the exclusive control of the princes.[47] Casanova describes this as the "passage, transfer, or relocation of persons, things, function, meanings, and so forth, from their traditional location in the religious sphere to the secular spheres."[48] This meaning of secularization predominated at the 1648 Peace of Westphalia and onward; on November 2, 1789, Talleyrand announced to the French National Assembly that all ecclesiastical goods were at the disposal of the French nation.[49]

In a third transformation and from the nineteenth century onward, secularism began to take on the meaning recognized in the vernacular today. It described a movement that was "expressly intended to provide a certain theory of life and conduct without reference to a deity or a future life."[50] Coined officially by George Jacob Holyoake in 1851, who led a rationalist movement of protest in England, the term secularism was at this time "built into the ideology of progress."[51] As Madan concludes, "secularization, though nowhere more than a fragmentary and incomplete process, has ever since retained a positive connotation."[52] Secularists were those who believed that the "Church and the world are caught up in an historical struggle in which slowly, irreversibly worldliness is getting the upper hand."[53] By the nineteenth century, the *seculere* had "emerged historically within North American and European Christian culture as a subordinate space in which the mundane and the material could be given due attention."[54]

The idea of the separation of church and state remains the most influential popular narrative of secularism in contemporary Europe and the United States. As Mahmood argues, however, "secular liberalism cannot be addressed simply as a doctrine of the state, or as a set of juridical conventions: in its vast implications, it defines, in effect, something like a way of life."[55] Secularism identifies something called religion and posits its differentiation from the domains of the state, the economy, and science.[56] The secular is associated with the worldly or temporal; it carries no overt references to transcendent order or divine being. The secularist separation between religion and politics makes it possible to speak of religion as privatized on the level of the individual, the community, the state, and the international system. Secularism is therefore part of what Taylor describes as a "modern social imaginary."[57] It is a lingua franca in which influential narratives of modernity, development, and progress have been constructed.[58] Secularism also is part of what Hunt refers to as "the intellectual underpinnings of foreign policy."[59] It is an ideological formation, defined as "an interrelated set of convictions or assumptions that reduces the complexities of a particular slice of reality to easily comprehensible terms and suggests appropriate ways of dealing with that reality."[60]

Secularism helps constitute the political culture of international relations, described by Bukovansky as "that set of implicit or explicit propositions, shared by the major actors in the system, about the nature of legitimate political authority, state identity, and political power, and the rules and norms derived from these propositions that pertain to interstate relations within the system."[61] Secularism is a normative formation that is widely perceived as legitimate.[62] It is what Halliday describes as "informal ideology," part of the broader underlying political culture and context in which decisions are made.[63] Like Bukovansky, this book is concerned with "how the terms of legitimate authority are constructed and contested," both domestically and internationally.[64]

In international relations secularism helps to generate and organize collective belief systems, defined by Page as "sets of attitudes, beliefs, and orientations concerning world affairs that are linked both logically and empirically with support for particular policy alternatives."[65] These basic values affect perceptions of international threats and problems, lead people to embrace particular foreign policy goals, and influence specific foreign policy preferences.[66] As Page argues, "Americans tend to organize their foreign policy attitudes into *purposive belief systems*, in which their policy preferences reflect logically related goals for foreign policy, perceptions of international threats, feelings about foreign countries and foreign leaders, and predispositions toward international activity or isolationism."[67] The forms of secularism described in this book are part of the basic values and fundamental beliefs that "feed into a set of *political predispositions*."[68] Secularism is part of the "climates of opinion" and the "context of public opinion" described by Cohen and Key. Cohen refers to the foreign policy decision-making "environment and cultural milieu" that shapes thinking and behavior.[69] Key suggests that the context that conditions the substance, form, and manner of actions "consists of opinion irregularly distributed among the people and of varying intensity, of attitudes of differing convertibility into votes, and of sentiments not always readily capable of appraisal."[70]

Key implies that the study of social phenomenon like secularism is a complex undertaking. To adapt Calhoun's observation about nationalism, secularism "is not the solution to the puzzle [of politics and religion] but the discourse within which struggles to settle the question are most commonly waged."[71] Secularism is what Shotter describes as a "tradition of argumenta-tion."[72] It is a resource for collective mobilization and legitimization, forming what Özkırımlı has described as "the mould within which all kinds of political claims have been cast."[73] Secularism is a historically articulated site of moral and political judgment.[74] Like nationalism and democracy, it is a language in which moral and political questions are defined, contested, settled, and legitimated. As an important site of moral and political authority, secularism inhabits and extends beyond the jurisdiction of the state. It sustains complex relations to global capitalism and other more heavily theorized sites of power in both domestic and international politics. As Chakrabarty sug-gests, "the phenomenon of 'political modernity'—namely, the rule by modern institutions of the state, bureaucracy and capitalist enterprise—is impossible to *think* of anywhere in the world without invoking certain categories and concepts, the genealogies of which go deep into the intellectual and even theological traditions of Europe."[75] Secularism is a foundational category of political modernity.

Finally, and critically for the argument of this book, secularism is a global discourse insofar as "new groups of people could take it up, could participate in it, and could in varying degrees innovate with it."[76] Many varieties and forms of secularization have set in motion different historical processes in predominantly Catholic countries as opposed to in Protestant countries, for example, and have taken on yet another set of connotations in the Eastern Orthodox context, particularly under communism. India has no wall of separa-tion between church and state because, as Madan notes, "there is no church to wall off, but only the notion of neutrality or equidistance between the state and the religious identity of the people."[77] In the postcolonial Middle East, secularization has been associated with the attempt to consolidate state power, reflecting "the desire of these states to reduce, or break, the power of an alter-native centre of power, the *ulema* in the Arab world, the *mullahs* in Iran, the *hocas* in Turkey, who had hitherto exercised such influence."[78] Since the term entered the lexicon in the Arab world in the mid-nineteenth century, the debate over secularism has been cast in terms of the opposition between *din* (religion) and *'aql* (reason), *asalah* (nobility) and *mu'asarah* (modernity), *din* and *dawlah* (state), and *din* and *'ilm* (science or knowledge). The term secu-larism or laicism has been translated as *'ilmaniyah* (from *'ilm*, or science) or as *'alamaniyah* (from *'alam*, or world). Others translate it as *dunyawiyah*, or that which is worldly, mundane, and temporal.[79] Secularism in this region and elsewhere has come to be associated with universalist pretensions and claims to superiority over nonsecular alternatives. "Secular nationalism," ac-cording to Juergensmeyer, "was thought to be not only natural but also univer-sally applicable and morally right."[80] As Casanova notes, "the theory of secular-ization may be the only theory which was able to attain a truly paradigmatic status within the modern social sciences."[81]

Despite its authoritative status, however, secularist boundaries between politics and religion exist not as a result of teleology or God's hand or chance, but as a result of historical and political processes that create distinctions and then lean upon these distinctions to maintain power. A secularist frame of reference has become, to borrow Wittgenstein's formulation, the invisible "scaffolding of our thoughts."[82] It responds to what Hunt describes as a "vaguely felt need for continuity or stability."[83] Yet secularism remains an exercise of power. It is an authoritative discourse.[84] As Calhoun suggests, "what gives tradition (or culture generally) its force is not its antiquity but its immediacy and givenness."[85] Secularism is taken as a given. Secularist ideological formations are notable for the absence of self-consciousness surrounding them.[86] The secularist construction of religion is generally accepted as immediate and natural.[87] Like Said's Orientalism, secularism is "a discourse that is by no means in direct, corresponding relationship with political power in the raw, but rather is produced and exists in an uneven exchange with various kinds of power, shaped to a degree by the exchange with power political, power intellectual, power cultural, power moral.[88] Secularism produces authoritative settlements of religion and politics, while simultaneously claiming to be exempt from this process of production.[89] This is a formidable exercise of power.[90] As Hunt concludes, "the case could be made that ideologies assume formal, explicit, systematic form precisely because there is resistance to them within the culture, whereas an ideology left implicit rests on a consensus and therefore exercises a greater (if more subtle) power."[91]

The question, then, is not "What is religion and how does it relate to politics?" For, according to Asad, "there cannot be a universal definition of religion, not only because its constituent elements and relationships are historically specific, but because that definition is itself the historical product of discursive processes."[92] Rather, the question is, *How* do processes, institutions, and states come to be understood as religious versus political, or religious versus secular, and how might we ascertain the political effects of such demarcation? To define the boundaries of the secular and the religious is itself a political decision.[93] Theories of international relations that depend upon stable and universal conceptions of the secular or the religious displace the politics involved in these authoritative designations.[94]

METHODS AND ASSUMPTIONS

As Connolly wrote of William James, "one attraction of James is that he fesses up to the motives that underlie his philosophical reflection."[95] This final section "fesses up" to my motives, explaining my approach to the metaphysical and ontological assumptions that animate this book and describing my methodology and sources. There are many epistemological and ontological traps in the study of secularism. By describing my assumptions up front, I hope to avoid them.

The principle substantive objective of this book is to deconstruct the secular-theological oppositional binary and open the way for religiopolitical possibilities that are structured less antagonistically, softening the rigid oppositions that often characterize the assumptions brought to the study and practice of both secularism and religion.[96] I do the same methodologically, such that my philosophy of inquiry mirrors what I am doing substantively in the book. First, I do not assume that I have access to criteria of knowledge that leave ontological questions behind, nor do I assume that my own epistemology provides neutral procedures through which I can pose and resolve ontological questions.[97] I agree with Wendt's observation that "ontology gets controversial when it invokes unobservables."[98] In response, I adopt a "bicameral" approach both to the metaphysical assumptions of this study and those of the secular, Christian, Judeo-Christian, and Islamic traditions that form my objects of analysis.[99] I argue on the one hand in favor of the view that people and institutions are social constructions in a pervasive sense of the term, while on the other hand acknowledging that this assumption of the constructed character of being is itself profoundly contestable.[100] My approach to social construction gives priority "not to a disengaged subject in its relation to independent objects, but to historically specific discursive practices within which people are engaged prior to achieving a capacity to reflect upon them."[101] Humans engage with each other and with the world within previously established contexts that help to constitute us and the objects represented to and by us.[102] As Barnett and Duvall argue, "constitutive relations cannot be reduced to the attributes, actions, or interactions of pregiven actors. Power, accordingly, is irreducibly social."[103]

My approach to social construction is influenced by what White describes as "weak ontology."[104] Weak ontologists assume that an ethical orientation to life does not "depend upon the demand to lock all reverence for life into some universal theistic faith, rational consensus, secular contract, transcendental argument, or interior attunement to a deep identity."[105] The task of the analyst is to interpret "actively, specifically, and comparatively, without praying for the day (or deferring until the time) when the indispensability of interpretation is matched by the solidity of its grounds."[106] This approach to social construction is the operative "faith" that animates this study, with the latter defined as "a creed or philosophy plus the sensibility mixed into it."[107] This approach shares lines of connection with Gramsci's recognition in his later writings that "all commitments pose an element of belief—that is, an active conviction and commitment—that one could interpret as religious."[108] It shares different lines of connection with Buddhist thought. As King writes, "in ancient Buddhist thought there has been no postulation of an all-powerful deity nor of an immortal soul constituting our real and essential identity. The spat between the

Church and the secular humanists simply did not occur. In contrast, Buddhist philosophy and practice is grounded upon a realization of the impermanent and fluctuating nature of the self and a deeply empathetic realization of the interconnectedness of all sentient beings as impermanent, multifaceted and 'relational' processes."[109]

Those who place the soul at the very center of being may find this approach to social construction challenging or even unacceptable. To mediate between these views I acknowledge that at its deepest level my own assumptions are contestable.[110] As Epicurus observed, "one must not be so much in love with the explanation by a single way as wrongly to reject all the others from ignorance of what can, and what cannot, be within human knowledge, and consequent longing to discover the undiscoverable."[111]

This book seeks to engage those who do not share my assumptions. Readers who come to this book who are believers in a traditional sense, for example, will find many points on which we agree. Take, for example, the ways in which my bicameral commitment to my metaphysics and its contingency resonates with the approach to religious liberty taken at the Second Vatican Council as described by religious historian Jaroslav Pelikan. As Pelikan recounts, "at the Second Vatican Council the declaration on religious liberty, largely written by my late friend Father John Courtney Murray of the Society of Jesus, declared the right of religious liberty not on the basis of saying, 'Well, it doesn't matter much what you believe.' Quite the opposite. Because you believe in the Christian tradition, which affirms creation of the human race in the image of God — the title of the declaration is 'Dignitatis Humanae,' 'Human Dignity.' Because of that, because therefore, religious faith is so important rather than because it's so trivial, therefore, you must not constrain others because faith can only be given freely."[112]

My position, like the one articulated by Pelikan, seeks to avoid bracketing what Berger describes as "metahuman" experiences, thereby slipping into what Porpora criticizes as "methodological atheism."[113] In methodological atheism, "the reality of any supernatural object of religious experience is forever debarred from consideration within sociology as a possible—even if partial—explanation of the experience."[114] Instead, my approach comes closer to what Porpora describes as "methodological agnosticism," but with a slightly different approach to social construction.

Social constructivists are often criticized for asserting or assuming that religion is no more than a human projection. This accusation, however, presumes that the human realm is an accessible, mundane, and sensible domain populated with autonomous human agents who are engaged in the social construction of religion, among other things. It also presumes that this human realm is distinct and separate from the true realm of religion, which is conceptualized variously as the domain of God,[115] the supermundane,[116] the transcendent, the nonsocially constructed or what Porpora refers to as the "extra-social."[117] I do not adopt these distinctions. Instead, I operate on the assumption that these two realms are configured differently on an ontological level, reflecting neither a philosophy of transcendence nor a philosophy of radical atheism but a "Deleuzean metaphysic":

> The Deleuzean metaphysic reconfigures the standing and shape of the Kantian transcendental field without eliminating it altogether. It is transcendental in residing above or below appearance, but not in being unquestionable or in authorizing a morality of command. This, then, is metaphysics without the claim to apodictic authority or epistemic certainty, a combination that eludes the Habermasian division between metaphysical and postmetaphysical thought.[118]

I do not (and cannot) authoritatively and "illegitimately liquidate transcendental phenomena from within," as Porpora accuses Berger of attempting to do in his sociological writings.[119] This is because, in this view, the transcendent is immanent.[120] This transcendental empiricism resembles Spinoza's metaphysical monism, "in which 'God or Nature' is conceived as *immanent* in the movement of things rather than forming a commanding, juridical order above them."[121] This tradition, reflected in the work of Stuart Hampshire and neuroscientist Antonio Damasio, is described by Connolly as a "minor tradition" of the Enlightenment that can be traced from Epicurus and Lucretius through Spinoza's nonsecular and nonecclesiastical monism of substance to Deleuze's mobile or "pure" immanence.[122] In this tradition the transcendent is both immanent and emergent, residing both above and below appearance.[123] It is neither directly accessible to experience nor outside experience, but immanent to it.[124] A philosophy of radical atheism, like other philosophies, depends upon a particular series of metaphysical assumptions. Radical atheism is itself a form of faith. As Asad has written, "the idea that there is a single clear 'logic of atheism' is itself the product of a modern binary—belief or unbelief in a supernatural being."[125] This has important implications for the politics of secularism.

Porpora wrestles with and ultimately gestures toward these possibilities at the end of his essay when he concludes that if we were to "integrate putatively super-mundane objects of experience with the rest of the causal order . . . the objects certainly would not cease being what they are, but we might cease regarding them as super-mundane. Instead, our conception of the mundane might just expand. We might, for example, come to regard a certain depth or sacred dimension as one of the natural features of our universe."[126] On this view, which I share, the original problem posed by a rigid divide between mundane and metaphysical realms, as well as the accusation that political scientists fail to engage the extrasocial because they merely construct religion as a social projection, appears in a different light. The conception of the mundane has now been reworked to accommodate a non-Kantian transcendental field in which what Kantians designate as the "supersensible" is replaced by an "infrasensible" transcendental field.[127] The infrasensible is real but not actual. Its elements cannot be fully captured, projected, or represented by the analyst.

This lends itself to a particular approach to the aspirations and limitations of social inquiry more broadly and social construction specifically. It allows for the elaboration of a constructivism that, as Price and Reus-Smit argue, rejects the search for timeless laws in favor of historically, culturally, and onto-logically contingent generalizations.[128] However, it also takes a step beyond their critique of positivism by insisting that the broader context, systems of knowledge, operations of power, and discursive practices within which social actors are produced cannot be fully captured or represented by the analyst. Thus, on the one hand a focus on structural power that assumes that "the social relational capacities, subjectivities, and interests of actors are directly shaped by the social positions that they occupy"[129] is insufficient because it neglects the role of "agency," construed here to include elements emanating from both the sensible and the infrasensible, in the production and transfor-mation of structure. On the other hand, the combination of individualism and materialism that underlies both neorealism and neoliberalism in international relations, which assumes that the structure constraining state behavior derives from the aggregation of properties of the actors such as the distribution of power, technology, and geography,[130] is also problematic. It disregards the so-cial constitution of subjectivity by assuming that social actors are preconsti-tuted and downplays or ignores the social processes through which material factors gain meaning for actors.[131] My approach therefore comes closest to, while slightly modifying, Barnett and Duvall's concept of "productive power," insofar as it emphasizes the elusive yet significant context within which the social production of subjectivity takes place. In their insistence that productive power constitutes "*all* social subjects with various social powers through sys-tems of knowledge and discursive practices of broad and general social scope,"[132] Barnett and Duvall, like Berger in his sociological writings, teeter on the precipice of methodological atheism.

This study operates on the assumption that people and institutions are so-cially constructed along the distinctive lines and within the (weak) ontological parameters described previously. At the same time, like James and Connolly, I think it "unlikely that any specific combination of evidence and argument will suffice to reduce the number of defensible philosophical faiths to one."[133] I seek to open lines of connection and communication with other approaches, to pursue commonalities that may have been foreclosed in the past by the rigid secular-theological binaries problematized in the substantive chapters of this book. These connections are pursued through a style of theorizing de-scribed by Bennett as "includ[ing] a set of claims about human being and the fundamental character of the world, even as these claims are presented as essentially contestable."[134]

Finally, I want to describe my sources and methodology. At the end of the day, secularism is intangible. Like nationalism, it is most powerful when experienced as natural and given. Unlike economic indicators or election results, it is extraordinarily difficult to measure or quantify. To deal with the inevitable empirical challenges of studying forms of political authority that are felt but not seen, I draw on multiple sources and use multiple methodologies. My theoretical orientation is given depth and breadth through the course of the study. Building on Çinar's definition, I approach secularism as a series of interlinked political projects that continually seek to "transform and reinstitute a sociopolitical order on the basis of a set of constitutive norms and principles."[135] Any particular instantiation of the secular involves the reproduction and transformation of a particular series of norms and principles. It also invokes, creates, and expresses particular sensibilities, habits, and practices. As Asad argues, according to Scott and Hirschkind, the secular must be approached "not simply in terms of the doctrinal separation of religious and political authority but as a concept that has brought together sensibilities, knowledges, and behaviors in new and distinct ways."[136] The two trajectories of secularism developed in this book attempt to capture the histories, sensibilities, and habits that are carried and transformed by and through collective secularist norms, identities, and institutions.

To investigate the political consequences of these forms of secularism in international relations, this study draws in the first instance upon analyses of public discourse in the United States and Europe, such as government policy statements, pundit commentaries, international agreements, presidential speeches, print media, radio talk shows, opinion polls, court decisions, and conference proceedings from research institutions and universities. Additional evidence and historical background used to support my empirical arguments are drawn from secondary sources in political science, history, anthropology, and Middle East studies on relations between the West and the Middle East. I am indebted in particular to several excellent historical accounts on relations between France and North Africa, the European Union and Turkey, and the United States and Iran. The collection and analysis of these various sources, historical and contemporary, academic and nonacademic, allowed me to piece together evidence attesting to the presence and power of the cultural and political sensibilities, the collective dispositions and tendencies, identified as laicism and Judeo-Christian secularism. This study takes the collective cultural, religious, and political pulse of the United States and Europe vis-à-vis secularism, Islam, and Judeo-Christianity from a position that strives to achieve critical distance from the collective cultural formations and authoritative traditions under study.

The relationship between metaphysics, ethics, and politics is complex and fluid. As McClay argues, "it is futile to imagine that the proper boundaries between religion and politics can be fixed once and for all, in all times and cultures, separated by an abstract fiat. Instead, their relationship evolves out of a process of constant negotiation and renegotiation."[137] The evolving and ever-elusive idea and practice of religion is interwoven with political authority in ways that align only fleetingly, if ever, with state boundaries, secularist assumption, Christian doctrine, Islamic law, or Deleuzean metaphysics. International relations theorists and practitioners need to reconsider the ontological and epistemological foundations of the discipline that govern what counts as politics in international politics. They need to rethink the assumptions about religion and politics embedded in the hypotheses and empirical tests of international relations scholarship. This book contributes to that effort.

CHAPTER TWO

Varieties of Secularism

SOCIOLOGISTS HAVE DEBATED the secularization thesis for decades.[1] Political theorists have analyzed the public-private divide since the founding of the discipline.[2] These debates have only just begun to enter the field of international relations. When Christine Sylvester wrote that international relations "smacks of debates within the hierarchy of one church," she might have been right in more ways than one.[3] For the most part, it is a secular church.[4] Contemporary international relations takes the Euro-American definition of religion and its separation from politics as the natural starting point for social scientific inquiry.

This book adopts a different starting point. Secularism is one of the most important organizing principles of modern politics. It is a discursive tradition defined and infused by power.[5] The social construction of secularism has taken two distinct paths in international relations: a laicist trajectory, in which religion is seen as an adversary and an impediment to modern politics, and a Judeo-Christian secularist trajectory, in which religion is seen as a source of unity and identity that generates conflict in modern international politics. These two varieties of secularism, and their history and consequences for international relations, are the subject of this chapter.

Each of these traditions of secularism is associated with particular sets of practices. Laicism, which comes out of the Enlightenment critique of religion, is associated with attempts to force religion out of politics. The secular spheres are emancipated and expanded "at the expense of a much-diminished and confined religious sphere."[6] Judeo-Christian secularism is associated with attempts to claim and reinforce the "secular" as a unique Western achievement that both distills and expresses the essence of Euro-American history, civilization, and culture. Each of these forms of secularism is a contingent and productive form of power located on a much broader spectrum of theological politics.[7] They are not mutually exclusive. There is no strong or necessary dividing line between them. An individual or an institution may draw upon the substantial discursive resources of both traditions simultaneously to legitimate a particular political position.

The forms of secularism delineated in this book are indebted to three different bodies of work by Charles Taylor, José Casanova, and Talal Asad. In "Modes of Secularism," Taylor describes an "independent political ethic" variety of secularism and a "common ground strategy" of secularism which, he argues, turn out to be "ancestral to rather different understandings of secularism today."[8] He then develops a new model of secularism, which he calls the "overlapping consensus model." A modified version of Rawls's blueprint for a just society, it is similar to the independent political ethic but without the requirement of a common foundation of universally accepted political principles. Taylor argues that there can be no universal basis for these principles, whether religious or not.[9] In *Public Religions in the Modern World*, Casanova refers to two distinct paths for managing the public-private distinction: liberal and civic-republican. Like Taylor and myself, he is cautiously critical of both of these traditions, "the liberal perspective because it insists on the need to confine religion to a private sphere, fearing that public religions must necessarily threaten individual freedoms and secular differentiated structures; the civic-republican perspective because . . . like the liberal perspective it also conceives of public or civil religions in premodern terms as coextensive with the political or societal community."[10] Casanova reconsiders three ethnocentric prejudices embedded in the theory of secularization: a bias for Protestant subjective forms of religion, a bias for "liberal" conceptions of politics and the public sphere, and a bias for the sovereign nation-state as the systemic unit of analysis. In *Formations of the Secular*, Asad explores the construction of modern categories of the secular and the religious and unpacks the assumptions that govern Western forms of secularism, including the concepts of religion, ethics, and politics that they presuppose.[11]

As to the geographical scope of my argument, the secular formations identified here are influential within and between countries that inherited, borrowed, had imposed upon them, or somehow ended up living with and against the traditions (both secular and religious) of historical Latin Christendom, including Europe and its settler colonies, Turkey, Iran, and elsewhere. Practitioners, theorists, and others rely upon these discursive traditions to frame and respond to events and processes involving religion, politics, and international relations. Laicism and Judeo-Christian secularism prestructure discourse and practice involving politics and religion in international relations.[12] They are productive modalities of power that work "through diffuse constitutive relations" to contribute to the "situated social capacities of actors."[13] They are vehicles through which shared interests, identities, and understandings involving religion and politics developed primarily at the domestic and regional levels become influential at the systemic level in international relations.

Charting the influence of these forms of secularism in international politics challenges the "clash of civilizations" narrative in which religion is seen as a fixed source of communal unity and identity that generates conflict in international politics. If the secular is socially constructed along the weak ontological lines described in chapter 1, then at least two considerations emerge with regard to the clash narrative. The first is that the attempt to identify something called "religion" and to assign it a stable and unchanging role in "politics," whether domestic or international, is a contestable move that is called into question through a genealogy of the secular. The second is that elements of religion always escape such attempts to represent, define, and confine religion to particular roles, spaces, and moments in politics.

This argument also presents an alternative to realist and liberal approaches in which religion is considered to be a private affair.[14] According to these traditions, religion was privatized in 1648 at the Peace of Westphalia as a solution to sectarian violence in Europe. This attempt to privatize religion, to which I will return in my discussion of laicism, emerged out of a series of political and philosophical attempts to manage and moderate sectarianism in European politics. No philosopher was more committed to this effort than Immanuel Kant.

KANT'S SECULAR VARIANT OF CHRISTIANITY

Though perhaps most widely known in academic international relations for his contributions to idealist theories of cosmopolitanism, Kant was also an important forerunner of modern forms of secularism.[15] In contemporary international relations, the legacy of Kant's "rational religion" may even outweigh his contribution to theories of cosmopolitanism and idealism.[16] One of the principle objectives of Kantian universal moral philosophy involved the attempt to address the adversarial effects of religious sectarianism in Europe. To do so, Kant laid a template for a generic form of Christianity that was intended to supersede sectarian faith. This template served as an important historical precursor of and political resource for later articulations of the forms of secularism described in this book. Understanding Kant's rational religion thus makes it possible to discern some of the historical, religious, and philosophical contingencies embedded in and transmitted through contemporary forms of modern secularism.

To overcome sectarianism, Kant proposed elevating "universal philosophy," or rational religion," to the position previously reserved for Christian theology.[17] This rational religion was essentially a generic form of Christianity that would replace and render publicly inert sectarian faith. As Connolly argues, the key to this Kantian rational religion is that it is anchored in a metaphysic of the supersensible that is presupposed by *any* agent of morality.[18] "Kant anchors rational religion in the law of morality rather than anchoring morality in ecclesiastical faith."[19] This allows Kant to retain the command model of morality from Augustinian Christianity while shifting the proximate point of command from the Christian God to the individual moral subject.[20] By shifting the point of command to the individual moral subject, however, Kant also ensures that "authoritative moral philosophy and rational religion are now only as secure as the source of morality upon which they draw"—individual apodictic recognition.[21] In this way, Kant's rational religion, although it seeks to displace Christian ecclesiastical theology, also shares several significant qualities with it. Connolly identifies four of these common qualities shared by rational religion and the church doctrine that it sought to displace:

> First, it places singular conceptions of reason and command morality above question. Second, it sets up (Kantian) philosophy as the highest potential authority in adjudicating questions in these two domains and in guiding the people toward eventual enlightenment. Third, it defines the greatest danger to public morality as sectarianism within Christianity. Fourth, in the process of defrocking ecclesiastical theology and crowning philosophy as judge in the last instance, it also delegitimates a place for several non-Kantian, nontheistic perspectives in public life.[22]

Kant was a forerunner of secularism rather than a secularist himself.[23] Yet forms of secularism that evolved out of the Kantian settlement consisted of "a series of attempts to secure these four effects without open recourse to the Kantian metaphysic of the supersensible. Secularism, in its dominant Western forms, *is* this Kantian fourfold without metaphysical portfolio."[24]

This describes laicism and, to a certain extent, Judeo-Christian secularism. Laicism pursues the Kantian effect of an authoritative public morality based in a singular conception of reason. It rejects theology in public life as dangerous sectarianism. It harbors an antipathy toward nontheistic and non-Kantian philosophies, as well as philosophies of public order derived from Islamic tradition. Laicism attempts to contain ecclesiastical intrusions into public life.[25] Its overarching objective is to provide "an authoritative and self-sufficient public space equipped to regulate and limit 'religious' disputes in public life."[26] There is an emphasis on "protecting the authority of deliberative argument in the secular public sphere."[27] To achieve this Kantian effect, laicism constantly reinscribes the boundary between public and private, secular and sacred, mundane and metaphysical.

The specific contours of this separation, if made explicit, are often legitimated through reference to the dictates of logic, reason, or nature. As Connolly argues, "many secularists who have lost confidence in a god replace it with an overweening confidence in the power of logic, reason, or nature as a guide to life."[28] The suggestion that a single logical, reasonable, or natural universal moral order is slowly replacing religion is an example of how Kantian-inspired laicism influences contemporary international relations theory.[29] Elements of this tradition are reflected in the work of David Held, Martha Nussbaum, and Francis Fukuyama.[30] Connolly describes this move toward moral universality as "the secular variant of Christianity."[31] The spheres of social control are divided between the realm of the Judeo-Christian sacred, on the one hand, and the realm of secular morality, international law, and international order on the other. A consensus separating the Judeo-Christian sacred from universal secular reason thus defines the terms through which the sacred and the secular are conceptualized in the field of international relations.

Like laicism, Judeo-Christian secularism also pursues the Kantian effect of an authoritative public morality based in a singular conception of reason. It also shuns nontheistic and non-Kantian philosophies, including Islamic ones. Like laicism, this variety of secularism also seeks to regulate and limit religious intrusions in public discourse. The difference is that unlike laicism, which claims to have superseded religion and religious origins altogether, Judeo-Christian secularism elevates and emphasizes a different aspect of Kant's moral philosophy: his insistence that among all ecclesiastical creeds available Christianity comes closest to his version of "universal rational religion."[32] Judeo-Christian secularism thus positions itself differently and more warmly toward the "metaphysical portfolio" eschewed by laicism. Judeo-Christian secularism draws upon these insistences in Kantian philosophy to sustain a distinct narrative about the origins, nature, and significance of modern secularism. In this narrative, Christianity informs and sustains the moral foundations of modern secular order. The Christian origins of modern secularism are valued; claims to secular order are emboldened and not scuttled through reference to these origins.

The concept of Judeo-Christian secularism captures elements of modern secularism that escape the laicist framework of interpretation yet are important in sustaining modern secularist settlements. Consider, for example, Gilles Deleuze's observation that the "apodictic recognition" upon which Kantian morality is grounded is no more than "a secondary formation reflecting the predominantly Christian culture in which it is set."[33] Unlike laicism, in which secularism is considered universal, or at least universalizable, in Judeo-Christian secularism modern habits of secularism are culturally embedded, fixed, and largely unproblematic. This is not the case for Deleuze. I return to this important distinction later, but the point is that the concept of Judeo-Christian secularism allows us to access cultural, religious, and embodied elements and practices of modern forms of secularism that are occluded by the assumptions of laicism.

The assumptions about Christianity and secularism that animate Judeo-Christian secularism have long been debated among philosophers, theologians, and historians.[34] John Milbank, for example, has suggested that "all the most important governing assumptions of [secular social] theory are bound up with the modification or the rejection of orthodox Christian positions. These fundamental intellectual shifts are . . . no more rationally 'justifiable' than the Christian positions themselves."[35] Milbank concludes that only Christian theology offers a viable alternative to both secular reason and "nihilism." Christian theologian Arend Theodor van Leeuwen, according to Juergensmeyer, argues that "the idea of a secular basis for politics is not only culturally European but specifically Christian."[36] For van Leeuwen, according to Juergensmeyer, "secular culture was, in his mind, Christianity's gift to the world."[37] While Juergensmeyer argues that van Leeuwen's thesis about the Christian origins of modern secularism "is increasingly regarded as true, especially in Third World countries," he also criticizes van Leeuwen for suggesting that secularism was *uniquely* Christian and argues that other civilizations do indeed have distinctions between priestly and secular authority.[38] This distinction is important for my argument. Juergensmeyer does not suggest, as does van Leeuwen, that Christianity is the *unique* foundation of secular democracy. Instead, he gestures toward the argument that particular forms of secularism are historically specific and contingent formations. Juergensmeyer therefore supports van Leeuwen's argument, as do I, that "the particular form of secular society that has evolved in the modern West is a direct extension of its past, including its religious past, and is not some supracultural entity that came into being only after a radical juncture in history."[39]

In reaching these conclusions, however, Juergensmeyer wrestles with and ultimately leaves unresolved an important tension in the study of secularism. Like van Leeuwen, he acknowledges the complex yet also much-interrupted relation between Christian history and doctrine and modern forms of Euro-American secularism. Unlike van Leeuwen, however, he wants to leave open the possibility that alternative forms of secularism can and have emerged in non-Christian settings. Yet, in the same moment that Juergensmeyer gestures toward this need to disaggregate secularism and examine its diverse historical trajectories and complex relation to religion in different historical and political circumstances, he also (somewhat apodictically) recognizes religion and secular nationalism as opposing "ideologies of order" and then concludes that "there can ultimately be no convergence between religious and secular political ideologies."[40]

I take a different approach. Rather than close off inquiry by setting up the "religious" and the "secular" as mutually exclusive, this book examines the ways in which particular trajectories of secularism are socially constructed in particular historical circumstances and assesses their political consequences for international relations.[41] The two forms of secularism examined in the following sections emerged out of the theopolitical history and traditions of Latin Christendom, which was richly informed by but not limited to Kantian philosophy and tradition. Other traditions, such as Spinozism and Lockean liberalism, for example, also profoundly influenced the forms of secularism analyzed here.[42] These forms of secularism represent only two points on a much broader spectrum of theological politics.[43] As I argue later, other forms of secularism that do not share the same philosophical, religious, historical, and institutional legacies are likely to appear quite differently.

LAICISM

In his classic 1965 text *The Secular City*, Harvey Cox suggests that "it will do no good to cling to our religious and metaphysical versions of Christianity in the hope that one day religion or metaphysics will once again be back. They are disappearing forever and that means we can now let go and immerse ourselves in the new world of the secular city."[44] This perspective emerges more recently in Hardt and Negri's *Empire*, which describes the evanescent quality of religion and suggests that "every metaphysical tradition is now completely worn out."[45] This assumption has been influential in the academy, in which, as Esposito observes, "religious faith was at best supposed to be a private matter. The degree of one's intellectual sophistication and objectivity in academia was often equated with a secular liberalism and relativism that seemed antithetical to religion . . . Neither development theory nor international relations considered religion a significant variable for political analysis."[46] In this view, "the mixing of religion and politics is regarded as necessarily abnormal (departing from the norm), irrational, dangerous, and extremist."[47]

Laicism is a powerful tradition of the secular city, world "empire," and Western academy that presumes that metaphysical traditions of all kinds have been exhausted and transcended. It is one of the founding principles of modern political thought and one of the practical pillars of the secular separation of church and state. There are many dimensions of laicism, including the exclusion of religion from the spheres of power and authority in modern societies (structural differentiation), the privatization of religion, and a decline in church membership and potential disappearance of individual religious belief.[48] I focus on the exclusion of religion from spheres of modern power and authority because this dimension of laicism is most relevant to my argument about international relations.

Laicism is a powerful organizing principle of modern politics that has been influential in France, the former Soviet Union, Turkey, China, and elsewhere. It is derived from the Jacobin tradition of *laïcisme* and associated with what Chatterjee describes as "a coercive process in which the legal powers of the state, the disciplinary powers of family and school, and the persuasive powers of government and media have been used to produce the secular citizen who agrees to keep religion in the private domain."[49] Casanova argues that this privatization of religion is "mandated ideologically by liberal categories of thought which permeate not only political ideologies and constitutional theories but the entire structure of modern Western thought."[50] According to Taylor, the overarching objective of the "independent political ethic" mode of secularism, pursued by Grotius and others, is to identify features of the human condition that allow the deduction of exceptionless norms about peace and political obedience, making religion irrelevant to politics.[51] As Grotius argued, "*etsi Deus non daretur* ... even if God didn't exist, these norms would be binding on us."[52] The result is that "the state upholds no religion, pursues no religious goals, and religiously-defined goods have no place in the catalogue of ends it promotes."[53] Asad notes that laicism seeks to confine religious belief and practice "to a space where they cannot threaten political stability or the liberties of "free-thinking" citizens."[54] Van der Veer and Lehmann observe that "it is a fundamental assumption of the discourse of modernity that religion in modern societies loses its social creativity and is forced to choose between a sterile conservation of its premodern characteristics and a self-effacing assimilation to the secularized world."[55] Richard King describes laicism as the attempt to define and then exclude (whatever laicists identify as) religion:

> The Enlightenment preoccupation with defining the "essence" of phenomena such as "religion" or "mysticism" serves precisely to exclude such phenomena from the realms of politics, law and science, etc.—that is, from the spheres of power and authority in modern Western societies. Privatized religion becomes both clearly defined and securely contained by excluding it from the public realm of politics.[56]

International relations theory assumes that religion was privatized in the course of creating the modern state and thus excluded from spheres of power and authority in modern societies. Realist and liberal approaches to international relations are part of a broad tradition in social theory that operates on the assumption that religion has been confined to the private sphere or has diminished altogether.[57] As Katzenstein observes, "because they are expressions of rationalist thought deeply antithetical to religion, the silence of realist and liberal theories of international relations on the role of religion in European and world politics is thus not surprising."[58] The operative assumption, characteristic of these approaches, that religion has been privatized is what Thomas refers to as the "Westphalian presumption."[59]

There is a vast literature on religion, the Protestant reformation, and the Westphalian settlement (which ended the Thirty Years' War between 1618 and 1648), most of which emphasizes the declining role of religion in European public life.[60] Skinner, for instance, observes that after Luther "the idea of the Pope and Emperor as parallel and universal powers disappears, and the independent jurisdictions of the *sacerdotium* are handed over to the secular authorities."[61] Pizzorno refers to this transition as the "Gregorian moment," and describes it as the most emblematic episode of what he calls "absolute politics" in Western history, which "lies at the root of the transfer, as it were, of the collective responsibility for ultimate ends from a collectivity having the boundaries of Christianity, and including all believers tied by this particular bond of faith, to separate collectivities defined by the territorial boundaries of one state and including all the individuals identified by their living within those boundaries."[62] Philpott emphasizes the important role of the Reformation and processes of secularization that emerged out of it to challenge the temporal powers and decrease the public role of the church.[63] Krasner suggests that "the idea of sovereignty was used to legitimate the right of the sovereign to collect taxes, and thereby strengthen the position of the state, and to deny such right to the church, and thereby weaken the position of the papacy."[64] He argues that Westphalia "delegitimized the already waning transnational role of the Catholic Church and validated the idea that international relations should be driven by balance-of-power considerations rather than the ideals of Christendom."[65] Cavanaugh argues that the conflicts of the sixteenth and seventeenth centuries inverted the dominance of the ecclesiastical over the civil authorities through the creation of the modern state, preparing the way for the eventual elimination of the church from the public sphere.[66]

Westphalian republicanism was organized on a modern conception of social and political order in which individual subjects assembled a society under a single sovereign authority. By challenging the arbitrary rights of kings in the name of the common good,[67] the new republicanism did delegitimize and transform preexisting hierarchic forms of order, as most conventional accounts have it.[68] As Taylor argues, however, this new republicanism also reinforced a particular distinction between natural order and supernatural order, and this distinction itself came out of and remained indebted to a broader Christian framework.[69] Early republican order was characterized by a strong idea of providence and a pervasive sense that men were enacting a master plan that was providentially preordained. As Taylor suggests, the idea of moral order underlying this arrangement is in fact unrecognizable to non-Westerners due to its emphasis on a providential plan to be realized by humans.[70] That early republicanism was situated within a broader Christian context also fits with Krasner's observation that religious toleration in the Treaty of Osnabrück (one of the two treaties that made up the Peace of Westphalia along with the Treaty of Münster) was limited to Lutherans, Calvinists, and Catholics.[71] Westphalia, as Nexon concludes, thus contributed to a "territorialization of religion" leading toward the "formation of polities in which territory, state, and confession were closely linked."[72]

The forms of secular authority identified in this book emerged out of this Christian-influenced Westphalian moral and political order. Although laicism presents itself as a universalizable discourse that emerged out of the Westphalian settlement as a solution to the "wars of religion," it is actually "a specific fashioning of spiritual life . . . carved out of Christendom."[73] As Mitchell observes, even "the idea of the sovereign self, the autonomous consenting self, emerged out of Christianity . . . paying attention to the religious roots of consent in the West alert us to the fact, that it is in fact a provincial development, not necessarily universalizable."[74] The influence of Christian tradition upon the original Westphalian "secular" settlement makes it difficult to subsume modern international order into realist and liberal frameworks that operate on the assumption that religion has been completely privatized. This is because the traditions of secularism identified here contribute to the constitution of particular modern forms of state sovereignty that *purport* to be universal in part by defining the limits of state-centered politics with religion on the outside.

Modernization theory is the policy expression of this commitment to build a modern Westphalian state. The dominant paradigm in this theory is that "managing the public realm is a science which is essentially universal and that religion, to the extent it is opposed to the Baconian world-image of science, is an open or potential threat to any polity."[75] As Falk argues, the exclusion of religion from the spheres of power and authority "was intended to facilitate governmental efficiency as well as to provide the basis for a unified politics of the state in the face of religious pluralism, and a background of devastating sectarian warfare. Ostensibly, in the modern world religious identity was declared irrelevant to the rational enterprise of administering the political life of society."[76] In viewing religion as an impediment to the scientific management of the domestic and international public realms, modernization theory reflects laicist assumptions. Religion, however defined, was to be confined to the private realm in order to ensure the proper demarcation of public and private, sacred and secular. This paradigm was considered to be universal, or at least universalizable. As T. N. Madan concludes, "the idea of secularism, a gift of Christianity, has been built into Western social theories' paradigms of modernization, and since these paradigms are believed to have universal applicability, the elements, which converged historically — that is in a unique manner — to constitute modern life in Europe in the sixteenth and the following three centuries, have come to be presented as the requirements of modernization elsewhere."[77]

Structuralist and materialist approaches to international relations such as neorealism and historical materialism are also influenced by laicism insofar as religion is seen as epiphenomenal to more fundamental material interests. Neorealism proceeds on the assumption that states have a set of fixed and innate interests and that their behavior is constrained by international structure defined by factors such as the distribution of power, technology, and geography. Historical materialism, following Marx, dismisses religion as "a mode of consciousness which is other than consciousness of reality, external to the relations of production, producing no knowledge, but expressing at once the anguish of the oppressed and a spurious consolation."[78] As with the realists and liberals, materialist approaches to state interests neglect the constitutive and productive role of social norms and practices.[79] As Bukovansky argues, "materialist approaches tend to view rules and norms as being contingent upon, and thus reducible to, material configurations of power or resources."[80] The forms of secularism identified here are not reducible to material power or resources but instead play a constitutive role both in creating agents and contributing to the normative structure in which they interact.[81]

Like their realist and liberal counterparts, constructivists have paid little attention to the important role of the secular-sacred dichotomy in constituting state sovereignty. Although much constructivist literature examines the interaction of preexisting state units to explain how international norms influence state interests, identity, and behavior,[82] the literature on the social construction of states and the state system has ignored the secular and sacred or treated religion as essentially private by prior assumption.[83] Despite offering important insights into world politics, neither of these strands of constructivist theorizing provides space for examining, either historically or conceptually, the political authority of secularism.

The most significant implication for international relations of these differing attempts either to expel religion from politics or to assume that it has been successfully privatized within the state is that they demand "not only the sharing of the (independent political) ethic but also of its foundation — in this case, one supposedly independent of religion."[84] Laicism defines religion by designating that which is *not* religious: the secular. As Asad argues, "in the discourse of modernity 'the secular' presents itself as the ground from which theological discourse was generated."[85] In doing so, laicism implicitly demarcates the limits and boundaries of public space. In defining the temporal, laicists aspire to define or at least delimit the transcendental. The laicist settlement is a form of politics that, as Pizzorno argues in reference to absolute politics, "sets the boundaries between itself and other activities. To define what is within or without the scope of politics, one needs laws, or abolition of laws, hence political decisions, political activities, and discourse."[86] Laicism attempts to set the terms for what constitutes politics and religion. This move is ambitious and contestable. As Scott observes, "part of the problem to be sketched and investigated therefore has precisely to do with the instability of what gets identified and counted by authorized knowledges as 'religion': how, by whom, and under what conditions of power. In other words, the determining conditions and effects of what gets categorized as 'religion' are historically and culturally variable."[87] The traditions of secularism described in this book are forms of authorized knowledge that emerged out of the contested theopolitics of Latin Christendom and rely upon particular assumptions about the secular and the religious.

These are historically contingent forms of knowledge. The contingency of their assumptions may be illustrated through a look at the derivation of the English term "religion" from the Latin *religio*.[88] In the pre-Christian era, Cicero provided an etymology of the term linking it to the Latin verb *relegere*, "to retrace or reread."[89] In pre-Christian times, *religio* referred to retracing the ritual of one's ancestors. As King observes, "this understanding of the term seems to have gained provenance in the 'pagan' Roman empire and made *religio* virtually synonymous with *traditio*." The Roman idea of *religio* tolerated different traditions, since the exclusion of one tradition in order for another to be practiced was not required.[90] At the time, early Christians were referred to as atheists because they did not belong to a recognizable *traditio* and did not acknowledge the gods of others.[91] As Christians increased their power among the Romans, they also transformed the meaning of *religio* by severing its association with ancestral traditions:

> It became increasingly important within early Christian discourses to drive a wedge between the traditional association of *religio* with *traditio*. This occurred through a transformation of the notion of *religio*. Thus in the third century CE we find the Christian writer Lactantius explicitly rejecting Cicero's etymology, arguing instead that *religio* derives from *re-ligare*, meaning to bind together or link.[92]

Over time, *religio* came to be associated with "a worship of the true and a superstition of the false."[93] For Christians and Westerners more generally, religion came to denote a "bond of piety" between *one true* God and man. Cavanaugh argues that this modern concept of religion dates to the late fifteenth century and the writings of Marsilio Ficino, whose 1474 *De Christiana Religione* represents religion as a universal human impulse. In the sixteenth and seventeenth centuries, "religion moves from a virtue to a set of propositions . . . at the same time the plural 'religions' arises, an impossibility under the medieval usage."[94]

This reconceptualization of *religio*, as King argues, established "the monotheistic exclusivism of Christianity as the normative paradigm for understanding what a religion is."[95] This monotheistic exclusivism influenced European social order, European perceptions of others, and, later, European forms of secularism. Kant, for instance, was famously unable to fathom the idea of more than one valid religion:

> *Differences in religion*: an odd expression! Just as if one spoke of different *moralities*. No doubt there can be different kinds of historical *faiths*, though these do not pertain to religion, but only to the history of the means used to promote it, and these are the province of learned investigation; the same holds of different religious *books* (Zendavest, the Vedas, Koran, and so on). But there is only a single *religion*, valid for all men in all times. Those [faiths and books] can thus be nothing more than the accidental vehicles of religion and can only thereby be different in different times and places.[96]

Writing in the same decade as Kant, Joseph Endelin de Joinville, the surveyor general in the administration of Frederic North, first governor of British possessions in Ceylon, also suggests that religion could refer only to a Christian belief system.

> An uncreated world, and moral souls, are ideas to be held only in an infant state of society, and as society advances such ideas must vanish. A *fortiori*, they cannot be established in opposition to a religion already prevailing in a country, the fundamen-

tal articles of which are the creation of the world, and the immortality of the soul. Ideas in opposition to all religion cannot gain ground, at least cannot make head, when there is already an established faith.[97]

The spread of this particular concept of religion in Europe meant that the term came to be associated with a set of *beliefs* as opposed to "the inherent pluralism of the Ciceronian understanding of *religio* and *traditio*."[98] As King concludes, "modern discussions of the meaning and denotation of the term *religio* tend to follow Lactantius's etymology, thereby constructing a Christianized model of religion that strongly emphasized *theistic belief* (whether mono-, poly-, heno-, or pantheistic in nature), exclusivity, and a fundamental dualism between the human world and the transcendent world of the divine to which one "binds" *(religare)* oneself."[99] According to Cavanaugh, "religion as a transhistorical phenomenon separate from 'politics' is a creation of Western modernity."[100]

Modern forms of secularism inherited this specifically Christian approach to religion. Attempts to regulate the terms through which religion is defined and confined lead to conflict between laicists, who police the boundary of what they define as the public sphere, and others, who view this policing as an extension of religion in the name of a rival (laicist) set of metaphysical assumptions and practices.[101] As Taylor explains,

> What to one side is a more strict and consistent application of the principles of neutrality is seen by the other side as partisanship. What this other side sees as legitimate public expressions of religious belonging will often be castigated by the first as the exaltation of some peoples' beliefs over others. This problem is compounded when society diversifies to contain substantial numbers of adherents of non-Judaeo-Christian religions. If even some Christians find the "post-Christian" independent ethic partisan, how much harder will Muslims find it to swallow it.[102]

By defining something called religion and working to exclude it from politics, laicism constructs and delimits the temporal domain in a particular fashion. This is a political move. It is also a theological one. Laicism marks out the domain of the secular and associates that domain with public authority, common sense, rational argument, justice, tolerance, and the public interest.[103] It reserves the religious as that which it is not, and associates it with a personal God and beliefs about that God.[104] Laicism, then, is not the opposite of theological discourse. It enacts a particular kind of theological discourse in its own right. In this discourse, religion is "treated as a universal term, as if 'it' could always be distilled from a variety of cultures in a variety of times rather than representing a specific fashioning of spiritual life engendered by the secular public space carved out of Christendom."[105] As Milbank argues in his critique of secular reason, "a theology 'positioned' by secular reason . . . is confined to intimations of a sublimity beyond representation, so functioning to confirm negatively the questionable idea of an autonomous secular realm, completely transparent to rational understanding."[106]

Milbank also refers to the "critical non-avoidability of the theological and metaphysical" and observes that differing approximations of it appear in the work of Alasdair MacIntyre, Gillian Rose, René Girard, Guy Lardreau, and Christian Jambet.[107] Similarly, White argues that "the supposedly neutral, 'freestanding' nonontological standpoint is, in fact, a perspective constitutively infused with an ontological desire to hold an authoritative center in the flux of political life . . . the desire for a definitive center is what needs to be diffused."[108] Although laicism purports to stand outside the contested territory of religion and politics, it does not and cannot. Laicism is located on the spectrum of theological politics.

In international relations, laicism works to exclude alternative approaches to the negotiation of the secular that threaten its concept and practice of modern politics. As Taylor observes with regard to global politics, "defined and pursued out of the context of Western unbelief, it understandably comes across as the imposition of one metaphysical view over others, and an alien one at that."[109] In attempting to legislate the terms through which the secular and the sacred are defined, laicism rules out in advance linkages between religion and spheres of power and authority such as law, science, and politics within states. In defining the limits of state-centered politics with religion on the outside, it contributes to the constitution of a particular form of state sovereignty above states. The exercise of this productive power matters because, as Casanova has observed regarding religious interventions in the secular public sphere, "the purpose of such interventions in the undifferentiated public sphere is not simply to 'enrich public debate' but to challenge the very claims of the secular sphere to differentiated autonomy exempt from extrinsic normative constraints."[110] Challenges to dominant formations of secular order, including secular concepts of state sovereignty, are often particularly pronounced in non-Western contexts where Western-imposed or Western-inspired forms of laicism do not correspond neatly to local political and religious traditions. This theme is revisited in chapter 4 in the discussion of contested secularisms in Turkey and Iran.

A second consequence of laicism for international relations involves the definition of religion and the production of particular kinds of religious subjects. Laicism presumes to distinguish cleanly between the transcendent or supernatural and the temporal or mundane. As Casanova has remarked, "the secular, as a concept, only makes sense in relation to its counterpart, the religious."[111] Laicism defines itself as the starting point in relation to which the religious is constructed. It therefore effectively contributes to the production of the categories that it presupposes. It is most powerful when this process of construction, this mode of production, remains invisible or unseen. In this way, laicism aspires to represent itself as the natural order that emerges when there is no ideology present.[112] This makes it exceptionally powerful. In it most influential legal, social, and political instantiations, laicism succeeds in positing itself as public, neutral, and value-free, while assigning religion the role of its private, affective, and value-laden counterpart. Religion becomes the domain of the violent, the irrational, the undemocratic, the "other." Thus Cavanaugh argues that "liberal theorists . . . assume that public faith has a dangerous tendency to violence,"[113] and Appleby refers to the "conventional wisdom that religious fervor—unrestrained religious commitment—inevitably expresses itself in violence and intolerance."[114] Laicism is the "conventional wisdom" adopted by Cavanaugh's "liberal theorists." The secular public sphere is constructed as the domain of reason, objectivity, deliberation, and justice. The religious private sphere is construed as the domain of subjectivity, transcendence, effeminacy, and affect. Laicism guards against what it defines as religion in the public sphere. Religious presence is seen as unnatural, undemocratic, and even theocratic. Adapting Honig's insight about virtue theorists, laicists "distance themselves from the remainders of their politics and that distance enables them to adopt a not terribly democratic intolerance and derision for the other to whom their democratic institutions are supposed to be (indeed claim to be) reaching out."[115] As Euben argues, these "religious" subjects in turn become repositories for laicist anxieties about relations between politics, religion, and violence.[116]

By pushing dissenters to the laicist settlement out of the domain of the political and into the domain of the religious, laicism incites counterreactions in contemporary politics, including international politics. As both the religious and the internal "remainders" of laicism are shut out of politics, as they come to sense that this domain itself is in fact purportedly *defined* by laicism, some resort to extreme tactics to air their grievances. As Nandy argues, "modern scholarship sees zealotry as a retrogression into primitivism and as a pathology of traditions. At closer sight it proves to be a by-product and a pathology of modernity."[117] Zealotry is not always attributable to pathological religious beliefs. It can result from overzealous attempts to universalize laicism.

JUDEO-CHRISTIAN SECULARISM

George W. Bush supported secular democracy in Iraq. Yet he acknowledged that religion played an important role in his strategic vision, policy decisions, and leadership style. In a 2003 speech to the National Endowment for Democracy Bush stated that "liberty is both the plan of Heaven for humanity and the best hope for progress here on earth."[118] In his second inaugural address in 2005, Bush described his commitment to human rights as founded in the belief "that every man and woman on this earth . . . bear[s] the image of the Maker of Heaven and Earth."[119] President Bush was not a laicist. He did not support the exclusion of religion from the spheres of power and authority in modern societies. Instead, he invoked what Wolterstorff has described as a theistic account of political authority. "Among the ways in which a theistic account of political authority is distinct from all others," according to Wolterstorff, "is that it regards the authority of the state to do certain things as transmitted to it from someone or something which already has that very same authority."[120] The United States, for Bush, is empowered by a transcendental authority. It is a secular republic that is realizing (a Christian) God's will. This joint invocation of secular and Christian discourse displays a familiar logic.[121] This is Judeo-Christian secularism.

Judeo-Christian secularism is a discursive tradition that aspires to negotiate the modern relationship between religion and politics. While laicism seeks to define and confine religion to the private sphere, Judeo-Christian secularism connects contemporary Western secular formations to a legacy of "Western" (Christian, later Judeo-Christian) values, cultural and religious beliefs, historical practices, legal traditions, governing institutions, and forms of identification. Many Christians and Jews are not Judeo-Christian secularists, and it is possible to adopt the assumptions of Judeo-Christian secularism without being either Jewish or Christian. Like laicism, Judeo-Christian secularism is a discursive formation that comes in many different variations. George W. Bush, for example, invokes a particular version of Judeo-Christian secularism: while Christian discourse is inseparable from the practice of secular authority, it is not the case that *only* Christianity holds the key to secularization. The common claim of Judeo-Christian secularism of all varieties, however, is that Western political order is grounded in a set of core values with their origins in (Judeo)-Christian tradition.

The religious populism of Richard John Neuhaus is one variation of this tradition.[122] Neuhaus argues that universally valid traditional Catholic moral arguments should replace "secular" public godlessness and reclothe the naked public square as the basis of American identity, community, and foreign policy. Americans, for Neuhaus, are a "Christian people," and Catholic natural law theorizing should serve as a universal moral-religious vocabulary in American public life.[123] Drawing on the arguments of John Courtney Murray, Neuhaus argues that Catholicism is not the enemy of liberalism but "its true source and indispensable foundation."[124] For Neuhaus and others who articulate different variations of this tradition, religion (Catholicism, Christianity, and/or Judeo-Christianity) is the elemental defining feature and moral basis of Western civilization. As Jelen argues, "in the United States, a 'Judeo-Christian' tradition is thought to provide a moral basis for political life — what some analysts have described as a 'sacred canopy' beneath which political affairs can be conducted. Religion is thought to perform a 'priestly' function of legitimating political authority."[125] Judeo-Christian forms of secular order, in this view, are among the core values of Western civilization. They do not merely contribute to but actually help to constitute the common ground upon which Western democratic order rests. Religion plays an important constitutive role in this form of secular politics. It constitutes what Jelen describes as "the basis of an ethical consensus without which popular government could not operate."[126] This form of secularism draws on a long tradition that Casanova has described as a "celebratory Protestant reading of modernity, going from Hegel's _Early Theological Writings_ through the Weber-Troeltsch axis to Talcott Parson's interpretation of modern societies as the institutionalization of Christian principles."[127]

In the laicist account of secularization, the Christian identity of the West was superseded, radically transformed, and for all practical purposes rendered irrelevant. A modern, rational West was reinvented and rejuvenated by democratic tendencies inherited from its earlier Greek and Roman predecessors. Judeo-Christian secularism does not share this assumption that after the Protestant Reformation and the Enlightenment linkages between Western politics and public forms of Christianity were definitively severed. It works out of a different set of traditions involving the relationship between Christianity and modern political identities and institutions. Rather than eschewing religion, this tradition of secularism draws sustenance from earlier European traditions and institutional arrangements in which church and state were unified, with "each representing a different aspect of the same divine authority."[128] Gedicks describes this arrangement:

> Prior to the Reformation . . . the concepts "religious" and "secular" did not exist as descriptions of fundamentally different aspects of society. Although there clearly was tension and conflict in the relation between church and state during this time, the state was not considered to be nonreligious. Both church and state were part of the Christian foundation upon which medieval society was built.[129]

The Reformation, Gedicks argues, led to the distillation of two separate spheres of influence: the spiritual, which was led by the church, and the temporal, overseen by the state. Luther and Calvin revived and strengthened Augustine's concepts of the "city of God" and the "city of men," which described two aspects of the sovereign authority of God as embodied in the church and the state. However, they also made this split more fundamental by claiming that "God had instituted two kingdoms on earth, one spiritual to be ruled by the church, and the other temporal to be ruled by a civil sovereign."[130]

In the case of the United States, according to Gedicks, this larger Christian context within which both church and state were set during the Reformation in turn set the terms of American public discourse at least through the nineteenth century:

> There was no explicit 19th century ethic that required the divorce of religion from politics and government . . . there was no division of society into spheres of the

religious and the secular . . . rather religion and government emerged as competing centers of institutional authority, each of which tacitly recognized the pre-eminence of the other in certain matters.[131]

It was both legally and culturally acceptable at this time for Americans to argue public policy in openly religious terms.[132] Following the influx of immigrants to the United States in the late nineteenth and early twentieth centuries, however, it became politically expedient to couch political programs in increasingly nonsectarian terms in order to ensure success at the polls.[133] While Protestant discourse at that point took a back seat to a more general civic religion, a de facto Protestant establishment continued to set the ground rules. As Gedicks notes, "Protestantism still affected public business, but implicitly, more as the source and background of political movements than as the movements themselves."[134]

Judeo-Christian secularism is part of the source and background of contemporary domestic and international politics. It draws on a long tradition in which particular religious traditions are linked implicitly to the possibility of civilization, as described most famously in reference to the United States by Tocqueville:

In the United States it is not only mores that are controlled by religion, but its sway extends over reason. . . . So Christianity reigns without obstacles by universal consent. . . . Thus while the law allows the American people to do everything; there are things which religion prevents them from imagining and forbids them to become. . . . Religion, which never intervenes directly in the government of American society should therefore be considered as the first of their political institutions.[135]

The religious beliefs of the Protestant majority in early America formed the basis of a particular understanding of modern democratic politics, which is discussed at length in chapter 3 with regard to the constitutive relation between Islam and modern secular democratic identities. The influence of the Protestant majority in early America was evident in legislative prayer, state acknowledgment of Easter, Christmas, Thanksgiving, and the Christian Sabbath, and the outlawing of blasphemy and the punishment of atheism.[136] As Gedicks explains, Protestants "opposed a particular Protestant denomination to Protestantism in general, which later they did not equate with an establishment. The notion of prayer and worship based on the Bible accepted by all Protestants did not amount to a general establishment, but constituted an essential foundation of civilization."[137] To be secular, in this line of reasoning, meant to not privilege one Protestant denomination over another. The common ground of Christian civilization was taken for granted. A similar situation prevailed contemporaneously in England. In his analysis of nineteenth-century debates between British evangelicals and their utilitarian rivals, van der Veer notes that despite their differences both sides agreed that "civil society and the forms of knowledge on which it was based were ultimately part and parcel of Christian civilization."[138]

This Protestant common ground, though slowly eroded by the increasing religious diversification of the American population and eventually modified to incorporate both Catholic[139] and (after World War II) Jewish influences, has retained a cultural foothold. It is out of a celebratory reading of this cultural inheritance that Judeo-Christian secularism emerged and continues to shape modern sensibilities and attitudes regarding the secular. Stephen L. Carter refers to this tradition when he suggests that "the image of America as a Christian nation is more firmly ingrained in both our politics and our practices than the adjustment of a few words will ever cure."[140] Along with Carter, other scholars of religion including Bellah, Connolly, Taylor, van der Veer, Morone, and Pizzorno have gestured toward the apparatus that is identified here as Judeo-Christian secularism by chronicling the ways in which Judeo-Christian tradition resonates in and through contemporary politics, including in modern forms of liberalism and secularism.[141]

Morone, for example, draws a portrait of American history in which the nation develops "not from religious to secular but from revival to revival."[142] Connolly points to a tendency in canonical liberal thinkers, such as J. S. Mill, to rely quietly upon Judeo-Christian tradition as the moral basis of civilizational unity and identity. As he reads Mill, "it is therefore through Jewish and Christian culture above all that a territorial people acquires the civilizational conditions of possibility for representative government."[143] Mill, then, contributed to the cultural and political inheritance that I identify as Judeo-Christian secularism. Van der Veer identifies a long tradition of combining liberalism and evangelical moralism in Anglo-American political thought. He describes British Liberal leader Gladstone's (1809–98) writings as invoking a "liberal view of progress . . . but added to this is the notion that progress is the Christian improvement of society and that in such progress we see the hand of God."[144] This understanding is reflected in Bush's rhetoric described earlier. Taylor describes what he calls "common ground" secularism, in which members of a political community agree upon an ethic of peaceful coexistence and political order based on doctrines common to all Christian sects, or even to all theists.[145] Historically, this represented a successful compromise in Europe for warring sects because "political injunctions that flowed from this common core trumped the demands of a particular confessional allegiance."[146] The objective was not to expel religion from politics in the name of an independent ethic, as in laicism. Rather, it was to prevent the state from backing one (Christian) confession over another by appealing to that which all held in common. This evenhandedness between religious traditions was, according to Taylor, the basis of the original American separation of church and state.[147] Finally, Pizzorno suggests that the "fundamental, long-term function of the church in the formation of Western civilization" was to offer "a set of symbols of common identity, which made it possible to establish who belonged and who was excluded."[148]

The tradition that I identify as Judeo-Christian secularism, as these different accounts suggest, is beholden to religion in a particular way. It is not the opposite of theological discourse. Instead, it enacts a particular kind of theological discourse in its own right. Like laicism, it is located on the spectrum of theological politics. Judeo-Christian secularism differs from laicism in that it does not aspire to absent or exclude religion from modern spheres of power and authority. It diverges from laicism with regard to the role of Judeo-Christian tradition in the establishment and maintenance of the secularist "separation" of church and state. While laicism assumes that religion has receded out of modern spheres of authority and into the private realm or diminished altogether, Judeo-Christian secularism does not make this assumption. Instead, Judeo-Christian secularism is a variant of what Jelen describes as religious "accommodationism" insofar as it maintains that "religion (singular) is ultimately good for democratic politics, because a *shared* adherence to a common religious tradition provides a set of publicly accessible assumptions within which democratic politics can be conducted."[149] For Judeo-Christian secularists, the separation of church and state is a unique Western achievement that grew out of a shared adherence to a common set of European religious and political traditions. Christianity, as van Leeuwen argued, led to secularism.

International relations theory has not escaped the influence of this powerful tradition. The most influential variation is found in arguments suggesting that religious history and tradition play a specific and determinative role as the source of particular styles and institutions of governance, forms of civilizational identity, and entrenched and violent clashes between so-called civilizations. Judeo-Christian tradition, in this view, culminated in and contributes to the unique Western achievement of the separation of church and state and forms of liberal democracy.[150] As Huntington argues, "Western Christianity, first Catholicism and then Protestantism, is historically the single most important characteristic of Western civilization."[151] This prevailing dualism between "God and Caesar, church and state, spiritual and temporal authority . . . contributed immeasurably to the development of freedom in the West" and forms part of "the factors which enabled the West to take the lead in modernizing itself and the world."[152] Religion is the bedrock of this cultural inheritance and is closely tied to geographic location. It is responsible for differentiating between civilizations and between individuals: "in the modern world, religion is a central, perhaps *the* central, force that motivates and mobilizes people."[153] It is the glue that holds civilizations together. Religion and culture are dictated not by "political ideology or economic interest," but "faith and family, blood and belief."[154] There is solidarity in civilizational consciousness, and religious diversity is dangerous because it threatens this solidarity.

As Huntington argues, "multiculturalism at home threatens the United States and the West; universalism abroad threatens the West and the World. Both deny the uniqueness of Western culture."[155] If the United States becomes "de-Westernized," and "Americans cease to adhere to their liberal democratic and European-rooted political ideology, the United States as we have known it will cease to exist and will follow the other ideologically defined superpower onto the ash heap of history."[156]

This account divides the world into two categories, those who share the Judeo-Christian common ground and those who do not. This is often accompanied by an implicit hierarchy between these two groupings. This framework for understanding the world is strikingly similar to the divisions proposed in the fourteenth-century by Italian jurist Bartolus de Sassoferato.[157] Bartolus divided the world into five classes: the *populus Romanus* or "almost all those who obey the Holy Mother Church," and four classes of *populus extranei*: the Turks, the Jews, the Greeks, and the Saracens.[158] Bartolus's scheme is similar to Huntington's seven or eight "major civilizations": Western, Confucian, Japanese, Islamic, Hindu, Slavic-Orthodox, Latin American, and "possibly African." Pagden describes the effects of these divisions:

> The effect of Bartolus's ethnic division is once again to limit "the world" to a distinct cultural, political, and in this case religious, community. And again it places boundaries between what may be counted as the domain of the fully human world, and those others—which because of their rejection of the hegemony of the Western Church now also included the Greeks—who have no place within the civitas, and so no certain claim upon the moral considerations of those who do.[159]

The position that a Judeo-Christian secular common ground ends abruptly at the edge of Western (Judeo-Christian) civilization leads to the defense of this ground against both internal and external enemies, resulting in what Connolly has described as "civilizational wars of aggressive defense of Western uniqueness."[160] These wars of defense become aggressive as the common ground is challenged and reconfigured under the stress of an increasing pluralistic West made up not only of Judeo-Christians but also Muslims, Hindus, Buddhists, atheists, agnostics, and Deleuzeans. As Taylor notes, "with the widening band of religious and metaphysical commitments in society, the ground originally defined as common becomes that of one party among others."[161] At this critical junction the common ground is either renegotiated or the "aggressive defense" of the common ground is set in motion. Neuhaus opts for the latter, arguing that the godless are incapable of a "morally convincing account" of the nation and concluding that "those who believe in the God of Abraham, Isaac, Jacob, and Jesus turn out to be the best citizens."[162]

This kind of thinking is expressed in international relations in the idea that the secular West has a monopoly over the proper relationship between religion and politics. As Keane argues,

The principle of secularism, which "represents a realisation of crucial motifs of Christianity itself" (Bonhoffer), is arguably founded upon a sublimated version of the Christian belief that Christianity is "the religion of religions" (Schleiermacher), and that Christianity is entitled to decide for non-Christian others what they can think or say — or even whether they are capable of thinking and saying anything at all.[163]

This kind of thinking results in the marginalization of non-Western and non-Judeo-Christian perspectives on religion and politics. If the dualism between spiritual and temporary authority is uniquely Western and Christian, then non-Westerners who want to democratize have no alternative but to adopt Western forms of secularism. A recent statement by Bernard Lewis reflects this assumption:

> Separation of church and state was derided in the past by Muslims when they said this is a Christian remedy for a Christian disease. It doesn't apply to us or to our world. Lately, I think some of them are beginning to reconsider that, and to concede that perhaps they may have caught a Christian disease and would therefore be well advised to try a Christian remedy.[164]

In this way of thinking, on the one hand non-Westerners who do not advocate for Western forms of secularism are portrayed as children who refuse to acknowledge that they are sick and need to stay in. On the other hand, those who *do* advocate for some form of secularism are subject to the charge from either abroad or at home that they are advancing pale imitations of a robust Western ideal, thereby departing from (and potentially betraying) indigenous tradition. As I argue in the coming chapters, this binary has the effect of delegitimizing alternative trajectories of secularization as they are automatically associated with Western power and domination.

Charting the influence of secularist traditions in international relations calls into question the assumptions upon which the "clash of civilizations" narrative rests. Understanding secularism as a set of discursive traditions that seeks to construct both the secular and the religious in particular ways makes it clear that defining religion as a fixed and final source of unity and identity with a particular relationship to politics is itself a political move. It is also a theological one. Both are contestable. Any attempt to fix the meaning of religion and then define its relationship either in or out of politics is inherently political and inherently unstable. Elements of religion always escape such attempts to represent, define, and confine it to particular roles, spaces, or moments either within or outside modern politics.

SECULARISM AND THE DISPLACEMENT OF POLITICS

In *Political Theory and the Displacement of Politics*, Bonnie Honig discusses two conflicting political impulses: the desire to decide "undecidabilities," and the will to contest established institutions and identities.[165] She criticizes theorists who limit their definition of politics to the "juridical, administrative or regulative tasks of stabilizing moral and political subjects, building consensus, maintaining agreements, or consolidating communities and identities."[166] Rather than theorizing politics, she argues, they "displace" it. Honig explores a contrasting impulse in the work of Nietzsche, Arendt, and Derrida, for whom politics is a "disruptive practice that resists the consolidations and closures of administrative and juridical settlement for the sake of the perpetuity of political contest."[167]

Like their counterparts in political theory, scholars of international relations yearn for closure and consensus, at least regarding the relation between religion and politics. As Barnett argues, "actors struggle over the power and the right to impose a legitimate vision of the world because doing so helps to construct social reality as much as it expresses it."[168] For most political scientists, this is a secular social reality. Most of us, perhaps unconsciously, perhaps less so, think, work, struggle against, and live in and around variations of the two traditions of secularism described in this chapter. These secular visions and the attitudes, sensibilities, and habits that sustain and shape them do not merely reflect social reality; they construct it along the lines described in chapter 1. They provide what Bukovansky describes as "a set of parameters, focal points, or even points of contention around which political discourse revolves."[169] They also provide attitudes, sensibilities, and habits that facilitate closure and agreement around particular cultural, political, and legal settlements of the separation of church and state. Secularism, it turns out, is a powerful "pattern of political rule."[170]

This pattern of rule is sustained by and through a constellation of related yet distinct authoritative discourses: secularization as the most recent step in the worldly realization of Judeo-Christian morality, secularization as the natural evolution toward a universal morality that has transcended any need for metaphysical moorings, secularization as a laudable side effect of democratization and economic and political modernization within the state, secularization as the globalization of the Westphalian state system in which religion has been privatized. These discursive formations shape and reproduce modern sensibilities and beliefs about the secular. They also contribute to the consolidation of modern national identities as secular and democratic. One way in which these traditions of secularism and the national identities with which they are intertwined have been consolidated is through opposition to the idea and practice of Islam. This constitutive opposition is the subject of chapter 3. Its political effects are the subject of chapters 5 and 6.

CHAPTER THREE

Secularism and Islam

> In conflict resistless each toil they endur'd,
> Till their foes shrunk dismay'd from the war's desolation:
> And pale beam'd the Crescent, its splendor obscured
> By the light of the star-spangled flag of our nation
> > Where each flaming star gleam'd a meteor of war,
> > And the turban'd head bowed to the terrible glare.
> > Then mixt with the olive the laurel shall wave,
> > And form a bright wreath for the brow of the brave.
>
> Our fathers who stand on the summit of fame,
> Shall exultingly hear, of their sons, the proud story,
> How the young bosoms glow'd with the patriot flame,
> How they fought, how they fell, in the midst of their glory,
> > How triumphant they rode, oe'r the wandering flood,
> > And stain'd the blue waters with infidel blood;
> > How mixt with the olive, the laurel did wave,
> > And form a bright wreath for the brow of the brave.[1]

WRITTEN BY MARYLAND LAWYER Francis Scott Key in 1805, these two verses of what would in 1814 become the American national anthem celebrate the accomplishments of postrevolutionary American soldiers in the war against Tripoli in the early years of the American republic. The lyrics suggest that early American national identity was composed at least in part of American ("star-spangled flag") opposition to, and victory over, Muslims (the "Crescent," "infidel blood").

There is a multidisciplinary attempt underway to understand how the West has been constituted through interactions with other societies. As Lockman argues, however, "exploration of how the modern West has in crucial ways been shaped, if not constituted, by its interactions with other societies is still at an early stage and remains vastly outweighed by the huge scholarly and popular literature that takes for granted the West's self-conception as a distinct and self-generated civilization and then focuses on the West's impact on the rest of the world."[2] In the field of international relations, Inayatullah and Blaney suggest that "each culture brings to the interactions (changeable) images of itself and others that are prefigured by myths, texts, and traditions. The study of international relations requires comparative and historical analysis of how cultures conceptualize others."[3] Wendt argues that "managing relationships and determining how we ought to act depend in part on answers to the explanatory question of how certain representations of Self and Other get created. This cannot be answered by unit-level theorizing alone."[4]

This chapter contributes to this effort by analyzing the relationship between secularism, Islam, and European and American national identities. Elements of both laicism and Judeo-Christian secularism compete and coexist in both European and American discourses on religion and politics. Here I trace a series of examples that illustrate the connections between French national identity and laicism and between American national identity and Judeo-Christian secularism. Each trajectory of secularism draws on a different set of historical representations of Islam: laicist assumptions contribute to depictions of Islam as a surmountable though formidable stumbling block to the rationalization and democratization of societies, whereas Judeo-Christian secularist assumptions lead to more ominous conclusions in which Islam is portrayed as a potential threat to the cultural, moral, and religious foundations of Western civilization that must be successfully defused. I conclude that the formations of secularism analyzed in this book, and the national identities in which they are embedded and through which they are expressed, have been generated in part through opposition to Islam.[5]

This argument makes two contributions to international relations theory. First, it challenges Hall's assertion, shared by most realist, liberal, and constructivist international relations theorists and contested throughout this book, that with the Westphalian settlement and the rise of nationalism in Europe "religious identity in the liberal west is thoroughly relegated to the status of a cultural attribute within domestic society, a matter of personal preference no more significant in the civic order than is the individual's taste in music, food, clothing, or any consumer commodity."[6] The norms and forms of secularism analyzed here emerged out of and remain indebted to both Enlightenment and Christian (and later Judeo-Christian) beliefs and practices.[7] These powerful traditions exercise significant influence in international relations such that they cannot be accurately characterized as matters of personal preference.

The argument developed here also contributes in two ways to the literature on "soft power" in international relations.[8] First, forms of secularism represent an important yet understudied part of the culture and values to which Joseph Nye has referred in his numerous discussions of soft power. As Nye suggests, "soft power grows out of a country's culture; it grows out of our values — democracy and human rights, when we live up to them; it grows out of our policies.[9] Second, as Samir Khalaf has suggested, the historical evidence presented here suggests that the United States' global projection of soft power began not after World War II as commonly assumed but much earlier with Protestant missions to the Middle East in the early nineteenth century.[10] Missionaries were, and remain, important transmitters of various forms of American culture and vehicles of American soft power.[11]

In making the argument that European and American forms of secularism are generated in part through opposition to particular appropriations of Islam, I am not suggesting that forms of secularist authority and the national identities in which they are embedded have been generated exclusively through this opposition. This is clearly not the case. Many factors unrelated to the politics of religion and entirely unrelated to representations of Islam have contributed to the consolidation of modern forms of secularism and modern European and American identities.[12] In addition, other religious traditions including Protestantism and Greek Orthodoxy also contribute in different ways to the consolidation and reproduction of the forms of secularism described in this book.[13] Finally, I do not want to suggest that there exists a direct and unmediated relationship between secularist authoritative traditions, national identities, and foreign policy outcomes. It would be unwise to assume "an easy or transparent relationship between representations of the foreign in cultural production and the world of foreign relations,"[14] as Brian Edwards points out in his analysis of the disjuncture between cultural production and political discourse:

> We are mistaken if we read literary and cultural production as somehow engaging political history on equal grounds — ground made equal by the space of criticism — as has been a common temptation in American studies in the wake of Said's work. Such a temptation, however well intended, is based on a misreading of Said and a failure to attend to his emphasis on questions of institutions rather than on "discourse."[15]

Yet, as Edwards himself demonstrates in his review of Paul Bowles's and General George Patton's writings, examining the overlap between cultural and political discourse also does make it possible to challenge the "perceived chasm separating cultural production from international politics" without equating the two indiscriminately.[16] Mary Ann Heiss bridges this chasm nicely in her analysis of the connection between paternalistic, demeaning, and gendered Anglo-American representations of Muhammad Mossadegh and the justification for the U.S.- and British-engineered coup in 1953 that removed him from power.[17] Heiss argues that representations of Mossadegh as effeminate, fickle, and irrational were significant obstacles in the effort to reach a negotiated resolution of the oil crisis in the wake of Mossadegh's attempted nationalization of the Iranian oil industry.

> Assessing the immediate influence of Western characterizations of Mossadeq on the formulation of Anglo-American policy is tricky because it is not possible to determine a direct causal relationship between Anglo-American perceptions and prejudices and specific events. We cannot say, for example, that Western stereotypes led

linearly to the coup that removed Mossadeq from office in the summer of 1953. But this does not mean that these stereotypes were unimportant. On the contrary, by shaping the mind-set of Anglo-American officials, they were part of the context within which those officials formulated policy. They buttressed claims of Western superiority over Iranians and other Middle Eastern peoples by perpetuating the idea that those peoples were weak and incapable. And their cumulative effect was to paint Mossadeq and others like him in unfavorable ways that rationalized and justified Western control.[18]

Like Edwards and Heiss, but with a focus on the construction of the political authority of two particular traditions of secularism, this chapter works this connection between cultural discourses, political identities, and forms of authority without assuming an easy or transparent relationship between them. If secularism is a multifaceted authoritative discourse that draws on a deep well of laicist and Judeo-Christian tradition, as argued in chapter 2, it is also the case that this same discourse has a very different yet also significant relationship to Islam. This relationship becomes the focus of this chapter. More than any other single religious or political tradition, Islam has come to represent the "nonsecular" in European and American political thought and practice. Laicism and Judeo-Christian secularism, and the collective identities in which these traditions are embodied and through which they are expressed, have been consolidated in part through opposition to the idea of an antimodern, anti-Christian, and theocratic Islamic Middle East.[19]

Secularist political authority, then, is produced performatively. Representations of Islam as antimodern, anti-Christian, and theocratic are not a coincidental by-product of an inert, pregiven secular political authority—they actually help to constitute it. As Homi Bhabha observes, "terms of cultural engagement, whether antagonistic or affiliative, are produced performatively. The representation of difference must not be hastily read as the reflection of *pre-given* ethnic or cultural traits set in the fixed tablet of tradition."[20] Traditions of secularism, and national identities in which they are embedded and through which they often become manifest, are produced performatively and relationally. As Özkırımlı has argued, "the meanings (and values) attributed to various constituents of the national culture, that is myths, symbols, and traditions, are interminably negotiated, revised and redefined."[21] Through this process of revision and redefinition, an opposition to Islam has been built into the secularist traditions analyzed in this book and has come to constitute part of the national identities with which these traditions are intertwined. Modern Euro-American forms of secular authority are, at least in part, an *effect* of the differentiation of a secular "self" from an Islamic "other." As Michael Dillon has argued,

> how the alien is alien . . . determines how the self-same, in both philosophy and politics, is itself not simply constituted, but continuously re-inaugurated in the process of trying to make the alien proper. There brews, therefore, beneath all identity

politics and beneath all allied philosophical systems a secret *horror alieni* that insidiously seeks to dispel all aliens—alienness itself—to divest things of everything enigmatic and strange.[22]

This argument about Western forms of secularism and their constitutive relation to particular ways of coming to terms with Islam adds depth and substance to Zachary Lockman's claim that "it was in part by differentiating themselves from Islam . . . that European Christians, and later their nominally secular descendants, defined their own identity."[23] Representations of Islam, the "Islamic Middle East," and Muslim subjects have underwritten the production and legitimization of secularist political authority and have made "various courses of action possible."[24] These representations have been appropriated historically to contribute to the construction of European and American national identities as laicist and Judeo-Christian secularist, respectively.

To develop this argument requires a genealogy of secularist authority in relation to Islam. This involves an attempt to "trace the small, discrete and disconnected beginnings of formations we now take for granted and now treat as if they were natural, given, or established by reason or expressive of an inner telos."[25] My approach to this endeavor, and to the politics and history of representation more generally, draws selectively upon the writings of Michel Foucault, Hayden White, William Connolly, and Talal Asad. Foucault was concerned with the rules governing a particular field of discourse, and sought to "explore scientific discourse not from the point of view of the individuals who are speaking, nor from the point of view of the formal structures of what they are saying, but from the point of view of the rules that come into play in the very existence of such discourse."[26] His approach leads to a concern for the rules, regulations, and enabling conditions that make particular kinds of discourse about Islam possible. White identifies three important political moments in the representational process, including the prefiguration of the historical or representational field, the figuration or writing of the representation, and the refiguration of the narrative as interpreted by different audiences.[27] This calls attention to the multifaceted nature of the representational process and the ways in which a single representation can have multiple and even contradictory political consequences. Connolly draws selectively from the arguments of both Foucault and White to emphasize the political nature of representations and the processes through which they are created and reinstantiated. He insists that representations get caught in a cycle of previous representations, resulting in a "doubling" effect:

> Representation occurs within historically particular contexts that fix both the things to be represented and the terms through which representation occurs. Representation always involves the representation of prior representations. This duality, or doubling, eventually confounds representation, not as an indispensable social practice but as a detached, neutral method of accumulating knowledge.[28]

This approach to the politics of representation directs attention to the changing historical contexts, and evolving philosophical and political terms, through which secularist representations of Islam have developed over time. Finally, in his study of the relationship between representation, knowledge, and religion, Asad underlines the importance of investigating two-way lines of connection between authoritative discourses and the production of knowledge about particular collective subjects. He suggests that "forms of interest in the production of knowledge are intrinsic to various structures of power, and they differ not according to the essential character of Islam or Christianity, but according to historically changing systems of discipline.["][29] These four approaches to politics, religion, and representation orient my attempt to understand select aspects of the historical constitution of the forms of secularist authority analyzed in this book, their relation to particular images of Islam, and the political consequences of these relations for the national identities that secularist authority shapes and through which it is legitimized.

ISLAM AND THE WEST

Bunyamin Simsek grew up in Aarhus, Denmark, the son of immigrants from the central Turkish village of Kizilcakisla. Working as a cabin attendant for a Danish charter airline company in the 1990s, he often was asked about his country of origin. His first response of "Aarhus" was usually met with incredulity, so he began asking customers to guess. Greece or Spain, they would venture, but never Turkey. To quote Simsek, "they think I'm nice, so they don't imagine I could be Turkish. Turkey, for them, is Islam, and Islam is fundamentalism.["][30]

Oleg Graber argues that European identity is sustained by "a vast fantasy of an Orient that is both a seminal creator (*ex oriente lux*, light comes from the east) and a threat from aliens with an 'oriental' mind.["][31] Mohja Kahf suggests that "if there is such a thing as a European outlook on the world, a sense of what is European as distinct from not-European, it began to develop and define itself in opposition to Islamic civilization.["][32] Neumann and Welsh agree that "the very idea of what Europe was was from the beginning defined partly in terms of what it was *not* . . . the non-European barbarian or savage played a decisive role in the evolution of the European identity and the maintenance of order among European states.["][33] Richard King connects the rise of secular rationality to the subordination of mystical elements of life associated with the Orient, in particular India:

> Since the Enlightenment . . . representations of Western cultures have tended to subordinate what one might call the "Dionysian" (as opposed to the Apollonian) aspects of its own culture and traditions (that is, those trends that have been con-

ceived as "poetic," "mystical," irrational, uncivilized and feminine). These characteristics represent precisely those qualities that have been "discovered" in the imaginary realm of "the Orient." Of course, this is a grand narrative about a highly complex and contradictory set of cultural processes, but it involves the ascendancy of secular rationality as an ideal within Western intellectual thought, a concomitant marginalization of "the mystical" and the projection of qualities associated with this concept onto a colonized and essentialized India.[34]

Finally, Asad has suggested that:

> The populations designated by the label "Islam" are, in part at least, the physical descendants and cultural heirs of the Hellenic world—the very world in which "Europe" also claims to have its roots. Yet "Islamic civilization" must somehow be denied a vital link to the very properties that define so much of what is essential to "Europe," for otherwise a civilisational difference cannot be postulated between them.[35]

As each of these authors suggests, negative associations of Islam and/or the Orient have played an important role in the establishment of European secular rationality, identity, and culture. Their observations are the starting point for my argument that negative associations of Islam have contributed not only to a general sense of Euro-American culture and civilization but to the elaboration of specific trajectories of secularism. This argument can be situated as part of a broader project described by historian Barbara Metcalf:

> Recent work by Benedict Anderson and others has placed metropolitan and colonized areas into a single historical space where many processes, in fact, have turned out to be simultaneous and the product of complex interactions. The most fundamental institutions of society and economy, even the very concept of nation, along with gender, class, and caste, prove to have been constituted as part of these interactions. One dimension of this is that terms that have been used as scientific categories, not least *modernity* and *secularism* on one side, and *tradition* and *religion* on the other, are increasingly studied as political categories dependent on each other.[36]

Metcalf emphasizes the collective intersubjective constitution of "fundamental institutions of society and economy," including the institutions of secularism. I argue that negative representations of Islam have contributed to the consolidation of French national identity as democratic and *laic*, and American national identity as democratic and Judeo-Christian secular. These representations contribute to the production and reproduction of the traditions of secularism analyzed here and the national identities in which these secularist commitments are embedded and expressed. Ann Laura Stoler makes a similar argument regarding the necessity of thinking through the domestic cultural and political effects of European imperial projects. In *Race and the Education of Desire,* for example, she argues that "the discursive practical field in which nineteenth-century bourgeois sexuality emerged was situated on an imperial landscape where the cultural accoutrements of bourgeois distinction were partially shaped through contrasts forged in the politics and language of race."[37] Like Stoler, I seek to contribute to a rethinking of the historiographical conventions that bracket histories of the West,[38] focusing on the discursive field in which particular forms of secularism emerged and their relationship to a broader imperial landscape.

The objects of analysis in this chapter are European and early American representations of Islam and their political and cultural effects, and not actual Islamic institutions or their relation to state politics and power in Muslim-majority societies. Mohja Kahf describes this important distinction in her book on Western representations of Muslim women:

> The actual condition of Muslim women is a serious and complex topic. Its study, however, does little to explain the development of the Western narrative. This narrative has a genealogy and logic of its own, emerging from developments in Western representations of gender, of the self, and of the foreign or other. . . . There is nothing essential or timeless behind Western representations of the Muslim woman; they are products of specific moments and developments in culture.[39]

Similar to Kahf's focus, my subject is not Muslim belief, Islamic tradition, or the relationship between Islam and actual modes of governance in any particular country; it is European and American representations of Islam and how these representations have contributed to the constitution of different forms of secularist authority and the production of particular national identities through which these forms of secularism are expressed and articulated. As Kahf's work illustrates, the ability to represent Islam in a particular way is itself an exercise of power. Edwards makes a similar argument in his discussion of how Western cultural and political representations of the Maghreb have reflected and reinforced a sense that there is no need to engage with actual North Africans.[40] Edwards describes this self-referential American mind-set as "Lucean" after Henry Luce's 1941 essay "The American Century," in which he expounds a "conservative vision of a circular or tautological American understanding of the world—where U.S. global positioning is imagined as supreme within an 'imaginative' American recreation of global power relations."[41] Before examining the American case, however, I turn to French representations of Islam and the construction of the republican ideal of *laïcité*.

COLONIALISM AND THE REPUBLICAN PROJECT: ISLAM AND FRENCH *LAÏCITÉ*

Laicism is a productive modality of power that organizes itself by establishing particular boundaries and producing particular kinds of collective (theo)political identities.[42] The ambition to realize a pure, universal form of laicism that expels religion from politics is one of the hallmarks of modern French political order and has been achieved by legislating the relationship between the realm of the sacred and the realm of the profane. Laicism insists upon a singular and universal set of relations between sacred and profane dimensions of existence that holds regardless of cultural or historical circumstances. This is achieved in part through exclusionary practices that represent Islam as antimodern, irrational, and tyrannical. In the political imaginary of laicism, Islam is represented as an impediment to the rationalization and democratization of modern society. Laicism therefore reproduces itself and the national identities with which it is affiliated as legitimate, democratic, and modern by representing Islam as irrational, despotic, and antimodern. As Eugenio Trias has observed, "it is in the struggle against religion that reason has sought to secure its own legitimacy."[43] Negative representations of Islam do not merely reflect the political authority of laicism. They help to constitute it. The following paragraphs document select elements of that process by drawing on historical and postcolonial accounts of French colonial rule and its relationship to the republican laicist project.

Napoleon's invasion of Egypt in 1798 inaugurated a self-proclaimed French "civilizing mission" to North Africa and the Middle East that was conceived as raising backward peoples to the level of a universal culture and civilization.[44] An alleged deficiency in the civil societies of the colonized created what many Europeans perceived as "a vacuum that was used to justify the moral necessity of western imperialism in North Africa, the Middle East, and the East Indies."[45] The development of a vibrant civil society in the West was cited as a contrast to an Eastern "system of absences" and served as a counterpart to the colonizing mentality that sought to correct those absences through colonial rule. This colonial mentality was fueled in part by a commitment to the theory of "Oriental despotism," a concept originally developed by Montesquieu in *The Spirit of the Laws* that was influential in the writings of Marx, Weber, James Mill, John Stuart Mill, and others.[46] The theory posited that Islamic societies lacked "many of the features and institutions which modern European societies seemed to possess and which had supposedly enabled Europeans to achieve progress, knowledge, wealth and power."[47] The theory of Oriental despotism also served as a means for Europeans to surreptitiously criticize despotic tendencies in their own societies, as in, most famously, Montesquieu's *Persian Letters* (1721).[48]

Oriental despotism fits into a broader tendency identified by Dipesh Chakrabarty as a "stagist theory" of history and by Michael Hanchard as "racial time"[49] through which European political and social thought has made room for what Chakrabarty describes as subaltern classes:[50]

> If "political modernity" was to be a bounded and definable phenomenon, it was not unreasonable to use its definition as a measuring rod for social progress. Within this thought, it could always be said with reason that some people were less modern

than others, and that the former needed a period of preparation and waiting before they could be recognized as full participants in political modernity.[51]

Laicism served as an ideological and practical measuring rod that helped to define and bound political modernity broadly and the European "civilizing mission" specifically. In French interventions in the Middle East and North Africa, the expulsion of religion from politics was identified with progress and civilization, while Islam was associated with Oriental despotism.[52] By appropriating Islam as a regressive and even transgressive nemesis, as a stumbling block to be overcome on the road leading to the French (theoretical though never actual) ideal of assimilation, French thinkers, writers, and colonial administrators contributed to the consolidation of republican identity and state authority as *laic*.[53] The concept and practice of a modern, civilized, and laicist French identity was consolidated, at least in part, through opposition to a series of Muslim colonial "others" that had not yet been, and perhaps never would be, fully civilized.[54] As Todd Shepard argues, "by the late nineteenth century assumptions about the inferiority of Algerian 'Muslims' joined continued assertions that France needed to respect the attachment of 'Muslims' to their Koranic or customary law status as explanations for the continued exclusion of most from full citizenship."[55]

Others have investigated the connections between colonialism and the construction of the domestic institutions of the colonizer. Shepard, for example, underscores the "crucial role that building an overseas empire had in structuring republican institutions in France."[56] Timothy Mitchell developed a similar argument regarding the effects of British colonial power in Egypt. Mitchell argues that one of the political effects of British colonial rule was the sense that the world was divided into two different domains: the colonial self and the colonized other.[57] Paul Silverstein has suggested that the French colonial project in Algeria functioned as an important element in the consolidation of a republican national regime:[58] "The Algerian colony, as a site of innovation and experimentation with the norms and forms of modernity, provided the tools for the French state to monopolize its authority at home, slough off its undesirable masses, and gain a rotating reserve army of laborers necessary for building up the metropole."[59] Laicism was one of the "norms and forms of modernity" identified by Silverstein. Laicism was not a pregiven French standard that was exported to Algeria during the period of French rule between 1830 until the first Algerian war of 1954–62. Instead, *laic* republican collective subjectivity was in part the *effect* of the differentiation of a civilized laicist colonizer from an uncouth, Islamic colonized Algerian. Modern colonialism, as Shepard argues, was a republican project.[60] The process of colonizing Algeria helped to consolidate both the tradition of modern French laicism and French republican ideals with which it was closely intertwined while excluding Muslims from these allegedly universal forms of identification.[61]

There are numerous examples of the consolidation of French republican identity as laicist, scientific, and rational through the representation of Algerian Muslims as overly religious, backward, and irrational. Silverstein argues that "Islam served as the primary trope for explaining two opposed characteristics of the observed Arab personality: on the one hand, their bellicose, hostile nature, attributable to their religious fanaticism; and on the other hand, their inveterate laziness, resulting from their reverent fatalism."[62] Patricia Lorcin notes that "the spectre of Islam as a belligerent religion was ever-present throughout the 130 years of French occupation, and the French invariably imputed to Islam all forms of opposition to their rule."[63] Going back to the original sources, Auguste Pomel, in his 1871 treatise on the "indigenous races of Algeria and the role reserved for them by their aptitudes" wrote that "Mahometism appears specially adapted to societies whose social evolution arrested in the phase of barbarous patriarchy . . . a theocratic status of which absolutism is the pivot and fatalism the measure."[64] Muslims were portrayed by many French writers and administrators as unreceptive to change and hostile to progress. As Silverstein notes, "French administrators perceived this essential religiosity of Arabs as an inherent stumbling block to their administrative and legal incorporation into the French nation."[65]

Nowhere were French representations of Islam as the central impediment to the rationalization and modernization of Algerian society more evident than in the excessive French praise for the Berbers, and in particular the Kabyle minority, who were depicted as more modern and civilized than their Arab counterparts.[66] The French portrayed the Kabyles as only superficially Islamic and in every way the opposite of the Arabs.[67] As one French analyst observed in 1950, "the Berbers are part of the rational West in formal opposition to the Arabs, who are above all of the imaginative Orient."[68] These negative representations of Algerian Muslims did not merely reflect, but actually helped to consolidate and legitimize, the political authority and moral superiority of laicism. As Lorcin argues,

> natural tendencies to view European civilization as universally superior were exacerbated intellectually by three factors, namely, the received ideas that had first been elaborated during the Middle Ages and had undergone little subsequent modification, the commitment to secularization on the part of an essentially anti-clerical officer corps, and the awareness, on the part of Saint-Simonian officers in particular, of the nascent ideas connecting religion to human development.[69]

Depicting Algerian Muslims as tradition-bound, lazy, fatalistic, theocratic, and irrational helped to construct and defend an emergent French ambition to public order that embodied the opposite traits, an objective that was to be achieved at least in part through the exclusion of religion from public life.[70]

The fact that French thinkers and members of the Algerian officer corps had such strong views concerning the connections between religion, politics, morality, and public order in French Algeria in the mid- to late nineteenth century suggests that these same connections were undergoing revision in France at that time. Indeed, a new legal, institutional and political French commitment to *laïcité* emerged in the late nineteenth century,[71] part of a vast assemblage of modernizing developments that have been traced meticulously in the history of French domestic politics but only rarely explicitly connected to French colonial politics.[72] Although its formal origins can be traced at least to the French Revolution, the nineteenth century witnessed a series of events and reforms that embedded a particular tradition of laicism in French law, including the political victory of the anticlerical movement in the founding of the Third Republic in 1871[73] and legislative acts limiting the role of religion in public education through the institution of *morale laïque* in the 1880s.[74] These developments culminated in the French Law of 1905, which ensured liberty of conscience, guaranteed the free exercise of religion (Article I), and acknowledged that the Republic would not recognize, remunerate, or subsidize any religious denomination (Article II).[75] As Lorcin observes, "from the 1789–99 revolution, when the Church was divested of its territorial wealth, to 1905 when Church and state were finally separated, the tide between clerical and anti-clerical elements in France ebbed and flowed as France was gradually transformed into a secular state."[76]

Conventional accounts of these developments portray them "as part of the constant tug-of-war between the Church and the liberalizing forces of the society over the *pouvoir éducateur*."[77] As Peter McPhee argues, "central to the Third Republic's educational project was the assumption that republican values could only finally be embedded in French society if the power of the Catholic Church over the minds of the young could be broken."[78] I would argue that in addition to these domestic considerations, the entrenchment of a particular form of laicism in France both contributed to and benefited from specific French colonial policies, in particular a more assertive and deliberate overseas colonial policy that developed after the military defeat of 1870—the same year that France made Algeria an integral part of France with three départements.[79] As McPhee notes, this new policy "united the small but influential colonial lobby" concerning the just nature of the French civilizing mission abroad, assumptions that were "not seriously questioned across the political spectrum."[80] One powerful proponent of this colonial policy was Jules Ferry (mayor of Paris in 1870–71 and prime minister in 1880–81), the leading figure in French secularizing educational reforms of this era.[81] Ferry supported the "obligation and duty that are imposed on all civilized people to make the signature of their representatives respected by all barbarous nations."[82] As McPhee argues, "colonialism took on a rehabilitating, 'civilizing' mission for France as well as for its colonial subjects."[83] French colonial representations of Algerian Muslims as nonsecular, uncivilized, and disorderly contributed to the establishment of French civilization as modern, demo-

cratic, and *laic*. As Lorcin concludes, "allegiance to the nation served to coun-
teract internal political or regional schisms and to unite the country behind
a secular banner."[84]

It is difficult and perhaps risky to trace causal connections between the
historical constitution and legal instantiations of French *laïcité* and contemporary French politics. However, one possible legacy of these negative representations of Islam in current debates surrounding French identity is the relative lack of toleration in these discussions for the public accommodation of
Islamic expression and identification. Up to the present, being a French sup-
porter of laicism has generally meant *not* being Muslim, at least not openly
and publicly. One could be Jewish (at times) or Christian, but within the
concept of "secular Muslim European" has been lodged an assumption that
the "Muslim" part is subordinate to the "secular" and "European" parts. Recent illustrations of this tension between received traditions of French republican identity and the realities of a diversifying theopolitical landscape in contemporary France include support for the legal ban on veiling and other
ostensible forms of religious expression in French public spaces enacted in
2004, as well as opposition to Turkish membership in the European Union.
The latter is the subject of chapter 4.

"LIKE APPLES AND ORANGES": ISLAM AND JUDEO-CHRISTIAN SECULARISM

In March 2000 the Al Salam Mosque Foundation signed a $2.1 million dollar
contract to purchase a Reformed Church in Palos Heights, Illinois.[85] When
the Mosque Foundation sought the city's assurance that the building could
be used as a religious institution, as it had been previously, residents and two
city council members protested. In defense of her opposition to the mosque,
one alderwoman commented that "what you are proposing is like upside-
down . . . yours (referring to the Muslim day of worship) is on Friday, and
then you are not going to use it on Sunday. It's kind of like comparing apples
and oranges." In a newspaper interview a second alderman (who later apolo-
gized) stated, "if someone had intervened early on to stop Adolph Hitler, there
might not have been a world war." At public meetings Muslims were told to
"go back to their own countries," and one woman described Islam as a "false
religion."[86] In an attempt to resolve this conflict, the Palos Heights City Council voted to pay the Al Salam Mosque Foundation $200,000 to walk away from
the deal. Although the foundation initially accepted this compromise, the
mayor of Palos Heights later vetoed the buyout on the grounds that it was an
insult to Muslims. The foundation responded by suing the city in federal civil
court for $6.2 million on the grounds that "the city's handling of the situation
amounted to religious discrimination, conspiracy, and unwarranted meddling
in a private real estate transaction."[87]

This resistance among "average" Americans in Palos Heights to the presence of a mosque in their community reminds me of a billboard that I saw in the early 1990s alongside Route 9 in Connecticut that read, "Exercise your freedom of religion: attend the Church of your choice." Both the Palos Heights controversy and the billboard in Connecticut suggest in differing ways that religious freedom in the United States has on occasion been conflated with the right to practice Christianity. In Palos Heights, the "apples and oranges" defense expressed deep-seated anxieties about the presence of Muslim religious institutions. The residents' discomfort with the idea of a mosque in their community, expressed in one individual's suggestion that allowing Muslims to worship in Palos Heights would be equivalent to accepting Hitler, suggests that the (Judeo)-Christian tradition of secularism that informs American discourse on religion and politics stands in a tense relation with Islam. The practice of Judeo-Christian secularism seems to carry within it a philosophical, historical, visceral, and institutionalized opposition to Islam, as witnessed in Palos Heights. In this instance, as in others,[88] Judeo-Christian secularism fails to provide the ethical resources required for an actual pluralization of public life in suburban Illinois and elsewhere.

Negative representations of Islam have a long and active history in American politics[89] and remain influential in contemporary references to "natural" links between Christianity and American democracy, "natural" links between Islam and theocracy, suggestions that democratic secular order is a unique Western achievement, and the sense that Islam poses a special kind of threat to the cultural, moral, and religious foundations of Western ways of life. This section argues that these unflattering contemporary representations of Islam are the direct descendants of early American attempts to consolidate a democratic, secular national identity that was achieved in part through opposition to particular understandings and representations of Islam.[90] Like republican laic identity in France, the consolidation of early American identity as Christian and democratic was achieved in part through negative appropriations of Islam. (The prefix Judeo was not added to Judeo-Christian until after World War II and is therefore not relevant to this discussion, which focuses on the relationship between Christianity, Islam, and early American national identity.)

In his excellent work on this subject, Timothy Marr has shown that early American identity was constituted as morally righteous, democratic, and modern by representing Islam as the epitome of "antichristian darkness and political tyranny."[91] Marr demonstrates that unfavorable early American representations of Islam by Protestant missionaries contributed to the construction of early American national identity as modern, democratic, and Christian. Drawing on Marr's work, I argue that these representations also laid a template not only for domestic American hostility toward Islam as witnessed on an individual and communal scale in Palos Heights, but also for much larger state-level Euro-American collective approaches to international relations with Muslim-majority states. Missions abroad, religious in the American case and colonial in the French one, have played a critical role in the construction of domestic forms of identification and the emergence of particular kinds of political institutions and traditions.

Robert Allison notes that "the American encounter with the Muslim world actually began before there was a United States and almost before Europeans became aware that America existed."[92] Early American Protestant missionaries, who saw Islam as the antichrist, were among the earliest actors to frame Islam as the nemesis of American identity, which was construed as Christian and democratic.[93] As one female Protestant missionary to Syria in the early nineteenth century wrote, "what else but evil can be told of the undisputed dominions of the enemy of God?"[94] As Marr chronicles, the missionaries believed that Islam "claimed a direct revelation from God after that of Christ, [and] could not be placed within a Christian world-view. Its very existence shook the foundations of Christian belief, spelling spiritual ruin and a return to moral chaos."[95] In seeking to explain why God would allow the foundations of Christian belief to be shaken, Protestant eschatology placed the blame on Christians themselves, insisting that Islam was "as an enemy whose existence was solely a result of Christian mistakes."[96] According to Martin Luther, the Turkish invasions of Europe were "the rod of punishment of the wrath of God" for their infidelity to the spirit of Christ.[97] John Cotton claimed that "popish idolatry causes Turkish tyrannie."[98]

Many early Americans also believed that the Day of Judgment and the final destruction of the Muslim antichrist would follow the fall of Islam, and religious authorities competed to confirm signs of the coming fall.[99] Protestant biblical commentators in the seventeenth through nineteenth centuries established a link between the fall of Islam and the return of Christ by arguing that Islam as a historical phenomenon was expressed by the fifth and sixth trumpets, "whose blasts were called the first two trumpets of woe," described in the ninth chapter of Revelation.[100] They believed that the sixth trumpet was passing and that the Day of Judgment was near. As Marr argues, "it was mainly through the agency of this 'Turkish theory' that the fate of Islam came to be intimately connected with the possibility of Christ's return."[101] The missionaries' religious zeal notwithstanding, they encountered difficulties in their attempts to convert Muslims to Christianity. Within five years of starting their mission to the Middle East in 1820, Pliny Fisk and Levi Parsons had both fallen ill and died. To make matters more difficult, Ottoman law punished apostasy from Islam. In addition, as Marr notes, "to this date there has been no large-scale conversion of Muslims to Christianity in large part because the Qur'an acknowledges the divine mission of Christ."[102]

Despite their relatively limited success abroad, the missionaries were extremely influential in the United States itself. Samir Khalaf, for example, argues that between 1820 and 1920 U.S. foreign policy to the Middle East was based on reports filed by these missionaries.[103] In addition, at home the missionaries inaugurated a tradition of interpreting Islam through a Christian worldview that approached Muslim-Christian relations as part of a divine plan. A powerful interpretive tradition that spanned three centuries and a wide range of thinkers,[104] Protestant eschatology figured prominently in the formation of early American attitudes toward Islam. In part as a result of these representations, American national identity was constructed in terms of Christian superiority over a despotic Islamic infidel. The threat posed by Islam had been repackaged into a confirmation of Christian superiority.[105] As Marr argues, "dehumanizing notions about one of the world's major religions were implanted within the cultural perspective, and even the religious faith, of many educated Americans."[106]

Missionaries Pliny Fisk, Jonas King, and Levi Parsons all contributed to this anti-Islamic mind-set. Convinced of the superiority of Christianity over Islam, Parsons referred to Islam as "this great empire of sin."[107] Colorful biblical interpretations fueled this political and religious imaginary. Biblical commentators attempted to establish links between the "perceived qualities of the Arabian peoples and the behavior of natural locusts" in order to assure readers that Revelation's locusts referred to Saracens from the east.[108] The drying up of the Euphrates, the commentators assured their readers, "signified the declension of the Turkish empire to make room for the restoration of the Jews to Israel and their subsequent conversion to Christianity, a harbinger of the end of the antichristian empire."[109] Marr describes the influence of this discourse upon the American public:

The combined elements of these theories of the eastern antichrist—which identified the fifth trumpet with the rise of Islam, the sixth trumpet with the establishment of the Turkish empire, and the sixth vial with its imminent demise—was a mainstay of many American biblical commentaries in the first half century after the formation of the United States. The most popular resources—handbooks, dictionaries, family Bible commentaries, and reference compendia—incorporated the Turkish theory in their explanatory notes. . . . These sources spread these views of Islam, while validating them as the authoritative judgments of experts, into the studies of ministers and living rooms of lay people.[110]

This biblical prophecy was interpreted as suggesting that Islam was fated to fall. As Reverend Pliny Fisk argued, "it is not more certain, that the walls of Jericho fell before the ancient people of God, than it is, that the whole Mahommedan world will be subdued by the Gospel."[111]

At the same time, American engagement in the Mediterranean increased dramatically during the early nineteenth century as a result of mounting commercial, missionary, and trade interests. Disputes arose between the United States and Algiers between 1785 and 1815; the United States was involved in the Tripolitan War of 1801–15 and the Greek War of Independence of 1821–

28, and the United States bombed Sumatra in 1831. As the United States became militarily and economically more powerful, Americans worked to legitimize both their foreign policy and their newly established domestic government. Marr notes that "events in the Muslim Mediterranean thereby performed necessary functions in the affirmation of American nationalism and functioned as a stage of legitimization, both historically and rhetorically, upon which Americans could dramatize the humanity and heroism of their own cultural practices and the global relevance of their form of government."[112] Americans consolidated this common national identity against what they represented as the anti-Christian tyranny of Islamic rule. "This orientalist construction of Islam as a cultural enemy, maligned as both antichristian and antidemocratic, served as an idealized antithesis against which Americans of diverse denominational, ethnic, and partisan stripes could unite in defining republican identities from the nation's founding up until the Age of Jackson."[113] The link between the superiority of Christianity and American exceptionalism was strengthened by the widespread belief that the new nation had been created to assist in bringing about the millennium—the thousand-year reign of Christian peace.[114]

Early American democratic nationalism combined Orientalism, ideals of Christian superiority, and the American approach to government.[115] One consequence of the popularization of these connections in the United States was that Americans conceived of Islam as synonymous with despotic rule. "Islam, as the Americans saw it, was against liberty, and being against liberty, it stopped progress."[116] At the same time, commentators interpreted the political disintegration of Mediterranean governments as confirmation of the virtues of American republican government. "The construction of tyranny and despotism was thus an inherent part of the process of reinventing republicanism."[117] Montesquieu and other Enlightenment thinkers were an important source of the idea that American ideals of governance should be posited as the opposite of Islamic political order. According to Allison, "Enlightenment writers created a picture of the Muslim world that served as a sober warning about the dangers of submitting to despotism, about the dangers of suppressing public debate, and about the twin evils of tyranny and anarchy."[118] Montesquieu's writings on the virtues of checks and balances, the separation of powers, and civic virtue were, according to Marr, "only fully understood in dialectic relation to the despotism that arose in their absence."[119] Thus Montesquieu not only contributed to an understanding of republican government but also "helped to form early American views of Islamic government . . . as the oppositional model of the excesses to be avoided in the new American system."[120]

Islamic imagery thus functioned in postrevolutionary America as an "interpretive horizon against which Americans oriented the direction of their national project, the morality of their cultural institutions, and the shape of their romantic imaginations."[121] Even literary productions produced consensus around the virtues of republicanism, Christianity, and democracy in opposition to Islamic despotism and exploitation. As Allison observes:

> A flood of books on the Muslim world poured from American presses in the 1790s: captivity narratives; histories, including two biographies of Muhammad; novels and poems; and the first American edition of the *Arabian Nights*. This literature conveyed a consistent picture of the Muslim world, an inverted image of the world the Americans were trying to create anew.[122]

Moralizing, fictional oriental tales stood in as the "secular counterpart to eschatological utopianism," "an important cultural enterprise of counterdespotism [that] stimulated the expression of a sublime moral idealism which Americans harnessed for nationalist ends."[123] Themes of these productions included the family as the vehicle of virtue and bedrock of moral democracy, the harem as the seedbed of despotism, and the conversion of the infidel and the naturalization of the despotic (and spying) alien.

The production of early American national identity as Christian, secular, and democratic was at least in part an *effect* of the attempt to differentiate a modern, republican Christian America from an antimodern, despotic Islamic Middle East. Long before any Muslims settled in the United States, Islam played an important role in the construction of American identity as Christian (later Judeo-Christian), secular, and democratic.[124] This process of collective self-identification laid important cultural templates for powerful contemporary connections between American identity, manifest destiny, and Christianity. This is illustrated in a response to a poll given by a forty-six-year-old engineering technician from Ohio, who stated that "this country was set up to lead the rest of the world. God picked this country."[125] These same templates contribute to American constructions of Muslim deviance at home and abroad, including contemporary notions of the "rogue state," the Islamist terrorist, and the portrayal of Islam as a "false religion."[126]

CONCLUSION

This chapter has argued that French and American national identities and the two traditions of secularism described in this book that are embedded in them have been constituted in part through opposition to particular representations of Islam. These representations are not the by-product of a pregiven form of secularist authority. They are constitutive of it. They help to define, reproduce, elaborate upon, and patrol the boundaries of the authoritative secularist traditions described in chapter 2.

The next chapter bridges the historical and conceptual work accomplished thus far with the more applied arguments that make up the middle chapters of the book, introducing the cases of Turkey and Iran to illustrate how the "secular" has been constructed, contested, and renegotiated in these countries. Chapters 5 and 6 describe the implications of laicism and Judeo-Christian secularism for international relations through empirical analyses of the cultural and normative foundations of European opposition to Turkish accession to the European Union and American responses to the Iranian revolution of 1978–79, respectively. Neither the controversy over EU enlargement nor ongoing hostility between the United States and Iran may be understood through recourse to the rationalist accounts that dominate contemporary international relations theory and take state interests as objective and pregiven. Understanding these empirical puzzles requires reframing the question to account for the effects of secularist tradition, forms of collective identification, and epistemology upon international politics.

CHAPTER FOUR

Contested Secularisms in Turkey and Iran

> Post-Enlightenment thought defines modern politics in terms
> of a public realm that is or should be . . . animated either by
> apparently objective socioeconomic interests or secular ideals, or
> both; by contrast the very definition of irrationalism is historically
> and culturally linked with the authority of religion, faith, and
> tradition. The attempt to remake the public realm in terms of
> religious imperatives, to (re-)define the boundary between public
> and private, to (re-)interpret the collective good in terms of a
> divine mandate comes to seem no less than an attempt to destroy
> the foundations of modern politics itself.[1]

THIS CHAPTER BRIDGES the conceptual and historical arguments of the two preceding chapters and the more applied arguments of chapters 5 and 6. Its primary objective is to introduce domestic Turkish and Iranian renegotiations of the secular. Woven into these historical accounts are examples of how the epistemological and evaluative stances described in the preceding chapters as laicism and Judeo-Christian secularism have operated in practice to condition Western responses to religiopolitical developments in Turkey and Iran. Developments in these countries do not fall easily into categories available to Western observers for understanding religion and politics. The cases in this chapter are examples of religiopolitical accommodation and contestation that are neither laicist nor Judeo-Christian secularist. They illustrate my argument that the attempt to remake the public realm is not necessarily a threat to the foundation of modern politics. It is a modern contestation of the concept and practice of the secular authorized and regulated by state authorities since the founding of the modern Turkish Republic by Atatürk in 1923 and the rise of Reza Shah in Iran in 1925. It *is* modern politics. Renarrating these historical episodes poses a challenge to what Anthony Marx has referred to as the "long cherished consensus and conventions of Western historiography."[2] It contributes to "a rethinking of the historiographic conventions that have bracketed histories" of Turkey and Iran.[3] Finally, the background presented in this chapter is part of a broader historical and political context that is referred to but not described in detail in later chapters. This chapter therefore also serves as an important preface to chapters 5 and 6, which focus on the role of secularist authority in European and American representations of and relations with Turkey and Iran.

TURKEY

At the founding of the modern Turkish republic in 1923, Mustafa Kemal (Atatürk, or "father of the Turks") adapted the French model of laicism, emphasizing state control of religious expression and institutions,[4] into a unique mixture of Turkish nationalist, Sunni Islamic, and European laicist traditions that became known as Kemalism.[5] For Kemalists, progress was defined as the management and control over local Islamic culture.[6] Atatürk's reforms were codified in a new Turkish Civil Code enacted in 1926 (a translation of the Swiss Code civile), which legalized state attempts to regulate religion. This included a ban on Sufi *tarikats* (religious brotherhoods) and state suppression of Sufi activities. The national capital was moved from Istanbul to Ankara to sever ties with the Byzantine and Ottoman past. The caliphate and the religious courts were abolished in 1924, the calendar changed from the Islamic to the Gregorian, and Arabic script replaced with the Latin alphabet. The Turkish language was "purified" of all words with Arabic roots; and "within three months all books, newspapers, street signs, school papers, and public documents had to be written using the new letters."[7] Clocks were set to European time, rather than Muslim time in which the date changed at sunset. Women were discouraged from wearing traditional dresses and, in at least one instance, were forbidden from entering prominent public places in Ankara in traditional attire.[8] *Tekkes* (lodges) and *türbes* (shrines of saints) were ordered closed by the state.

It is usually assumed that Kemalism was strictly separationist.[9] Yavuz, for example, describes Kemalist reforms as an attempt "to guide an exodus from the Ottoman-Islamic past . . . [using] the French conception of rigid secularism as a compass to determine the direction of the exodus."[10] However, Davison takes a slightly different view, which I share, suggesting that the Turkish state "never made religion or Islam an entirely separate (and thus, 'private') matter. . . . The separation of religion from its previous position of influence constituted a shift in Islam's institutional and legitimation position, not its formal, full elimination . . . Islam was not disestablished, it was differently established."[11] This was Kemalism.

Kemalism, a new and different establishment of Ottoman and Islamic tradition that also brought in elements of French laicist tradition, incited a range of responses. Some Turks were quick to adopt what they perceived to be Western ways. According to a Turkish colleague quoted by sociologist Nicolas Demerath, "Turkey became a nation of forgetters. Many in my parents' generation were eager to renounce the past in favor of a new westward-looking way of life. My family even got rid of our heirloom Turkish rugs in favor of chic, wall-to-wall carpeting. I recently learned that some of those rugs are now in museum shows in the United States."[12] Others sought to explicitly adopt elements of both Kemalist and Ottoman tradition. Ihsan Yilmaz, for example, argues that, despite the imposition of secular law, Turks effectively combined unofficial Islamic law and official secular law into a hybrid permitting the retention of traditional ties to Islamic practice. "In all sorts of spheres of life, Muslim law is referred to and obeyed by many people despite the non-recognition of the state."[13] Others opposed the reforms. Özdalga describes the rise of a "silent suspicion" of Kemalism among rural individuals sympathetic to popular forms of Islam and the cultural resources of the *tarikats*.[14]

Various attempts to renegotiate the Kemalist settlement began to emerge with the opening of the Turkish political system to multiparty competition in the 1950s and the end of single-party rule by the staunchly Kemalist Republican People's Party. In 1970 the first party to self-identify as "Islamic" was established, the National Order Party (NOP). After the military coup of 1971 the government closed down the NOP, and its leaders went into exile. In 1973 the party reopened as the National Salvation Party (NSP), led by Necmettin Erbakan. After a coup in 1980 shut down all political parties, the former NSP arose as the Welfare Party (*Refah Partisi*, or RP) in July 1983. The Iranian revolution and anger over government corruption added momentum to the RP's program in the early 1980s, at the same time that state-sponsored political and economic reforms favored an accommodationist approach to Islamic and Sufi activism in an attempt to co-opt the Islamists and suppress the left.[15] After a 1987 referendum allowed ex-politicians to reenter politics, Erbakan assumed the leadership of RP and took a strong stance against Kemalism, advocated an Islamic currency, Islamic United Nations, Islamic NATO, and an Islamic version of the European Union. He condemned imperialism and Zionism and publicly supported a campaign to recapture Jerusalem.

During the 1980s and 1990s, the RP's appeal spread from its rural constituents to the urban lower middle classes.[16] On March 27, 1994, RP won 19.09 percent of the vote in municipal elections, with the two leading center-right parties obtaining about 20 percent each, with electoral participation at 94 percent.[17] The party won the mayorships of thirty main cities, including the business and cultural capital, Istanbul, and the national capital, Ankara. Shortly thereafter in the 1995 general elections, RP received 21.4 percent of the vote, and Erbakan became prime minister in a coalition government with Çiller's True Path Party to form the first religious-secular coalition government in Turkey's seventy-three-year history. By the mid-1990s, RP had established itself as one of the most influential political actors in Turkey, although it remained internally divided between conservatives supporting an Islamic-friendly form of modernization and radicals skeptical of all universalist approaches to law and governance.[18]

RP drew support from Islamist intellectuals seeking freedom of religious expression, Sunni Kurds seeking state recognition, the urban poor seeking social justice, and the new bourgeoisie advocating liberalization and the eradication of state subsidies for large corporations.[19] As White notes, "the political interests of its constituents ranged widely, from social and economic reform to replacing the secular state system with one founded on Islamic law."[20] Gülalp describes the social base of the movement as "a vertical bloc comprising segments of different socio-economic classes . . . united in their common opposition to Kemalism and their expression of political will through the assertion of an Islamic identity."[21] Göle traces the party's success to the participation of critical Islamist elites such as engineers, intellectuals, and women in a system supportive of their social mobility and political participation.[22] The RP also contained within its ranks "the peripheral groups, the urban underclasses who, in a context of frustration and despair, can easily turn toward terrorism and crime."[23] It brought in the Kurdish vote "timidly in discourse, but forcefully in election results."[24] It offered a means of identification for individuals sympathetic to Islamic or Ottoman tradition by seeking to "incorporate the Ottoman times into national memory, unsettling the secularist constructions of national history centered around the Kemalist/Republican era of the twentieth century."[25]

The Kemalist establishment's response to the rise of RP was to "drown the party at the bottom of the sea."[26] On February 28, 1997, the National Security Council forced Erbakan to accept eighteen recommendations reaffirming the secular nature of the Turkish state and designating political Islam the top national security concern.[27] The military briefed governmental, judicial, and nongovernmental organizations on the presence of an "Islamic threat" in Turkey. Succumbing to the pressure, Erbakan resigned on June 18, 1997. In this "soft coup," the army enjoyed the backing of the Kemalist establishment, including much of the military, civil service, and intelligentsia. In January 1998 the Turkish Constitutional Court banned the RP, expelled Erbakan from Parliament, tried him for sedition, banned him from politics for five years, and seized the party's assets. The court argued that "*laicism* is not only a separation between religion and politics but also a necessary division between religion and society."[28] Defying the official ban, the RP was succeeded by the Virtue (Fazilet) Party, which was "eager to distance itself from the Welfare legacy, even though it inherited Welfare's political cadres and most of its parliamentary seats."[29] Virtue was banned in June 2001, charged with serving as a "center for antisecular activities." It split into two factions: conservatives led by Necmettin Erbakan became the Felicity (Saadet) party and reformists under Recep Tayyip Erdogan became the Justice and Development Party (AKP). In national elections on November 3, 2002, AKP received 34 percent of the vote, far more than any other party and enough to form a government and nominate a prime minister. Disposing of nine out of ten members of the previous parliament, voters granted a mandate to a party with Islamic connections for the first time in the history of modern republican Turkey.

Whereas some argue that AKP successfully renegotiated the Kemalist settlement since taking power in late 2002, others counter that the party distanced itself from its previous affiliations so as to render its challenge to Kemalism insubstantial or even nonexistent.[30] In any case, despite trepidation on the part of the military and its Western allies concerning the "Islamicization" of Turkish politics, AKP did not impose Islamic law but instead endorsed what White describes as a "Muslimhood" model in which "religious ethics inspire public service but overt religiosity is not part of an individual's public political identity."[31]

In Europe and the United States, this process of renegotiating the secular in Turkey is portrayed as a lurking danger that may need to be suppressed in defense of democratic norms and institutions. The Kemalist establishment and its allies abroad, including the United States, are wary of the rise of "Islamic" political identification. According to Yavuz, the Turkish military had the full support of Israel and the United States in the 1998 ouster of the Erbakan government.[32] Caliskan and Taskin have suggested that "no party generally accepted as Islamist can be a welcome part of the ruling civilian-military bureaucracy, who embrace militant secularism, neo-liberalism, authoritarian rule and a hawkish foreign policy as the main principles of government."[33]

Laicist assumptions and sensibilities underlie both Turkish domestic and international actors' responses to this renegotiation of the secular in Turkey. Islamic political identification is regarded as a form of backsliding away from modernization and toward archaic forms of political order that threaten domestic stability and international security. As Gülalp writes, from this perspective Islam is merely "a remnant of underdevelopment that is bound to disappear with industrialization and urbanization."[34] Laicist dispositions, for example, contributed to a July 31, 2001, decision by the European Court of Human Rights (ECHR) to support the Turkish establishment's suppression of the Welfare Party. The ECHR was founded in Strasbourg in 1959 to deal with alleged violations of the 1950 European Convention on Human Rights. Originally a two-tier system of a part-time commission and court, a full-time court was established in November 1998. Although the ECHR is not officially an EU institution, decisions by influential European institutions on such matters are regarded as significant in Turkey, particularly at a time when Turkey is seeking accession to the European Union.[35] In the Welfare case the ECHR ruled 4–3 that the government's action to ban the party did not violate human rights because Turkey had legitimate concerns about the party's threatening its democratic society. The court argued that the party leadership's intention to establish Islamic law conflicted with values embodied in the European Convention on Human Rights, and that statements by the leadership suggested that it might resort to force in order to gain and retain power.[36] The following excerpt from the summary of the judgment of the court's decision suggests that for the majority of the judges a political party must either support the state-sponsored version of laicism (Kemalism) *or* represent a threat to democratic politics:

> The Court held that the sanctions imposed on the applicants could reasonably be considered to meet a pressing social need for the protection of democratic society, since, *on the pretext of giving a different meaning to the principle of secularism*, the leaders of the Refah Partisi had declared their intention to establish a plurality of legal systems based on differences in religious belief, to institute Islamic law (the *Sharia*), a system of law that was in marked contrast to the values embodied in the Convention. They had also left in doubt their position regarding recourse to force in order to come to power and, more particularly, to retain power.
>
> The Court considered that even if States' margin of appreciation was narrow in the area of the dissolution of political parties, since pluralism of ideas and parties was an inherent element of democracy, the State concerned could reasonably prevent the implementation of such a political programme, which was incompatible with Convention norms, before it was given effect through specific acts that might jeopardise civil peace and the country's democratic regime.[37]

As Göle has argued, however, RP was a complex phenomenon insofar as it contained significant elements that did not advocate a radical stance against the West, democracy, or the concept of secularism, though it did oppose the Kemalist instantiation of secularism.[38] These complexities, and particularly the possibility (expressed to a lesser degree in Refah's policies and rhetoric and to a greater degree by its successor AKP) that one could oppose Kemalism while supporting a different *form* of secularism, eluded the laicist categorizations and dispositions available to European and Turkish judicial authorities sitting on the Turkish Constitutional Court and the European Court of Human Rights. Working out of the assumptions of laicism, the courts presumed the only two available alternatives to be benevolent secular democracy (in its Kemalist form) or menacing Islamic theocracy (overturning Kemalism). The judges dismissed the possibility of a reformulated or entirely different instantiation of secularism as a "pretext," arguing that the real intention of the party was to "institute Islamic law." They viewed Kemalism in its current form as the closest approximation to laicism available, and the latter was assumed to be a universal good, or at least a decent approximation of the "values embodied in the Convention."

Judeo-Christian secularist collective dispositions present a similar yet slightly less optimistic account of attempts to refashion the secular in Turkey. In this view, secular democracy is felt to be a unique Western achievement with deep roots in Euro-American culture, religion, and civilization that cannot be fully replicated in Muslim-majority societies. The renegotiation of the secular in Turkey according to this set of assumptions is seen as confirmation of the incommensurability of different civilizations and the futility of attempting to "export" secularism outside historical Latin Christendom and its settler colonies. From this perspective, Islamic political identification, unlike "softer" and more familiar forms of Christian political identification, is an aggravating yet persistent throwback to premodern politics and a threat to public and international order to be met with strong opposition both domestically and internationally.[39] As Lewis observed in reference to Turkey, "the path that the revival will take is still not clear. If simple reaction has its way, much of the work of the last century will be undone, and Turkey will slip back into the darkness from which she so painfully emerged."[40] In this narrative a "heavy state" that acts against the ever-present threat of "political Islam" appears an undesirable but necessary solution in Muslim-majority societies.

Yet the rise of Islamic political identification in Turkey does not represent a return to Islamic tradition but a renegotiation of the Kemalist settlement, which establishes and continually reproduces a particular relationship to and control over what the state defines as (a particular Sunni-Hanefi form of) Islam. The Turkish state controls all of the 80,000 mosques in Turkey and employs their imams as state functionaries. Sunni Hanefi Islam is the doctrine of the State Directorate of Religious Affairs (DRA). Other sects, including the Alevis, which compose 20–30 percent of the Turkish population, are not recognized by the state.[41] Yavuz concludes that "the main source of conservatism in the DRA is the widespread insecurity among its clergy about Islamic knowledge, faith, and supremacy."[42]

Kemalism, in other words, also lies on the spectrum of theological politics. The rise in religiously inspired political identification in Turkey is part of a broader public struggle over authoritative Kemalist designations of the secular authorized and enforced by state authorities. It is a challenge to Kemalist attempts to create and regulate the definition of and division between the secular, the sacred, and the political. This argument, developed further in the two final chapters of this book, challenges the depiction of the rise of political Islam as a side effect of economic or political woes, a stage in the rocky transition to Western modernity, or evidence of an intractable clash of civilizations. Challenges to Kemalism in Turkey are not merely an irrational backlash against secularization nor are they evidence of a clash of civilizations spawned by commitments to premodern Islamic ideals. They are part of a series of efforts to grant cultural and historical legitimacy to alternative models of religious separation and accommodation.[43] They are attempts to refashion the secular. They are attempts to relocate the secularist settlement to a different position on the spectrum of theological politics. Such attempts reflect not only what Yavuz has described as "an ongoing internal liberalization process of establishment political Islam" but also a relocating and refashioning of the boundaries upon which the categorization of political Islam depends. I would thus modify Yavuz's suggestion that the AKP "aimed to reposition the party as a center-right party by accepting the secular nature of the political system and pursuing integration of the country with the EU."[44] Rather than merely accepting the secular nature of the system, the AKP and other actors have contributed to a collective contestation and refashioning of what it means to *be* secular in contemporary Turkish politics.

Alfred Stepan defines the twin tolerations as "the minimal boundaries of freedom of action that must somehow be crafted for political institutions vis-à-vis religious authorities, and for religious individuals and groups vis-à-vis political institutions."[45] As he concludes, "when we consider the question of non-Western religions and their relationship to democracy, it would seem appropriate not to assume univocality but to explore whether these doctrines contain multivocal components that are usable for (or at least compatible with) the construction of the twin tolerations."[46] The multiple forms of religious politics in contemporary Turkey offer concrete evidence of the multivocality, rather than univocality, of Islamic tradition.[47] The challenge to Kemalism testifies both to the inability of the Kemalists to monopolize definitions of and divisions between religion and politics and to the multivocality of Islamic tradition and its potential compatibility with Stepan's "twin tolerations." The attempt to remake the Kemalist public realm is not a threat to the foundation of modern politics as conventional accounts would have it. It is a modern contestation of an authoritative secularist tradition (Kemalism) that has been authorized and regulated by state authorities since the founding of the modern Turkish Republic in 1923. It is modern politics.

IRAN

Like Turkey, modern Iran has also witnessed attempts to contest authoritative forms of secularism authorized and regulated by state authorities. While it is common knowledge that a strict Islamic dress code was implemented by the Iranian government that came to power in 1979, it is less well known that the government of the first shah, Reza Shah Pahlavi (r. 1925–41) also implemented a restrictive dress code early in the twentieth century as part of the attempt to "modernize" Iran. Pahlavi mandated secular Western dress for men, restricted clerical attire, and banned the veil for women.[48] Iranians' discomfort with Pahlavi state-sponsored secularization policies thus dates to the early part of the twentieth century and the regime of Reza Shah Pahlavi. His policies incited a counterreaction that accelerated over the following decades under the regime of the shah's son, Muhammad Reza Pahlavi (r. 1941–78). Following the violent government repression of September 8, 1978, "women who had worn modern attire now joined their more traditional sisters in donning the veil as a symbol of protest against a monarch whose modernization program had once attempted to ban it."[49] This recalls Frantz Fanon's description of the symbolic politics of veiling in Algeria, in which "the veil was worn because tradition demanded a rigid separation of the sexes, but also because the occupier *was bent on unveiling Algeria.*"[50]

Despite these early attempts at modernization, the consolidation of an autocratic modernist state did not fully take hold in Iran until the 1950s when the Shah's repression displaced a lively democratic period between 1941 and 1953. After invading Iran in 1941, Britain and the Soviet Union demanded the expulsion of German advisers from Iran, seized control of the Trans-Iranian Railway, and forced Reza Shah to abdicate in favor of his son. In 1953, after the shah had been forced into exile by Prime Minister Muhammad Mossadegh's nationalist movement that threatened Western oil interests by nationalizing Iranian oil, the CIA in conjunction with the Anglo-Iranian Oil Company organized a coup to overthrow Mossadegh. Known as Operation Ajax, it was considered a resounding success for both U.S. and British intelligence.[51] After the coup, the United States escorted the shah from Rome back to Tehran aboard an American military plane accompanied by the head of the U.S. Central Intelligence Agency.[52] As a result of the coup, Iran became part of the "Northern Tier" of anti-Communist states along the southern border of the Soviet Union running from Turkey to Pakistan, and in 1955 Iran joined the Baghdad Pact.[53]

On the domestic front, the returning shah severely limited or destroyed all forms of democratic political association. Opposition groups active before the coup, located in unions, parties, and the media, were forced after the coup into mosques, seminary schools, bazaars, and universities.[54] Although the shah brutally suppressed secular dissenters, he was obliged to tolerate Shi'i independence. Ali Mirsepassi has suggested that "one of the reasons why the movement against the Shah and his modernization policies was translated into an Islamic discourse was that the only existing sub-culture to survive the political terror of the Pahlavi State were the institutions of Shi'i Islam."[55]

The close relationship between the shah and the United States became increasingly politically, strategically, and economically significant for both countries during the 1960s and 1970s, as Esposito suggests:

> At a time when the United States was heavily committed in Vietnam and Britain was withdrawing its forces from the Persian Gulf, the Shah's Iran represented policies and interests that coincided with those of the United States, from the Shah's rejection of Nasserism and pragmatic relations with Israel, and his nation's stable presence in the Gulf, to its oil wealth and market for American products. American and European bankers and businessmen along with diplomats and military advisors enjoyed a high-profile presence in Iran.[56]

The shah was particularly close to the administration of Richard Nixon (1969–74).[57] In the early 1970s, and in return for assurances that he would serve as a virtual proxy of American interests in the Persian Gulf (and in accordance with the Nixon Doctrine of 1969),[58] the shah received access to all nonnuclear hardware in the U.S. arsenal, including F-14 and F-15 supersonic jets, purchases funded with his rising reservoir of petrodollars.[59] As Douglas Little writes, "Never known for restraint when it came to shopping lists, during the next five years the shah would shell out $16.2 billion—nearly seven times what he had spent during the preceding two decades—for U.S. planes, tanks, warships, and other sophisticated weapons systems."[60] The shah used this equipment to assist the sultan of Oman in putting down a Soviet-backed uprising in 1973, which delighted his supporters in Washington. In addition to containing the Soviet Union, the shah advanced two other important goals of U.S. policy in the region: support for Israel and assurance of a continual supply of oil to the West. Iran was one of the few Middle Eastern nations that did not participate in the oil embargo of 1973. (Iraq also elected not to participate in this embargo due to its rivalry with Saudi Arabia and other conservative oil-producing states.)

The shah's domestic policies were, as Suzanne Maloney observes, "defiantly secular and vehemently nationalist."[61] As she explains, "the Shah was repelled by traditionalism; he swore to raze all of the country's *bazaars* in order to build supermarkets, and he boasted of plans to boost the Iranian economy beyond that of Germany and France by the turn of the century."[62] To further his modernizing objectives, the shah instituted a series of economic policies drawing on oil revenues (known as the White Revolution) that benefited mainly elites and led to unrest among merchants (*bazaari*), the religious classes, and the urban poor, who felt threatened by the influx of Western banks and the rise of a state-supported entrepreneurial Western-oriented class. Many also suffered from food shortages and rampant inflation.[63] Modernization led to urbanization and a rise in slums. While a small minority prospered as a result of the modernization programs, Iran, once agriculturally self-sufficient, was now spending more than $1 billion annually on imports.[64] The living conditions of the urban poor and the increasing economic disparities in Iranian society contributed to general hostility toward the shah's regime and the West. As Halliday observes, "as early as 1971 a cautious observer of Iran remarked that, on walking through the streets of the southern, poorer part of Tehran, he encountered 'more expressed hatred than I have ever heard before' from 'people who watch the cars of those people who are doing well.' "[65] With the exception of a small Shi'i elite, however, internal dissenters were silenced.[66] After the coup of 1953, Colonel H. Norman Schwarzkopf (father of the Desert Storm commander) aided the shah in organizing a brutally effective secret police force known as the SAVAK.[67] As McAlister notes, "the internal security police in Iran, SAVAK, were known for torture and murder; they were also trained and funded by the CIA."[68] Halliday argues that "Iran is a society where, since the 1920s, the regime has been based on the army, and where repression is the main means of ensuring the government's political control."[69]

As a result of the suppression of internal opposition, during the 1960s and 1970s a diverse coalition of dissenters, including Iranian students in Iran and abroad, began to organize to protest the shah's domestic policies and the terms and consequences of his alliance with the United States.[70] Nationalists, leftists, secularists and religionists, merchants, clergy, modern elites, and what Keddie has described as the urban subproletariat all participated in a growing broad-based opposition movement.[71] Halliday writes that "these people, many of whom paid with their lives for their hostility to the Shah's government, were not organized from abroad, or Marxists, or reactionaries. They were people who could no longer tolerate the stifling political atmosphere and the gross inequalities of Iranian urban life."[72] By the late 1970s, the opposition, which also included many women, was active and vocal. As Keddie notes, "as the threat of violence grew, women often marched bravely at the head of processions; participants recognized that this put the police and regime in a difficult position."[73] Rising external pressure from the Carter administration and international organizations and human rights groups such as Amnesty International, the International Commission of the Red Cross, and the International Commission of Jurists also encouraged the shah to amend his repressive internal policies.[74]

On January 8, 1978, following an attack on Khomeini in the semiofficial newspaper *Ettela'at* and the death of Khomeini's son in a car accident that the shah's government was suspected to have orchestrated, a group of students and mullahs loyal to Khomeini (who had been exiled in Turkey, France, and Iraq) gathered in Qom to protest the shah's regime. Government forces opened fire on the meeting, killing two-dozen demonstrators. This sparked a wave of anti-Pahlavi outbursts. In the spring and summer of 1978 there were enormous street demonstrations, and on September 8 (Black Friday), the shah's troops fired on 20,000 pro-Khomeini protestors in Tehran's Jaleh Square, killing between 400 and 900 protestors and wounding 4,000.[75] This event placed what Abrahamian describes as "a sea of blood between the shah and the people."[76] As the protests intensified, it became evident that the shah's downfall was imminent. Massive strikes against the shah throughout the government and oil industry paralyzed the country. In November, recognizing the increasingly precarious nature of his hold on power and uncertain of American support for his regime,[77] the shah appointed General Gholam Reza Ashari prime minister in a military government, closed the schools and universities, suspended newspapers, and prohibited meetings of over three persons in Tehran.[78] Despite the new government's effort to end the strikes, they increased, and "attempts to reimpose censorship were met by press strikes."[79]

On January 16, 1979, the shah fled to Egypt. Khomeini returned from exile on February 1, after a brief delay due to the fact that the shah's new premier (Bakhtiar) had closed the Tehran airport as a stalling tactic. Khomeini denounced the United States as a vile traitor and dismissed the shah's White

Revolution as an affront to Muslim tradition. On February 2, 1979, he told a huge crowd just outside Tehran that the shah had "enacted his so-called reforms in order to create markets for America and to increase our dependence upon America." Power was officially transferred to Khomeini and his followers on February 11, 1979.

The Iranian revolution was the culmination of a gradual rejection of the shah's domestic policies, including his authoritarian form of secularism, and a rejection of American influence in Iran. Richard Cottam writes that "by 1979 the United States had become the preeminent imperial presence in Iran and the primary external target of the revolution."[80] The revolutionaries sought to overturn and then refashion the shah's authoritarian secularist settlement. Michel Foucault, who served as a special correspondent for the Italian daily *Corriere della Sera* at the time, sensed what was at stake when he described the revolutionary movement as an outbreak of "political spirituality," as an attempt to "open up a spiritual dimension in politics."[81] As in the case of challengers to Turkish Kemalism, the question among the revolutionaries was not whether the shah's secularist settlement should be overturned, but how, and to what ends. The revolutionary movement set in motion an attempt to fashion a new public settlement on the spectrum of theological politics. At the time of the revolution, the exact terms of this settlement were unknown. Had they been negotiated in advance, it is possible that the fragile coalition that brought the revolution would have crumbled in disagreement. The fact that the renegotiation of the secular was at stake is perhaps why Foucault described the revolutionary movement as an outbreak of political spirituality.

Although the diverse coalition that coalesced in opposition to the shah's rule held together through the revolution, deep philosophical and political cleavages began to emerge not long thereafter. McAlister observes that initially "the Iranian government under Khomeini's leadership was . . . composed of a complex set of disparate elements that had little in common but their desire to get ride of the Shah and a broadly shared hatred of the United States as the Shah's backer."[82] As Esposito argues, "the Revolutionary coalition comprised a diverse assortment of liberal, leftist, and religious groups that agreed on little other than their antipathy for the shah and the institution of absolute monarchy. Their negative consensus and the sheer breadth of their ideological and socioeconomic agendas set the stage for a bitter feud after the coup."[83] Bashiriyeh refers to two "strands" of discourse at this time, liberal democrats in the Provisional Government who supported the democratic ideals of the Constitutional Revolution (1906–11) and clerical fundamentalists of the Islamic Republican Party.[84] In addition to disagreeing over foreign policy and the nature of the constitution, these power struggles involved a dispute over the future terms of the authoritative Iranian public settlement of religion and politics, with one side advocating moderation and the other clerical absolutism. Two of the most prominent antagonists in this dispute were Ayatollah

Ruhollah Khomeini and reformer and sociologist Ali Shariati, each representing two starkly contrasting alternatives to the shah. As Esposito observes,

> The political opposition ranged from those for whom an Irano-Islamic alternative simply meant Iran's cultural heritage and values, to those who wished to see the establishment of Islamic state and society. Similar differences existed among the Islamically committed. Clergy as well as laity differed sharply in their Islamic ideologies . . . nowhere was this clearer than in the juxtaposition of the Ayatollah Khomeini and Dr. Ali Shariati—Khomeini who embodied clerical authority and power; Shariati and other Islamic modernists who represented a far more nonclerical, innovative, creative reformist approach.[85]

For nearly a year following the revolution several factions struggled for power in Iran, including the clergy (Islamic Republican Party), the liberals (Bazargan), a group of liberal to leftist Islamic parties (Bani-Sadr), and the non-Islamic left.[86] The hard-line clerics prevailed.[87]

Mirsepassi attributes the rise of clerical hard-liners and the eclipse of moderates such as Mehdi Barzargan and Abolhassan Bani-Sadr to three factors: the formation of an autocratic state in post-1953 Iran; a sense of social alienation due to modernization processes during the 1960s and 1970s; and the transformation of the Shi'i hierarchy and construction of a new political Islamic ideology.[88] Political Islam, argues Mirsepassi, represented a uniquely compelling alternative discourse to modernization: "the hegemony of political Islam was made possible through capturing the 'imaginary' of the Iranians in a way that presented itself as the only desirable answer to the country's dilemmas."[89] The shah's systematic repression of all socialist and liberal alternatives, and the secular opposition itself, contributed to the rise of popular Shi'ism by romanticizing the Islamist movement. As Keddie argues, "the government had been largely successful over many years in suppressing secular protests and had left a clearer field for the less manageable religious opposition."[90]

Contrary to conventional accounts, however, the secular opposition to the shah *also* sought to refashion the shah's authoritarian secularist settlement. Revolutionaries of very different (theo)political persuasions, who might be labeled either secular, religious, or perhaps neither, all sought to refashion the state-imposed secular settlement supported by the shah. The Iranian revolution, then, was not simply a "religious" backlash against "secular" modernity as it is often portrayed. It was a challenge to and an attempt to reconfigure the fundamental categories through which the religious and the secular are conceived and practiced, and a challenge to the institutions and ways of life that made particular versions of these categorizations authoritative. Some of these institutions and ways of life were associated with the West.[91] This explains Robert Allison's provocative suggestion that "the Iranian people did not rebel against their own failed rulers but against ours,"[92] and Juergensmeyer's argument that "the goal of the Islamic Revolution in Iran, then, was not only to free Iranians politically from the shah but also to liberate them conceptually from Western ways of thinking."[93]

The Iranian revolution of 1978–79 was not an attempt to return to Islam. It was an attempt to overturn and renegotiate the prevailing state-sponsored secular modernist settlement, widely perceived as connected to illegitimate and culturally distant outside interests. After the revolution many Iranians argued and worked in support of the development of a nondogmatic and nonhegemonic Islamic tradition of secularism. They worked for a new form of theopolitics that was neither secular nor theocratic, as those terms are commonly understood in the West. They lost to Khomeini. This was not inevitable. At the time of the revolution Iran had no direct historical precedent for governance by the clergy; as Maloney argues, "the basis for Khomeini's theory of Islamic governance—the guardianship of the religious jurist (*veliyet-e faqih*)—rests on a novel and almost unprecedented reinterpretation of religious canon that continues to be contested by senior theologians."[94] Khomeini's support of direct clerical rule and government by Islamic jurists was "neither a prominent Shii doctrine nor one which had enjoyed widespread support among Iran's religious establishment."[95] Instead, an imperial form of secular modernity had been challenged and was ultimately replaced by an imperial form of religious modernity. Said Arjomand has described this as a shift "from temporal to theocratic absolutism."[96] Casanova describes Khomeini's regime as a "mobilizational state religion," in which religion is deprivatized in such a way that it creates "a totalitarian participatory publicness that tends to destroy the very boundaries between the private and the public spheres by infringing upon private rights . . . and destroying public liberties."[97]

Khomeini's settlement was consolidated in opposition to what Iranian writer and activist Jalal al-e Ahmad denounced as "Westoxification," or *gharbzadegi*, defined by its opponents as "the profound psychological dislocation produced by an internationally orchestrated economy and a bifurcated culture . . . compared to cholera infecting Iran."[98] A sense of Iranian identity coalesced around opposition to the shah and support for "de-Westoxification." Displeased with Khomeini's ascendance, many of his former political allies in opposition to the shah either resigned or were executed; according to Esposito, "the Islamic Republic's first prime minister, Mehdi Bazargan, resigned in disgust; Bani-Sadr, its first elected president, fled to exile in France; Sadeq Gobtzadeh, who had held a number of government posts, was executed for his participation in an alleged plot to assassinate Khomeini."[99]

The overthrow of the secularist establishment in Iran was received angrily in the West, and the effect of these developments upon U.S.-Iranian relations is the subject of chapter 6. "Islam" and the "Islamic republic" became synonymous with the violation of laicist conceptions of neutral public space, common sense, and the public good. As Jonathan Rée has suggested,

Back home, liberal commentators were doing their best to fit the new political possibilities into the old progressive narratives. But Iran did not present the familiar lineaments of a struggle between pure-hearted youthful rebels and dark-souled reactionaries ... meanwhile, the very idea of "political spirituality" seemed like an anachronism that could never get any traction in the modern world.[100]

One effect of the tendency to categorically reject the revolutionaries in Iran, like the RP in Turkey, was to deny support for potentially nonhegemonic and nondogmatic forms of Islamic secularism that were contending for power in each of these circumstances. In the Iranian case, Shariati and other Islamic "modernists"[101] who represented what Esposito describes as "a far more nonclerical, innovative, creative reformist approach" articulated a very different political vision from Khomeini and the hard-liners supporting him. As Said has argued, however, "very little of this struggle was reported in the United States while it was taking place. So strong was the ideological commitment to the idea of a monolithic and unchanging Islam that no note was taken of the political process *within* this or any other particular Islamic country."[102] Richard Cottam concurs, noting that "only rarely did an article discuss the historic struggle among competing political philosophies in Iran."[103]

Had the social and historical contingencies of Euro-American trajectories of secularism, including the laicist trajectory of modernization imposed by the shah, been acknowledged, it is possible that Khomeini's more moderate rivals might have received more internal and, perhaps, external support and been able to assume power, or at least a power-sharing arrangement as opposed to exile or death. I therefore disagree with Keddie when she concludes that "popular ayatollahs who stressed rather a return to full implementation of the 1906–07 constitution, whether the moderate Shariatmadari or the socially conscious Mahmud Taleqani ... were bound to lose influence to the more uncompromising Khomeini in revolutionary circumstances."[104] Moderate clerics were not "bound to lose." Khomeini's victory over his rivals was not predetermined. As Rée notes, "if things were indeed turning out badly in Iran, that did not invalidate [Foucault's] remarks about how they might have been different; nor did it show that events were bound to revert to a familiar pattern and lose their capacity to surprise us."[105]

In an alternative path, the United States would not have supported the suppression of multiple forms of politics in Iran, both secular and religious (thereby empowering the most radical elements of the oppositional Islamist movement) under the shah, but would have instead encouraged the shah to open space for religious and secular oppositional politics. After the revolution, and perhaps even more critically during the transitional situation that emerged, the United States would have distanced itself from the shah and supported Khomeini's moderate opponents, both secular and religious, who were also opponents of the shah. It is likely that these dissenters would have been open to such dialogue. As Mirsepassi notes, "in retrospect it is astounding that the many left-wing groups and organizations ignored the obvious fact that post-revolutionary Iranian society was being transformed into an Islamic-totalitarian state and made no effort to form a broad secular-radical united front to oppose this trend."[106] The views of dissenters from Khomeini's program offer a glimpse of the potential represented by a third path rejecting the binary of secularism and political Islam and the restrictive forms of politics that often attach themselves to it. This path would have entailed a more nuanced approach to the interplay between religion and political authority. It would have engaged moderate dissidents and reformers who sought to work outside the confines of the strictly oppositional binary discourses of tradition versus modernity and Islamic versus secular so effectively monopolized by both the shah and Khomeini.[107]

Jalal-e-Ahmad, Mehdi Bazargan, and Ali Shariati are examples of such dissidents and reformers. Jalel-e-Ahmad (1923–69) was a secular socialist who opposed what he called "Westruckness." Ahmad called for continuity between modern Iran's identity and culture and its past, and he condemned efforts either to Westernize *or* to attempt to recreate or retreat to the past. As Esposito argues,

> Jalal-e-Ahmad did not see a simplistic world of monolithic, stereotypical choices, either a path of modernization/Westernization of society or a retreat to the past. He opted for a third alternative, a return to Irano-Islamic culture as a source of national identity, unity, history, and values. His secular intellectual indictment of Westernization . . . was a primary agenda for others as well, religiously oriented lay and clerical ideologists, laymen like Mehdi Bazargan and Ali Shariati and clerics like the Ayatollah Khomeini.[108]

A second dissident and ideologue of the revolution who conformed to neither the shah's nor Khomeini's politics was Mehdi Bazargan (1907–95), who became famous for a lecture he gave in 1962 entitled "The Boundary between Religion and Social Affairs." A French-trained engineer who voluntarily joined the French army to fight Nazi Germany while studying in France, Bazargan was jailed under both shahs for his "strong Islamic commitment." He was also active under Mossadegh's National Front and became provisional prime minister of the Islamic Republic in 1979. Bazargan cofounded the Liberation Movement of Iran to "bridge the gap between modern secular and traditional religious Iranians and work toward a more Islamic state and society."[109] He resigned his post in Khomeini's government in disagreement with the violent repression of dissidents by the Khomeini regime.

Dr. Ali Shariati (1933–77), an ideologue of the revolution with a Ph.D. from the Sorbonne, also worked outside the confines of both Western secular and militant Islamic traditions. Shariati was imprisoned for opposition to the shah as a student and later drew enormous audiences in Tehran before being forced into exile where he died under mysterious circumstances. Shariati preached what Esposito describes as an "Islamic theology of Third World liberation, an indigenous populist Shii ideology for sociopolitical reform."[110] He combined Weber's and Durkheim's modern sociology with the Third World socialist outlooks of Fanon and Guevara and sought to revitalize and reinterpret Islamic identity and roots. Shariati supported a strong role for "religiously minded lay intelligentsia, Islamically oriented but with a knowledge and command of modern thought and methods."[111] Author of *Man and Islam* and *On the Sociology of Islam*, Shariati was often at odds with both religious traditional *ulama and* more Westernized secular university professors. As Le-Vine and Salvatore conclude, "for both Shariati and Foucault, the project of self-realization involved the politicization of an ethical sensibility, one that like Nietzsche's calls us to 'think differently,' that solicits us to join the quest for a different future. And if one considers this ethical sensibility on a political register, we understand the relationships it might establish with religiously motivated movements of resistance."[112] Had the United States worked to engage Khomeini's opposition differently after the revolution rather than antagonizing its proponents in categorical terms according to Euro-American secularist presumptions, it is possible that a less violent postrevolutionary order might have emerged.

CONCLUSION

The forms of secularism described in this book are discursive frames, habits of speech and thought, and collective dispositions that place secular democratic practices and Islamic religious practices in opposition as incompatible.[113] Nonlaicist and non–Judeo-Christian secularist modes of religious separation and accommodation are dismissed as threats to the foundations of modern politics, as a backlash against modernization and globalization, or as evidence of the clash of civilizations. The tenacity of particular post-Enlightenment conceptions of politics, and the secularist dispositions lodged deeply within them, effectively delegitimize non-Western movements working toward different formations of democracy and secularism, exemplified to some degree by the RP in Turkey, to a greater extent by the AKP, and by the moderate postrevolutionary Islamic opposition in Iran. These actors and movements endorsed alternative models of separation and accommodation between politics and religion. They sought to refashion the secular, not to get rid of it, by endorsing various forms of nontheocratic politics.[114] These attempts to renegotiate the secular nontheocratically, however, escape the confines of Euro-American secularist epistemology. For secularists, the only two available options are Islamic fundamentalism or a weak imitation of Western secularism. Non-Westerners must (inevitably) abandon tradition in the face of Western power and superiority. Within this form of thinking, democratic alternatives to *both* fundamentalism *and* Western-derived forms of secularism either do not exist or pale in comparison to their more robust Western counterparts.

This chapter has elaborated upon modern Turkish and Iranian attempts to renegotiate the secular. It has illustrated that modern forms of politics often exceed and disable the secularist conceptual apparatus used to interpret them. The Iranian rebellion, as Foucault noted, was "irréductible."[115] Poor concepts lead to poor policy, as opportunities to work outside the secular-theocratic binary as traditionally conceived are repeatedly missed. The Euro-American traditions of secularism described in this book fail to acknowledge and engage alternative forms of religious accommodation, such as the clerical moderates in postrevolutionary Iran. Neglecting these forms of nontheocratic politics inadvertently gives way to ideologues like Khomeini who seek to dissolve the boundary between public and private and use the disciplinary powers of the state to police both spheres.[116] Countering conventional images of Islam and politics, Hefner argues that this usurpation of the public-private divide is historically foreign to Muslim-majority societies:

> The Qur'an knows no such concept of an "Islamic" state, least of all one with the coercive appetites of modern totalitarianism. In fact, in their uncritical appropriation of the idea of a centralized state with a monopoly of social and ideological power, conservative Islamists show their debt to, not traditional Muslim conceptions, but the corporatist ambitions of high modernist political ideology.[117]

Viable, local alternative forms of religious separation and accommodation drawn out of multivocal Islamic traditions are needed to render radical Islamism inert and irrelevant. As Göle observes, "if channels of upward social mobility and political participation are repressed and the social ascent of Islamist elites thus blocked, the Islamist movement will, in most likelihood, evolve toward a logic of reaction and/or to a logic of violence, one evident in the Egyptian and Algerian cases."[118]

The rise of Islamic forms of modern politics is not merely a backlash against modernization or a revival of premodern Islamic tradition. It is part of an ongoing controversy over the relationship between metaphysics and politics, including how each of these categories is defined by and relates to the state. The rise in religiously inspired political identification in Turkey and Iran reflects a public struggle over the authoritative designation of the secular authorized and imposed by Kemalists in Turkey and the shah in Iran. In this struggle, "Islam" is a powerful set of discursive traditions mobilized in different ways and with differing political effects by Kemalists in Turkey, the shah in Iran, and their various challengers to legitimate their respective political positions.[119] I return to and expand upon this argument in chapters 7 and 8. The forms of secularism described in this book are discursive traditions that rely upon particular inherited dispositions, habits, and beliefs about religion and politics. These traditions have influenced Western historiographical conventions, as suggested in this chapter, and they also have found their way into contemporary international politics, helping to shape and structure the controversy over Turkish accession to the European Union and American relations with Iran.

CHAPTER FIVE

The European Union and Turkey

SOCIAL AND RELIGIOUS factors have played a significant role in European opposition to Turkish accession to the European Union (EU). To identify the presence and political effects of the cultural and political sensibilities, collective dispositions, and discourses identified in earlier chapters as laicism and Judeo-Christian secularism, this chapter draws on policy statements, pundit commentaries, international agreements, opinion polls, court decisions, conference proceedings, and popular and academic accounts of Turkish and European politics. Using a similar methodology but a different set of sources, the next chapter examines the influence of these two forms of secularism upon U.S.-Iranian relations.

Most observers depict the cultural and religious dimensions of the European debate over Turkish accession as a disagreement between those who see Europe as a Christian club and those open to a more religiously pluralistic European identity. However, polls suggest that cultural and religiously based doubts about Turkish accession resonate with a much larger proportion of the European population than those who publicly defend the idea of an exclusivist Christian Europe. Both secularists *and* Christian exclusivists (or traditionalists) express hesitations about Turkish membership:

> Opposition to Turkish accession is coming from secular as well as religious quarters in Europe. Some nonreligious Europeans worry that bringing a large Muslim country into the EU could endanger the Continent's tradition of gender equality and tolerance of alternative lifestyles, for instance. For traditionalists, Turkish accession threatens the very idea of Europe as a Christian civilization.[1]

Prevailing explanations of European resistance to Turkish accession that rely upon the assumption that opposition is based exclusively upon support for a Christian Europe miss a crucial part of the story concerning the cultural and religious basis of this resistance. Cultural and religious opposition to Turkey's accession is not only about defending the idea of a Christian Europe, though this is a significant consideration. The prospect of Turkish accession has stirred up a more fundamental controversy about European identity and the politics of religion within Europe itself. Turkey has turned toward a different trajectory of secularism that conforms to neither Kemalism (a Turkish version of laicism described in chapter 4) nor the two prevailing trajectories of secularism described in this book: laicism and Judeo-Christian secularism. This form of secularism threatens not only the Kemalist establishment in Turkey but European secularists as well. As a result, Turkey's potential accession to the EU has propelled the controversial question of what it means to be both secular and European into the public spotlight. There is a sense of urgency in Europe that the religion-politics question and its relationship to an ever-evolving European identity be resolved before Turkey is admitted to the EU.[2] The Turkish case is therefore controversial in cultural and religious terms not only because it involves the potential accession of a Muslim-majority country to an arguably, at least historically, Christian Europe, though this is important, but also and more fundamentally because it brings up long dormant dilemmas *internal* to Europe regarding how religion and politics relate to each other.[3] Turkey's candidacy destabilizes the European secular social imaginary.[4] It involves unfinished business in the social fabric of the core EU members, including what it means to be secular (both in Europe and in Turkey) and how religion, including but not limited to Islam, should relate to European public life.[5] This cultural sticking point is what the debate over Turkish accession is really about, and it is for this reason that it is culturally—in addition to economically and politically—so contentious.[6]

This argument suggests that even if economic and political obstacles to Turkish accession are lifted, even if Turkey is deemed to be in unambiguous conformity with the Copenhagen criteria, European opposition to Turkish membership will persist. This is due to nagging discord within Europe on two counts: how religion relates to European identity and institutions; and whether alternative trajectories of secularism such as the current Turkish one, which moves *away* from European-inspired Kemalism toward a different variety of secularism, can ever be considered fully European. This is a more complex story than the assertion that European cultural and religious opposition to Turkey is based on the defense of the concept of a Christian Europe. It also explains why many laicists in Europe have expressed ambivalence and, in some cases, opposition to Turkish accession despite their discomfort with the idea of a Christian Europe. The implications of this argument for international relations theory are described in the concluding section of the chapter.

Turkish accession to the EU has become one among several symbolic carriers of domestic European angst about religion, and particularly Islam, and politics.[7] The powerful foundations and formulations of secularism that structure the debate in Europe and in (Kemalist) Turkey make it difficult to cope with what is often described as an "Islamic challenge" to Europe, both internally and externally. Turkish candidacy for the EU makes these stumbling blocks in the European secularist imaginary explicit. Turkey's candidacy makes it evident that European approaches to religion and to religious minorities within its own borders are not set in stone but must be constantly renegotiated, and that expanding Europe to include Turkey will force a renegotiation of those standards by introducing new forms of secularism on the European horizon.

EUROPE AND TURKEY: 1963–2006

Although Turkey and the EU signed an Association Agreement in 1963, it was not until 1987 that Turkey first applied for EU membership. In 1989 the European Commission rejected the application on the grounds that the Turkish economy was not sufficiently developed, Turkish democracy failed to adequately guarantee political and civil rights, unemployment in Turkey would pose a threat to the EU markets, and the dispute with Greece over Cyprus remained unresolved.[8] Recognizing their common political, economic, and security interests, however, the EU and Turkey reached a Customs Agreement that went into effect on December 31, 1995, granting the Turks "closer economic ties with the EU than any other nonmember country at the time, with the exception of Iceland, Norway, and Switzerland, and opened the Turkish market of 65 million customers to EU companies."[9] Relations cooled following the commission's decision not to grant candidate status to Turkey at the Luxembourg summit in 1997. Angered by this decision, the Turks announced that they would no longer consider the EU as a third-party mediator in Greek-Turkish affairs and in the Cyprus controversy, vetoed the European allies' European Security and Defense Initiative plans on agenda setting in NATO, and opted not to purchase military hardware from EU states.[10]

In December 1999, after a thaw in EU-Turkish relations precipitated by Greek-Turkish cooperation following the Turkish earthquake that year, the European Council met in Helsinki and reversed course, inviting Turkey to join candidates for membership from the Central and Eastern European countries, with the assumption that Turkey would be admitted to the EU if it met the same criteria as the other candidates.[11] This landmark decision resulted from a compromise in which the EU agreed to lift the Greek veto, and in return Turkey agreed to adapt to the *acquis communitaire* and work cooperatively to solve disputes with Greece.[12] The EU agreed to review Turkish progress by the end of 2004. After 1999 successive governments began to implement democratizing reforms in the areas of civil-military relations, human rights, cultural rights, judicial procedure, economic policy, and Cyprus policy.[13] Although the EU did not name Turkey as part of the official strategy of expansion (until 2010) at the Nice summit in December 2000, in February 2001 the European Council did declare an Accession Partnership with Turkey. In response, the Turkish government prepared its national program for the adoption of EU membership in March of that year.[14] However, relations soured again in Copenhagen in 2002 when the European Commission refused to set up a timetable for starting membership accession talks, outlining instead the political and economic conditions that Ankara would have to satisfy before talks would begin.[15] In a reflection of Turkish progress toward satisfying the Copenhagen criteria, however, in December 2004 the EU extended a conditional start date of October 2005 for the talks.

On October 4, 2005, Turkey officially opened negotiations with the EU on the thirty-one chapters of the *acquis*. As Gordon and Taspiner have observed, however, "even if the Council does agree to start accession talks, that process will be long, and would only be completed if and when all EU members— and the EU Parliament—were ready to take the revolutionary step of welcoming Turkey into the EU."[16] To accede to the EU, Turkey will have to be deemed in compliance with the Copenhagen criteria, adopted at the EU summit in Denmark in June 1993, which stipulate that member countries must be stable democracies, respect human rights, the rule of law, and the protection of minorities; have a functioning market economy and the capacity to cope with the competitive pressure and market forces within the Union; and adopt the common rules, standards, and policies that make up the body of EU law (*acquis communitaire*).[17] Negotiations are expected to take at least a decade to complete; for budgetary reasons, 2014 is the earliest date that Turkey could join the EU, and some analysts suggest that it could be as late as 2020.[18]

Although a majority of Turks support joining Europe,[19] there is widespread disagreement in Europe itself regarding the benefits and drawbacks of Turkish accession.[20] In both France and Germany, for instance, polls taken in February 2004 suggest that nearly 60 percent of the population opposes Turkish membership in the EU.[21] "Turco-skeptics" cite a host of reasons for their opposition. Economic concerns are paramount, including fear of a reallocation of scarce resources to Anatolia that would strain EU structural funds, concerns about Turkey's ability to adapt to European common policies including the common agricultural policy[22] and the social market economic model, fear of unwanted immigration of Turks to Europe in search of jobs, and other demographic implications of admitting Turkey—whose population exceeds the populations of all ten of the new states admitted to the EU in 2004 combined.[23]

A second line of oppositional arguments cites Turkish domestic political shortcomings, including lack of protection of minority rights;[24] limited freedom of expression, including freedom of religion; the constrained independence of the judiciary; excessive military control of political and civilian affairs; and the failure to come to terms with the Armenian genocide in the early twentieth century. Turkish relations with the "near abroad," including Turkish policy in Cyprus (depicted as an illegal occupation of EU territory) are a subset of these domestic political difficulties, as is the issue of how the future borders of Europe would be patrolled should they extend into Asia Minor. One senior EU diplomat summarized his view of Turkish domestic politics to Douglas Frantz of the *New York Times*, stating that "the Turks have to find a way to get the pashas out of politics."[25] Frantz points out that military-owned businesses, which are exempt from taxation, are among some of Turkey's largest enterprises: "The businesses operate outside government control and profits pay for pensions, resorts, and other benefits for members of the armed forces, helping attract and retain top personnel and cementing the soldiers' elevated social standing."[26] Franz notes that through the holding company Oyak (Armed Forces Trust and Pension Fund) with its 30,000 employees, the military has financial interests in twenty-four Turkish companies, including a bank, supermarket chain, real estate, and 47 percent of one of the country's two most prominent automobile makers.

The controversy surrounding free expression in Turkey is illustrated by the charges brought in 2005 against the acclaimed novelist Orhan Pamuk, who won the Nobel Prize in 2006 for his books *My Name Is Red, Snow,* and *The White Castle,* among others. Because the Justice Ministry refused to issue a ruling as to whether the charges should stand, his trial was suspended shortly after opening in December 2005. Though charges were dropped, Pamuk stood accused under Article 301 of Turkey's criminal code for "insulting Turkishness" after telling a Swiss newspaper in February 2005 that "30,000 Kurds and one million Armenians were killed in these lands, and nobody but me dares talk about it."[27] Though the motivations behind the charges remain murky, they may have been an attempt by Turkish anti-EU forces to jeopardize Turkey's chances of accession by provoking the EU on a subject it is known to defend adamantly: freedom of expression. The charges called attention to the fact that Turkish law makes it illegal to insult the republic, parliament, or any organs of state—thereby restricting freedom of expression. As the BBC concluded, "many in Turkey see his trial as part of a wider struggle between conflicting forces in the country—those who want to open up and join Europe and those opposed to the EU."[28]

A third category of concern related to Turkish accession involves the geopolitical implications of further EU expansion, in particular in an era when a significant proportion of the population in France—one of the two founding nations of the EU—is questioning the viability of the European project.[29] Some argue that if Turkey is admitted, a long list of central Asian states such as Georgia, Armenia, Moldavia, Ukraine, Belarus, and perhaps Russia also will qualify for consideration for EU membership. Gordon and Taspinar also have observed that "many Europeans worry about taking in a country that is geographically largely outside of Europe[30] and situated in a region plagued with conflict, instability, and terrorism."[31]

Fourth, critics cite procedural issues within the EU, including governance issues, as a reason to reject Turkey's candidacy. According to this argument, if admitted, Turkey would exercise an inordinate amount of voting weight in the EU (particularly the European Council and the European Parliament) due to the structure of the new constitution, in which political representation and voting weight in EU institutions is determined by population.[32] Other critics object to how negotiations by European leaders on the Turkish issue have been conducted, accusing the former of acting undemocratically and without transparency in decision-making procedures involving Turkish candidacy.[33]

Although each of the preceding factors is significant in its own right, European resistance to Turkish accession is rooted differently and more deeply than is suggested by an exclusive focus on economic and political considerations within the EU or domestic politics within Turkey. In 2002 former French president Valéry Giscard d'Estaing observed that Turkey was "not a European country" and that admitting Turkey to the EU would mean "the end of Europe."[34] Former West German chancellor and Social Democratic Party leader Helmut Schmidt suggested that Turkey should be excluded from the EU due to its unsuitable civilization[35] and that by opening the door to EU admission for other Muslim nations Turkey's accession could result "in the political union degenerating into nothing more than a free trade community."[36] In September 2004 EU internal market chief Frederik (Frits) Bolkestein stated "the American Islam expert Bernard Lewis has said that Europe will be Islamic at the end of this century. I do not know if this is right, or whether it will be at that speed, but if he is right, the liberation of Vienna in 1683 would have been in vain."[37]

These anxieties surrounding Turkish accession have been aggravated by heightened emotions in Europe following a series of recent episodes touching upon politics, religion, violence, and the challenges of pluralism in the context of postcoloniality, including the debate over God in the preamble of the EU Constitution (not included);[38] the murder of Dutch film maker Theo van Gogh; the dispute in France regarding the veil and the passage of the anti-headscarf law in 2004; the terrorist attacks of 3/11 in Madrid; the failure of the French state and society to integrate poor and marginalized citizens, many descended from immigrant families from former French colonies as evidenced by the violence in France in late 2005;[39] and the controversy surrounding the publication of cartoons perceived as offensive to Muslims in several European newspapers in early 2006.

Circulating within this charged environment, it is tempting to ascribe culturally and religiously based hesitations about Turkish accession to support for a Christian Europe in the face of a potential threat from a Muslim-majority state or civilization. However, like the violence in the French *cités*,[40] the story is more complex than is suggested by this "clash of civilizations" framework. Cultural and religious opposition to Turkey is not simply about defending the idea of a Christian Europe from an outside threat. This opposition is the cultural and political manifestation of the unsettled nature of the relation between religion, politics, and European identity. It attests to the presence of unresolved issues concerning the politics of religion *within* Europe itself. By challenging prevailing notions of what it means to be secular and European, Turkey's candidacy propels a series of difficult questions into the public spotlight and contributes to a sense of urgency among Europeans that they be settled before Turkey is admitted to the union. The contestation and recon-figuration of dominant forms of European secularism—both inside and out-side Europe—is at the heart of the debate over Turkish accession.

The next two sections fill in the content of this domestic cultural opposition to Turkish accession. I do so by charting the influence of Judeo-Christian secularism and laicism upon the debate over Turkish accession to the EU. Drawing on Rumelili's argument concerning two different dimensions of Eu-ropean identity—exclusive and inclusive—I explain how these two trajecto-ries of secularism have conditioned EU-Turkey relations.[41] Keyman and Onis allude to this distinction between laicist and Judeo-Christian secular perspec-tives on Turkey in their discussion of the effects of European political cleav-ages upon the debate over Turkish accession:

> A clear dividing line has emerged between the social democrat and Christian demo-crat perspectives. The former . . . proved more receptive to Turkey's eventual acces-sion provided that the country undertook the reforms necessary to satisfy the Copen-hagen criteria. Christian democrats, in contrast, found it more difficult to come to terms with Turkey's eventual membership, given their narrow conception of Euro-pean identity.[42]

The argument developed in this chapter suggests that only when Europe ac-knowledges the historical particularism of its own traditions of secularization, as well as the possibility of legitimate alternatives to them, will Turkish integra-tion into the EU be successful. The challenge to Kemalism, a Turkish form of secularism that approximates the laicist approach to religion and politics, is not a religious threat to secular democracy that should be suppressed at almost any cost, as laicists argue. It is also not a retreat to archaic Muslim forms of political order. It is an alternative trajectory of secularization that is part of a logical protest against the Kemalist attempt to monopolize what would otherwise be an ongoing, public debate over what it means to be a secular Muslim-majority state. This "third tradition" is an attempt to legiti-mate Turkish public order as both modern and Ottoman, as both secular and Islamic, thereby distinguishing itself from *both* Kemalism and the formations of secularism that emerged from Latin Christendom. Only when the EU rede-fines itself such that the inclusion of Turkey no longer threatens both exclusi-vist and inclusivist dimensions of the cultural and religious foundations of *European* identity will full Turkish integration become a possibility.

JUDEO-CHRISTIAN SECULARISM AND TURKISH ACCESSION

Charles Taylor defines a social imaginary as "the ways in which people imag-ine their social existence, how they fit together with others, how things go on between them and their fellows, the expectations that are normally met, and the deeper normative notions and images that underlie these expectations."[43] Laicism and Judeo-Christian secularism are important components of the European social imaginary. Together with the economic and political factors discussed previously, these two strands of secularist political discourse contribute to a climate of skepticism in Europe regarding Turkish accession.

In chapter 1 I referred to Çinar's definition of secularism as a series of interlinked political projects that continually seek to "transform and reinstitute a sociopolitical order on the basis of a set of constitutive norms and principles."[44] This chapter explains how secularist norms, principles, sensibilities, and attitudes continually transform and recreate international sociopolitical order in a specific time and place: contemporary Europe. Judeo-Christian secularism, as described in earlier chapters, is a constellation of norms and sensibilities that constitutes a political project in which Judeo-Christian religious traditions and modern politics are seen as commingling in a particular way, each strengthening the other. Secularization, in this view, is the realization of a Western religious tradition. Religion is part of the moral basis of civilization.[45] A significant implication of this authoritative discourse is that the secularist separation of religion from politics and the democratic settlement of which it is a part is perceived as a unique Western achievement that is superior to its non-Western rivals. If Judeo-Christianity is the fount and foundation of secular democracy, and the separation of church and state is a unique achievement that evolved out of Christianity, then in this narrative the potential for secularization is tied to a particular cultural identity, civilizational history, and geographic location.[46] Civilizational differences in the designation of the secular and the religious are fixed rather than fleeting. They cannot be transcended. This exclusivist approach to the cultural boundaries of democracy is the hallmark of Judeo-Christian secularism.[47]

Judeo-Christian secularism has significant implications for the debate over Turkish accession. In *Vers un Islam européen,* for example, Olivier Roy argues that "Turkey will be rejected from the European Union not because the Turkish state fails to satisfy the EU's demands to democratize, which would be a good reason, but because Turkish society is not [European], meaning that it does not share the fund of Christianity that serves as the foundation of laicism itself."[48] In other words, Turkey, though secular in some sense, will not be admitted to the EU because key decision makers in Europe and the majority of the European public do not believe it to be sufficiently secular in the European sense. Specifically, Turkey does not share the common cultural and religious ground that serves to anchor European secularism and, by extension, European democracy. Huntington expresses this idea succinctly in *The Clash of Civilizations*: "Where does Europe end? Where Western Christianity ends and Islam and Orthodoxy begin."[49] The Judeo-Christian secular formula for Europe relies upon the assumption that full secular democracy can be fully realized *only* in societies possessing a (Judeo)-Christian heritage. In this view, the Judeo-Christian foundation of European secularism and democracy, and of Europe itself, is the only foundation possible. A 2005 BBC poll in the United Kingdom confirmed the popular resonance of this connection between British identity and Christianity. The poll found that nearly 75 percent of respondents believed the United Kingdom should retain Christian values — including 69 percent of Jews, and nearly 50 percent of Muslims, Sikhs, and Hindus. Even among those individuals who claimed to have no faith, 44 percent favored retaining a "Christian ethos."[50]

Both Roy and Huntington allude to a set of assumptions, in the former case without endorsing them, that suggest that full-fledged European-style secular democracy can *only* be achieved in societies possessing a (Judeo)-Christian heritage. As Huntington argues, "Turkey will not become a member of the European Community, and the real reason, as President Özal said, 'is that we are Muslim and they are Christian and they don't say that.' "[51] The Christian foundation of European secularism, from this perspective, is the only possible one. As Göle has argued, Turkish candidacy renders these tacit assumptions connecting Christian heritage with European identity explicit, thereby revealing the limits of European democracy.[52] Walter Russell Mead agrees:

> There is still a symbolic connection between identity and religion, whether the connection is felt historically or in other ways. . . . One certainly sees it in the debate over Turkish membership in the European Union. Many people who rarely or never attend church still feel that Europe has a Christian identity and believe that identity is threatened by the membership of a secular Turkish republic.[53]

Turkish EU candidacy consolidates these tacit and sometimes conflicting assumptions regarding Christian values and Christian heritage and their relevance to European identity and propels them into the public spotlight.[54] The presumed connection between Christian values and European forms of democracy contributes to an aversion to Turkish Islamic identity and skepticism about Turkey's potential as a non-Christian-majority secular democratic member of the EU. In this view, Turkey is inherently different from Europe due to the existence of an exclusive European identity based on geography, culture, and religion.[55] European identity is conceived in bounded, fixed, and exclusive terms, "embodying a conception of difference that is based on inherent characteristics."[56] This contrasts with a more inclusive version of European identity emphasizing the possibility of a state *becoming* European by gradually acquiring a series of inclusive and (arguably) universal characteristics such as respect for liberty, human rights, and secular democracy.[57]

As an example of the influence of Judeo-Christian secularism upon European approaches to Turkey, consider the Judeo-Christian secularist response to the challenge to Kemalism in Turkey described in the previous chapter. From this perspective, the challenge to Kemalism confirms that secularization and democratization are unique to the (Judeo-Christian) West. Resistance to

Kemalism is taken as proof of the futility of "liberal" attempts to incorporate a Muslim-majority society into a democratic, secular (and Judeo-Christian) European Union. From this perspective, Turkey is and always will be at a disadvantage vis-à-vis the Copenhagen criteria due to its cultural and religious commitments and is therefore unfit to become fully European. Distinctions between religious and political authority are historically absent not only from Turkey but also from the Islamic world in general. The absence of such distinctions, it is argued, is attributable to the nature of Islam itself. Sociologist of religion David Martin, for example, has suggested that "the relative lack of the religious/secular distinction within Islam has serious consequences."[58] In this view, Muslim-majority civilizations simply do not enjoy indigenous forms of secularism, and then, to make matters worse, they insist upon rejecting the secularism imported from the West. For Judeo-Christian secularists, secularism is ultimately incompatible with Islam and unlikely to be realized in Turkey or any other Muslim-majority society.

This opposition to Turkey on exclusivist cultural and religious grounds also carries within it a position on the identity of the EU and the subordinate place of religious, and particularly Muslim, minorities within that identity. As Nexon argues, "a great many of the historical resources for articulating a common European identity are premised on a reduction of religious heterogeneity through the creation of Orthodoxy and Islam as important 'others.' "[59] By positing a unique set of connections between Judeo-Christianity, European identity, and the potential for successful democratization, this narrative creates and reinforces a particular image and tradition of Europe as (exclusively) Judeo-Christian. The divide between religious identities becomes a fixed marker of civilizational difference. This carries implications not only for Europe's external relations but also for non-Judeo-Christian Europeans, with the latter easily portrayed as "suspect citizens" and "potential enemies within."[60] The consequences of these divisions are evident in contemporary European politics. In this instance, Judeo-Christian secularism, following Asad, "is a way of trying to secure the power of *a particular* kind of state, by pronouncing the *illegitimacy* of certain kinds of citizen-subject who are thought to be incompatible with it because they do not share fundamental national values."[61]

LAICISM AND TURKISH ACCESSION

Laicism also contributes to a climate of skepticism in Europe regarding Turkish accession. Laicism, as described at length in chapter 2, refers to the attempt to purge religion from politics and is associated with both intensive and extensive state control of religious institutions, authorities, and expression. The laicist model, particularly in France, is distinct from the American secular "separation of church and state."[62] Laicists support a vigorous role for the state in the regulation of religion and are wary of religious infringements in public space. They are skeptical about the democratic potential of any relationship between religion and politics that diverges from strict separationism as defined by the state. Any increase in or reconfiguration of the public role of religion is viewed as an undesirable infringement upon would-be secular public life, a compromise of state authority, and, in the French and Turkish cases in particular, a threat to national identity.[63] Rigorous state regulation of public religious expression and institutions are the result, and any attempt to reconfigure the secular-religious divide away from a strict regulative model is perceived as a threat to democratic order. Andrew Davison, for example, defines Turkish Kemalism as "a structure of power in which Islam was separated from areas of governance in some respects within an overall and overarching integrated relationship of state control."[64]

In contrast to Judeo-Christian secularism, which emphasizes a fixed and exclusive version of European identity, laicism suggests that the exclusion of Turkey from Europe on cultural and religious grounds per se is unjustified. Laicism therefore leads to a different set of conclusions regarding European identity and its relationship to Turkish accession. Laicists emphasize the inclusive aspects of Europe and, as Rumelili argues, "construct Turkey as different from Europe solely in terms of acquired characteristics."[65] According to this argument, if Turkey conforms to European (laicist) norms regarding religion and politics, among other considerations, it should be admitted to the EU. The problem is not that Turkey is constitutionally and culturally incapable of complying with European standards, but rather that it has not *yet* satisfactorily achieved a particular level of (political, economic, and/or religiopolitical) development. As this argument goes, "if and when Turkey develops economic and political institutions in line with European values and standards, it will rightfully become a member of the EU, despite what others may claim to be its inherent differences."[66]

For laicists committed to the idea that Turkey will progress incrementally through a series of stages of development, culminating in its full Europeanization, there is a sense that contemporary Turkey is not "anti-Europe," but merely "less Europe," to borrow Wæver's useful formulation. As Wæver argues, "the dominant trend in European security rhetoric is that the Other is Europe's own past (fragmentation), and those further away from the center are not defined as anti-Europe, only less Europe. Europe has no clear border—it fades away as you move out over the Russian plains."[67] Laicists equate Europe's past experiences with Turkey's present "struggles" with secularization.

As is the case with their Judeo-Christian secularist counterparts, however, laicist commitments engender fear that this struggle, and specifically the challenge to the Kemalist settlement in Turkey, may be sufficient to derail Turkish progress toward modernization and Europeanization. While in recent decades organized religion has declined in Europe,[68] Turkey is experiencing a revival of public religion that challenges European universalist norms regarding the (laicist) division between religion and politics upon which Kemalism was modeled.[69] For some, this challenge is enough to question Turkey's qualification for EU membership. Kemalism, from this perspective, represents a laudable attempt to bring Turkey into a modern, laicist, and European present. Kemalism is reasonable. The revival of public religion—as a challenge to Kemalism—suggests that Turkey has not come far enough along the continuum of development. This challenge is unreasonable. In this view, Turkey has not come far enough along the continuum of development. It has not yet realized the progression out of a religious (Islamic) past into a laicist (European) present and is at risk of reverting to archaic practices regarding the public presence of religion and its formal control of the state. This fear is expressed in regretful terms as the "loss of Atatürk's legacy"[70] and manifests itself in conventional concerns about the intentions of the Justice and Development Party, or AKP: "Despite the AKP's continued popularity, some are skeptical of Erdogan's real intentions. Pointing to his more radical beginnings and recent AKP positions on women's rights and education, critics charge that the prime minister's commitment to secularism and liberalization is only superficial."[71]

Conventional laicist wisdom, exemplified in the decision by the European Court of Human Rights described in chapter 4, suggests that a post-Kemalist (assumed to be Islamist) Turkey is unfit to become fully European because it risks violating laicist norms that are among the founding principles of European democracy. Resistance to Kemalism, expressed in Islamic terms, appears as a threat to the laicist separationist public-private divide and concept and practice of religious freedom.[72]

For laicists, unlike for Judeo-Christian secularists, the shortcomings involved in the presence of Islam in Turkish politics are not irremediable but can be overcome through the importation of Western-style democracy and the secularization of politics and society. European identity itself is conceived as inclusive, based on a series of acquired characteristics rather than a series of pregiven cultural and civilizational traits. Because the solution to Turkey's potential problem is a renewed commitment to Kemalism, laicists often find themselves, whether intentionally or implicitly through received tradition, somewhat incongruously supporting the heavy-handed approach of the Turkish military vis-à-vis the regulation of public religion and find themselves suspicious of attempts to challenge the Kemalist establishment. They fear religious individuals and groups that are active in the public sphere as potential threats to democratic order and regretfully, often tacitly, support state suppression of such actors as legitimate and even warranted. As Kösebalaban points out, "while the European governments and human-rights organizations including the European Court of Human Rights have been very sensitive to Kurdish human rights, they have maintained a persistent indifference to political problems like the headscarf issue and the closure of Islamic-leaning political parties."[73] This makes for strange bedfellows, as laicists who otherwise support individual and human rights occasionally find themselves somewhat unhappily aligned politically with the repressive and interventionist Turkish army. Though not directly relevant to EU-Turkey relations, U.S. support for the army's ouster of Welfare Party also reflects the influence of laicist presuppositions. As Erhard Franz argues, "the USA, who had feared that Turkey under Erbakan would drift into the anti-American Islamic camp, views the Turkish military as the guarantor of the country's loyalty to the Western alliance."[74]

A June 2004 decision by the European Court of Human Rights (ECHR) illustrates the cultural foothold achieved in Europe by laicist commitments to exclude religion from the Turkish public sphere. The ECHR concluded in this decision, which was confirmed in 2005 by the Grand Chamber of the ECHR, that Article 9 of the European Convention on Human Rights had *not* been violated by the Turkish refusal to allow Turkish medical student Leyla Sahin to wear a headscarf while pursuing her studies at the University of Istanbul.[75] As Marshall summarizes the decision, "in all the cases, Convention institutions have found that in a democratic society, the relevant member state is entitled to ban adult women from wearing the Islamic headscarf on the basis that such bans have been prescribed by law, have a legitimate aim, that is, protecting the rights and freedoms of others, and are necessary in a democratic society."[76]

This decision reflects and reinforces the ECHR's commitment to a laicist understanding of the proper relationship between religious expression and democratic public space and discourse. The majority opinion in the Grand Chamber found secularism to be "consistent with the values underpinning the Convention. It finds that upholding that principle, which is undoubtedly one of the fundamental principles of the Turkish State which are in harmony with the rule of law and respect for human rights, may be considered necessary to protect the democratic system in Turkey. An attitude which fails to respect that principle will not necessarily be accepted as being covered by the freedom to manifest one's religion and will not enjoy the protection of Article 9 of the Convention."[77] One of the unexamined assumptions underlying this case and others decided in a similar way is the European tradition of laicism. Laicism appropriates to itself the power to define the "public" sphere in which an inappropriate and possibly illegal incursion of "private" religious belief and practice is alleged to have occurred.[78] Laicism, as argued in chapter 3, is also partially constituted through particular negative representations of Islam. This helps to explain why the court's decision, according to Marshall, relied upon a "largely unexamined assumption that their culture [Muslim women] and/ or religion is based on gender inequality and that they are some sort of duped victims."[79] The discursive power of laicism to set the terms within which debate over religion and public space proceeds is also exemplified in recent French legislation restricting public religious expression.[80] These developments suggest that individuals who have and choose to express an alternative understanding of the proper relationship between religious expression and public space, perhaps though not necessarily indebted to Islamic tradition, will have to work against a formidable European social and historical tradition to be accepted, at least in the near-term, as "European."

EUROPE, TURKEY, AND MULTIPLE SECULAR MODERNITIES

Halliday has observed that "if future relations between the Middle East/ Islamic world and the west are to be based on a solid foundation, then the fate of the still ongoing Turkish experience may be not just influential, but decisive."[81] Most observers of Europe-Turkey relations assume that Turkey needs to demonstrate its cultural, political, and economic fitness to participate in European institutions and society, and that Europe will in time render judgment in accordance with its own criteria. This assumption is reflected in the Negotiating Framework of October 2005, which states that, "in all areas of the *acquis*, Turkey must bring its institutions, management capacity and administrative and judicial systems up to Union standards, both at national and regional level, with a view to implementing the *acquis* effectively."[82] Fabrizio Barbaso, former director general for enlargement at the EU Commission, confirmed this expectation by insisting that Turkey conform to preexisting European standards: "the process of modernization of the Turkish political system and its adaptation to the EU standards is underway. . . . the further development of EU-Turkey relations . . . will depend on Turkey's capacity to demonstrate that it fulfils the Copenhagen political criteria, not only in legal provisions, but also in practice."[83]

The argument developed in this chapter challenges the assumption that Turkish compliance with the Copenhagen criteria will be sufficient to ensure a smooth incorporation of Turkey into Europe. As Göle suggests, the encounter between Turkey and Europe is a two-way street that transforms both Turkish politics *and* the European project itself.[84] Turkish candidacy challenges and may even change European concepts and practices of secularism. Before admitting Turkey, the EU will press Turkey to accept a variety of European legal, financial, and political institutions, standards, and practices. Yet, paradoxically, in the domain of religion and politics Turkish integration into the EU will be successful only insofar as Europeans revisit their own assumptions about politics, religion, and the moral foundations of democratization.

Turkish candidacy obligates Europeans to reconsider what it means to be a secular European. Up to the present, this generally has involved subscribing to laicism or Judeo-Christian secularism, or some version or combination thereof. Turkish candidacy changes and challenges the taken-for-grantedness of the equation between European identity and these particular traditions of secularism. It does so by introducing alternative trajectories of secularization that draw upon non–Judeo-Christian traditions and proposing that they be accepted as equally European. How Europe responds to this challenge remains to be seen. As long as Brussels continues to insist upon a "one-way" relationship between Turkey and the EU, it will remain impossible, or at least very difficult, for Turkey to fulfill the demands placed upon it to "modernize" along the lines of the European model as far as religion and politics are concerned. Turkey cannot be expected to follow either a Judeo-Christian secularist model of secularization or a laicist trajectory of secularization, both of which emerged over the course of centuries out of a set of disputes within Latin Christendom, as described in chapter 2.

Rather than impose either of these ill-fitting and arguably outdated secularist settlements upon the Turks and insist that they adhere to them to qualify for EU membership, successful negotiations will require that Europe both acknowledge alternative cultural and religious formulations and foundations of secularism and revisit its own collective assumptions about the relationship between religion, politics, and European identity. Within Europe, this means coming to terms with the multiple and diverse civilizational sources and varieties of secularism. It means acknowledging that the role of religion in European collective identity is far from settled and may well remain so.[85] Between Europe and Turkey, it requires an acknowledgment of the complexity of the challenge to Kemalism: such challenges are neither simply "religious" threats to "secular" democracy, as laicist inclusivists suggest, nor are they a predictable retreat to archaic Muslim forms of political order, as Judeo-Christian secularist exclusivists argue. Instead, these developments are part of a legitimate protest against the Kemalist attempt to monopolize what should be an ongoing public debate over what it means to be a secular Muslim-majority state. White has argued convincingly that democratic politics requires a continuing struggle over how the sacred and the secular are defined and practiced.[86] Challenges to Kemalism are part of this struggle insofar as they posit a rival Turkish public order that reconfigures the Kemalist settlement between secularism and Islamism, thereby forging a new model that is distinctive *both* from prevailing European modes of secularism and from Kemalism. As Yavuz has shown, the platform of Turkish "Islamist" parties did not amount to "an explicit program of Islamic revival but rather the reconstruction of Ottoman-Turkish norms and associations to challenge the alienating aspects of the Kemalist project."[87]

Norms that circulate globally adapt to local conditions and appear differently in different cultural and political circumstances. As Taylor observes, "we need to speak of *multiple* modernities, the plural reflecting the fact that non-Western cultures have modernized in their own ways and cannot be properly understood if we try to grasp them in a general theory that was originally designed with the Western case in mind."[88] Modern variations of Turkish Islamism, rather than simply a threat to secular democracy or a revival of religion in public life, are an example of how different forms of secularism emerge in different cultural and political circumstances. As Göle has argued, "although the cultural program of modernity has a great capacity to influence and circulate, the encounter between the two cultural codes leads not to a simple logic of emulation or rejection but to improvisations in social practices and cultural meanings."[89] Turkish Islamism is such an improvisation. Rather than a pre- or antimodern attempt to resuscitate a pristine Islamic past, Turkish Islamism is part of an attempt to reformulate "the borders and the meanings of the secular public sphere" itself, serving as a "destabilizing force" in secular (including secular European) social imaginaries.[90] As Çinar concludes, "in Turkey Islamism has advanced an alternative nationalist project that is equally modernizationist to that of secularism and hence has produced what can be referred to as Islamic modernism."[91] This challenge to Kemalism involves no less than "the reconfiguration of religion and politics in the public sphere."[92]

Secularism, this argument suggests, is a contingent and contested social construction. As Yavuz argues, it is "a terrain of contestation rather than a fixed ideological or behavioral understanding across time and space."[93] This chapter has illustrated that different foundations and formulations of secularism exist both within Europe and outside of it. Multiple forms of secularism exist in both Christian and Muslim-majority societies. Turkish candidacy for the EU is politically inflammatory in part because it makes the historical contingencies of these different forms of secularism explicit. As Çinar argues, "Islamist interventions served to reveal that secularism is neither natural nor a fact of public life, but indeed another forged and partial principle that is quite negotiable and contestable."[94] Although some varieties of secularism did emerge out of Christianity, Europeans hold no monopoly on the separation of civil and religious authorities, mundane and metaphysical spaces, or sacred and secular institutions. Turkey fails to conform to European secular standards only if Europeans define those standards a priori in terms of their political and religious history, and not their present or future.

The Negotiating Framework of October 2005 stipulates that "negotiations will be based on Turkey's own merits and the pace will depend on Turkey's progress in meeting the requirements for membership." A significant choice for Europe in the next decade is whether to recognize the differing historical trajectories of secularism both in Europe and in Turkey, or to impose its own historical secularist expectations upon new and aspiring "Europeans." My argument suggests that for Turkish integration into the EU to succeed, negotiations must encompass not only Turkish progress in meeting European standards but also a reevaluation of those standards to acknowledge and incorporate alternative ways of living the politics of religion. As Asad concludes, "if Europe cannot be articulated in terms of complex space and complex time that allow for multiple ways of life (and not merely multiple identities) to flourish, it may be fated to be no more than the common market of an imperial civilization, always anxious about (Muslim) exiles within its gates and (Muslim) barbarians beyond."[95]

POLITICAL CULTURE AND INTERNATIONAL RELATIONS

The traditions of secularism analyzed in this book contribute to the creation of what Peter van der Veer has described as "public spheres of political interaction central to the formation of national identities."[96] Yet connections between secularism, religion, national and supranational identities, and international relations are rarely investigated. One objective of this book is to open up this field of inquiry in the discipline of international relations. This chapter has clarified some of the ways in which particular formations of secularism become implicated in, and partially constitutive of, European identity. European responses to the possibility of Turkish accession illustrate the political salience of negotiations between domestic political culture, supranational forms of identification, and international politics.[97] Domestic secularist norms and practices contribute to the construction of European identities and interests. As Kowert and Legro argue, authoritative forms of secularism "interact powerfully with conceptions of identity," working to shape both the identities of actors and the rules for enacting those identities.[98] The ways of life associated with the forms of secularism described here as laicism and Judeo-Christian secularism also contribute to the production of particular forms of collective subjectivity and help to delimit the boundaries of what is defined as modern politics.

This argument complements the international relations literature focused on the processes through which domestic concerns shape foreign policy and allows us to make two important moves in international relations theory. First, it moves beyond models that sideline religious and cultural factors by assuming that international relations is a story of autonomous states pursuing stable, fixed, and pregiven interests. Second, and in engagement with theories that do acknowledge the role of cultural factors, it allows us to go beyond generic references to cultural or religious difference as causal factors in international relations and to examine the international political consequences of specific authoritative discourses—in this case, two variations of secularism —for attempts at multilateral cooperation and community formation. These moves are important because, as the Turkey-EU question suggests, there are questions in international relations that cannot be addressed without accounting for the political authority exercised by multidimensional cultural and religious norms, sensibilities, and habits of speech and thought whose origins lie in domestic political culture.

The question is not *whether* political culture matters in international relations but *how* it matters. Most international relations theory either sidelines cultural and religious issues altogether and thereby misses an important part of the story, or defaults to a paradigm in which the Western defense of secular democracy is counterpoised to some other group or other civilization's irrational defense of ideology, tradition, and/or authoritarianism. The merit of the latter approach is that it acknowledges the significance of political culture to international politics. The problem is that it is often accompanied by a series of untenable assumptions about religion and politics, such as the conviction that, unlike other parts of the world, the West has outgrown the need to rely upon religion in ordering its political affairs.[99] This is not the case. Authoritative cultural and religious systems of belief and practice are powerful determinants of modern domestic politics and contemporary international relations both in the West and outside of it. Recognizing how these forms of power operate allows a better understanding of crucial empirical puzzles in international relations, including the social and cultural politics of EU enlargement and relations between the United States and Iran.

The United States and Iran

> But over near the White House the nation's official Christmas
> tree is dark except for one star at the top, because the hostages
> in Iran have yet to receive the Christmas gift of freedom from
> the unwise men of the East.[1]

THE UNTHINKABLE REVOLUTION

An imposing calendar hung on the wall of Mrs. Soderlund's fourth-grade class
at Field Elementary School in Minneapolis. With each day that passed in
1979–80 during which fifty-two American diplomats were held hostage in the
U.S. Embassy in Tehran for 444 days, Mrs. Soderlund would cross out the
date with a thick red "X." Marking time in this way was not unusual during
the crisis. Melani McAlister notes that during those months "the United States
existed on two calendars, with the number of days in captivity superimposed
over the Gregorian dates."[2] The red marks on the calendar in my classroom
sparked a sense of curiosity about those whose actions warranted the symbolic
obliteration of an entire day, day after day, month after month. We were told
that the Iranians were angry at the United States and that they had taken
innocent Americans hostage. They were religious fanatics, very distant, and
completely different from us. Americans, as I interpreted the situation, were
not Iranian, not fanatical, and not particularly religious. Americans were rational, secular, and democratic. It was the first time that I had ever heard of Iran.

For U.S.-Iranian relations, the hostage crisis of November 1979 was the
most politically inflammatory episode in the rejection of the shah's power and
Western influence in Iran that was the Iranian revolution of 1979.[3] Iranians
were frustrated with what they perceived as long-standing and excessive U.S.
intervention in Iranian domestic affairs, evidenced at the time by a meeting
in Algiers on November 1, 1979, between U.S. National Security Advisor
Brzezinski and Iranian Prime Minister Bazargan and Deputy Prime Minister
Yazdik, and many believed that the United States was sheltering the shah in
exile in preparation for returning him to power.[4] Given the events surrounding
the coup of 1953, Iranians were suspicious of U.S. government claims that
the shah was being treated for cancer in the United States.[5] The hostage crisis
was significant inside Iran because, as Maloney observes, it "fused the extremist dimensions of the divergent worldviews remaining within the revolutionary

coalition: radical anti-Westernism and vehemently Islamist self-identifica-tion."[6] The hostages became "both symbol and stake in the internal struggle to define the nature of postrevolutionary Iran."[7]

Although pundits and commentators are quick to attribute negative Ameri-can views of postrevolutionary Iran to this crisis, to view American opposition to Iran as a mere reaction to the hostage taking would be a mistake. This opposition is not only a response to outside provocation but is deeply rooted in American political culture and history, including American religious his-tory. The two traditions of religion and politics — laicism and Judeo-Christian secularism — described in this book provide the conceptual apparatus and cul-tural backdrop through which American opposition to Iran has been consoli-dated and legitimized since the revolution. These forms of secularism are part of what Connolly describes as the "institutionally embedded ethos flowing into" modern practices of sovereignty in the United States.[8] They form part of the cultural and religious foundation of modern American relations with Iran, conditioning American foreign policy but also, and perhaps more funda-mentally, helping to constitute what it means to *be* American. These forms of secularism are the principal reason that for Americans the 1979 revolution was "unthinkable."[9]

One of the overarching themes of this book is that attempts to explain relations between Europe, the United States, and the Middle East and North Africa in terms of fixed and objective state interests, characteristics of individ-ual leaders or bureaucracies, Cold War politics, or other traditional variables that sideline the role of cultural and religious traditions are insufficient. The preceding chapter examined the controversy surrounding Turkey's potential accession to the European Union, suggesting that European resistance cannot be fully explained in economic or political terms, or even as a result of opposi-tion to a Muslim-majority country in a Christian-majority Europe. Cultural and religiously based opposition to Turkey has arisen because Turkish candi-dacy brings up long-dormant dilemmas internal to Europe regarding what it means to be a secular European. Turkey has turned toward a different trajec-tory of secularism that conforms to neither Kemalism nor the two prevailing trajectories of secularism in EU, laicism and Judeo-Christian secularism. This third way threatens not only the Kemalist establishment in Turkey but Euro-pean secularists as well. The Turkish case is therefore controversial not only because it involves the potential accession of a Muslim-majority country to a historically Christian Europe, but also because it involves unfinished current business in the social fabric of the core EU members, including what it means to be secular and how religion, including but not limited to Islam, relates to European identity. These cultural sticking points explain why this debate is so contentious.

The present chapter situates secularist authority in a different historical context, assessing the effects of secularist norms and practices upon American

understandings of the 1978–79 revolution in Iran and upon American relations with Iran after the revolution. A comprehensive understanding of the
history of U.S.-Iranian relations requires that we consider not just pregiven
geopolitical and material interests but the cultural and social practices, habits,
and social relations through which these interests take shape and are expressed. As Asad argues, "the specific practices, sensibilities and attitudes that
undergird secularism as a national arrangement—that give it solidity and support—remain largely unexplored."[10] This chapter explores these secularist
practices and attitudes and demonstrates that they are a productive part of
the social and cultural foundation of contemporary international relations.
Laicism and Judeo-Christian secularism are formative elements in the conceptual apparatus through which Americans interpreted and responded to the
Iranian revolution of 1979. These widely held and influential theses about
the relationship between religion and politics constitute an important part
of the cultural and religious backdrop through which the United States has
legitimized opposition to Iran.

Accounts that focus on objective state interests that dominate international
relations theory miss a key component of the Iranian-American relationship
and fail to capture the intensity and complexity of the antagonism between
these two countries. While such accounts offer important insights into this
relationship, they do not account for the effects of productive forms of power
that operate outside the purview of rationalist explanation, including the authoritative secularist discourses described in this book. My critique of these
explanations is not unlike van der Veer's criticism of Habermas, which suggests that "Habermas's analysis of the Enlightenment tradition very much belongs, at the theoretical level, to a discourse of modern, European self-representation. A striking element in this self-representation is the neglect of
religious, public opinion that cannot be regarded as 'rational' and 'critical.'"[11]
I argue that this religious public opinion is important not only in Iran, as is
commonly assumed, but also in the United States. The social bonds provided
by the forms of secularism described in this book serve as a basis of national
cohesion in the United States and as an important source of American identity
and American foreign policy.[12]

Anthony W. Marx makes a related claim about the exclusionary religious
foundations of nationalism in France, England, and, to a lesser degree, Spain.
Marx argues that the emergence of modern nationalism in Europe can be
traced to a "logic of exclusionary cohesion" in which the social bonds of religion were used as the basis of national collective identity. As he suggests,
"religion was thereby turned into a basis for selective and secular allegiance
. . . religious division thus made impossible inclusive unity, but at the same
time it provided a powerful alternative of building selective nationalism."[13]
Marx's nationalist logic of exclusionary cohesion in early modern Europe also
applies to the power of modern secular authority in the contemporary United

States. The "nationalization" of laic and Judeo-Christian secularism has significant political effects; as Marx argues state authority is "bolstered by exclusionary forms of faith, reinforced by enmity and encoded in nation."[14]

In addition to exploring the cultural and religious basis of U.S.-Iranian relations, this chapter offers an empirical contribution and an important corrective to the international relations literature involving how individual states construct their interests and identities. As Saideman argues, "identities shape perceptions of oneself and of others, which, in turn, influence foreign policy. Identity defines a state's reality—who it is, who the threats are, and which policies are possible."[15] The U.S.-Iran case demonstrates how shared interests and identities developed primarily at the domestic level become influential at the systemic level in international relations. As van der Veer and Lehmann argue, "it is essential to follow the transformation of religious notions when they are transferred from a purely religious context to the sphere of national politics."[16] It is also essential to follow the transformation of cultural and religious factors when they are transferred to the sphere of *inter*national politics. As Bukovansky argues, "understanding the cultural system is an essential component of understanding international politics; it is not merely a 'residual' that cleans up the random and unimportant variations for which interests cannot account. Rather, cultural contradictions and complementarities are critical enabling conditions for interest-driven political conflict and collective action."[17]

Secularism is a productive part of the cultural and normative foundation of American political order, American national identity, and contemporary international relations. Following Marx, I approach nationalism as "a collective sentiment of bounded solidarity or identity"[18] and argue that secularism helps to generate and organize these collective sentiments and the practices associated with them. Van der Veer and Lehmann suggest that nationalism "feeds on a symbolic repertoire that is already available but also transforms it in significant ways."[19] Secularist authority is part of this symbolic repertoire. It helps to "shape the context within which officials [have] formulated policy."[20] As Hall argues in reference to national collective identity, "sovereign state actors may well have autonomous interests that help shape state policy, but the influences, beliefs and prejudices of individuals and sub-state groups within society help to determine how ostensibly objective state interests get translated into policy."[21] This variation of constructivism requires what Wæver describes as a concern for "how each unit has to construct its own world . . . a more extorting approach, but in some sense more true to the basic constructivist premise that we can't start from some world 'as it really is,' but only from worlds as they are created."[22]

Two caveats are in order. First, because this chapter focuses on the cultural and religious bases of American secularist representations of and relations with a "religious" Iran, a caveat introduced earlier also applies here. Chapter

3 argued that Euro-American traditions of secularism and the national identities with which they are associated have been generated in part through opposition to particular appropriations of Islam. My object of analysis was not Muslim belief, Islamic tradition, or the relationship between Islam and modes of governance in the Middle East, but European and American representations of Islam and how these representations contributed to the construction of particular forms of secularist authority and the national identities in which these formations are embedded. Similarly, the object of analysis in the present chapter is neither Iranian representations of the United States[23] nor the relationship between Islamic tradition and domestic political authority within Iran,[24] but rather the political effects of secularist authority upon American representations of the revolution and relations with Iran.

Second, to argue that secularist authority is an influential part of the sociocultural context within which U.S. foreign policy is formulated is not to argue that secularism mono-causally drives U.S. policy toward Muslim-majority countries or transnational Islamic movements regardless of other circumstances. As indicated by current friendly U.S. relations with Saudi Arabia and American support during the 1980s for the Afghan *mujahideen* (described by President Reagan as "freedom fighters"), there are many factors that contribute to the process and context through which U.S. foreign policy is formulated, framed, and legitimized. In the Saudi case, geopolitical and material interests have been paramount; and in the Afghan case, Cold War politics (which was at least partly legitimized through references to fighting "Godless communists") dominated U.S. decision making. Material interests and Cold War politics also have been critical in U.S.-Iran relations. However, an exclusive focus on material forces or strategic interactions sidelines powerful social and cultural factors that influence relations between the United States and Iran.

"CRESCENT OF CRISIS": SECULARISM AND THE REVOLUTION[25]

Although the revolutionary movement in Iran had been gathering momentum for nearly three decades, the revolution and its aftermath, including the hostage crisis, baffled schoolchildren and Western experts alike.[26] It was difficult for informed Americans to imagine how this could have happened to the shah. Esposito writes that "the Pahlavis, like the Sadats, spoke English, dressed in well-tailored Western clothes, and appeared on American television, interviewed by the likes of Barbara Walters. (They were like 'us.')"[27] Mirsepassi notes that "every expectation was defied . . . the media, academia and public were overwhelmed by the vision of a modernizing and pro-Western monarchy being overthrown by a mass movement under the leadership of men whose image matched the most deeply entrenched Orientalist stereotypes."[28] The country that President Jimmy Carter had famously described in a December

1977 speech in Tehran as an "island of stability" had been torn apart by social and political upheaval that was unimaginable just weeks before it occurred. As Esposito concludes, "that such a shah would be overthrown was unthinkable . . . that the Pahlavi dynasty would come crashing down at the hands of a revolution led by a bearded, exiled ayatollah and conducted in the name of Islam was incomprehensible."[29]

Many factors contributed to American antipathy toward the Iranian revolutionaries, such as sympathy for the shah among American leaders, opposition to Ayatollah Khomeini and his religious politics, the geopolitics of the Cold War and the fear of losing ground to the Soviets in the Middle East, concerns about securing American access to Iranian oil, the outrage surrounding the hostage crisis, and concern about the fate of Israel in a rapidly changing Middle Eastern political landscape. Each of these factors has been discussed in a vast literature on the revolution, which spawned a cottage industry for Middle East specialists on Islam and the Islamic resurgence.[30] However, despite abundant commentary on the politics of religion within revolutionary Iran, including much discussion of the revolutionaries' aspirations to spread the revolution abroad, scant attention has been paid to how the politics of religion within the United States has influenced relations between the United States and Iran. Accounts of U.S.-Iranian relations that exclude such considerations from the start in favor of material capabilities and strategic interactions cannot account for the complex cultural and political topography of U.S.-Iranian relations.

The two trajectories of secularism described in this book, laicism and Judeo-Christian secularism, form the conceptual apparatus through which Americans framed the revolution and the cultural and religious backdrop through which the United States established and legitimized opposition to the Islamic Republic. Understanding the pull of these secularist traditions on American ways of living through and responding to the revolution reveals that the revolution was threatening to Americans not only because it attacked American interests in the Middle East but also because it threatened American national identity as secular and democratic. In rejecting the attempt to impose authoritarian secularism in Iran, the revolution demonstrated the contingent nature of the link between secularization and democratization. In challenging the connection between these two powerful components of modern politics, the revolution revealed the contestability of the American secularist settlement. It therefore posed a threat to American identity insofar as the latter is anchored in a series of connections between particular forms of secularism and prevailing notions of what it means to be American.

In her excellent analysis of American representations of terrorism and their relationship to U.S. "expansionist nationalism," McAlister writes that "the discourse of terrorist threat formed in the context of the Iran hostage crisis depended on the underlying structure of a captivity narrative—those stories of whites taken by Indians that had dominated the literature of early America."[31]

McAlister observes that when the captivity narrative was used to explain Iranian actions during the crisis, it did so through Islam rather than the history of U.S.-Iranian relations:

> "Militant Islam" quickly became the primary narrative device for the U.S. news media; long essays and editorials in many major publications explained "Islam" as a single, unchanging cultural proclivity to mix faith with politics, and to express both through violence. The vast variety of Muslim beliefs and practices, spread across four continents, were summarized in simplistic, often overtly hostile summaries of the "essence" of Islam, which was allegedly on display in Tehran.[32]

Although she offers compelling examples of how this narrative was put to use by the American media, McAlister does not discuss the broader context in which specific American approaches to religion and politics contributed to these representations of Islam. I explain this context and describe its impact on international relations. My argument is that it was due to the influence of laicism and Judeo-Christian secularism that Islam—and not the history of U.S.-Iranian relations—became the dominant explanatory trope for the events surrounding the Iranian revolution, including but not limited to the hostage crisis. These two trajectories of secularism help to explain *why* "many commentators . . . saw America as both egregiously wronged by Iran and innocent of anything but excessive benevolence towards Iranians."[33] The politics of secularism explains the shock and bewilderment of the Americans at the time of the revolution and contributes to understanding the intensity and persistence of American hostility toward Iran.

Laicism and the Revolution: Religion in the Public Sphere

As established in chapter 2, laicism presents itself as the starting point in relation to which the "religious" is defined.[34] It carves out the domain of the secular or the laic and declares it the realm of public authority, common sense, rational argument, democracy, and the public good.[35] The religious is denominated as that which the secular is *not*. For laicists, the Iranian revolution compromised the most basic tenet of their authoritative belief system by importing religion directly into the public sphere. Religion was intended (at least by the conservative clerics who eventually assumed power) to serve as the exclusive foundation of political order in the Islamic Republic. This was the mirror image of laicist ideology, which demands that religion be expelled entirely from public space. As a result, "Islam" and the "Islamic republic" became synonymous with the violation of laicist conceptions of neutral public space, common sense, and the public good. From this perspective, it was incomprehensible why the revolutionaries would want to stand in the way of progress and modernization, as represented by the shah's regime. Laicism therefore contributed to the sense, described by many Western analysts, that the revolution in Iran was unthinkable and impossible. Laicism functioned as what Linda Zerilli describes as a mythology:

> A mythology cannot be defeated in the sense that one wins over one's opponent through the rigor of logic or the force of evidence; a mythology cannot be defeated through arguments that would *reveal* it as groundless belief. . . . A mythology *is* utterly groundless, hence stable. What characterizes a mythology is not so much its crude or naïve character—mythologies can be extremely complex and sophisticated—but, rather, its capacity to elude our practices of verification and refutation.[36]

Americans were baffled and bewildered by the revolution, which was aptly described by Esposito as "beyond the imagination of experts and rulers alike."[37] This bewilderment makes sense from within a laicist mind-set. It was unthinkable that any rational individual could oppose the shah's, and by extension the Americans', benevolent attempt to modernize Iran. This attempt was part of the project of modernity, which as Asad argues, "consists not simply of looking and recording but of recording and remaking, and as such its discourses have sought to inscribe on the world a unity in its own image."[38] Recording and then remaking Iran in the image of the United States seemed natural to Americans, as Cottam argues:

> Seeing the American role in Iran as "modernizing" and "nation-building," Americans projected a benevolent paternalism in their self-image. However, because of a historical rejection of imperialism, they could not admit this even to themselves. Thus when anger and hatred toward the United States on the part of the Iranian mass public became undeniable during the hostage crisis, the American response was one of bewilderment and indignation.[39]

The revolution was seen as an irrational backlash against a generous fatherly attempt to spread modern ways of life and to defend the Iranians from communism. It was not that it never occurred to Americans that legitimate reasons might exist for rejecting the shah, the West, and secular modernity. Rather, this rejection was unimaginable from within a laicist worldview. It was unthinkable that secular modernization could be associated with SAVAK, with the repression of dissent, with inequality or injustice.

An episode recounted by McAlister involving one of the American hostages released in late November of 1979 illustrates this mind-set.[40] In a press conference after his release, Sergeant William Quarles told reporters that he had made some friends among his captors and "indicated that he had been receptive to some of the political frameworks the Iranians had presented."[41] Quarles stated, "I've learned a lot from what I've read and what I've seen, and I'm very saddened by some of the things that went on under the Shah's regime."[42] The American media quickly dismissed these statements and attributed Quarles's sympathy for his Iranian captors to a psychological syndrome common among former hostages.

Laicism is neither a coincidence nor a conspiracy. In this sense, I disagree with Said's portrayal in *Covering Islam* of the American media as caught up in a conspiracy against Islam. Said ascribes too much intentionality to individual journalists and neglects the influence of the broader discursive formations in which they inevitably participate. This is not a question of individual agency or choice on the part of any single journalist, academic, or pollster. As Saba Mahmood observes in her insightful analysis of the practices of mosque participants in Egypt, "these activities are the products of authoritative discursive traditions whose logic and power far exceeds the consciousness of the subjects they enable."[43] This explains why for many Americans, "despite the fact that some news accounts explained something of the history of U.S.-Iranian relations under the Shah, a determined incomprehension remained the dominant stance."[44] The American laicist perspective on Iran was a consequence of an often unacknowledged intellectual and visceral commitment to a particular formation of secular modernity, even in the face of a direct and violent challenge to this particular (Iran under the shah) version of it.

Judeo-Christian Secularism and the Revolution: The "Mobilization of Religion-as-Nation"

Judeo-Christian secularism also prestructured American interpretations of the Iranian revolution, contributing to a sense among American analysts and the public that the revolution was proof of the incompatibility of Islam and modernity. As explained previously, Judeo-Christian secularism invokes and relies upon the assumption that Christian, and later Judeo-Christian, religious tradition culminated in and contributed to the unique Western achievement of the separation of church and state. Secularization, in this context, is the realization of Judeo-Christian religious tradition. This powerful tradition is embedded within and expressed through certain instantiations of American national identity. As Marx argues with regard to early modern Europe, but which also fits the American case, "these identities still rested on religion as a crutch for long periods, before they were sufficiently consolidated to become more or less secular, or at least with religious foundations forgotten. And despite later denials, the reliance on religious identities to bolster secular solidarity was exclusionary."[45] Van der Veer argues along similar lines that "what happened to race and language in the age of nationalism also happened to religion. It becomes a defining feature of the nation and for that purpose it is transformed in a certain direction. Religion is nationalized, so to speak."[46] Following this thought, I have clarified how (Judeo)-Christian tradition becomes nationalized, secularized, and thereby transformed into Judeo-Christian secularism. In some variations, its religious foundations are forgotten or denied. In others, they are alive and active.

Opinion polls confirm a persistent public connection between (Judeo)-Christian tradition and American national identity. A 2002 survey conducted by the Pew Forum on Religion and Public Life and the Pew Research Center for the People and the Press found that two-thirds of American respondents consider the United States a "Christian nation" and 58 percent said that the strength of American society is based on the religious faith of its people.[47] A 2005 Associated Press—Ipsos poll found that nearly all U.S. respondents said faith was important to them and only 2 percent said they did not believe in God. In the same poll, almost 40 percent of Americans said religious leaders should try to sway policy makers, a percentage that was "notably higher than in other countries." As one respondent remarked in an interview after the polling, "our nation was founded on Judeo-Christian policies and religious leaders have an obligation to speak out on public policy."[48] This statement confirms Diana Eck's observation that "the language of a 'Christian America' has been voluminously invoked in the public square . . . display[ing] a confident, unselfconscious assumption that *religion* basically means Christianity, with traditional space made for the Jews."[49]

Judeo-Christian secularism posits a connection between secularization and attachment to political and religious traditions inherited from Christianity and Judaism. In strong versions of this view, distinctions between religious and political authority are not only historically absent from Muslim-majority societies such as Iran but are also unrealizable due to the nature of Islam. In short, Islam is incompatible with democracy.[50] These views prestructured American interpretations of the Iranian revolution.[51] Working out of this set of predispositions, the Iranian revolution was seen by many as confirmation of the "natural" linkages between Islam and theocracy, which stand in sharp contrast to the "natural" linkages between Christianity and democracy. Like van der Veer's observation about the nationalization of religion, McAlister describes the American reception of the revolution as the "mobilization of religion-as-nation," noting that at the time of the revolution "Islam was contrasted explicitly with Christianity, and perhaps in no other political situation in the 1970s did the mainstream media and politicians so insistently present the United States as a 'Christian' nation."[52] She concludes that although before the revolution it had been "relatively uncommon for the mainstream media to evoke Christianity as a public symbol of [American] nationalism . . . as 'Islam' emerged as the category for understanding Iran, Christianity became remarkably prominent in the media accounts."[53]

way to define oneself in opposition to the other

CONDEMNING THE REVOLUTION: SECULAR AMERICA AND THEOCRATIC IRAN

The most powerful American condemnation of the Iranian revolution on cultural and religious grounds occurred when these two interpretive frames and collective dispositions reached the same conclusion about developments in Iran, though for different reasons. In both laicist and Judeo-Christian secularist logic, in the former due to its inexplicable and irrational revolt against modernization and in the latter due to the resurgence of Islam and its theocratic proclivities, the Iranian revolution represented a setback for civilization. In both cases, as Cottam argues, "the Khomeini phenomenon was explained as a consequence of the shah's having moved too quickly for the ignorant, barely aware Iranian to be able to follow his lead."[54] This account became the standard-bearer among U.S. representations of the revolution. As Said notes, "the *Wall Street Journal* editorialized on Nov. 20, 1979 that 'civilization receding' came from 'the decline of the Western powers that spread these [civilized] ideals to begin with.'"[55] For laicists, because the revolution imported (any) *religion* directly into a modernizing public sphere in which the former was unwelcome, it was a defeat for the progress of *universal* values and civilization. For Judeo-Christian secularists, because the revolution imported *Islam* into a modernizing public sphere in which the former was unwelcome, it represented a defeat for the progress of *Western* values and civilization. Working in tandem, and combining at different moments with the considerable influence of the material and strategic interests mentioned earlier, these two narratives go some distance toward explaining the extraordinary vehemence of American opposition to the revolution. This confirms Van der Veer's argument that, "contrary to theory, religion is a major source of rational, moral subjects and a major organizational aspect of the public spheres they create."[56] How religion manifests in contemporary international relations is complex and, paradoxically at first, involves secularist authority. More than any other single factor, the authoritative forms of secularism described in this book account for the visceral nature of American antipathy vis-à-vis Iran and the Iranian revolution.

In addition to activating latent American cultural and religious dispositions about religion and politics, the Iranian revolution represented a direct affront to the powerful set of connections between American national identity, secularism, and democracy. In rejecting the attempt to impose authoritarian secularism in Iran, the revolution called into question any sort of necessary linkage between secular modernization and democratization. Indeed, one of the central messages of the revolutionaries was that in prerevolutionary Iran these two principles had been working at odds—secular modernization had led to repression and not democratization. The shah was secular yet undemocratic. Secular modernization had, in fact, served as a legitimizing principle for the suppression of local politics and practice.[57] In challenging Western assumptions about secularization and its allegedly irrefutable connection to democratization, the revolution illustrates empirically that the secularist division between religion and politics is not fixed but rather socially and historically constructed. It can be constructed very differently in different historical circumstances, with varying implications for democratization. The revolution demonstrated in concrete terms that secularism means different things in different cultural, historical, and political circumstances. By illustrating the contingent and constructed nature of the secularist settlement in Iran, the revolution made explicit the essentially contested nature of the secularist settlement in the United States. By illustrating the contingent relationship between secularization and democratization in Iran, the revolution called attention to the contested and controversial relation between religion, democracy, and national identity in the United States. The revolution therefore destabilized American national identity insofar as the latter is anchored in a series of assumptions about the pregiven and nonnegotiable compatibility between secularization and democratization.

One tangible result of this perceived affront to the American secularist settlement and way of life was that in the United States from 1979 onward to stand for a (laicist and Judeo-Christian) secular and democratic United States was to oppose an (Islamic) theocratic and authoritarian Iran.[58] As Casanova writes, "the secular, as a concept, only makes sense in relation to its counterpart, the religious."[59] Representing Islam and the Iranians as a threat to modern American civilization cemented the connections between American national identity, (laicist and Judeo-Christian) secularism, and democracy in opposition to Iranian Islamic theocracy and tyranny. As Marx argues, the basis of national identity and national unity is often exclusive:

> Nationalism may not then emerge as an imagined community of inclusion, a sort of literary trope, or an institutionalized process toward inclusion propelled by economic development and modernization. Instead, nationalism is often exclusive, with such exclusion emerging in fits and starts but encouraged or enforced to serve the explicit requirements for solidifying core loyalty to the nation.[60]

In one of these exclusionary "fits and starts," a secularist version of what Michael Dillon describes as a *horror alieni*[61] surfaced on the American political landscape at the time of the Iranian revolution, seeking to disassociate the United States from the injustices of the shah's secular yet undemocratic regime, to divest American identity of everything enigmatic and strange (Islam), and to shore up American nationalism as democratic, laicist, Judeo-Christian, and secular. This helps to explain the intensity of the American response to the revolution and the long life-span of American opposition to postrevolutionary Iran. This antagonism is a result not only of American economic and strategic interests in the Middle East, though these are critical, but also and perhaps even more fundamentally is part of an attempt to secure a particular conception of what it means to *be* secular, Judeo-Christian, democratic, and American.

CONCLUSION

In his landmark study of U.S.-Iranian relations, *The Eagle and the Lion: The Tragedy of American-Iranian Relations*, James Bill concludes that:

> Pervasive ignorance characterized American relations with Iran. The emphasis placed on interests such as personal gain, economic goals, Soviet imperialism, and Israeli needs, along with a preoccupation, both real and artificial, with the ideological challenge of communism inevitably brought about a sterility of understanding. The mutually reinforcing dialectics between interests and ideology effectively undercut the need for an in-depth understanding of the objective realities of Iranian society and politics.[62]

Bill notes that this "sterility of understanding" led to what became known as "the Pahlavi premise," a belief in the invincibility of the shah's regime and the mistaken yet powerful American conviction that his government "was stable and worthy of unquestioned support."[63] The forms of secularism described in this book are important contributors to the constellation of considerations identified by Bill as crucial determinants of U.S.-Iranian relations. Framing the question of U.S.-Iran relations in terms of autonomous states pursuing pregiven strategic and material interests cannot account for the sources and intensity of the hostility between these two countries.

These two varieties of secularism are part of the broader cultural, social, and normative context within which the United States and Iran relate to each other. Laicism and Judeo-Christian secularism formed the conceptual apparatus through which Americans interpreted the revolution and the cultural and religious backdrop through which the United States continues to legitimize opposition to the Islamic Republic. The revolution was threatening to the United States not only because it attacked American interests in the Middle East but also because it represented an affront to American national identity as secular and democratic. Domestic secularist authority, then, is a productive part of the cultural and normative foundations of contemporary Iranian-American relations. The tenacious hold of these particular secularist imaginaries in the United States helps to account for the "sterility of understanding" of Iran experienced by Americans and identified by James Bill.

This is not to suggest that American ignorance of Iranian society, history, and politics is solely a result of subscribing to a particular tradition of religion and politics. It is to suggest that authoritative secularist discourses have contributed in significant ways and in combination with other factors to the current state of affairs by determining how American decision makers, media, academics, and the public understand and respond to Iran, the revolution, and the role of Islam in Iranian public life. Secularist understandings, habits, and predispositions contribute to the environment and cultural milieu that shapes thinking and behavior.[64] They are part of the context and climate of public opinion described by public opinion scholars and discussed in the introductory chapter of this book. They contribute to a common sense of identity and a common way of life. As Saideman argues, "communal identity is relevant in foreign policy not just because of the existence or prominence of the identity but also because of its content. What does the identity imply for foreign policy or for domestic politics? What does it rule in or rule out?"[65] Laicism produces subjects for whom "Islam" and the "Islamic republic" are synonymous with the violation of laicist conceptions of neutral public space, common sense, and the public good, contributing to the sense that the revolution was unthinkable, irrational, and impossible. Judeo-Christian secularism produces subjects for whom the revolution was seen as proof of the existence of natural linkages between Islam and theocracy, in contrast to the natural linkages between Christianity and democracy. In both cases, the revolution was a setback for progress and modern civilization. These forms of secularism contributed to and help to explain what Bill identifies as "a distorted image of Iran" among "important individuals and groups in America."[66] They fuel American hostility toward Iran, an unwillingness to engage Iran diplomatically, and the assumption that the history of Iranian society and politics is less significant than the history of Islam for understanding contemporary Iran.

These forms of secularism remain active in contemporary American and European politics. Yet their influence upon international relations is not limited to EU-Turkey and U.S.-Iran relations. They also contribute to the epistemological underpinnings of the discipline of international relations by providing the terms through which crucial distinctions are made between public and private, secular and sacred, and religious and political. This epistemological context and its limitations are the subject of the final two chapters of the book, which focus on the implications of my argument for the study of political Islam and religious resurgence.

CHAPTER SEVEN

Political Islam

Il s'agit bien d'aborder la question de fond: l'islam est-il compatible avec la laïcité? Mais alors, de quelle laïcité parlons-nous?[1]

The attempt to understand Muslim traditions by insisting that in
them religion and politics (two essences modern society tries to
keep conceptually and practically apart) are coupled must, in my
view, lead to failure.[2]

IN RULE OF EXPERTS, Timothy Mitchell writes that "the possibility of social
science is based upon taking certain historical experiences of the West as
the template for a universal knowledge."[3] This observation applies to the
knowledge about "political Islam" generated by secularist epistemology in
the field of international relations. The conceptions of secularism underlying
social inquiry in this discipline determine the kinds of questions that can be
asked and are worth asking about secularism, religion, and politicized religion.[4] As Hirschkind argues, "greater recognition must be given to the way
Western concepts (religion, political, secular, temporal) reflect specific historical developments, and cannot be applied as a set of universal categories or
natural domains."[5]

Most attempts to theorize religion in international relations add a concern
for religious beliefs, actors, and institutions into the literature on sovereignty,
security, global governance, conflict resolution, human rights, intercivilizational dialogue, and the role of transnational actors.[6] This approach fails to
address a fundamental question that lies at the center of this book, which is
the extent to which assumptions about what religion is and how it relates to
politics determine both the kinds of questions worth asking about religion and
the kinds of answers one expects to find. These assumptions are generally
secularist.[7] Secularist habits, dispositions, and interpretive traditions are part
of the cultural and normative foundation of the field of contemporary international relations. They are an implicit part of the ontology of this research
tradition.[8] As a result, traditional forms of international relations require and
assume a particular kind of religious subject that is produced through a series
of practices that are at the core of modern secularist authority.[9] Recognizing
the epistemological contingencies of secularist authority and coming to terms
with its political consequences in international relations are the objectives of

the next two chapters. The present chapter focuses on secularist representations of political Islam, and chapter 8 analyzes religious resurgence. Secularist epistemology provides the terms through which crucial distinctions are made between public and private, religious and political, and sacred and secular. These modes of apprehending political Islam and religious resurgence have significant political consequences in international relations.

This chapter also explores the effects of these secularist understandings upon contemporary European and American foreign policy toward Islamic political actors and movements. I suggest that laicism contributes to a tendency to seek to engage and transform political Islamists both politically and economically, while Judeo-Christian secularism contributes to a tendency to try to eliminate Islamist actors and movements by starving them both diplomatically and economically. This chapter explains these policy divergences and opens possibilities for new ways of thinking about and relating to political Islam.

POLITICAL ISLAM AND INTERNATIONAL RELATIONS

The term "political Islam" was coined in the 1970s to refer to what Denoeux describes as the "rise of movements and ideologies drawing on Islamic referents—terms, symbols and events taken from the Islamic tradition—in order to articulate a distinctly political agenda."[10] For Ayubi political Islam refers to "the doctrine and/or movement which contends that Islam possesses a theory of politics and the State."[11] Hefner describes a "resurgence of piety and public religious activity unprecedented in modern history" in the Muslim world during the 1970s and 1980s, but emphasizes the diversity of commitments within this movement and distinguishes between public expressions of Muslim piety and identity and political Islam.[12] Salvatore approaches political Islam as a "conceptual and symbolic construct, and never as an unproblematic description of a clear phenomenon."[13] As he argues, "the attribution to Islam of an inherently political dimension states the degree of the divergence of this religion from the assumed normality, and the degree of the divergence of the 'Islamic' polity from a normal concept and practice of politics."[14]

Hefner and Salvatore are onto something important when they identify the diversity of commitments within these movements and extent to which political Islam is often presumed to diverge from "normal" politics. Political Islam is interpreted by secular analysts as epiphenomenal, as a divergence and/or infringement upon neutral secular public space, as a throwback to premodern forms of Muslim political order, or as a combination of all of these features. Widely held interpretive and evaluative frameworks about Islam and politics form the cultural and religious backdrop out of which Europeans and Americans understand and engage with political Islam.

Two sets of secularist assumptions are operative in this cultural backdrop. In laicism, political Islam appears as a superficial expression of more fundamental economic and political interests and an infringement of irrational forms of religion upon would-be secular public life in Muslim-majority societies. It threatens democratic public order and marks a step toward theocracy. In Judeo-Christian secularism, political Islam appears as an undemocratic commingling of Islam and politics that stands in sharp distinction to the modern (Christian or Judeo-Christian) separation of church and state. Distinctions between religious and political authority are not only historically absent from Muslim-majority societies but are unthinkable due to fixed characteristics of the Islamic religion. In both interpretive traditions, each of which is discussed at length below, political Islam appears as a refusal to acknowledge the privileged status of the private sphere and a transgression of secularist categories of public and private.[15]

The problem with this approach to political Islam is, as Connolly argues, that it adopts as "neutral terms of analysis several concepts and themes that became authoritative only through the hegemony of [particular forms of] Western secularism."[16] Euro-American secularist epistemologies produce particular understandings of political Islam, at the same time that, to follow Euben's formulation, they "conceal their 'mechanisms of production' within claims of objectivity resulting in images which say less about what [political Islam] 'really is' than about the ways in which [secularist] assumptions derived from Western history and experiences ... produce our understandings of [it]."[17] In other words, secularist epistemology and secularist authority rely upon and produce a particular kind of religious subject and a particular understanding of normal politics that lends a particular coloring to political practices in Muslim-majority societies. The effect of this production of religious subjectivity is to equate the appearance of Islamic religion in political practice with fundamentalism and intolerance.

These "framing effects" have not gone unnoticed. Baker, for example, alludes to a Western tendency to frame political Islam in negative terms in his account of the New Islamist movement in Egypt.[18] As he suggests, "there are no sound scholarly reasons for the critical gap in the Western understanding of Islam ... language barriers and cultural differences have meant that these important aspects of mainstream Islam that flow from New Islamist interpretations have been largely ignored in the West."[19] Gerges has remarked that "the underlying cultural values of Americans play a major role in shaping most policy makers' perceptions of Islamists."[20] The first step in my argument is to suggest that European and American forms of secularism are important contributors to these "cultural differences" and "cultural values" identified but not explained by Baker and Gerges. Although the causalities are complex, secularist epistemology contributes in crucial ways to the constitution of these otherwise inexplicable cultural barriers.

The second step is to argue that secularist evaluations of political Islam have significant policy consequences in international relations. First, in secular analyses forms of politics identified as Islamist appear almost exclusively in their transgressive and/or regressive capacity and tend to be equated and conflated with fundamentalism. As van der Veer and Lehmann note, "when religion manifests itself politically . . . it is conceptualized as fundamentalism. . . . It is almost always interpreted as a negative social force directed against science, rationality, secularism—in short, against modernity."[21] Gertrude Himmelfarb, for example, associates Islamic fundamentalism with "disagreeable images of female subjugation and abuse, religious intolerance and persecution, despotic governments and caste systems, child labor and illiteracy, and other unsavory practices that are hardly consonant with the vision of a universal 'moral community.' "[22] Secularists like Himmelfarb are quick to associate political Islam with the transgression of universal norms in part because "from the point of view of secularism, religion has the option either of confining itself to private belief and worship or of engaging in public talk that makes no demands on life."[23] Because the forms of politics identified by secularists as political Islam do not conform to either of these requirements, secularist epistemology equates them with dogmatism and fanaticism.[24] Political Islam is defined a priori as a threat to the privileged status of the private sphere and as a step toward theocracy. This presumptive transgression is often linked rhetorically to the alleged Muslim proclivity for terrorism and totalitarianism, both of which also refuse to honor the privileged status of the private sphere.[25]

A second policy consequence of Euro-American secularist epistemology is that the forms and degrees of separation between public and private, sacred and secular, Islam and politics that *do* exist in contemporary Muslim-majority societies either do not appear at all or appear as ill-fitting imitations of a Western secular ideal. On the one hand, attempts to negotiate secular modalities of differentiation between religion and politics are depicted as "derivative discourses" of a more successful and authentic Western secular ideal. Political Islam, on the other hand, is depicted in oppositional terms vis-à-vis these derivative secularist discourses and represented as a unitary and unified threat to otherwise viable local variations of Western secularism. As a result, legitimate negotiations over the terms in which religion enters into public life in Muslim-majority contexts that take place under the heading of political Islam are occluded.

Political Islam is neither merely a backlash against modernization, nor an epiphenomenal expression of more fundamental material interests, nor an attempt to revivify anachronistic local tradition, though each of these factors may be operative to some extent. Political Islam is a modern language of politics that challenges, sometimes works outside of, and (occasionally) overturns fundamental assumptions about religion and politics that are embedded in the forms of Western secularism that emerged out of Latin Christendom.

These forms of secularism are themselves social and historical constructs. The secularist settlement, as Connolly argues, is a "division of labor that fell out of that historic compromise within predominantly Christian states" that "provided fragile protection against sectarian conflict and intolerance for a few centuries." However, he continues, it also "spawned practices of public life too dogmatic and terse to sustain the creative tension needed between democratic governance and critical responsiveness to the politics of becoming. And the destructive orientations it supported to non-Christian countries left a lot to be desired too."[26] The impact of these destructive orientations is felt today in Western representations of political Islam.

This is not to deny that there are forms of Islamism, such as those espoused by Khomeini and his followers in postrevolutionary Iran, the Armed Islamic Group (French acronym GIA) in Algeria, the National Islamic Front (NIF) in Sudan, the Taliban in Afghanistan, and Al-Qaeda globally, that *are* transgressive or regressive by almost any standard of judgment. (The extent to which Al-Qaeda can be legitimately associated with any version of Islamic tradition is questionable, however, because the group adamantly rejects the authority of all established Islamic authorities. According to Carapico, members of "Al-Qaeda . . . do not respect or abide by Islamic law as understood by those who know what it is about. They are reactionary nihilist-anarchists with no positive vision or program: even the goal of an 'Islamic state' per se is more imputed than articulated.")[27] These parties and movements, however categorized, threaten the status of almost any conceptualization of a private sphere and any attempt to democratically negotiate the relationship between religion and politics, and deserve international condemnation. With regard to such cases, I agree with Algerian historian Mohammed Arkoun in his observation, summarized by Lee, that "the tyranny of faith in militant Islam is no more acceptable than the tyranny of reason."[28] Yet these extreme forms of Islamist politics are the exception rather than the rule.[29] As Carapico concludes, "there is no evidence of a mass following or widespread public support in North Africa, the Levant or the Arabian Peninsula for a group calling itself al-Qaeda, much less al-Qaeda in Europe. . . . Al-Qaeda is not representative of Islamism and its pronouncements are not consonant with those of any major Islamist party."[30]

My argument is that not *all* forms of what secularist authority designates as political Islam pose this kind of threat. There is more going on than is suggested by authoritative secularist categorizations. As LeVine and Salvatore argue, "the vocabulary of social science (in turn influenced by the grammar of theories of civil society) cannot completely capture the rich and complex idiom of these movements."[31] Political Islam raises important critical questions about the foundational principles of collective life, including secularist collective life. The shift of many Islamist movements in recent years away from radical politics and toward a more cultural orientation does not attest to the "failure of Islamism," as Roy has suggested.[32] As Göle has shown, the result of this shift is that "instead of disappearing as a reference, Islam penetrates even more into the social fiber and imaginary, thereby raising new political questions, questions not addressed solely to Muslims but concerning the foundational principles of collective life in general."[33]

In sum, most varieties of political Islam operate outside the epistemological and explanatory confines of secularist tradition and secularist international relations theory. By failing to conform to the categories available to international relations theorists for understanding religion and politics, these forms of politics pose a challenge to the epistemological and cultural assumptions of the academics and policy makers who are immersed in these secularist traditions. Like religious resurgence, the subject of the next chapter, the rise of different trajectories of political Islam provides an opportunity to revisit these assumptions and to rethink policy recommendations that follow from them.[34]

LAICISM AND POLITICAL ISLAM

Political scientists are socialized in the tenets of classical liberalism with its emphasis on the benefits of a strict laicist separation of religion and politics.[35] As a form of political authority, laicism is most powerful when it appears as the natural order that emerges "when there is no ideology present,"[36] rather than as "a specific fashioning of spiritual life . . . carved out of Christendom."[37] To recap the argument of chapter 2, laicism denominates itself as public, neutral, and value-free and denominates religion as its private, affective, and value-laden counterpart. The public sphere is the domain of reason, objectivity, deliberation, and justice; and the private the domain of subjectivity, transcendence, effeminacy, and affect. Laicism warns against religion in the public sphere and construes it as unnatural, undemocratic, and even theocratic. Religion is assigned a fixed place out of this sphere; it is excluded from the spheres of power and authority in modern societies as well as from political analyses of these spheres. The relationship between religion and politics is thus subject to a set of rules considered to be universally applicable regardless of cultural, historical, or political circumstance.

Two laicist representations of political Islam correspond to the two variations of laicism discussed in chapter 2. They also correspond roughly to what Daniel, in his discussion of Christian-Islamic relations in the nineteenth century, describes as "the two extremes of administrative pragmatism and missionary fanaticism."[38] In the former, political Islam is represented as an epiphenomenal expression of more fundamental structural, material, or psychological interests. As Gerges observes, the Islamic resurgence is seen as "a product of socioeconomic and political woes; it is locally rooted."[39] Roger Owen, Graham Fuller, Fred Halliday, Bassam Tibi, and, in some of his writings, John Esposito adopt variations of this approach. Owen describes political Islam as a response to "the perceived failures of the secular developmentalist ideologies and strategies which had been used to legitimate most newly independent regimes."[40] Fuller argues that "most regimes see almost any form of political Islam as a threat, since it embodies a major challenge to their unpopular, failing and illegitimate presidents-for-life or isolated monarchs."[41] Halliday attributes the rise of political Islam to "a general rejection of the secular modernity associated with radical nationalist politics and with the modernizing state";[42] and Tibi argues that "the foremost issue related to the pertinence of politicized religion for IR [international relations] is exactly the 'revolt against the West' directed against the existing secular order."[43] Esposito stresses that "the failures of increasingly discredited secular forms of nationalism . . . strengthened new voices who appealed to an Islamic alternative."[44] Political Islam is portrayed as a backlash against modernity in general and unjust domestic economic and political conditions in particular.

In a second variation of laicism, political Islam is represented as a threat to the scientific management of the modern public sphere. In Hirschkind's account of this position, "the term 'political Islam' has been adopted by many scholars in order to identify this seeming unprecedented irruption of Islamic religion into the secular domain of politics and thus to distinguish these practices from the forms of personal piety, belief, and ritual conventionally subsumed in Western scholarship under the unmarked category 'Islam.' "[45] In this view, political Islam is represented as "opposed to the principles of modern living and inconsistent with the game of modern politics, science and development, and therefore deservedly facing extinction."[46] It is a menacing departure from the norm of the separation of religion and politics and harbors the potential to be irrational, dangerous, and extremist. Political Islam is a refusal of the privileged status of the modern private sphere and a transgression against secular democratic categories of public and private.

Laicism is what Mahmood describes as an "evaluative stance"[47] in which political Islam emerges as either a reaction against unfavorable political and economic conditions and/or a dangerous infringement upon modern secular discourse and institutions. In both cases, "the neologism 'Islamism' . . . frames its object as an eruption of religion outside the supposedly 'normal' domain of private worship, and thus as a historical anomaly requiring explanation if not rectification."[48] Some approaches focus on explaining political Islam, whereas others are more concerned with rectifying it. These evaluative stances are politically significant because they are politically effective. Their importance, as Mahmood observes, "is not simply a question of ideological bias, but rather the way these critiques function within a vast number of institutional sites and practices aimed at transforming economic, political, and moral life in the Middle East—from international financial institutions to human rights associations to national and local administrative bureaucracies."[49] Framing political Islam as either epiphenomenal or as a reactive infringement upon secular public space contributes to the insistence on the part of the international community that Muslim-majority states follow a laicist trajectory of development and modernization, with its emphasis on a particular form of separation between Islam and politics.

This set of assumptions is particularly influential in contemporary European political relations with the Muslim-majority countries of North Africa and the Middle East. Gilles Kepel, for example, argues that the "separation of the secular and religious domains is the prerequisite for liberating the forces of reform in the Muslim world."[50] According to Kepel, Islam must be reconciled with modernity, meaning that the shortcomings of Islam in politics are to be remedied through the importation of Western-style democracy, the secularization of civil society, and the separation of mosque and state. Political Islam is constitutionally ill equipped to contribute to public life in Muslim-majority societies.

Laicist assumptions about political Islam are also influential among U.S. foreign policy makers engaged with Muslim-majority societies. As Gerges argues,

> Actual American policies toward Islamic movements and states reveal a deep residue of ambivalence, skepticism, and mistrust . . . the United States has not only supported its traditional friends—in their fight against Islamists—but has done little to persuade them to open up the political field to existing, legitimate opposition forces.[51]

Development and foreign assistance programs prioritize the privatization of religion in the name of modernization, development and democratization. This mentality peaked during the heyday of modernization theory in the 1950s and 1960s[52] and also stood behind the state imposition of secularism (much lauded in Western accounts) that accompanied the founding of the modern Turkish republic.[53]

At least three policy consequences follow from the commitments and assumptions identified here as laicism. First, the laicist framing of political Islam makes it difficult for oppositional politics cast in religious language to flourish in the public spheres of Muslim-majority societies. As Gerges observes, "a strain of skepticism exists within U.S. foreign policy-making circles regarding the compatibility between political Islam and democracy. U.S. discourse, replete with implicit references to Islamists' political behavior, views revolutionary Islam as antidemocratic and autocratic."[54] Nasr agrees: "as secularism is commonly viewed as a prerequisite for viable democracy, the rise in the fortunes of Islamic revivalism is viewed with alarm."[55] Yet, as Asad and others point out, given the structures of authority in these societies religious activists of any kind, extremist or not, have little choice but to engage state institutions and discourse: "Islamism's preoccupation with state power is the result not of its commitment to nationalist ideas but of the modern nation-state's enforced claim to constitute legitimate social identities."[56] Following Asad, Mahmood contends that "it is not that the pietists have 'politicized' the spiritual domain of Islam (as some scholars of Islamism claim) but that conditions of secular liberal modernity are such that for any world-making project (spiritual or otherwise) to succeed and be effective, it must engage with the all-encompassing institutions and structures of modern governance, whether it aspires to state power or not."[57] Hirschkind makes a similar point when he suggests that "to the extent that the institutions enabling the cultivation of religious virtue become subsumed within (and transformed by) legal and administrative structures linked to the state, the (traditional) project of preserving those virtues will necessarily be 'political' if it is to succeed."[58] Nonhegemonic articulations of Islamic political tradition must engage state structures in order to be effective in the public spheres of Muslim-majority societies, an outcome that is unacceptable to laicists yet, paradoxically, necessary for political engagement to occur.

A second consequence of the laicist framing of political Islam is that negotiations between public and private, sacred and secular, pietists and secularists that *are* currently taking place in Muslim-majority societies appear as unnatural and ill-fitted attempts to realize a modern (laicist) ideal. Attempts to negotiate modalities of separation between religion and politics are perceived to be what Partha Chatterjee and L. Carl Brown (though from very different perspectives) have described as derivative discourses of a more successful and authentic Western secular ideal.[59] Secularism is thus "dichotomized between a noble Western invention and an ignoble non-Western imitation."[60] Political Islam is construed in oppositional terms vis-à-vis these derivative laicist discourses. It is represented as a unitary and unified threat to otherwise viable local variations of Western secularism. Tibi advances a version of this argument when he suggests that "political Islam and its concept of order are based on hostile attitudes vis-à-vis the globalization of Western models and the universalisation of their values; it revives worldviews not consonant with European concepts of world order."[61] As Augustus Richard Norton has shown convincingly, however, this is simply not the case: "the Shi'i resurgence in Lebanon has not been a simple reflection of Shi'ism's supposed rejection of secular authority. . . . History is replete with examples of accommodation, and most Lebanese Shi' a do not reject the legitimacy of all temporal states, though they find the Lebanese state, as it has functioned, illegitimate."[62]

A third consequence of the laicist framing of political Islam is that it precludes effective engagement between secularists and what Hefner has identified as moderate "civil Islamists," such as the Muhammadiyah and Nahdlatul Ulama in Indonesia and the New Islamist movement in Egypt.[63] Baker describes the latter as an influential moderate Islamist movement that emerged out of the Muslim Brotherhood roughly two decades ago:

> Under authoritarian conditions, they have constituted themselves as a flexible and resilient "intellectual school," neither attached to one particular movement nor an extension of official authority, yet nevertheless able to give coherence to their collective interpretive and practical work in a multitude of fields.[64]

Framing political Islam as either epiphenomenal or as an infringement upon neutral public space eclipses the democratic potential of forms of Islamism pursued by the Egyptian New Islamists, the Turkish Justice and Development Party (AKP), Khatami's reform movement in Iran, Jamaat-i-Islami in Pakistan, and other similar movements. As Asad suggests, these instances of what Casanova describes as "deprivitized religion," and others such as the 1992 elections in Algeria and the 1997 rise of the Welfare Party in Turkey, "are intolerable to secularists primarily because of the motives imputed to their opponents rather than to anything the latter have actually done. The motives signal the potential entry of religion into space already occupied by the secular."[65] In short, laicism in foreign policy contributes to the perception that a particular Western version of the separation of religion and politics offers the only path toward liberal democracy, a position described by Amartya Sen: "The liberty that is increasingly taken in quick generalizations about the past literature of non-Western countries to justify authoritarian Asian governments seems to have its analogue in the equally rapid Western belief that thoughts about justice and democracy have flourished only in the West, with the presumption that the rest of the world would find it hard to keep up with the West."[66]

The term political Islam is an ambitious one, striving to encompass a range of different forms of politics many of which exist beyond the reach of secularist epistemology. As LeVine and Salvatore argue, "there are concepts of the common good deployed by contemporary Muslim socio-religious movements that do not adhere to the dynamics or norms—and indeed, as we learn from Foucault, the techniques of power and subjectivity—of the main historical trajectories of European public spheres."[67] To recognize these forms of politics and come to terms with their effects requires acknowledging that the secularist traditions used to interpret them generate and rely upon particular and contestable ontological and epistemological assumptions. Secularist epistemology is not pregiven but is socially and historically constructed. Forms of politics associated with political Islam pose therefore not only a political challenge but also and more fundamentally an epistemological and ontological challenge to European and American categorizations of religion and politics, to Euro-American conceptualizations of the secular. As Asad concludes, "if the secularization thesis no longer carries the weight it once did, this is because the categories of politics and religion turn out to implicate each other more profoundly than we thought."[68]

JUDEO-CHRISTIAN SECULARISM AND POLITICAL ISLAM

In 1907 President Theodore Roosevelt confessed privately that "it is impossible to expect moral, intellectual and material well-being where Mohammedanism is supreme."[69] Echoing these sentiments several decades later, Jeane Kirkpatrick observed that "the Arab world is the only part of the world where I've been shaken in my conviction that if you let the people decide, they will make fundamentally rational decisions."[70] Robert W. Merry, president and publisher of *Congressional Quarterly* and a former reporter for the *Wall Street Journal*, argued in his 2005 book *Sands of Empire* that the inseparability of religion and politics is "etched in the cultural consciousness" of the world's Muslims.[71]

In this evaluative stance, political Islam is the manifestation of a unique, culturally rooted and irrational commingling of religion and politics that is distinct from the Judeo-Christian separationist approach to religion and state. In this view there is a connection between the Islamic religion and the failure to modernize and secularize Muslim-majority societies.[72] The potential for secularization is a consequence of the inherent cultural and religious characteristics of particular communities. Muslim-majority societies are perceived as culturally and religiously unequipped or only weakly equipped to secularize in comparison to their Judeo-Christian counterparts. As a result, the religious-secular line becomes a fixed marker of civilizational difference. Forms of politics identified as political Islam, and specifically the unwelcome incursion of religion into public space, are seen as a natural, though regrettable, consequence of fixed differences between religions and civilizations. In short, "all forms of Islamism (from its more militant to its more quiescent) are seen as the products of a roving irrationality."[73]

Judeo-Christian secularism is one background source of the assumption that distinctions between religious and political authority are absent from the history of Muslim-majority societies and should not be expected to materialize in the future. As Lewis argues in an example of this thesis, "the identity of religion and government is indelibly stamped on the memories and awareness of the faithful from their own sacred writings, history and experience."[74] Harris has suggested that "a future in which Islam and the West do not stand on the brink of mutual annihilation is a future in which most Muslims have learned to ignore most of their canon, just as most Christians have learned to do. Such a transformation is by no means guaranteed to occur, however, given the tenets of Islam."[75] Islamic civilizations, according to this view, lack any indigenous form of secularism and reject the secularism imported from the West.[76] As Barber suggests, "Islam posits a world in which the Muslim religion and the Islamic state are cocreated and inseparable, and some observers argue it has less room for secularism than any other major world religion."[77] Lewis describes this scenario as a "clash of civilizations—the perhaps irrational but surely historic reaction of an ancient rival against our Judeo-Christian heritage, our secular present, and the worldwide expansion of both."[78] In *Islam and the West*, he argues that political and religious authorities have become increasingly separate in the West since the rise of secularism, and increasingly united in the Middle East since the rise of Islam in the seventh century:

Islam was . . . associated with the exercise of power from the very beginning. . . . This association between religion and power, between community and polity, can . . . be seen in . . . the religious texts in which Muslims base their beliefs. One consequence is that in Islam religion is not, as it is in Christendom, one sector or segment of life regulating some matters and excluding others; it is concerned with the whole of life, not a limited but a total jurisdiction.[79]

A. C. Grayling of the *Financial Times* echoed several of these themes in a 2003 book review:

It is hard not to feel that one of many things the Palestinian philosopher Edward Said criticizes western observers for—namely, seeing Islamic civilization as frozen and backward-looking, falling behind the scientific, technologised, industrialised west because it is locked in an unprogressive medievalism—may be right after all. Explanations for this are uncomfortable to offer, but both Wheatcroft and Fletcher imply a plausible one. *It is that the disjunction between religious and secular aspects of life in the west, and its openness to debate, self-questioning and change, is precisely what traditional Islam lacks.* As a result, it is in the west . . . that technological and industrial progress has occurred. And with this progress have come more flexible forms of social organization, leading (however fitfully) to the evolution of democracy and human rights.[80]

Judeo-Christian secularism is set of beliefs, practices, and dispositions that predisposes those influenced by it to see the Islamic "refusal" to honor the special status of the secular private sphere as confirmation of the hopelessness of Islamic civilization. Barber illustrates this in his suggestion that "Islam . . . is relatively inhospitable to democracy and that inhospitality in turn nurtures conditions favorable to parochialism, antimodernism, exclusiveness, and hostility to 'others'—the characteristics that constitute what I have called Jihad."[81] In such accounts, Islam and modernity are incommensurable worldviews that lead to the creation of incompatible social and political systems. Policy options are limited to either tense coexistence, violent confrontation, or, in some cases, conversion.[82] Political Islam is defined a priori as a threat to democracy, the privileged status of the private sphere, and a step toward theocracy. This presumptive transgression is often linked rhetorically to the alleged Muslim proclivity for terrorism and totalitarianism, both of which also refuse to honor the privileged status of the private sphere.[83] As with laicism, one result of this evaluative stance is that the varying forms and degrees of separation and accommodation between public and private, sacred and secular, religion and politics that *do* exist in contemporary Muslim-majority societies either do not appear at all or appear as unnatural and ill-fitted imitations of a superior yet ultimately unrealizable Western secular ideal.

The difference between laicism and Judeo-Christian secularism is that in the latter Islam is seen as incompatible with *any* modality of separation between politics and religion, whereas in the former it is not. For laicists, Muslim-majority societies can be "modernized" if, like Turkey, they follow in the footsteps of their secular European and American role models and enforce the exclusion of religion from politics. This line of reasoning has influenced the foreign policies of many European countries insofar as they seek to engage in diplomatic dialogue with political Islamists to lure them toward a European model of secularism and punish them economically and politically should they stray from this trajectory. An example is French and Russian advocacy of direct dialogue with Hamas after the Palestinian elections of January 2006. For Judeo-Christian secularists, on the other hand, the prospects for transformation are less optimistic, and foreign policy must operate on the assumption that it is necessary to stamp out Islamist political movements because conversion to modern secular politics is simply impossible. This line of reasoning is reflected in the American position toward Hamas, which refused engagement on the grounds that, according to President Bush, Hamas has "one foot in politics and another in terror."[84] As Hoagland observed in the *Washington Post*, "under the Bush doctrine, political Islam is to be fought country by country, through counterterrorism programs, diplomatic isolation and economic sanctions."[85] This approach to political Islam is reflected and reinforced in Merry's argument, cited earlier, that the inseparability of religion and politics is "etched in the cultural consciousness" of the world's Muslims and can be remedied only through opposition and force.

Political Islam Reconsidered

Contrary to the views that emerge from laicism and Judeo-Christian secularism, the relationship between public and private, sacred and secular, and Islam and democracy in Muslim-majority societies is complex and contested.[86] As Ayoob argues, "the distinction between temporal and religious affairs and the temporal authority's de facto primacy over the religious establishment continued through the reign of the three great Sunni dynasties — the Umayyad, the Abbasid, and the Ottoman."[87] Halliday maintains that "a separation of religion and state, indeed a rejection of all worldly, political activity, is just as possible an interpretation of Islamic thinking as anything the Islamists now offer."[88] Lapidus suggests that a "fundamental differentiation" between state and religion has existed in Muslim societies since classical Umayyad and Abbasid periods.[89] He argues that the integration of state and religious community has characterized only a small segment of Middle Eastern and other Muslim lineage or tribal societies.[90] Esposito notes that the relation between Muslim religious and temporal authorities, including Shi'i Islam in Iran, has been ambiguous. As he argues, "despite the popular Western image of Shi'i Islam as a religion of revolution and martyrdom, its relationship to the state in Iran throughout Islamic history has been diverse and multifaceted. . . . the relationship of the *ulama* to the state in Iranian history varied from royal patronage to opposition, depending on the sociopolitical context."[91] There is disagreement over the proper relationship that should obtain between political and religious authorities in Muslim-majority societies, and a range of institutional arrangements have reflected this conflicted relationship historically. As Muhammad Asad argues, "the political ordinances of Qur'an and Sunnah . . . do not lay down any specific form of state: that is to say, the shari'ah does not prescribe any definite pattern to which an Islamic state must conform, nor does it elaborate in detail a constitutional theory."[92] The relationship between Islam and democracy and the extent to which Islamic law is equipped to serve as a blueprint for governance is also a subject of debate.[93] As Hefner concludes, "rather than an unchanging religious ideology established 1400 years ago, Muslim politics . . . has been shaped by broad changes in the state and society, especially those related to mass education, urbanization, socioeconomic differentiation, and the popular desire for public participation."[94]

As suggested by the public presence of the New Islamists in Egypt, the Moroccan PJD (Parti pour la Justice et le Developpement), the AKP in Turkey, the democratic coalition in Indonesia that toppled Soeharto in 1998 (which included "a wealth of activists and intellectuals" involved in an "effort to effect a foundational reorientation of Muslim politics"),[95] the public and democratic negotiation of the relationship between religion and politics in Muslim-majority societies often takes place under the aegis of what is labeled by secularists as political Islam. Like secularism, political Islam is "a discursive tradition that connects variously with the formation of moral selves, the manipulation of populations (or resistance to it), and the production of appropriate knowledge."[96] It is "not an old doctrine that is currently being resurrected, but rather a new doctrine that is in the process now of being invented."[97] Political Islam refers to a diverse, contested, and evolving set of languages of religion and politics involving "a general mobilization of people around cultural, political, and social issues that are presented and interpreted through an Islamic idiom."[98] As Eickelman and Piscatori argue, Muslim politics "relate to a widely shared, although not doctrinally defined, tradition of ideas and practice,"[99] involving "the competition and contest over both the interpretation of symbols and control of the institutions, formal and informal, that produce and sustain them."[100] As Ayubi argues, "apart from a moral code and few 'fixations' related to dress, penalties, and *halal/haram* foods, drinks and social practices, there is no well-defined comprehensive social-political-economic programme that can be described as 'Islamic.' "[101] Islamic ideologies are "shaped by and encapsulated within a *multitude* of ideal social, political, and cultural identities that can contradict as well as complement one another."[102]

This historical dynamism in the relationship between Islam and politics suggests that the spectrum of movements, identities, individuals, and activities designated by secularist tradition as Islamist are not the expression of deeper structural, psychological, and/or material interests or the pathological side effect of antiquated religious commitments that are fundamentally incompatible with "modernity." Political Islam is not a reflection of a commitment to irrational theopolitics or simply an oppositional discourse reflecting economic and political malaise. It is a diverse and multifaceted set of discursive traditions in which moral and political order is negotiated and continuously renegotiated in contemporary Muslim-majority societies. Like secularism, it is a powerful tradition of argumentation and a resource for collective legitimation. It is neither merely an oppositional discourse nor a nostalgic one, though elements of both may be present. As Mahmood concludes, "to read the activities of the mosque movement primarily in terms of the resistance it has posed to the logic of secular-liberal governance and its concomitant modes of sociability ignores an entire dimension of politics that remains poorly understood and undertheorized within the literature on politics and agency."[103]

Secularist epistemology misses these dimensions of politics because political Islam works outside of the epistemological assumptions of the authoritative public settlements that emerged principally from Latin Christendom, including the forms of secularism described in this book. Political Islam contests the terms through which secularist epistemology organizes religion and politics. It stands apart from the most fundamental epistemological and ontological assumptions of the secularist settlement as it evolved out of Latin Christendom, including the rationalist assumptions that serve as the foundation of modern European-inspired formations of collective life.[104]

Identifying the epistemological limits of secularism makes it possible to identify some forms of political Islam as part of a broader critique of European traditions of rationalism and secularism, as Euben has done. Sayyid Qutb, for instance, appears as a dissenter from the epistemological and ontological foundations of the traditions of secularism analyzed in this book. Qutb criticized post-Enlightenment political theories that exclude religious authority from politics.[105] He argued that the European imposition of a division between faith and reason, or what Berman describes as the "liberal idea that religion should stay in one corner and secular life in another,"[106] upon the Muslim peoples had resulted in their alienation and humiliation.[107] Qutb's theory, as Euben has argued, challenges secularism in a way that parallels internal Western reassessments of Enlightenment tradition.[108] His critique of sovereignty, for example, stands as a "a rebuttal to the epistemological assumption that truths about the world—political or moral—can be reached by way of human faculties, and that knowledge of such truths can legitimate human mastery over nature and human nature, and the exclusion of divine authority from the public sphere."[109]

Identifying the epistemological limits of laicism and Judeo-Christian secularism also helps to explain why political Islam is perceived as more threatening to Western ways of life than political Christianity. The latter also challenges the secular public-private distinction on a variety of levels, often to a remarkable degree. Yet the reception of political Christianity in Western democracies differs from the reception of political Islam, as suggested by the fact that the term "political Christianity" is rarely if ever used, despite the public role of Christian tradition in European and, particularly, American politics and foreign policy. This is because Euro-American secularist traditions evolved out of Christianity and remain indebted to Christian traditions in significant ways. Even in many laicist trajectories of secularization, public forms of Christianity are seen as a way station on the road to liberal democracy, if not a significant contributor to it. As Tocqueville famously observed, "for Americans the ideas of Christianity and liberty are so completely mingled that it is almost impossible to get them to conceive of one without the other."[110] It is often suggested that Christian values (and, since World War II, Judeo-Christian values) serve as the basis of American national identity and the source of American political ideals. Islam, on the other hand, has a different history of negotiating the public-private distinction than does either Christianity or the particular forms of secularism that it spawned. From a Christian-secularist perspective, Muslim negotiations of public and private therefore appear foreign, unnatural, or even nonexistent.

Conclusion

Martha Nussbaum writes that "one of the greatest barriers to rational deliberation in politics is the unexamined feeling that one's own preferences and ways are neutral and natural."[111] We may never achieve pure rational deliberation in politics. Yet, in suggesting that we examine our unexamined ways and preferences, Nussbaum makes an important point. The traditions of secularism described in this book have quietly come to dominate Western ways of organizing religion and politics. They are among our most significant unexamined ways and preferences. They are widely held to be neutral and natural starting points for public deliberations on the subject of religion and politics. They are neither neutral nor natural. They are political settlements and not uncontestable dictates of public discourse.[112] They are social and historical constructs. These settlements have significant implications for how Europeans and European settler colonies, including the United States, understand and relate to the rest of the world, and, in particular, the Islamic world.

In contemporary international relations theory and practice, Euro-American forms of secularism are viewed as the standard-bearers. Non-Western models of religion and politics are seen as attempts either to approximate the

Western ideal or to react, often violently, against it. As Grovogui argues, "the vast majority of contemporary international theorists . . . have failed to recognize the validity of non-Western languages of politics and their intended moral orders as legitimate contexts for imagining the alternatives to the present moral order."[113] Many of the forms of politics designated by secularists as political Islam are such non-Western languages of politics and moral order. These forms of politics operate outside and beyond the epistemological confines of secularism and secularist international relations theory. They throw into disarray the fundamental terms through which Euro-American forms of secularism organize religion and politics. In some cases, these forms of politics also seek to challenge Western hegemony in international relations by refusing to "accept the current distribution of power in the international system as either legitimate or permanent."[114] As a result of both these epistemological limitations and political challenges, those influenced by secularist tradition are often quick to attribute the Muslim "refusal" to acknowledge the special status of the (Western) secularist private sphere as a harbinger of despotism in Muslim-majority societies and a threatening challenge to Western ways of organizing the public-private divide. This leads to an indictment of the potential of Islamic tradition to contribute to the public life of Muslim-majority societies, making it difficult, if not impossible, to imagine a nonhegemonic and nondogmatic role for Islam in public life, discourse, and institutions.

This epistemological narrowing presents a major stumbling block for secularist observers and policy makers. As Foucault observed, "the problem of Islam as a political force is an essential one for our time and for years to come, and we cannot approach it with a modicum of intelligence if we start out from a position of hatred."[115] The ascription of threat to all forms of Islamist politics starts out from such a position. It empowers radicals who argue that the West aspires to global hegemony through a crusade against Islam, while silencing their rivals who are either ignored or classified as radicals and dismissed as fundamentalists. It fails to address the nuanced realities of contemporary politics in Muslim-majority countries, in which movements like Hezbollah and Hamas have gained a strong and legitimate political and cultural foothold that cannot be effortlessly washed away. As Tamimi observed after the Palestinian elections of 2006, "Hamas is not isolated at all; it has more windows open to it today than ever before."[116] Blanket ascriptions of threat and anti-Islamic rhetoric and foreign policy serve to strengthen radical and violent elements of such groups and disenfranchise moderates. As Ottaway concludes, "No matter what the United States says or does, the Islamist parties will remain the strongest players in the politics of Arab countries. The only question is whether they will continue to manifest that strength by competing in elections, as they have done lately, or whether they will do so through violence."[117]

This argument leads to three conclusions. First, Euro-American forms of secularism need to be "parochialized" in Chakrabarty's sense of the term.[118] The forms and degrees of separation between Islam and politics that do exist in contemporary Muslim-majority societies are not ill-fitting imitations of a Western secular ideal but local modalities of separation that may or may not have any relation to the forms of secularism that emerged from European Christendom. Second, although they may contest fundamental assumptions embedded in Western traditions of secularism, modalities of politics designated by secularists as political Islam are not necessarily aberrant. The question of how any particular instantiation of political Islam measures up vis-à-vis indices of democratization or pluralization must be determined on a case-by-case basis. As Ayoob argues, "no two Islamisms are alike because they are determined by the contexts in which they operate."[119] Political Islam may appear in a transgressive or regressive capacity in some instances, but it will not appear exclusively in that capacity. Third, and consequently, democratic modalities of separation and accommodation between religion and politics in Muslim-majority settings may be promulgated by those currently identified as Islamists. For political Islam cannot be automatically situated in oppositional terms vis-à-vis secularist or other separationist discourses. It is not a monolithic threat to otherwise viable local variations of Western secularism. Instead, like the traditions of secularism analyzed in this book, it is a discursive tradition mobilized in different ways with differing consequences. It is a tradition of argumentation. It is a discourse in which relations between metaphysics, politics, and contemporary moral order are deliberated and contested. It is a language of politics.

Like political Islam, the forms of politics associated with the global religious resurgence need to be explained and theorized not through Western categories of the sacred and secular but as a process through which these foundational categories of political and religious order are themselves challenged and renegotiated. This is the subject of chapter 8.

CHAPTER EIGHT

Religious Resurgence

RELIGION AND POLITICS overlap and intersect in complex and multiple formations in different times and locations, composing political settlements that wax and wane in their influence. Religion and politics do not belong to distinct domains of culture and power. As King observes, "examples of religious and political association are no longer automatically seen as the inappropriate grouping of two separate spheres of human cultural existence."[1] Secularism is a social construction.

The challenge to conventional European and American secularist divisions between religion and politics is now being felt in the discipline of international relations. The problem of how religion fits with world politics has become a significant topic not because it was identified as theoretically important in international relations, but because real-world events forced it back into the consciousness of international relations theorists. For at least three reasons, it has now become impossible to maintain that religion is irrelevant to international outcomes, as most conventional accounts would have it.[2] First, the United States and others have had a hard time imposing their vision of secular democracy around the world. Second, there has been the advent of a U.S. foreign policy model in the George W. Bush administration that is officially secular but inspired by a kind of Christianity. Third, over the past several decades there has been a rise in religious movements and organizations with broad bases of national and transnational influence.[3] These developments and others like them have led analysts to refer to a "resurgence of religion" in international relations.[4] Thomas describes the resurgence as the result of "a collapse in the faith of modernizing religion . . . motivated by the desire . . . to rethink and reevaluate how religion and modernity are related."[5]

There is good evidence for the resurgence.[6] It is now unsustainable to claim that religion plays no significant role in international relations; it has become a critical consideration in international security, global politics, and U.S. foreign policy.[7] Anson Shupe describes organized religion as a "stubbornly persistent and often integral factor in contemporary national and international politics."[8] Timothy Shah testified before the House International Relations Committee in 2004 that "the importance of the religion factor in public life is not decreasing or remaining static but is increasing in almost every part of the world."[9] Peter Berger, one of the foremost proponents of secularization theory in the 1960s, observed that, "put simply, most of the world is bubbling with religious passions."[10] Hatzopoulos and Petito have suggested that "the global resurgence of religion confronts IR theory with a theoretical challenge comparable to that raised by the end of the Cold War or the emergence of globalization."[11]

This chapter tackles this challenge. Although religious politics is not new, there has been an increase in the scope and intensity of the politicization of religion around the world in recent decades. Viewing secularism as a social construction as this book does opens the way for a new understanding of these developments. Çinar, it will be recalled, defines secularism as a series of political projects that transforms and reinstitutes sociopolitical order on the basis of a set of constitutive norms and principles.[12] I have suggested that any particular formation of the secular invokes a particular set of norms, principles, and practices that can be challenged and renegotiated, and often are. That is what this chapter is about. This is what religious resurgence is about. "Religious resurgence" is a term that relies upon particular secularist epistemological assumptions. It is used to refer to activities, movements, and processes that challenge authoritative secularist settlements of the relationship between metaphysics, politics, and state power. From this perspective, religious resurgence is neither a passing aberration on the road to modernization nor is it confirmation of insurmountable cultural and religious difference in world politics, as conventional accounts have it. It is instead an attempt to refashion the secular. It is a dispute over the very terms of the debate that structure the discussion of religion and politics, a dispute that is often presumed to have been resolved once and for all long ago. Religious resurgence directs attention to a controversy over how metaphysics, ethics, and politics relate to each other and to the state that calls into question the most fundamental received definitions and traditions of the secular analyzed in this book. It is a challenge to authoritative secularist settlements of the relationship between religion, politics, and state power in India, the United States, Turkey, Latin America, and elsewhere. There are multiple variations of this challenge, located on a spectrum that includes Al-Qaeda, the Hindutva movement in India, the Pakistan Awami Tehreek, the Turkish Justice and Development Party, and the Evangelical Christian movement in the United States.[13]

Secularist assumptions prestructure our understanding of religious resurgence. Conventional assumptions about what religion is and how it relates to politics determine the kinds of questions deemed worth asking about the "return of religion" and the kinds of answers one expects to find. The traditions of secularism described in this book are embedded at a preconscious level. Working together with other factors, they condition how the secular and religious are imagined and affect how religious resurgence is theorized. These formations of secularism are part of the epistemological and ontological foundation of the discipline of political science and so are embedded in the hypotheses and empirical tests of much international relations scholarship. As a result, most attempts to explain the religious resurgence reveal more about the epistemological assumptions of secularism than they do about the resurgence itself. As was the case with political Islam as described in chapter 7, by failing to conform to the categories available to international relations theorists for understanding the relationship between religion and politics, religious resurgence calls into question the ontological foundations of the discipline and practice of international relations. It also provides an opportunity to revisit these foundations.

My objective in this chapter is neither to explain nor to predict when religious resurgence will occur or why certain forms of political religion emerge at a particular time or place. As Haynes argues in reference to the resurgence, "there is no simple, clearcut reason, no single theoretical explanation to cover all cases."[14] Instead, my objective is twofold: first, to demonstrate how the forms of secularism described in this book structure knowledge and understanding of religious resurgence in contemporary international relations theory; and, second, to produce an alternative account of these developments that opens the way for new thinking about the politics of religion in international relations. I begin by revisiting the two trajectories of secularism that form the conceptual backbone of this book and prestructure attempts in international relations to theorize religious resurgence: laicism and Judeo-Christian secularism. I argue that each of these interpretive dispositions relies upon particular assumptions about the relation between religion and politics that condition their interpretations of the resurgence. Laicism, which suggests that religion will disappear as societies modernize, approaches the resurgence as a surface manifestation of deeper social, economic, and political grievances. Judeo-Christian secularism, which operates on the assumption that only Judeo-Christianity can serve as the basis of modern secular democracy, approaches the resurgence as proof of the entrenched differences between different religions and the civilizations influenced by these religions.

These paradigms miss a crucial insight about the resurgence. The increasing presence of religious phenomena, identities, and actors in international relations is not merely a protest against modernization, a retreat to archaic traditional forms of political order, or a backlash against "global modernity, authenticity and development."[15] Though some of these factors may also be operative, what is identified as religious resurgence is actually a political contestation of the most fundamental contours and content of the secular, a contest that signals the disruption of preexisting standards of what religion is and how it relates to politics. This apparent resurgence is evidence of the unsettling of convention and the eruption of fundamental contention over the relationship between metaphysics and politics that calls into question foundational secularist divisions between the secular and the religious. Religious resurgence therefore must be understood not through Euro-American categorizations of the religious and the political, but as a process through which these basic ontologies of political and religious order themselves are being renegotiated and refashioned.[16] It is a live and ongoing refashioning of the relation between the sacred, the profane, and the political that cuts through and calls into question the very definition of, and boundaries between, mundane and metaphysical, secular and sacred.[17]

Following this line of argument, one might expect religious resurgence to occur whenever there is growing public dissatisfaction with the prevailing terms of the current secularist settlement, and indeed this is the case. Mobilization against any particular secularist settlement, however, may not be spearheaded by those conventionally defined as religious. The reasons for seeking to overturn or refashion any particular instantiation of the secular are diverse, and so are the metaphysical and ontological commitments of the constituencies that seek to do so. It is for this reason that I hesitate and ultimately decline to adopt the term "religious resurgence." Designating the challenge to any particular form of secularism as religious defines in advance, in secularist terms, the commitments of those who are allegedly "resurging." This forecloses on interesting and important forms of politics that my alternative approach works hard to represent. Approaching religious resurgence as a challenge to authoritative *secularist* settlements reframes the kind of questions that are asked about oppositional politics and secularist authority. These forms of politics appear as neither epiphenomenal nor symptomatic of a return to religion. Instead, they are indicative of a public struggle over authoritative, historically contingent, and often state-enforced divisions between the secular, the sacred, and the political.

The final section of the chapter argues that international relations theory has not been able to fully account for the role of religion because it has not theorized the politics involved in the designation and enforcement of particular formations of the secular. International relations has not come to terms with the social and historical construction of the secular. This is because the religious and the political, the sacred and the secular, are generally presumed to be stable categories aligned with familiar and well-established modern divisions between public and private that date back to the Westphalian settlement.[18] This assumption concerning the stability and normativity of these categories is unsustainable given the evidence of change and contestation of the secular and the varieties of secularism that exist in the world today, as illustrated throughout this book. Religion and politics are not fully and finally differentiable, in Turkey, Iran, India, the United States, or elsewhere. This changes how we approach religion in both the theory and practice of international relations.

LAICISM AND RELIGIOUS RESURGENCE

Since the end of the Cold War, most political scientists have approached religion as either an inexplicable obstacle on the road to secular democracy or as evidence of entrenched cultural and civilizational difference in world politics.[19] As Euben argues, "both pessimistic and optimistic prognoses of the post–Cold War world are content implicitly to assume and thus reinforce the idea that religio-political movements (among others) stand in relation to Western, secular power and international order as the chaos of the particularistic, irrational, and archaic stand in relation to the universalistic, rational, and modern."[20]

This book has argued that two forms of secularism have been particularly influential in the attempt to come to terms with religion in international relations. Laicism and Judeo-Christian secularism are strategies for managing the relationship between religion and politics. Both are secularist in that they defend some form of the separation of church and state, but they do so in different ways and with different justifications. Both emphasize, though to differing degrees, what Casanova refers to as the "core and central thesis of the theory of secularization": the functional differentiation of the secular and the religious spheres.[21]

Laicism adopts two corollaries to this differentiation argument, advocating the privatization and, in some cases, the decline and/or elimination of religious belief and practice altogether.[22] The objective of laicism is to create a public life in which religious belief, practices, and institutions have lost their political significance, fallen below the threshold of political contestation, or been pushed into the private sphere. Laicism presents itself as the absence of ideology; as the resting point that is attained after having moved beyond the debate over religion and politics. Laicism works hard to appear to stand outside and above the religion-politics melee in a neutral space of its own creation. From this lofty vantage point, as noted by van der Veer and Lehman, "when religion manifests itself politically in the contemporary world, it is conceptualized as *fundamentalism*. . . . It is almost always interpreted as a negative social force directed against science, rationality, secularism—in short, against modernity."[23] In this view religion and the religious resurgence represent a threat to modern social order. Falk describes laicists as "those who view religion as disposed toward extremism, even terrorism, as soon as it abandons its proper modernist role as a matter of private faith and intrudes upon public space, especially on governance."[24] As Haynes suggests, this perspective has been especially influential in the social sciences:

> The commanding figures of 19th century social science—Durkheim, Weber, Marx—argued that secularisation was an integral facet of modernisation, a global trend. Everywhere, so the argument goes, religion would become privatised, losing its grip on culture, becoming a purely personal matter, no longer a collective force with mobilising potential for social change.[25]

From within this perspective, the two principal alternatives for public order are liberal (laicist) democracy or illiberal religious theocracy. In reference to the states of the Middle East, for example, Deborah Gerner and Philip Schrodt have argued that "virtually every state in the region is experiencing tensions from competing political perspectives advocating *either* increased democracy *or* greater religious influence in government."[26] The assumption is that democratization is tied to the expulsion of religious influence from governance. A country is either democratic and laicist, or it is undemocratic and religious, and perhaps theocratic. Any role for religion in public life is a step toward theocracy.

The assumptions about religion and politics underlying laicism lead to a particular approach to religious resurgence. For laicists democratic public order is separationist, in accordance with Rawls's famous liberal injunction to "take the truths of religion off the political agenda."[27] Marx illustrates this view in a more extreme form: "[religions are] no more than stages in the development of the human mind—snake skins which have been cast off by history, and man [is] the snake who clothed himself in them."[28] For secular international relations theorists following in the intellectual footsteps of either of these thinkers, as many do, religious resurgence appears as a reaction against the changes imposed by modernization and globalization, a moment of irrationality to be overcome or outgrown on the road to secular democracy, an epiphenomenal manifestation of structural social, economic, and political grievances, or all of the above. The resurgence is seen as a backlash against the effects of government efforts to modernize, for example. As governments and ruling elites came under criticism for corruption, economic failure, and political repression, so the argument goes, "people turned to other leaders and institutions to champion their interests."[29] At other times it is explained as a side effect and symptom of a range of existential hardships including economic difficulties, political instability, and natural disasters.[30] The essential element tying these accounts together is their assumption that the resurgence is epiphenomenal: it is the surface manifestation of other underlying grievances. From this perspective, the key question for international relations becomes, as Rinehart argues, "the extent to which changes in the international system since World War II have contributed to a resurgence in the role of religion in the politics of the developing world."[31] This leads to a focus on material and structural causes of religious resurgence rather than a consideration of the contested politics of secularism that lie at the core of this contestation.

JUDEO-CHRISTIAN SECULARISM AND RELIGIOUS RESURGENCE

According to Judeo-Christian secularism, Christianity and/or Judeo-Christian tradition is the unique and inimitable foundation of secular public order and modern political institutions.[32] Unlike laicism, Judeo-Christian secularism does not assume or promote a decline in or privatization of religion, although it does assume some degree of differentiation between the temporal and the religious spheres. In this view political order in the West is based in a common set of values with their roots in Western Christianity. The idea, as Buruma observes, is that "only if secular government [were] firmly embedded in the Christian faith could its democratic institutions survive."[33] Judeo-Christian secularism, to borrow from Anthony D. Smith, is an "example of the tendency to understand contemporary society and politics in terms of the primordial attachments of kinship, language, race, custom, and territory."[34] It represents a very different story about religion and politics than laicism, one in which the potential for secularization is linked to a particular religious heritage. In this tradition of secularism, democratic political order in the West is based in a common set of values with their roots in Latin Christendom.

In contrast to laicism, Judeo-Christian secularism celebrates the contributions of Western religious tradition to modern secularism. Reflecting this, Bernard Lewis has suggested that "the notion that religion and political authority, church and state, are different and that they can or should be separated is, in a profound sense, Christian."[35] In this view the West's religious heritage bolsters democracy by offering a set of common assumptions within which politics can be conducted. Religious tradition is a source of political cohesion, and citizens who share religious sensibilities and enter into democratic deliberation will produce something approaching a moral consensus.[36] Judeo-Christian secularism draws sustenance from the religious origins of this cultural consensus. The West is uniquely privileged to be secular, liberal, and democratic as a result of its religious heritage. For Huntington, secular democracy is deeply rooted in Protestant Christianity. Western Protestant secularism provides the cultural and political ground in which liberal democracy flourishes. The West is defined by its secular and Christian nature, and this characteristic is seen as an important determinant of world order and international conflict.

For Judeo-Christian secularists such as Lewis and Huntington, religious resurgence confirms two fundamental elements of world order. First, it demonstrates the moral, religious, and (therefore) political incommensurability of different civilizations. Second, it confirms the "natural" relationship between Judeo-Christianity and secular democracy. Despite attempts to imitate Western institutions and legal codes, other civilizations are seen as incapable of fully grasping and successfully replicating the separation of religion and state as realized in Judeo-Christian majority settings such as Europe, the United States, and Israel. Religious resurgence thus confirms the existence of deep cultural divides that cannot be overcome with modernization, economic or moral development, or the globalization of secular democratic norms and institutions.

Lewis and Huntington are correct that Judeo-Christian tradition has played a significant role in processes of secularization and democratization. As Philpott and others argue, Protestantism played a significant role in bringing about the specific form of differentiation between the religious and temporal spheres that took hold in the West.[37] There also have been important developments in the now relatively accommodative relationship between the Catholic Church and modern liberal democracies, cautiously evolving into what Stepan refers to as the "twin tolerations."[38] Philpott suggests that "today it is difficult to think of an influential Catholic sector in any state that actively opposes liberal democracy," while cautioning that "the Church's support for democracy has not been the same everywhere . . . the Church's democratizing influence . . . was complex, varying in time, manner and extent."[39]

The problem therefore is not that Judeo-Christian secularism posits connections between Christianity and secularization, which certainly exist on multiple levels,[40] but that it often posits culturally exclusive boundaries to secularization and democratization. This tradition of secularism fails to acknowledge the potentiality and actuality of multiple traditions of secularism and trajectories of secularization. It fails to entertain the possibility that connections between religious tradition and alternative forms of secularism also exist in *non*-Judeo-Christian traditions. In short, it posits exclusivist cultural boundaries of democracy that fail to account for non-Western democratic practices that seek cultural and political legitimacy through recourse to religious tradition broadly defined. As Stepan argues, "a central thrust of Huntington's message is not only that democracy emerged *first* within Western civilization but that the other great religious civilizations of the world lack the unique bundle of cultural characteristics necessary to support Western-style democracy."[41] Islamic law, from this perspective, cannot offer fertile ground for democratization but sets the preconditions for totalitarianism by attempting to regulate all aspects of life. As Hashemi has observed of Lewis, "according to Bernard Lewis, Islamic tradition and liberal democracy are fundamentally incompatible and the ultimate choice facing the Muslim world at the beginning of the twenty-first century is between religious fanaticism and modernization."[42] For Lewis secular democracy is a unique Western achievement, and non-Western civilizations and in particular Islamic civilization are simply missing this crucial (Christian) distinction between the secular and the sacred, between the metaphysical and the mundane. Stepan rightly criticizes this view as "the fallacy of unique founding conditions."[43]

Laicism serves as a reminder of the dangers of mixing singular interpretations of religion with the powers of the state, and Judeo-Christian secularism calls attention to the elusive connections between religious tradition and contemporary international politics. However, the assumptions about religion and politics underpinning these forms of secularism also impose significant epistemological costs, and explanations that rely exclusively upon them reflect these costs. Challenges to laicism are framed automatically as religious, in accordance with laicist definitions of that term, and quickly dismissed as irrational and antimodern. Yet laicism is itself a social construction and does not stand above the melee surrounding religion and politics but is deeply immersed in

it. While Judeo-Christian secularism acknowledges its own social and historical origins, it also has a tendency to rule out comparable settlements outside
Judeo-Christian-majority societies. Challenges are dismissed as a "return to
tradition" and confirmation of entrenched cultural and civilizational differences. Explanations relying upon either or, as is often the case, both of these
evaluative stances account poorly for the ways in which ethics, metaphysics,
and politics are negotiated, particularly in non-Judeo-Christian majority societies. Religious revival is neither a rebellion against secular modernity nor
confirmation of intractable religious and civilizational difference. It is a dispute over the very terms of the debate involving religion and politics that
secular analysts take for granted. It is a dispute over the terms of a particular
secularist settlement. It is a controversy over how metaphysics and politics
relate to each other and to the state that calls into question fundamental
received definitions of both secular and sacred. It therefore needs to be understood and explained not only through Western categories of sacred and secular, or private and public, but also and more fundamentally as a process
through which the terms of theopolitical order are socially constructed and
politically renegotiated.

Those familiar with Asad's *Formations of the Secular* may recognize his
influence in this argument, in particular in my attempt to move beyond Durk-
heimian attempts to universalize a single concept of religion and the sacred.
The idea, as Asad explains, is to "shift our preoccupation with definitions of
'the sacred' as an object of experience to the wider question of how a heteroge-
neous landscape of power (moral, political, economic) is constituted, what
disciplines (individual and collective) are necessary to it."[44] Religious resurgence thus appears on the secularist epistemological landscape whenever authoritative secularist settlements of the relationship between metaphysics, politics, and state power are challenged. The central concern for scholars of
religion and international relations from this perspective is not only the *degree*
to which religion penetrates international, transnational, or domestic politics,
which it certainly does, but also and more fundamentally *how* secularist epistemologies and the metaphysical assumptions and institutional and individual
sites of power that sustain them are challenged and ultimately transformed by
the developments associated with religious resurgence. This shift in focus
makes it possible to see religious resurgence as an attempt to remake the
boundaries of the secular and to refashion the frontiers of the political.

THE SOCIAL CONSTRUCTION OF SECULAR
INTERNATIONAL RELATIONS THEORY

Various instantiations of secular order in the United States, Turkey, India, and
elsewhere are facing what Cutler has referred to as a "crisis of legitimacy."[45]

This crisis has been identified as religious resurgence. Yet the utility of traditional secularist interpretive assumptions about religion and politics for understanding these developments is limited. The global religious revival calls into question the secularist apparatus used to interpret it. Policy makers who continue to work within the secular-religious binary as traditionally conceived stumble repeatedly, both epistemologically and politically, in their efforts to understand and respond to the range of phenomena associated with religious resurgence. Religion is neither fading from domestic and international life as modernization proceeds, as laicists predict, nor is it necessarily a dangerous source of conflict when it makes its way into the public sphere in non-Western contexts, as Judeo-Christian secularists assume. The resurgence is neither an epiphenomenal expression of deep socioeconomic and political grievances that will be overcome with the globalization of Western secular norms and international development nor evidence of the triumph of archaic cultural and religious commitments. It is a series of challenges to the fundamental assumptions that sustain particular authoritative secularist settlements. The renegotiation and reconfiguration of these settlements on a global scale suggests that secularism is a social, historical, and political construct.

In her foreword to *The Sacred and the Sovereign*, Elshtain observes of religion that "no one quite knows how to capture the energies unleashed in our world conceptually."[46] My argument suggests that this conceptual confusion results from the fact that religious and political, like sacred and secular, are assumed to be unchanging categories aligned with familiar modern divisions between public and private. This is a mistaken assumption. Secularism refers to a series of social and historical traditions that both rely upon and produce particular understandings of religion, religious resurgence, and religious subjectivity. Religion and politics are not well defined and stable subcategories of a broader set of fixed binary divisions between public and private with their origins in the European Enlightenment. Secularist divisions between religion and politics are neither stable nor universal. They are fundamentally contested categories.

Cutler develops an analogous argument in the international political economy literature in her analysis of the inherently political nature of the "private" sphere and its implications for the legitimacy of the state, international law, and international organization.[47] Her approach to claims of public and private parallels my argument about claims to secular and religious. A process of differentiating between subject and object associates the former with secular actors, states, and processes, and the latter with religious actors, states, and processes, and then objectifies this condition by allowing the secular subject to drop out of sight. In the case of law and the state, according to Cutler, this process has enabled international law "to stand alone as the embodiment of sovereign will, authority and legitimacy."[48] In the case of secular authority, it has enabled particular traditions of secularism to stand as the fixed and unalterable embodiment of authority and legitimacy in international relations. The sacred sphere (as defined by secularists), like the private sphere for Cutler, is then defined out of existence as a political domain.

Cutler argues that a "crisis of legitimacy" has arisen in the field of international political economy because contemporary international relations and international political economy do not conform to a theoretical image of the state as the unique subject of international law and private corporate actors as its object. Thus a crisis arises because "the actors, structures, and processes identified and theorized as determinative by the dominant approaches to the study of international law and organization have ceased to be of singular importance."[49] This argument is relevant to the study of religion in the field of international relations. The (secular) modalities of order, actors, structures, and processes theorized as fixed and determinative by dominant approaches to international relations are no longer of singular importance, if they ever were. The foundational categories that sustain contemporary approaches to religion in international relations are like a desert oasis; the closer one gets to them, the more difficult and elusive they appear.

This is because contemporary international relations do not conform to the theoretical image of the secular subject as the unique subject of international relations and private religious actors, processes, and institutions as its object. The sacred sphere, like Cutler's private sphere, cannot simply be defined out of existence as a political domain. As Cutler, Strange, Helleiner, and others have argued in international political economy and Derrida, Connolly, Asad, and King have suggested in philosophy, political theory, anthropology, and religious studies, the processes through which these spheres are designated as sacred or private are fraught with controversy.[50] This also applies to international relations. Secular and religious are contested and relational constructs. Like public and private, they are "contingent categorizations, reposing on specific cultural traditions."[51] As Honig suggests with regard to the public-private distinction, the distinction between sacred and secular must be seen as "the performative product of political struggle, hard won and always temporary."[52]

Secularist settlements are hard won and always temporary. Theorists have stumbled in the attempt to theorize the return of religion because their concepts of authority fail to recognize the politics inherent in the definition, enforcement, and contestation of authoritative forms of secularism and processes of secularization. International relations has not come to terms with the actors, structures, and processes that are shaped by and contribute to these secular settlements. In foreign policy, this has contributed to a tendency to see (benevolent) Western forms of secular democracy and (menacing) non-Western forms of religious theocracy as the only two alternative forms of theopolitical order. Coming to terms with religious resurgence therefore requires rethinking the ontological and epistemological foundations of the discipline that govern what counts as politics in international politics. It requires rethinking Euro-American categorizations and practices of the secular, the religious, and the political. As Chakrabarty argues, "European thought . . . is both indispensable and inadequate in helping us to think through the various life practices that constitute the political and the historical in India."[53] This also applies to the discipline and practice of international relations.

This argument brings together concerns that cut across and occasionally move beyond debates over the past few decades in international relations theory surrounding the relative merits of realism, liberalism, and constructivism. While constructivism offers promising tools for considering how state interests and identities are constituted as secular or religious,[54] post-positivist theorizing has only just begun to work through the ontological and epistemological challenges posed by the question of the sacred and the secular. Religion and politics do not instinctively sort themselves out into distinct domains of power. Modern forms of secularism, like modern forms of nationalism, are made rather than found. They are continually forged and reforged. Secularist settlements always rest on a disintegrating sandbar. The return of religion is not a "special atavistic anomaly"[55] but is integral to modern politics itself. Several foundational categories in the discipline of international relations tacitly or overtly rely upon (moving) constructs of the secular, including the (secular) state, theories of modernization and development, sources of international law, theories of nationalism, and the concept of politics itself. Delineating how particular formations of the secular tacitly or explicitly influence these categories allows us to access the complex locations of religion in international relations.

This chapter has argued that the two forms of secularism analyzed in this book lead to accounts of religious resurgence as either a backlash against modernization and globalization or a harbinger of cultural and civilizational conflict. I have proposed that it is instead an attempt to refashion the secular. It is a dispute over the core terms of the debate that structure discussions of religion and politics. This dispute questions the received definitions and traditions of secularism analyzed in this book. It also suggests that there are many possible social constructions of the secular. Traditions of social inquiry in international relations that assume a fixed and unchanging definition of the secular and the political are unable to come to terms with the processes through which these constructions become authoritative. They miss the politics involved in the establishment of any particular authoritative secularist settlement on the spectrum of theological politics. These settlements, and the broader spectrum of theopolitical possibilities from which they are drawn, are the context from which particular conceptualizations of the secular and the political emerge and become authoritative. When a particular settlement is challenged, so are the concepts of the secular and the political that accompany and sustain it. This challenge is then designated as religious resurgence. This designation, however, is itself a product of the epistemological assumptions of the authoritative formation that is being contested. How to think productively, on a case-by-case basis, about these contestants or resurgents in their own terms and outside the binaries produced and maintained by secularist rigid authority is the next challenge.

CHAPTER NINE

Conclusion

IF THE TRADITIONS of secularism discussed in this book are not fixed but socially constructed, then they are also subject to modification. One way in which modification could occur is through the cultivation of a practice of agonistic or agonal secular democracy. Agonistic secular democracy elicits and seeks out public expression of contending views on religion and its relationship to the political: "a democracy infused with a spirit of agonism is one in which divergent orientations to the mysteries of existence find overt expression in public life."[1] At the same time, such a practice of democracy also continually interrupts attempts to impose a final and static solution to the relationship between religion and politics.[2] Agonistic democracy encourages contestation and shuns final settlements. It departs from the political minimalism of democratic individualism; and is not confined to the institutions of the territorial state.[3] This approach to religion and politics, this rewriting or refashioning of contemporary traditions of secularism, is uniquely suited to the challenge of incorporating both theistic and nontheistic perspectives on and into politics both domestically and internationally: As Connolly suggests, "The need today . . . is to rewrite secularism to pursue an ethos of engagement among a plurality of controversial metaphysical perspectives, including, for starters, Christian and other monotheistic perspectives, secular thought, and asecular, nontheistic perspectives."[4]

The prospects for agonal democracy seem reasonably good. Debate in the United States, for example, occasionally moves beyond the standoff between "religious conservatives" and "liberal secularists" toward an acknowledgment that "what is problematic is not vibrant religious activism in the public sphere, but the consistent association of religious devotion with a particular set of dogmatic political opinions."[5] Intolerance of a final settlement between a single religious perspective and the state was confirmed in the 2002 case of the 5,300-pound monument to the Ten Commandments that stood in the Alabama Supreme Court. Chief Justice Roy Moore, who placed the monument in the courthouse, stated that his intention was to remind citizens of the "sovereignty of God over the affairs of men." When pushed further, Moore admitted that he was referring to Jesus Christ and that other deities would deny our freedoms and specifically would "not allow for freedom of conscience."[6] A federal court ordered the removal of the monument and noted that Moore's views came "uncomfortably . . . close to . . . a theocracy."[7]

As the activities of Justice Moore and his many supporters suggest, however, "a generalized secularization story will not do."[8] The primary argument of this book is that secularism is a socially constructed form of political authority, and that recognizing this allows for a better understanding of critical theoretical and empirical puzzles in international relations, including the cultural foundations of conflict between the United States and Iran, the social and religious basis of European opposition to Turkish accession to the European Union, and the attempt to understand and respond to political Islam and religious resurgence. The difficulty in coming to terms with religion in international relations is traced to the unquestioned acceptance of the secularist separation between religion and politics. The secularist settlement is not fixed but rather socially constructed. This conclusion summarizes six contributions of this argument.

First, the book introduces two powerful traditions of secularism, laicism and Judeo-Christian secularism, describes their distinctive relationship to both Enlightenment critiques of religion and Judeo-Christian tradition, and analyzes their consequences for international relations between Europe, the United States, Turkey, and Iran. Laicism seeks to create a neutral public space in which religious belief, practices, and institutions have lost their political significance, fallen below the threshold of political contestation, or been pushed into the private sphere. Judeo-Christian secularism does not attempt to fully expel religion—or at least Judeo-Christian religion—from politics and public life. Instead, this narrative suggests that Judeo-Christianity culminated in and contributed to the unique Western achievement of the separation of church and state. Political order in the West is based in a common set of values with their roots in Latin Christendom. Secularism is one of these core values.

In Europe, the United States, and to varying degrees elsewhere, shared definitions and dispositions involving the relation between religion and politics have crystallized around these two forms of secularism.[9] These socially shared systems of belief and practice form an important part of the cultural and religious backdrop out of which Europeans and Americans engage in international relations. These traditions of secularism are powerful and persuasive collective dispositions that shape modern sensibilities, habits, and beliefs concerning the meaning of religion and its relationship to the political. They are significant examples of productive and constitutive power at work in contemporary international relations.

In developing this argument I have sought to avoid the cognitivist trap criticized by Krasner and other critics of constructivism in international relations. As Krasner argues, "norms, though not irrelevant, do not have the weight that constructivism has attributed to them."[10] I agree. Norms alone do not carry the weight often ascribed to them in constructivist analyses.[11] In response, I have pursued an approach to secularism that works to accommodate the "weightiness" of secular authority, as expressed not only through beliefs but through habits of speech and thought, sensibilities, conventional practices, and ways of being in and responding to the world. Though it is perhaps a way of dealing with the "inevitable lightness of norms" that differs from what Krasner envisions, this approach opens possibilities for constructivist theorizing in international relations that seeks to account for the influence of norms without reducing them to individual thoughts and beliefs. Norms cannot be analyzed outside of the structures of power and specific embodied social practices in which they are embedded and through which they are expressed. This is the case not only for the traditions of secularism discussed in this book but also for different formations of nationalism, varieties of capitalism, and other powerful organizing principles and practices of modern collective life.

Second, this book discusses the constitutive relationship between modern Euro-American forms of secularism and particular representations of Islam. The two varieties of secularism described in this book have been socially and historically constructed through opposition to particular representations of Islam and the Islamic Middle East. More than any other single religious or political tradition, Islam represents the nonsecular in European and American secularist thought and practice. The concept of a modern (laicist and Judeo-Christian) secular West was constituted in part through opposition to the idea of antimodern, anti-Christian, and theocratic Islamic Middle East. Opposition to Islam is built into secular political authority and the national identities with which it is associated. This suggests that negative associations of Islam not only run deep in Euro-American secular political traditions but help to constitute them.

Third, this argument about the constitution of modern forms of secular authority, together with the discussion of the United States and Iran in chapter 6, demonstrates the significance of the politics of secularism to national identity and international relations. Conventional international relations scholarship has operated on the assumption that secular nationalism and national identity transcend religion and religious identity. As van der Veer and Lehmann observes, "with few exceptions and for many years, the debates about the relationship of modern nationalism and the modern state have ignored the role of religion."[12] According to Metcalf this is because "the modernity of nationalism is defined by the presumed archaism of religion."[13] This book has provided evidence to the contrary. Modern forms of nationalism feed on a secular repertoire but also transform it in significant ways.[14] Secularist traditions and the multifaceted religious commitments that operate in and through them are implicated in and often partially constitutive of national identity. Historians, sociologists, and religious studies scholars have studied these "indissoluble links" between the modern nation-state and religion in a variety of contexts.[15] The Hindu nationalist movement (Hindutva) in India has been cited as an example of how a particular version of Indian nationalism draws upon the symbolic repertoire of religion and transforms it to create a blueprint for a pure form of Hindu identity.[16] Harootunian looks at the relationship between religion and the modern Japanese state, arguing that the rearticulation of Japanese common religious memories in nationalist institutional forms represents "a condition of modern, secular society, not a rejection of it."[17] McClay traces the connection between 9/11 and the revitalization of American civil religion, defined as "that strain of American piety that bestows many of the elements of religious sentiment and faith upon the fundamental political and social institutions of the United States."[18] In each of these cases, religion has contributed to the creation of what van der Veer describes as "public spheres of political interaction central to the formation of national identities."[19] Yet the connection between the contours and content of secular and religiously infused national identities and international relations is rarely investigated. One of my objectives has been to open up this field of inquiry in the discipline of international relations.

Fourth, drawing on contemporary EU-Turkey and U.S.-Iranian relations, the book shows why a comprehensive understanding of relations between the West and the Middle East requires consideration of the politics of secularism and analyzes the implications of this argument for international relations. Attempts to explain relations between Europe, the United States, and the Islamic Middle East and North Africa that rely upon conventional variables such as state interests, geopolitical imperatives, material factors, the characteristics of individual leaders, bureaucratic politics, and the international system fail to account for the international political effects of the authoritative forms of secularism described in this book. I demonstrate that secularist authority is a productive part of the cultural and normative foundation of contemporary international relations that contributes to political outcomes both in relations between states and between states and suprastate entities.

Chapter 5 began with the observation that most analyses of EU enlargement attribute European doubts about Turkey's fitness for membership to economic considerations, concerns over immigration, and hesitations about the democratization of Turkish domestic politics. Yet controversy over EU enlargement to include Turkey cannot be understood without taking account of the influence of authoritative traditions about religion and politics circulating within Europe. These collective dispositions have concrete effects upon the debate over religion and European political identity and in particular the role of Islam within that identity. Judeo-Christian secularism, in many of its forms, holds that Muslim-majority countries like Turkey are unequipped to fully democratize and therefore unfit to become fully European. In this view Turkey is missing one of the essential ingredients of European identity: a Judeo-Christian heritage that predisposes it toward democratic secularism. Laicism holds that religion should be kept out of politics and that the resurgence of Islamic political identification in Turkey poses a threat to European collective identity in which religion is considered a private affair. The revival of public religion in Turkey challenges European laicist, and Turkish Kemalist, constructions of the secular. A post-Kemalist Turkey therefore represents a potential threat to laicist and Kemalist standards regarding the separation of religion and state and is preceived as unfit to become fully European. I concluded that successful Turkish accession to the EU requires a reconsideration of the governing assumptions of these various trajectories of secularism and their relationship to European identity and institutions. The possibility that a Muslim-majority country could be equipped to democratize without any recourse whatsoever to Judeo-Christian history, politics, or institutions would have to be entertained. The assumed link between the laicist privatization of religion and democratization would need to be scrutinized. This will require work in Europe and among Europeans. This helps to explain why many Europeans perceive Turkish membership as a potential threat to European identity. In some ways, it is. Bringing Turkey in will require that Europeans create a series of more pluralistic settlements involving how religion and politics relate to European identity.

Chapter 6 examined U.S.-Iranian relations. Although the politics of religion within revolutionary Iran has been exhaustively analyzed, the question of how the politics of religion within the United States has affected relations between the United States and Iran has received less attention. I argued that both trajectories of secularism discussed in this book have played a critical role in relations between the United States and Iran. Laicism has been the prevailing American framework for interpreting the Islamic revolution. In this account the revolution was unacceptable because it imported religion into public life, compromising the most basic tenet of laicism. In the Judeo-Christian secularist account, the revolution was seen as confirming "natural" linkages between Islam and theocracy, in sharp contrast to the "natural" linkages between Christianity and democracy. Islam was contrasted explicitly with Christianity, and the United States was portrayed as a Christian nation. These two varieties of secularism led to powerful condemnations of the revolution and the representation of Iran as a threat not only to American national interests but also to the national identity of the United States as secular and democratic. It was in part due to the powerful influence of laicism and Judeo-Christian secularism that Islam—and not the history of U.S.-Iranian relations—became the dominant explanatory trope for the events surrounding the Iranian revolution. These two varieties of secularism help to explain *why* "many commentators . . . saw America as both egregiously wronged by Iran and innocent of anything but excessive benevolence towards Iranians."[20] The political authority of these forms of secularism explains the shock and bewilderment of the Americans at the time of the revolution and the intensity and persistence of American hostility toward Iran.

These two cases also contribute to the theoretical literature in international relations concerning how individual states and suprastate entities construct their interests and identities. Chapters 5 and 6 demonstrated *how* shared interests and identities about religion and politics developed primarily at the domestic level become influential at the systemic level in international relations. Domestic secularist authority is a productive part of the cultural and religious foundations of Euro-American political orders, national identities, and contemporary international relations. Situated at the interface of domestic and international politics, this book has sought to redress this structural, systemic, and cultural bias by demonstrating how shared interests, identities, and understandings involving politics and religion developed at the domestic or local level become influential at the systemic or global level.

Fifth, the argument of this book presents an alternative to realist, liberal, and most constructivist accounts of international relations that work on the assumption that religion has been privatized. I have challenged the assumption that since the Westphalian settlement religion has been marginalized and privatized in international relations, rendering it largely irrelevant to power politics. I argue instead that the modern forms of secular authority analyzed in this book emerged out of a profoundly Christian Westphalian moral order. The influence of Christian tradition upon the Westphalian secular settlement makes it difficult to subsume the current international order into realist and liberal frameworks that assume that religion has been privatized. As argued in chapter 2, modern forms of secularism contribute to the constitution of a particular idea and practice of state sovereignty that *claims* to be universal in part by defining the limits of state-centered politics with religion on the outside. This claim to delimit the terms and boundaries of politics, and to define religion as its private counterpart, is a highly politicized and historically and culturally variable process. Secularism is a form of authorized knowledge that creates and perpetuates particular claims about the limits of modern politics. These claims have become established settlements that operate below the threshold of public international discourse.[21] These settlements lie at the core of modern assumptions about and practices of state sovereignty.

Sixth, the argument helps to resolve long-standing challenges in international relations theory concerning how to approach political Islam and religious resurgence. I argue that these developments offer a unique opportunity to revisit the secularist epistemological and ontological foundations of the discipline. Chapter 6 analyzed two predominant secularist narratives of political Islam in the discipline of international relations that correspond to the two trajectories of secularism described in chapter 2. Laicism represents political Islam as an unnatural infringement of religion upon would-be secular public life in Muslim societies, while Judeo-Christian secularism represents it as a regrettable commingling of religion and politics to be distinguished from the Western separation of religion and state. These two evaluative stances reflect particular modern assumptions about the possibility of public religion in modern societies. As van der Veer and Lehmann observe, "it is a fundamental assumption of the discourse of modernity that religion in modern societies loses its social creativity and is forced to choose between a sterile conservation of its premodern characteristics and a self-effacing assimilation to the secularized world."[22] In failing to conform to either of these modern prescriptions, I argue that many of the forms of politics designated by secularists as political Islam operate outside the epistemological and explanatory confines of modern international relations theory. By failing to conform to the secularist categories available to international relations theorists for understanding religion and politics, these forms of politics challenge the epistemological foundations of international relations. Grasping these forms of politics and understanding their political consequences therefore require coming to terms with the limits of secularist epistemology. Doing so reveals that the forms of politics that secularists refer to as political Islam should not be automatically situated in oppositional terms vis-à-vis secularist or separationist discourses. Political Islam is not necessarily an ontological threat to these discourses. It is instead a multifaceted set of discursive traditions that, like the Euro-American forms of secularism described in this book, are variously engaged in the perennial controversy over religion and politics.

Chapter 8 examined the global religious resurgence in India, the United States, Turkey, Latin America, and elsewhere in light of my discussion of political Islam. I argue that the processes associated with the resurgence need to be understood and explained not through Western categories of the sacred and secular, or public and private, but as a process through which the most basic terms of political and religious order are themselves renegotiated. What secularists designate as religious resurgence is an ongoing contest over the fundamental contours and content of authoritative designations of the secular. It is a live controversy over the relationship between the sacred, the profane, and the political that cuts through and calls into question the definition of, and boundaries between, these authoritative categories.

The secularist division between religion and politics is not fixed but socially and historically constructed. The discipline of international relations has not been able to account for religion because it has not come to terms with the politics involved in defining and enforcing particular concepts and practices of the secular. Religion and politics, like sacred and secular, are assumed to be stable and unchanging categories aligned with familiar divisions between public and private. This is not the case. Religion and politics do not belong to distinct domains of power and authority. The designation of the religious and the political is itself a political act. It is not possible to make the contents of the religious sphere disappear by defining it out of existence as a political domain and refusing to acknowledge its constitutive role within modern politics. It is not possible to pinpoint the essence of any particular religion and associate it definitively and determinatively with a particular form of politics or set of political outcomes.

Secularism comes in many different varieties. All are located on a spectrum of theological politics. The failure to recognize that secularism is socially constructed explains why theorists of international relations have struggled to understand the power of religion in world politics. The failure to recognize the moral, political, and epistemological consequences of the rigid secularist constructions of religion analyzed in this book explains why practitioners in international relations have struggled to respond to the power of religion in world politics.

Notes

1. Michael Barnett and Raymond Duvall, "Power in International Politics," *International Organization* 59 (Winter 2005): 43.

2. Ibid., p. 44.

3. David Scott and Charles Hirschkind, "Introduction: The Anthropological Skepticism of Talal Asad," in Scott and Hirschkind (Eds.), *Powers of the Secular Modern: Talal Asad and His Interlocutors* (Stanford: Stanford University Press, 2006), p. 3.

4. Alasdair MacIntyre, *After Virtue: A Study in Moral Theory*, 2nd ed. (Notre Dame: University of Notre Dame Press, 1997), p. 61.

5. Anthony W. Marx, *Faith in Nation: Exclusionary Origins of Nationalism* (New York: Oxford University Press, 2003), p. 198.

6. Talal Asad, "Responses," in Scott and Hirschkind, *Powers of the Secular Modern*, p. 217.

7. Ole Wæver, "Insecurity, Security and Asecurity in the West European Non-war Community," in Emanuel Adler and Michael Barnett (Eds.), *Security Communities* (Cambridge: Cambridge University Press, 1998), p. 118, n. 89.

8. Eric Ringmar, "Alexander Wendt: A Social Scientist Struggling with History," in Iver B. Neumann and Ole Wæver (Eds.), *The Future of International Relations: Masters in the Making?* (London: Routledge, 1997), p. 285.

9. Stephen Saideman, "Thinking Theoretically about Identity and Foreign Policy," in Shibley Telhami and Michael Barnett (Eds.), *Identity and Foreign Policy in the Middle East* (Ithaca: Cornell University Press, 2002), p. 177; Marc Lynch, *State Interests and Public Spheres: The International Politics of Jordan's Identity* (New York: Columbia University Press, 1999); Michael Barnett, *Dialogues in Arab Politics: Negotiations in Regional Order* (New York: Columbia University Press, 1998).

10. Rodney Bruce Hall, *National Collective Identity: Social Constructs and International Systems* (New York: Columbia University Press, 1999), p. 4. Payne argues similarly that, "since World War II, the importance of domestic cultural factors in the shaping of a country's external behavior has been downplayed by scholars." Richard J. Payne, *The Clash with Distant Cultures: Values, Interests and Force in American Foreign Policy* (Albany: State University of New York Press, 1995), p. 3.

11. Interesting attempts to negotiate this divide in history and political science include Lynch, *State Interests and Public Spheres*; Azzedine Layachi, *The United States and North Africa: A Cognitive Approach to Foreign Policy* (New York: Praeger, 1990); Matthew Frye Jacobson, *Barbarian Virtues: The United States Encounters Foreign Peoples at Home and Abroad, 1876–1917* (New York: Hill & Wang, 2001); Anders Stephanson, *Manifest Destiny: American Expansion and the Empire of Right*, 5th ed. (New York: Hill & Wang, 2000); Naoko Shibusawa, *America's Geisha Ally: Reimagining the Japanese Enemy* (Cambridge, Mass.: Harvard University Press, 2006); and Petra

Goedde, *GIs and Germans: Culture, Gender, and Foreign Relations, 1945–1949* (New Haven: Yale University Press, 2002).

12. Hall, *National Collective Identity*, p. 4.

13. Scott M. Thomas, "Taking Religious and Cultural Pluralism Seriously: The Global Resurgence of Religion and the Transformation of International Society," in Fabio Petito and Pavlos Hatzopoulos (Eds.), *Religion in International Relations: The Return from Exile* (New York: Palgrave Macmillan, 2003), pp. 21–53. On the argument that the social power of Protestants was the central cause of the evolution of the Westphalian state system, see Daniel Philpott, "The Religious Roots of Modern International Relations," *World Politics* 52 (2000): 206–45.

14. John D. Carlson and Erik C. Owens, "Reconsidering Westphalia's Legacy for Religion and International Politics," in Carlson and Owens (Eds.), *The Sacred and the Sovereign: Religion and International Politics* (Washington, D.C.: Georgetown University Press, 2003), p. 14.

15. Teschke argues that the modern sovereign state system began not in 1648 but only following the rise of capitalist social property relations and modern state-formation in Britain. Benno Teschke, *The Myth of 1648: Class, Geopolitics and the Making of Modern International Relations* (London: Verso, 2003).

16. Charles Taylor, "Modes of Secularism," in Rajeev Bhargava (Ed.), *Secularism and Its Critics* (Oxford: Oxford University Press, 1998), p. 32 (emphasis added).

17. Carlson and Owens, "Reconsidering Westphalia's Legacy," p. 15.

18. I am grateful to John Mearsheimer and Lloyd Gruber for their helpful comments on this material.

19. José Casanova, *Public Religions in the Modern World* (Chicago: University of Chicago Press, 1994), p. 17.

20. Nikki Keddie, "Secularism and the State: Towards Clarity and Global Comparison," *New Left Review* 226 (November–December 1997): 32.

21. David Brooks, "Kicking the Secularist Habit: A Six-Step Program," *Atlantic Monthly* 291, no. 2 (March 2003): 27–28.

22. Saba Mahmood, *Politics of Piety: The Islamic Revival and the Feminist Subject* (Princeton: Princeton University Press, 2005), p. 17.

23. Ibid.

24. Partha Chatterjee, *The Nation and Its Fragments: Colonial and Postcolonial Histories* (Princeton: Princeton University Press, 1993), p. 13.

25. Hall, *National Collective Identity*, p. 27.

26. Like Asad, I approach traditions as "discourses that seek to instruct practitioners regarding the correct form and purpose of a given practice that, precisely because it is established, has a history." Talal Asad, "The Idea of an Anthropology of Islam," *Center for Contemporary Arab Studies Occasional Paper Series* (Washington, D.C.: Georgetown University, 1996), p. 14. See also Alasdair MacIntyre, *After Virtue*, and MacIntyre, *Whose Justice? Whose Rationality?* (London: Duckworth, 1988).

27. Casanova, *Public Religions*, p. 19.

28. Ibid., pp. 19–20.

29. Mark LeVine and Armando Salvatore, "Socio-Religious Movements and the Transformation of 'Common Sense' into a Politics of 'Common Good,' " in Armando Salvatore and Mark LeVine (Eds.), *Religion, Social Practice, and Contested Hegemonies* (New York: Palgrave Macmillan, 2005), p. 33.

30. Tamimi defines *laïcité* as "a doctrine of complete freedom from, and non-interference by, religion . . . the belief that functions previously performed by a priesthood should be transferred to the laity, especially in the judicial and educational spheres." Azzam Tamimi, "The Origins of Arab Secularism," in John L. Esposito and Azzam Tamimi (Eds.), *Islam and Secularism in the Middle East* (New York: New York University Press, 2000), p. 15.

31. The historical origins of this trajectory of secularization are diverse. Keddie emphasizes that, "while secularism is frequently traced to intellectual roots, in Locke and Mill on toleration, or Voltaire and other Enlightenment figures who attacked the Church and organized religion, it could equally be traced to Henry III, who confiscated monasteries and increased state control of the church, to enlightened despots who sponsored power over the Church, and certainly to the activities of the French Revolution, Napoleon, the new American republic, and increasingly secular European Governments." Keddie, "Secularism and the State," p. 36.

32. Peter L. Berger, *The Social Reality of Religion* (London: Allen Lane, 1973), p. 113.

33. William E. Connolly, *Why I Am Not a Secularist* (Minneapolis: University of Minnesota Press, 1999), p. 24.

34. Ibid.

35. See Ted G. Jelen, *To Serve God and Mammon: Church-State Relations in American Politics* (Boulder: Westview Press, 2000).

36. Richard Price and Christian Reus-Smit, "Dangerous Liaisons? Critical International Relations Theory and Constructivism," *European Journal of International Relations* 4, no. 3 (September 1998): 274–75.

37. Mlada Bukovansky, *Legitimacy and Power Politics: The American and French Revolutions in International Political Culture* (Princeton: Princeton University Press, 2002), p. 59.

38. Ibid. As to whether actors can be considered strategic, I agree with MacIntyre's argument (*After Virtue*, p. 222) that "all reasoning takes place within the context of some traditional mode of thought, transcending through criticism and invention the limitations of what had hitherto been reasoned in that tradition; this is as true of modern physics as of medieval logic."

39. Nilüfer Göle, "Islam in Public: New Visibilities and New Imaginaries," *Public Culture* 14, no. 1 (2002): 183.

40. Asad, "The Idea of an Anthropology of Islam," p. 11.

41. Thanks to Michael Loriaux for his suggestions on this passage.

42. Roxanne L. Euben, *Enemy in the Mirror: Islamic Fundamentalism and the Limits of Modern Rationalism* (Princeton: Princeton University Press, 1999), p. xiv.

43. Melani McAlister, *Epic Encounters: Culture, Media and U.S. Interests in the Middle East, 1945–2000* (Berkeley: University of California Press, 2001).

44. See Casanova, *Public Religions*.

45. Ibid., p. 13.

46. John Keane, "Secularism?" in David Marquand and Ronald L. Nettler (Eds.), *Religion and Democracy* (Oxford: Blackwell, 2000), p. 6.

47. T. N. Madan, "Secularism in Its Place," *Journal of Asian Studies* 46, no. 4 (November 1987): 747.

48. Casanova, *Public Religions*, p. 13.

49. Madan, "Secularism in Its Place," p. 748.

50. Tamimi, "Origins of Arab Secularism," p. 14.

51. Madan, "Secularism in Its Place," p. 748.

52. Ibid.

53. Keane, "Secularism?" p. 7.

54. William E. Connolly, *The Ethos of Pluralization* (Minneapolis: University of Minnesota Press, 1995), p. 189.

55. Mahmood, *Politics of Piety*, p. 191.

56. Casanova defines it as a "process of functional differentiation and emancipation of the secular spheres—primarily the state, the economy, and science—from the religious sphere and the concomitant differentiation and specialization of religion within its own newly found religious sphere." *Public Religions*, p. 19. For an interesting, if ultimately unconvincing, attempt to refute secularization theory empirically by arguing that the "golden age of Faith" (in contrast to the age of secularization) actually never existed, see Rodney Stark, "Secularization, R.I.P.," *Sociology of Religion* 60, no. 3 (Fall 1999): 249–73.

57. Charles Taylor, *Modern Social Imaginaries* (Durham, N.C.: Duke University Press, 2004).

58. As Wallis and Bruce argue, "the secularization thesis asserts that modernization . . . brings in its wake (and may itself be accelerated by) 'the diminution of the social significance of religion.' " Roy Wallis and Steve Bruce, "Secularization: The Orthodox Model," in Bruce (Ed.), *Religion and Modernization: Sociologists and Historians Debate the Secularization Thesis* (New York: Oxford University Press, 1992), p. 11.

59. Michael Hunt, *Ideology and U.S. Foreign Policy* (New Haven: Yale University Press, 1987), p. xi. "Suppose," Hunt suggests (p. 3), "that ideology is central, not incidental, to policymaking."

60. Ibid., p. xi. Hunt bases his approach on Geertz's work on ideologies as "integrated and coherent systems of symbols, values and beliefs" and then expands upon this to describe them as resulting from "cultural impulses" that sometimes become institutionalized and other times survive as forms of "folk wisdom." Ibid., pp. 12–13.

61. Bukovansky, *Legitimacy and Power Politics*, p. 2. Berger and Luckman define culture as "an all-embracing socially constructed world of subjectively experienced meanings." Peter L. Berger and Thomas Luckman, *The Social Construction of Reality* (New York: Doubleday, 1966), p. 118.

62. On the concept of legitimacy in international relations, see Ian Hurd, *After Anarchy: Legitimacy and Power in the United Nations* (Princeton: Princeton University, 2007), ch. 2.

63. Fred Halliday, *The Middle East in International Relations: Power, Politics and Ideology* (New York: Cambridge University Press, 2005), p. 221. On forms of politics that operate on the unconscious level, see Benedict Anderson, *Imagined Communities* (London: Verso, 1983), pp. 182–83.

64. Bukovansky, *Legitimacy and Power Politics*, p. 231.

65. Benjamin I. Page and Marshall Bouton, *The Foreign Policy Disconnect: What Americans Want from Our Leaders but Don't Get* (Chicago: University of Chicago Press, 2006), p. 236. On purposive belief systems, see also pp. 28–32. Thanks to Ben Page for making his proofs available.

66. Ibid., p. 236.

67. Ibid., p. 233 (emphasis in original).

68. Ibid., p. 30 (emphasis in original).

69. Bernard Cohen, *The Political Process and Foreign Policy: The Making of the Japanese Peace Settlement* (Princeton: Princeton University Press, 1957), p. 29.

70. V. O. Key, *Public Opinion and American Democracy* (New York: Alfred A. Knopf, 1961), p. 423.

71. Craig Calhoun, *Nationalism* (Minneapolis: University of Minnesota Press, 1997), p. 76.

72. John Shotter, *The Cultural Politics of Everyday Life* (Toronto: University of Toronto Press, 1993), p. 200.

73. Umut Özkırımlı, *Theories of Nationalism: A Critical Introduction* (New York: Palgrave, 2000), p. 233.

74. Judith Butler, "Universality in Culture," in Martha C. Nussbaum, *For Love of Country?: Debating the Limits of Patriotism*, ed. Joshua Cohen (Boston: Beacon Press, 1996), p. 47.

75. Dipesh Chakrabarty, *Provincializing Europe: Postcolonial Thought and Historical Difference* (Princeton: Princeton University Press, 2000), p. 4 (emphasis in original).

76. Calhoun, *Nationalism*, p. 107.

77. Madan, "Secularism in Its Place," p. 755. On India, see Gary C. Jacobsohn, *The Wheel of Law: India's Secularism in Comparative Constitutional Context* (Princeton: Princeton University Press, 2005), and Ashis Nandy, *Time Warps: Silent and Evasive Pacts in Indian Politics and Religion* (New Brunswick, N.J.: Rutgers University Press, 2002).

78. Halliday, *The Middle East in International Relations*, p. 88. See also Keddie, "Secularism and the State."

79. Tamimi, "Origins of Arab Secularism," p. 13. As Tamimi notes (p. 17), "the meaning of *ʿilmaniyah* or *ʿalamaniyah* in the Arabic literature is no less varied and confused than it is in the Western literature. In his four-volume encyclopedia on secularism, Elmessiri lists eighteen different definitions of 'secularism' collected from modern Arabic literature." The volume referred to is Elmessiri's *Tafkik al-Khitab al-ʿIlmani* (Deconstructing Secular Discourse), a four-volume encyclopedia in Arabic. For a survey of Arab secularist thought, see Nazik Saba Yared, *Secularism and the Arab World: 1850–1939* (London: Saqi, 2002).

80. Juergensmeyer cites as examples Hans Kohn, Rupert Emerson, and nationalist leaders such as Nasser and Nehru. Mark Juergensmeyer, *The New Cold War? Religious Nationalism Confronts the Secular State* (Berkeley: University of California Press, 1993), pp. 27, 15.

81. Casanova, *Public Religions*, p. 17.

82. Ludwig Wittgenstein, *On Certainty*, ed. Anscombe and von Wright (New York: Harper & Row, 1972), § 211, cited in Linda M. G. Zerilli, "Doing without Knowing: Feminism's Politics of the Ordinary," *Political Theory* 26, no. 4 (August 1998): 436.

83. Hunt, *Ideology and U.S. Foreign Policy*, p. 13. On the interesting distinction between interpretations of history that are "felt" as opposed to "intellected," see Anderson, *Imagined Communities*, p. 144.

84. I adopt Asad's definition of an authoritative discourse as a "a materially founded discourse which seeks continually to pre-empt the space of radically opposed utterances

and so to prevent them from being uttered." Talal Asad, "Anthropology and the Analysis of Ideology," *Man* 14, no. 4. (1979): 621. See also Hubert L. Dreyfus and Paul Rabinow, *Michel Foucault: Beyond Structuralism and Hermeneutics* (Chicago: University of Chicago Press, 1983), p. 77, and Michel Foucault, *The Archaeology of Knowledge* (New York: Pantheon, 1972), p. 157.

85. Calhoun, *Nationalism*, p. 34.

86. See Hunt, *Ideology and U.S. Foreign Policy*, p. 13.

87. Mahmood, *Politics of Piety*, p. 77.

88. Edward Said, *Orientalism* (New York: Random House, 1987), p. 12.

89. Asad, "Anthropology and the Analysis of Ideology," p. 623.

90. Elizabeth Shakman Hurd, "The Political Authority of Secularism in International Relations," *European Journal of International Relations* 10, no. 2 (June 2004): 235–62.

91. Hunt, *Ideology and U.S. Foreign Policy*, p. 14.

92. Talal Asad, *Genealogies of Religion: Discipline and Reasons of Power in Christianity and Islam* (Baltimore: Johns Hopkins University Press, 1993), p. 29.

93. See Jacques Derrida, "Faith and Knowledge: The Two Sources of 'Religion' at the Limits of Reason Alone," in Jacques Derrida and Gianni Vattimo (Eds.), *Religion* (Stanford: Stanford University Press, 1998), pp. 1–78, and Richard King, *Orientalism and Religion: Postcolonial Theory, India and "the Mystic East"* (London: Routledge, 1999).

94. Bonnie Honig, *Political Theory and the Displacement of Politics* (Ithaca: Cornell University Press, 1993).

95. William E. Connolly, *Pluralism* (Durham: Duke University Press, 2005), p. 79.

96. Thanks to Bonnie Honig for her helpful suggestions on this passage.

97. Connolly, *Ethos*, p. 5; see in particular chapter 1, "Nothing Is Fundamental."

98. Alexander Wendt, *Social Theory of International Politics* (Cambridge: Cambridge University Press, 1999), p. 22.

99. This approach is drawn from Connolly's "bicameral" approach to citizenship, which "requires a tolerance of ambiguity in politics . . . there is, first, the faith, creed, or philosophy that you adopt as an engaged partisan in the world . . . there is, second, the engrained sense that you should exercise presumptive receptivity toward others when drawing that faith, creed, or philosophy into the public realm." Connolly, *Pluralism*, p. 4.

100. I am grateful to Bill Connolly for this formulation.

101. Connolly, *Ethos*, p. 9.

102. Ibid. One result is that "each time the results of a new analysis of itself are brought back to the subject it is moved; it never reaches the solid ground it seeks to stand upon. This pursuit itself has become irreducible. The subject ('man') is haunted by an indispensable and unconquerable double—an immense expanse of shade—that repeatedly compromises its sovereignty, transparency, freedom, and wholeness" (p. 11).

103. Barnett and Duvall, "Power in International Politics," p. 46.

104. Stephen K. White, *Sustaining Affirmation: The Strengths of Weak Ontology in Political Theory* (Princeton: Princeton University Press, 2000).

105. Connolly, *Ethos*, p. 27.

106. Ibid., p. 29.

107. Connolly, *Pluralism*, pp. 4, 7. Other operative faiths include Marxism, Christianity, Islam, Kantianism, Rawlsianism, neoconservativism, and pragmatism.

108. John Fulton, "Religion and Politics in Gramsci: An Introduction," *Sociological Analysis* 48, no. 3 (1987): 201, cited in Salvatore and LeVine, "Socio-Religious Movements and the Transformation of 'Common Sense,' " pp. 36–42. This may be compared and contrasted with Plantinga's understanding of faith as "belief in the great things of the gospel that results from the internal instigation of the Holy Spirit." Alvin Plantinga, *Warranted Christian Belief* (New York: Oxford, 2000), p. 252.

109. King, *Orientalism and Religion*, pp. 198–99.

110. It is unlikely that we possess the resources to resolve this contest definitively, because "no perspective has at its disposal a consensual, pastoral, or transcendental strategy capable of reducing competitors in this domain to a small set of friendly alternatives." Connolly, *Ethos*, p. 16.

111. Epicurus, "On Terrestrial and Celestial Phenomena: Letter to Pythocles," in John Gaskin (Ed.), *The Epicurean Philosophers* (London: J. M. Dent, 1995), p. 34.

112. Jaroslav Pelikan, radio interview with Krista Tippett, *Speaking of Faith*," May 21, 2006 (transcript available at http://speakingoffaith.publicradio.org/programs/pelikan/transcript.shtml). See also Pelikan's *Credo: Historical and Theological Guide to Creeds and Confessions of Faith in the Christian Tradition* (New Haven: Yale University Press, 2005) and John Courtney Murray's classic text *We Hold These Truths: Catholic Reflections on the American Proposition* (New York: Rowman & Littlefield, 2005). For different approaches to the epistemological status of Christian belief, see Plantinga, *Warranted Christian Belief*, and John Milbank, *Theology and Social Theory: Beyond Secular Reason* (Oxford: Blackwell, 1993); for a historicist approach to Christian theology, see Sheila Davaney, *Pragmatic Historicism: A Theology for the Twenty-First Century* (Albany: State University of New York Press, 2000).

113. Douglas V. Porpora, "Methodological Atheism, Methodological Agnosticism and Religious Experience," *Journal for the Theory of Social Behaviour* 36, no. 1 (March 2006): 60. Thanks to Alex Wendt for this reference. On the necessity of bracketing "metahuman explanations" to achieve a position of (alleged) ontological neutrality, see Peter L. Berger, *The Heretical Imperative: Contemporary Possibilities of Religious Affirmation* (Garden City, N.Y.: Anchor, 1979), p. 36.

114. Porpora, "Methodological Atheism," p. 58. For Berger's classic articulation of methodological atheism, see *The Sacred Canopy: Elements of a Sociological Theory of Religion* (New York: Doubleday, 1967), p. 100.

115. Theologian Gordon Kaufman adopts this distinction when he argues that "the central problem of theological discourse, not shared with any other 'language game' is the meaning of the term 'God.' 'God' raises special problems of meaning because it is a noun which by definition refers to a reality transcendent of, and thus not locatable within, experience." Gordon Kaufman, *God the Problem* (Cambridge, Mass.: Harvard University Press, 1972), p. 8, cited in Plantinga, *Warranted Christian Belief*, p. 4.

116. On the supermundane, see Andrew Greeley, *Ecstasy: A Way of Knowing* (Englewood Cliffs, N.J.: Prentice-Hall, 1974).

117. Porpora, "Methodological Atheism," p. 70. I do not share Porpora's relatively rigid construction of the noumenal-phenomenal divide that propels his argument forward through much of his paper. This rigidity is surprising, given the skeptical

undertones of his argument, and softens in interesting and provocative ways in the concluding section.

118. Connolly, *Why I Am Not a Secularist*, p. 41.

119. Porpora, "Methodological Atheism," p. 70.

120. On Deleuze's transcendental empiricism, see Gilles Deleuze, *Difference and Repetition*, trans. Paul Patton (New York: Columbia University Press, 1994), ch. 3 "The Image of Thought," pp. 129–67; Gilles Deleuze and Félix Guattari, *What Is Philosophy?* (New York: Columbia University Press, 1994), pp. 35–60; Connolly, *Why I Am Not a Secularist*, ch. 1; and the essays in Paul Patton (Ed.) *Deleuze: A Critical Reader* (Oxford: Blackwell, 1996).

121. William E. Connolly, "Europe: A Minor Tradition," in Scott and Hirschkind, *Powers of the Secular Modern*, p. 83.

122. Ibid., p. 87. Stuart Hampshire, *Freedom of Mind, and Other Essays* (Princeton: Princeton University Press, 1971); Antonio Damasio, *Looking for Spinoza: Joy, Sorrow, and the Feeling Brain* (New York: Harcourt, 2003); and Antonio Damasio, *Descartes' Error: Emotion, Reason, and the Human Brain* (New York: G. P. Putnam, 1994).

123. See Brian Massumi, "The Autonomy of Affect," *Cultural Critique* 31 (Autumn 1995): 83–109.

124. Ibid., p. 94. As Artaud observed, "it is through the skin that metaphysics will be made to reenter our minds." Antonin Artaud, "The Theater of Cruelty: First Manifesto," in Susan Sontag (Ed.), *Antonin Artaud: Selected Writings* (Berkeley: University of California Press, 1988), p. 251.

125. Talal Asad, *Formations of the Secular: Christianity, Islam, Modernity* (Stanford: Stanford University Press, 2003), p. 55.

126. Porpora, "Methodological Atheism," p. 73.

127. The infrasensible is "a virtual field made up of elements too small to be perceptible and/or too fast to be actual, [that] insists below and within culturally organized registers of sensibility, appearance, discourse, justice, and identity." Connolly, *Why I Am Not a Secularist*, p. 40.

128. "When constructivists draw general conclusions about norm formation, maintenance and change the factors they focus upon are not treated as context-free independent variables that may be transferred unproblematically to any and all situations to produce a necessary outcome. Constructivists do offer analytics that travel, but systematic conclusions at the level of abstraction and in the form of causal determinism demanded by the most insistent proponents of the positivist legacy are not forthcoming from constructivism." Price and Reus-Smit, "Dangerous Liaisons?" pp. 274–75.

129. Barnett and Duvall, "Power in International Politics," p. 55.

130. Michael Barnett, "Social Constructivism," in John Baylis and Steve Smith (Eds.), *The Globalization of World Politics: An Introduction to International Relations*, 3rd ed. (Oxford: Oxford University Press, 2005), p. 253.

131. Wendt, *Social Theory*.

132. Barnett and Duvall, "Power in International Politics," p. 55 (emphasis added).

133. Connolly, *Pluralism*, p. 70.

134. Jane Bennett, *The Enchantment of Modern Life: Attachments, Crossings, and Ethics* (Princeton: Princeton University Press, 2001), p. 15. As Bennett argues (pp. 160–61), "What distinguishes a weak ontologist from a traditional metaphysician is

that the former emphasizes the necessarily speculative and contestable character of her onto-story and thus does not try to demonstrate its truth in any strong sense."

135. Alev Çinar, *Modernity, Islam, and Secularism in Turkey* (Minneapolis: University of Minnesota Press, 2005), p. 9.

136. Scott and Hirschkind, "The Anthropological Skepticism of Talal Asad," p. 10.

137. Wilfred M. McClay, "The Soul of a Nation," *Public Interest* 155 (Spring 2004): 7.

CHAPTER TWO
VARIETIES OF SECULARISM

1. See, for example, David Yamane, "Secularization on Trial: In Defense of a Neo-secularization Paradigm," *Journal for the Scientific Study of Religion* 36, no. 1 (March 1997): 109–22; Steve Bruce (Ed.), *Religion and Modernization: Sociologists and Historians Debate the Secularization Thesis* (Oxford: Oxford University Press, 2001); Max Weber, *The Sociology of Religion*, trans. Ephraim Fischoff (Boston: Beacon Press, 1993); José Casanova, *Public Religions in the Modern World* (Chicago: University of Chicago Press, 1994); Malcolm B. Hamilton, *The Sociology of Religion: Theoretical and Comparative Perspectives* (London: Routledge, 1995); Phillip Hammond (Ed.), *The Sacred in a Secular Age* (Berkeley: University of California Press, 1985); Bryan Wilson, *Religion in Sociological Perspective* (Oxford: Oxford University Press, 1982); Mark Chaves, "Secularization as Declining Religious Authority," *Social Forces* 72 (1994): 749–74; Olivier Tschannen, "The Secularization Paradigm: A Systematization," *Journal for the Scientific Study of Religion* 30 (1991): 395–415; and the special issue of the journal *Sociology of Religion* 60, no. 3 (1999).

2. See Hannah Arendt, *The Human Condition* (Chicago: University of Chicago Press, 1958), and Arendt, *On Revolution* (New York: Viking, 1963); Jürgen Habermas, *Structural Transformation of the Public Sphere* (Cambridge, Mass.: MIT Press, 1989), and Habermas, *Postmetaphysical Thinking*, trans. William M. Hohengarten (Cambridge, Mass.: MIT Press, 1992); Seyla Benhabib, "Models of Public Space: Hannah Arendt, the Liberal Tradition and Jürgen Habermas," in Craig Calhoun (Ed.), *Habermas and the Public Sphere* (Cambridge, Mass.: MIT Press, 1991), pp. 73–98; Alasdair MacIntyre, *After Virtue: A Study in Moral Theory* (Notre Dame: University of Notre Dame Press, 1984); and William E. Connolly, *Why I Am Not a Secularist* (Minneapolis: University of Minnesota Press, 1999).

3. Christine Sylvester, *Feminist Theory and International Relations in a Post-Modern Era* (Cambridge: Cambridge University Press, 1994), p. 9.

4. There are dissenters. On religious movements and conflict resolution, see R. Scott Appleby, *The Ambivalence of the Sacred: Religion, Violence, and Reconciliation* (Lanham, Md.: Rowman & Littlefield, 2000). On religion and international relations, see Jonathan Fox, "Religion as an Overlooked Element of International Relations," *International Studies Review* 3, no. 3 (Fall 2001): 53–73; the special issue of *Millennium: Journal of International Studies* 29, no. 3 (2000); and Barry Rubin, "Religion and International Affairs," *Washington Quarterly* 13, no. 2 (1990): 51–64. On the Protestant Reformation and the modern state system, see Daniel Philpott, *Revolutions in Sovereignty: How Ideas Shaped Modern International Relations* (Princeton: Prince-

ton University Press, 2001), and Philpott, "The Religious Roots of Modern International Relations," *World Politics* 52 (2000): 206–45. On the rise of religious violence, see Mark Juergensmeyer, *Terror in the Mind of God: The Global Rise of Religious Violence* (Berkeley: University of California Press, 2001).

5. Michael Barnett and Raymond Duvall, "Power in International Politics," *International Organization* 59 (Winter 2005): 41.

6. José Casanova, "A Reply to Talal Asad," in David Scott and Charles Hirschkind (Eds.), *Powers of the Secular Modern: Talal Asad and His Interlocutors* (Stanford: Stanford University Press, 2006), p. 23.

7. Thanks to Bonnie Honig for suggesting this phrase.

8. Charles Taylor, "Modes of Secularism," in Rajeev Bhargava (Ed.), *Secularism and Its Critics* (Oxford: Oxford University Press, 1998), pp. 33–36.

9. Ibid., p. 38.

10. Casanova, *Public Religions*, p. 216.

11. Talal Asad, *Formations of the Secular: Christianity, Islam, Modernity* (Stanford: Stanford University Press, 2003), p. 2.

12. On the prestructuration of discourse, see Hayden White, *The Content of the Form* (Baltimore: Johns Hopkins University Press, 1989).

13. Barnett and Duvall, "Power in International Politics," p. 48.

14. See the discussion in chapter 1, p. 3.

15. Connolly, *Why I Am Not a Secularist*, p. 33.

16. On these contributions, see Andrew Hurrell, "Kant and the Kantian Paradigm in International Relations," *Review of International Studies* 16 (1990): 183–205.

17. Connolly, *Why I Am Not a Secularist*, p. 30. See Immanuel Kant, *The Conflict of the Faculties*, trans. Mary J. Gregor (Lincoln: University of Nebraska Press, 1979).

18. Connolly, *Why I Am Not a Secularist*, p. 30.

19. Ibid., p. 31.

20. Ibid.

21. "Morality as law now itself becomes anchored only in the 'apodictic' recognition by ordinary human beings of its binding authority." Ibid., p. 31.

22. Ibid., p. 32.

23. "His obsequious deference to the prince, his explicit dependence on the supersensible, his hope that a natural teleology of public life will promote rationality in the public sphere by automatic means, and his hesitancy to include most subjects within the realm of public discourse render him a forerunner rather than a partisan of secularism." Ibid., p. 33.

24. Ibid., p. 32 (emphasis in original).

25. Ibid., p. 26.

26. Ibid., p. 5.

27. Ibid., p. 22.

28. William E. Connolly, *The Ethos of Pluralization* (Minneapolis: University of Minnesota Press, 1995), p. 189.

29. Immanuel Kant, *Perpetual Peace, and Other Essays on Politics, History, and Morals*, trans. Ted Humphrey (Indianapolis: Hackett, 1983).

30. David Held, *Democracy and the Global Order: From the Modern State to Cosmopolitan Governance* (Stanford: Stanford University Press, 1995); Martha C. Nussbaum, *For Love of Country?: Debating the Limits of Patriotism*, ed. Joshua Cohen

(Boston: Beacon Press, 1996); and Francis Fukuyama, "The End of History?" *National Interest* 16 (1989): 3–18.

31. Connolly, *Ethos*, p. 181.

32. William E. Connolly, "Europe: A Minor Tradition," in Scott and Hirschkind, *Powers of the Secular Modern*, p. 80.

33. Connolly, *Why I Am Not a Secularist*, p. 33.

34. See Carl Schmitt, *Political Theology: Four Chapters on the Concept of Sovereignty*, trans. George Schwab (Cambridge, Mass.: MIT Press, 1985); Karl Löwith, *Meaning in History* (Chicago: University of Chicago Press, 1949); and Hans Blumenberg, *The Legitimacy of the Modern Age*, trans. Robert M. Wallace (Cambridge, Mass.: MIT Press, 1986).

35. John Milbank, *Theology and Social Theory: Beyond Secular Reason* (Oxford: Blackwell, 1993), p. 1.

36. Mark Juergensmeyer, *The New Cold War? Religious Nationalism Confronts the Secular State* (Berkeley: University of California Press, 1993), p. 16. See Arend Theodor van Leeuwen, *Christianity in World History: The Meeting of the Faiths of East and West*, trans. H. H. Hoskins (New York: Scribner's, 1964).

37. Juergensmeyer, *The New Cold War?* p. 17.

38. Ibid., pp. 17–18.

39. Ibid., p. 18.

40. Ibid., p. 197. On Juergensmeyer, see Elizabeth Shakman Hurd, "The International Politics of Secularism: U.S. Foreign Policy and the Islamic Republic of Iran," *Alternatives: Global, Local, Political* 29, no. 2 (March–May 2004): 115–38.

41. On my approach to social construction, see chapter 1, pp. 16–20.

42. On this fascinating alternative challenge to established religion, see Benedict de Spinoza, *Ethics*, trans. Edwin Curley (New York: Penguin, 2005). On the contrast between Spinoza's "freedom to philosophize" and the liberal "freedom of conscience," see Jonathan I. Israel, "Spinoza, Locke and the Enlightenment Battle for Toleration," in Ole Peter Grell and Roy Porter (Eds.), *Toleration in Enlightenment Europe* (Cambridge: Cambridge University Press, 1999), pp. 102–13, and Miguel Vatter, "Strauss and Schmitt as Readers of Hobbes and Spinoza: On the Relation between Political Theology and Liberalism," *New Centennial Review* 4 (Winter 2004): 161–214.

43. For a different attempt to negotiate the demands of Christian faith and public life, see Hobbes's *Leviathan*, in which according to Taylor the "independent ethic reigns supreme." Taylor, "Modes of Secularism," p. 34. For a different reading of Hobbes, see Cavanaugh, who suggests that "in Hobbes it is not so much that the Church has been subordinated to the civil power; Leviathan has rather swallowed the Church whole into its yawning maw. . . . The body of Christ is thereby severely nominalized, scattered and absorbed into the body of the State." William T. Cavanaugh, "A Fire Strong Enough to Consume the House: The Wars of Religion and the Rise of the State," *Modern Theology* 11, no. 4 (October 1995): 406.

44. Harvey Cox, *The Secular City* (New York: Macmillan, 1965), p. 4.

45. Michael Hardt and Antonio Negri, *Empire* (Cambridge, Mass.: Harvard University Press, 2000), cited in William E. Connolly, *Pluralism* (Durham, N.C.: Duke University Press, 2005), p. 150.

46. John L. Esposito, *The Islamic Threat: Myth or Reality?* 2nd ed. (New York: Oxford University Press, 1992), p. 200. Daniel Lerner's *The Passing of Traditional Soci-*

ety: Modernizing the Middle East (New York: Macmillan, 1958) is the classic example. For a challenge to modernization and development theory, see James Ferguson, *The Anti-Politics Machine: "Development," Depoliticization, and Bureaucratic Power in Lesotho,* 4th ed. (Minneapolis: University of Minnesota Press, 1997).

47. John L. Esposito, "Islam and Secularism in the Twenty-First Century," in John L. Esposito and Azzam Tamini (Eds.), *Islam and Secularism in the Middle East* (New York: New York University Press, 2000), p. 9.

48. I thank Peter Berger for encouraging me to consider these different dimensions of secularization.

49. Partha Chatterjee, "The Politics of Secularization in Contemporary India," in Scott and Hirschkind, *Powers of the Secular Modern,* p. 60.

50. Casanova, *Public Religions,* p. 215.

51. Taylor, "Modes of Secularism," p. 33.

52. Ibid., pp. 33–34.

53. Ibid., p. 35.

54. Asad, *Formations of the Secular,* p. 191.

55. Peter van der Veer and Hartmut Lehmann, introduction to *Nation and Religion: Perspectives on Europe and Asia* (Princeton: Princeton University Press, 1999), p. 10.

56. Richard King, *Orientalism and Religion: Postcolonial Theory, India and "the Mystic East"* (London: Routledge, 1999), p. 11. In 1951 Adiver described Western positivism as "the official dogma of irreligion." Advan Adiver, "Interaction of Islamic and Western Thought in Turkey," in T. C. Young (Ed.), *Near Eastern Culture and Society* (Princeton: Princeton University Press, 1951), p. 126, cited in Esposito, *Islam and Secularism in the Middle East,* p. 7.

57. Thomas argues that this applies to the English School as well, in which "questions about war and religion, and the formation of practices and religious traditions in international relations, are unfortunately ignored." Scott M. Thomas, "Faith, History and Martin Wight: The Role of Religion in the Historical Sociology of the English School of International Relations," *International Affairs* 77, no. 4 (2001): 926.

58. Peter Katzenstein, "Multiple Modernities and Secular Europeanization?" in Peter Katzenstein and Timothy Byrnes (Eds.), *Religion in an Expanding Europe* (Cambridge: Cambridge University Press, 2006), p. 31.

59. Scott M. Thomas, *The Global Resurgence of Religion and the Transformation of International Relations: The Struggle for the Soul of the Twenty-First Century* (New York: Palgrave Macmillan, 2005), p. 33.

60. On the emergence of the Westphalian settlement and potential alternatives to it, see Hendrik Spruyt, *The Sovereign State and Its Competitors* (Princeton: Princeton University Press, 1994).

61. Quentin Skinner, *The Foundations of Modern Political Thought,* vol. 2 (Cambridge: Cambridge University Press, 1978), p. 353.

62. Alessandro Pizzorno, "Politics Unbound," in Charles S. Maier (Ed.), *Changing Boundaries of the Political: Essays on the Evolving Balance between the State and Society, Public and Private in Europe* (Cambridge: Cambridge University Press, 1987), p. 34. Thanks to Hendrik Spruyt for this reference.

63. Daniel Philpott, *Revolutions in Sovereignty: How Ideas Shaped Modern International Relations* (Princeton: Princeton University Press, 2001).

64. Stephen D. Krasner, "Westphalia and All That," in Judith Goldstein and Robert Keohane (Eds.), *Ideas and Foreign Policy: Beliefs, Institutions and Political Change* (Ithaca: Cornell University Press, 1993), p. 238.

65. Stephen D. Krasner, "Sovereignty," *Foreign Policy*, January–February 2001, p. 21. On the violation of state autonomy embedded within the Westphalian settlement through provisions enforcing religious toleration that undermined the principle of *cuius regio, eius religio*, see Stephen D. Krasner, *Sovereignty: Organized Hypocrisy* (Princeton: Princeton University Press, 1999), pp. 77–84.

66. Cavanaugh, "A Fire Strong Enough to Consume the House," pp. 398–400.

67. Craig Calhoun, *Nationalism* (Minneapolis: University of Minnesota, 1997), p. 70.

68. For a discussion of the emergence of the concept of politics as a separate activity in early modern Europe and the argument that "spiritual" or "ultimate" ends can always be found "in the pursuance of those activities to which it is today usual to assign the generic name of politics," see Pizzorno, "Politics Unbound," pp. 30–32.

69. Charles Taylor, seminar on "Secularization," Northwestern University (Spring 2003). Nexon argues similarly that "when we view Europeanization as a long historical process, we inevitably confront the creation of Europe as a community through, first, the extrusion of religious difference and, second, the management of religious schism within a broader Latin Christian community." Daniel Nexon, "Religion, European Identity, and Political Contention in Historical Perspective," in Katzenstein and Byrnes (Eds.), *Religion in an Expanding Europe*, p. 260.

70. Charles Taylor, seminar on "Secularization," Northwestern University (Spring 2003). On the argument that theological contributions underlie key components of the Westphalian settlement, including the legitimacy of private property, absolute sovereignty, and active rights, see Milbank, *Theology and Social Theory*, pp. 9–26.

71. Krasner, *Sovereignty: Organized Hypocrisy*, p. 81, citing Treaty of Osnabrück, 1648, Article VII.

72. Nexon, "Religion, European Identity, and Political Contention," p. 277.

73. Connolly, *Why I Am Not a Secularist*, p. 23.

74. Joshua Mitchell, comments presented at the Pew Forum on Religion and Public Life and the Pew Christian Scholars Program conference on "Theology, Morality, and Public Life" (University of Chicago Divinity School, February 25–27, 2003).

75. Ashis Nandy, "The Politics of Secularism and the Recovery of Religious Tolerance," in Rajeev Bhargava (Ed.), *Secularism and Its Critics* (Oxford: Oxford University Press, 1998), p. 129.

76. Richard Falk, "Religion and Politics: Verging on the Postmodern," *Alternatives* 13 (1988): 381.

77. T. N. Madan, "Secularism in Its Place," *Journal of Asian Studies* 46, no. 4 (November 1987): 754.

78. Talal Asad, *Genealogies of Religion: Discipline and Reasons of Power in Christianity and Islam* (Baltimore: Johns Hopkins University Press, 1993), p. 46.

79. On historical materialism, see Justin Rosenberg, *The Empire of Civil Society* (London: Verso, 1994), and B. K. Gills, "Historical Materialism and International Relations Theory," *Millennium* 16 (1987): 265–72; on neorealism, see Kenneth Waltz, *Man, the State and War* (New York: Columbia University Press, 1954), and Waltz's

chapter "Political Structures," in Robert Keohane (Ed.), *Neorealism and Its Critics* (New York: Columbia University Press, 1986), pp. 70–97.

80. Mlada Bukovansky, *Legitimacy and Power Politics: The American and French Revolutions in International Political Culture* (Princeton: Princeton University Press, 2002), p. 19.

81. See Friedrich V. Kratochwil, *Rules, Norms, and Decisions: On the Conditions of Practical and Legal Reasoning in International Relations and Domestic Affairs* (Cambridge: Cambridge University Press, 1989), and Alexander Wendt, *Social Theory of International Politics* (Cambridge: Cambridge University Press, 1999), chs. 1–3.

82. See Peter J. Katzenstein (Ed.), *The Culture of National Security: Norms and Identity in World Politics* (New York: Columbia University Press, 1996). For a critique, see Sujata Chakrabarti Pasic, "Culturing International Relations Theory: A Call for Extension," in Yosef Lapid and Friedrich V. Kratochwil (Eds.), *The Return of Culture and Identity in IR Theory* (Boulder: Lynne Rienner, 1996), pp. 85–104.

83. See Thomas Biersteker and Cynthia Weber (Eds.), *State Sovereignty as a Social Construct* (Cambridge: Cambridge University Press, 1996).

84. Taylor, "Modes of Secularism," p. 38.

85. Asad, *Formations of the Secular*, p. 192.

86. Pizzorno, "Politics Unbound," p. 28.

87. David Scott, "Conversion and Demonism: Colonial Christian Discourse and Religion in Sri Lanka." *Comparative Studies in Society and History* 34, no. 2 (1992): 333.

88. King, *Orientalism and Religion*, pp. 35–36.

89. In his analysis of the applications of the lexical resources associated with "religion," Derrida argues that *relegere* is from *legere*, "to harvest or gather," and is a Ciceronian tradition cited by W. Otto, J.-B. Hollmann, and Benveniste. He also points to a second etymological source of the word *religio*: *religare*, from *ligare*, "to tie or bind," and traces this tradition from Lactantius and Tertullian in Kobbert, Ernout-Meillet, and Pauly-Wissowa. Jacques Derrida, "Faith and Knowledge: The Two Sources of 'Religion' at the Limits of Reason Alone," in Jacques Derrida and Gianni Vattimo (Eds.), *Religion* (Stanford: Stanford University Press, 1998), pp. 34–35.

90. King, *Orientalism and Religion*, p. 36. The only restriction on *religio* in the Roman context was that practices were not allowed to "impinge upon acceptance of civic responsibilities."

91. Ibid., p. 36.

92. Ibid.

93. Lactantius, *Institutiones Divinae* IV.28, trans. Sister McConald (1964), 318–20, cited in King, *Orientalism and Religion*, p. 36.

94. Cavanaugh, "A Fire Strong Enough to Consume the House," p. 404.

95. King, *Orientalism and Religion*, p. 37.

96. Kant, "To Perpetual Peace: a Philosophical Sketch," in *Perpetual Peace and Other Essays*, p. 125.

97. Joseph Endelin de Joinville, "On the Religion and Manners of the People of Ceylon," *Asiatick Researches* 7 (1803): 397–444, cited in Scott, "Conversion and Demonism," p. 347.

98. King, *Orientalism and Religion*, p. 37.

99. Ibid., p. 37 (emphasis in original).

100. Cavanaugh, "A Fire Strong Enough to Consume the House," p. 411.

101. Taylor, "Modes of Secularism," pp. 36–37.

102. Ibid., For an analysis and critique of the justificatory liberal position on religious conviction in politics from a Christian perspective, see Christopher J. Eberle, *Religious Conviction in Liberal Politics* (Cambridge: Cambridge University Press, 2002).

103. Connolly, *Why I Am Not a Secularist*, p. 21.

104. Ibid.

105. Ibid., p. 23.

106. Milbank, *Theology and Social Theory*, p. 1.

107. Ibid., p. 3. Juergensmeyer alludes to this possibility in his reference to secular nationalism as "a suprareligion of its own." *The New Cold War?* p. 13.

108. Stephen K. White, *Sustaining Affirmation: The Strengths of Weak Ontology in Political Theory* (Princeton: Princeton University Press, 2000), p. 140.

109. Taylor, "Modes of Secularism," p. 37.

110. José Casanova, "Secularization Revisited: A Reply to Talal Asad," presented at a workshop on "Secularization and Religion" (Erfurt, Germany, July 2003), p. 5.

111. Casanova, *Public Religions*, p. 20.

112. Melani McAlister makes this argument with regard to gender in *Epic Encounters: Culture, Media and U.S. Interests in the Middle East, 1945–2000* (Berkeley: University of California Press, 2001), p. 232.

113. Cavanaugh, "A Fire Strong Enough to Consume the House," p. 409. Cavanaugh concludes that this liberal assumption precludes "the possibility of any truly social Christian ethic."

114. Appleby, *The Ambivalence of the Sacred*, p. 5.

115. Bonnie Honig, *Political Theory and the Displacement of Politics* (Ithaca: Cornell University Press, 1993), p. 6.

116. Roxanne L. Euben, *Enemy in the Mirror: Islamic Fundamentalism and the Limits of Modern Rationalism* (Princeton: Princeton University Press, 1999).

117. Nandy, "The Politics of Secularism," p. 335.

118. George W. Bush, "Remarks at the 20th Anniversary of the National Endowment for Democracy" (United States Chamber of Commerce, Washington, D.C., November 6, 2003).

119. George W. Bush, cited in Peter Ford, "What Place for God in Europe?" *Christian Science Monitor*, February 22, 2005 (www.csmonitor.com/2005/0222/p01s04-woeu.html).

120. Nicholas Wolterstorff, "'For the Authorities Are God's Servants': Is a Theological Account of Political Authority Viable?" comments on a paper presented at the Pew Forum on Religion and Public Life and the Pew Christian Scholars Program conference on "Theology, Morality, and Public Life" (University of Chicago Divinity School, February 25–27, 2003).

121. On the rich history of this discourse in the United States, see Anders Stephanson, *Manifest Destiny: American Expansion and the Empire of Right*, 5th ed. (New York: Hill & Wang, 2000), and Jon Meacham, *American Gospel: God, the Founding Fathers, and the Making of a Nation* (New York: Random House, 2006). For a darker picture, see Kevin Phillips, *American Theocracy: The Peril and Politics of Radical Religion, Oil, and Borrowed Money in the 21st Century* (New York: Viking, 2006).

122. For a different variation on this argument, see Rodney Stark, *The Victory of Reason: How Christianity Led to Freedom, Capitalism and Western Success* (New York: Random House, 2005).

123. Damon Linker, "Without a Doubt: A Catholic Priest, a Pious President, and the Christianizing of America," *New Republic*, April 3, 2006. On Neuhaus's philosophy, see his *Catholic Matters: Confusion, Controversy and the Splendor of Truth* (New York: Basic Books, 2006), *The Naked Public Square* (Grand Rapids, Mich.: Eerdmans, 1984), and *The Catholic Moment: The Paradox of the Church in the Postmodern World* (New York: HarperCollins, 1990). For two very different critiques, see Damon Linker, *The Theocons: Secular America under Siege* (New York: Doubleday, 2006), and Cavanaugh, "A Fire Strong Enough to Consume the House," pp. 410–12.

124. Linker, "Without a Doubt." For other examples of this tradition in American history, see this article.

125. Ted G. Jelen, *To Serve God and Mammon: Church-State Relations in American Politics* (Boulder: Westview Press, 2000), p. 11. See also Peter L. Berger, *The Sacred Canopy: Elements of a Sociological Theory of Religion* (New York: Doubleday, 1967), and Neuhaus, *The Naked Public Square*.

126. Jelen, *To Serve God and Mammon*, p. 34.

127. Casanova, "A Reply to Talal Asad," in Scott and Hirschkind, *Powers of the Secular Modern*, p. 21.

128. Frederick Mark Gedicks, "The Religious, the Secular, and the Antithetical," *Capital University Law Review* 20, no. 1 (1991): 116.

129. Ibid.

130. Ibid., pp. 117–18.

131. Ibid., p. 120.

132. Ibid., p. 121.

133. Ibid., p. 122.

134. Ibid. American Catholics in the late nineteenth century responded to Protestant bias in the schools by withdrawing from the public system and establishing parochial education. Ibid., p. 122, n. 29.

135. Alexis de Tocqueville, *Democracy in America*, trans. George Lawrence (New York: Harper & Row, 1969), p. 292.

136. Ibid., p. 123.

137. Thomas Curry, *The First Freedoms*, pp. 123–24, quoted in Gedicks, "The Religious, the Secular, and the Antithetical," p. 123, n. 30.

138. Peter van der Veer, "The Moral State: Religion, Nation, and Empire in Victorian Britain and British India," in van der Veer and Lehmann, *Nation and Religion*, p. 28.

139. On Catholicism in American public life, see John T. McGreevy, *Catholicism and American Freedom: A History* (New York: W. W. Norton, 2003).

140. Stephen L. Carter, *The Culture of Disbelief: How American Law and Politics Trivialize Religious Devotion* (New York: Doubleday, 1993), p. 86. See in particular his chapter "The 'Christian Nation' and Other Horrors."

141. See Robert Bellah's concept of American civil religion in *Beyond Belief: Essays on Religion in a Post-Traditional World* (Berkeley: University of California Press, 1991) and Juergensmeyer's argument that American nationalism blends secular nationalism

and the symbols of Christianity into a form of civil religion. Juergensmeyer, *The New Cold War?* p. 28.

142. James A. Morone, *Hellfire Nation: The Politics of Sin in American History* (New Haven: Yale University Press, 2003), p. 3.

143. Connolly, *Why I Am Not a Secularist*, p. 78.

144. Van der Veer, "The Moral State: Religion, Nation, and Empire in Victorian Britain and British India," p. 24.

145. Taylor, "Modes of Secularism."

146. Ibid., p. 33. Taylor cites Pufendorf and Locke as examples.

147. Ibid., p. 35.

148. Pizzorno, "Politics Unbound," p. 39.

149. Jelen, *To Serve God and Mammon*, p. 90. On democracy, religious pluralism and accommodationism, see Nancy Rosenblum (Ed.), *Obligations of Citizenship and Demands of Faith: Religious Accommodation in Pluralist Democracies* (Princeton: Princeton University Press, 2000).

150. Samuel P. Huntington, "Religious Persecution and Religious Relevance in Today's World," in Elliot Abrams (Ed.), *The Influence of Faith: Religious Groups and U.S. Foreign Policy* (New York: Rowman & Littlefield, 2001), p. 60. Huntington's thesis has been challenged from a range of perspectives. On the continued primacy of the state as the basic unit of analysis in international relations, see Ajami, "The Summoning," in Samuel P. Huntington (Ed.), *The Clash of Civilizations: The Debate* (New York: Foreign Affairs, 1996), p. 27. For a challenge to Huntington's portrayal of civilizations as unitary, see the responses of Binyan, Mahbubani, and Kirkpatrick to Huntington in *The Clash of Civilizations: The Debate*. On the problems with Huntington's essentialist ontology, see Patrick Thaddeus Jackson, " 'Civilization' on Trial," *Millennium: Journal of International Studies* 28, no. 1 (1999): especially 143, 152. For the argument that Huntington's book "is a construct of a sort of fundamentalism that has as its analogue exactly that type of Iranian or Sudanese fundamentalism that it sees as a bogey," see Stephan Chan, "Too Neat and Under-Thought a World Order: Huntington and Civilizations," *Millennium: Journal of International Studies*, 26, no. 1 (1997): 139. For a critique of the ethical implications of his argument, see Michael Shapiro, "Samuel Huntington's Moral Geography," *Theory and Event* 2, no. 4 (1999).

151. Samuel P. Huntington, *The Clash of Civilizations and the Remaking of World Order* (New York: Simon & Schuster, 1996), p. 70.

152. Ibid., pp. 70, 72.

153. Samuel P. Huntington, "If Not Civilizations, What?" in Huntington, *The Clash of Civilizations: The Debate*, p. 63.

154. Ibid., p. 67.

155. Huntington, *The Clash of Civilizations and the Remaking of World Order*, p. 318.

156. Huntington, "If Not Civilizations, What?" p. 62.

157. Anthony Pagden, *Lords of All the World: Ideologies of Empire in Spain, Britain and France, c. 1500–c. 1800* (New Haven: Yale University Press, 1995), p. 28.

158. Saracen is a Greek word that was synonymous with Arab in pre-Islamic times and referred to Arabic-speaking Muslims of indeterminate race in medieval times. After the twelfth century, along with other terms such as Turk and Moor, it generally came to be synonymous with Muslim. Mohja Kahf, *Western Representations of the*

Muslim Woman: From Termagant to Odalisque. (Austin: University of Texas Press, 1999), p. 181, n. 5.

159. Pagden, *Lords of All the World*, p. 28.

160. William E. Connolly, "The New Cult of Civilizational Superiority," *Theory and Event* 2, no. 4 (1999): 4.

161. Taylor, "Modes of Secularism," p. 33.

162. Neuhaus, cited in Linker, "Without a Doubt," p. 32.

163. John Keane, "Secularism?" in David Marquand and Ronald L. Nettler (Eds.), *Religion and Democracy* (Oxford: Blackwell, 2000), p. 14.

164. Bernard Lewis, "Islam and the West: A Conversation with Bernard Lewis," Pew Forum on Religion and Public Life, Luis Lugo, moderator (Washington, D.C., April 27, 2006; http://pewforum.org/events/index.php?EventID=107, accessed May 25, 2006).

165. Honig, *Political Theory*, p. 201.

166. Ibid., p. 2.

167. Ibid.

168. Michael Barnett, *Dialogues in Arab Politics: Negotiations in Regional Order* (New York: Columbia University Press, 1998), p. 250, citing Michael Williams, "Hobbes and International Relations: A Reconsideration," *International Organization* 50, no. 2 (Spring 1996): 213–37.

169. Bukovansky, *Legitimacy and Power Politics*, p. 25.

170. Talal Asad, "Responses," in Scott and Hirschkind, *Powers of the Secular Modern*, p. 219.

CHAPTER THREE
SECULARISM AND ISLAM

1. Francis Scott Key, excerpt from song written in 1805 in honor of Tripolitan war hero Decatur. Robert J. Allison, *The Crescent Obscured: The United States and the Muslim World, 1776–1815*, 2nd ed. (Chicago: University of Chicago Press, 2000), pp. 205–6.

2. Zachary Lockman, *Contending Visions of the Middle East: The History and Politics of Orientalism* (Cambridge: Cambridge University Press, 2004), p. 62. For the argument that modernity was not achieved in Europe alone but through conflicts between Europe and Islam, see Almut Höfert and Armando Salvatore (Eds.), *Between Europe and Islam: Shaping Modernity in a Transcultural Space* (New York: Peter Lang, 2000). For a renarration of history that develops the idea of "Islamo-Christian" civilization while rejecting the concept of "Judeo-Christian" civilization, see Richard W. Bulliet, *The Case for Islamo-Christian Civilization* (New York: Columbia University Press, 2004).

3. Naeem Inayatullah and David L. Blaney, "Knowing Encounters: Beyond Parochialism in International Relations Theory," in Yosef Lapid and Friedrich Kratochwil (Eds.), *The Return of Culture and Identity in IR Theory* (Boulder: Lynne Rienner, 1996), p. 82. See also Iver B. Neumann, *Uses of the Other: "The East" in European Identity Formation* (Minneapolis: University of Minnesota Press, 1998).

4. Alexander Wendt, *Social Theory of International Politics* (Cambridge: Cambridge University Press), p. 22.

5. This chapter deals with *representations* of Islam rather than actual Islamic beliefs or practices.

6. Rodney Bruce Hall, *National Collective Identity: Social Constructs and International Systems* (New York: Columbia University Press, 1999), p. 67.

7. See chapter 2.

8. Joseph S. Nye Jr., *The Paradox of American Power: Why the World's Only Superpower Can't Go It Alone* (Oxford: Oxford University Press, 2002), and Joseph S. Nye Jr., *Bound to Lead: The Changing Nature of American Power* (New York: Basic Books, 1990).

9. Joseph S. Nye Jr., "Soft Power: The Means to Success in World Politics" (Carnegie Council Books for Breakfast, New York: April 13, 2004; transcript available at http://www.cceia.org/viewMedia.php/prmTemplateID/8/prmID/4466, accessed May 8, 2006).

10. Samir Khalaf, "American Missionaries in the Levant: Precursors to Soft Power and High Culture," paper presented at the "Globalizing American Studies" conference (Northwestern University, Evanston, Illinois, May 5, 2006).

11. See Steve Brouwer, Paul Gifford, and Susan Rose, *Exporting the American Gospel: Global Christian Fundamentalism* (New York: Routledge, 1996).

12. Halliday, for instance, suggests that "the modern identities of the major western European powers—Britain, France, Germany—were formed in conflict with each other and through endogenous state and economic growth." Fred Halliday, *The Middle East in International Relations: Power, Politics and Ideology* (New York: Cambridge University Press, 2005), pp. 77–78; and Rich argues that "European identity has really been characterized by the emergence of a disparate and rather amorphous series of different identities that have been formed in a variety of contexts and historical situations." Paul Rich, "European Identity and the Myth of Islam: A Reassessment," *Review of International Studies* 25 (1999): 451.

13. I thank Paul Silverstein for pointing this out to me. On Protestantism and secularism, see the discussion in chapter 2.

14. Brian Edwards, *Morocco Bound: Disorienting America's Maghreb, from Casablanca to the Marrakech Express* (Durham, N.C.: Duke University Press, 2005), pp. 9, 18.

15. Ibid., p. 101.

16. Ibid., pp. 78, 82. "That Patton took time at all to describe the cultural forms of the land that he briefly administered and saw himself as the American heir to Marco Polo helps us to identify the intertwined nature of representations of Maghrebi people and culture and the military and diplomatic objectives of the North African campaign" (p. 32).

17. Mary Ann Heiss, "Real Men Don't Wear Pajamas: Anglo-American Cultural Perceptions of Mohammed Mossadeq and the Iranian Oil Nationalization Dispute," in Peter L. Hahn and Mary Ann Heiss (Eds.), *Empire and Revolution: The United States and the Third World since 1945* (Columbus: Ohio State University Press, 2001), pp. 178–94. On parallels between the 1953 coup and the 2003 American invasion of Iraq, see Elizabeth Shakman Hurd, "Chain Reactions: U.S. and Britain Got What

They Wanted in Iran in 1953, but Where Did It Lead?" *Chicago Tribune*, March 9, 2003.

18. Heiss, "Real Men Don't Wear Pajamas," pp. 189–90.

19. Both the "West" and the "Middle East" are contested, evolving, and relational political constructs. Originating with Latin Christendom, the West evolved to include the European West and its settler colonies and in the twentieth century became a proxy for the developed world. See further Martin Lewis and Karen Wigen, *The Myth of Continents: A Critique of Metageography* (Berkeley: University of California Press, 1997), and Maria Rosa Menocal, *The Arabic Role in Medieval Literature: A Forgotten Heritage* (Philadelphia: University of Pennsylvania Press, 1987). Lockman argues that "calling this region the Middle East obviously manifests a Eurocentric perspective: it is 'middle' and 'eastern' only in relation to western Europe." Lockman, *Contending Visions*, p. 98.

20. Homi K. Bhabha, *The Location of Culture* (London: Routledge, 2002), p. 2.

21. Umut Özkırımlı, *Theories of Nationalism: A Critical Introduction* (New York: Palgrave, 2000), p. 217.

22. Michael Dillon, "The Scandal of the Refugee: Some Reflections on the 'Inter' of International Relations and Continental Thought," in David Campbell and Michael J. Shapiro (Eds.), *Moral Spaces: Rethinking Ethics and World Politics* (Minneapolis: University of Minnesota Press, 1999), p. 104.

23. Lockman, *Contending Visions*, p. 37.

24. Roxanne Lynn Doty, *Imperial Encounters: The Politics of Representation in North-South Relations* (Minneapolis: University of Minnesota Press, 1996), p. 5.

25. William E. Connolly, *Political Theory and Modernity* (Ithaca: Cornell University Press, 1993), pp. 150–51.

26. Michel Foucault, *The Order of Things: An Archaeology of the Human Sciences* (New York: Random House, 1994), p. xiv.

27. Hayden White, *The Content of the Form* (Baltimore: Johns Hopkins University Press, 1989).

28. William E. Connolly, *The Ethos of Pluralization* (Minneapolis: University of Minnesota Press, 1995), p. 9.

29. Talal Asad, "The Idea of an Anthropology of Islam," *Center for Contemporary Arab Studies Occasional Paper Series* (Washington, D.C.: Georgetown University, 1996), p. 5.

30. Roger Cohen, "For 'New Danes,' Differences Create a Divide," *New York Times*, December 18, 2000, pp. A1, A10.

31. Oleg Graber, "Roots and Others," in Holly Edwards et al., *Noble Dreams, Wicked Pleasures: Orientalism in America, 1870–1930* (Princeton: Princeton University Press and Sterling and Francine Clark Art Institute, 2000), p. 3.

32. Mohja Kahf, *Western Representations of the Muslim Woman: From Termagant to Odalisque* (Austin: University of Texas Press, 1999), p. 14.

33. Iver B. Neumann and Jennifer M. Welsh, "The Other in European Self-Definition: An Addendum to the Literature on International Society," *Review of International Studies* 17 (1991): 329.

34. Richard King, *Orientalism and Religion: Postcolonial Theory, India and "the Mystic East"* (London: Routledge, 1999), pp. 3–4. On Western representations

of India, see Ronald B. Inden, *Imagining India* (Bloomington: Indiana University Press, 2001).

35. Talal Asad, "Muslims and European Identity: Can Europe Represent Islam?" in Elizabeth Hallam and Brian V. Street (Eds.), *Cultural Encounters: Representing "Otherness"* (New York: Routledge, 2000), p. 10.

36. Barbara D. Metcalf, "Nationalism, Modernity, and Muslim Identity in India before 1947," in Peter van der Veer and Hartmut Lehmann (Eds.), *Nation and Religion: Perspectives on Europe and Asia* (Princeton: Princeton University Press, 1999), p. 129 (emphasis in original).

37. Ann Laura Stoler, *Race and the Education of Desire: Foucault's History of Sexuality and the Colonial Order of Things* (Durham, N.C.: Duke University Press, 1995), p. 5.

38. Ibid.

39. "My subject is not 'women who are Muslim' but 'Western representations of the Muslim woman,' a category shaped by the literary conventions, linguistic tropes, and narrative processes within Western cultural traditions." Kahf, *Western Representations*, pp. 2–4. On Western representations of Islam generally, see Norman Daniel, *Islam and the West: The Making of an Image* (New York: Columbia University Press, 1989); Edward W. Said, *Covering Islam: How the Media and the Experts Determine How We See the Rest of the World*, 2nd ed. (New York: Random House, 1997); and Bernard Lewis, *Islam and the West* (Oxford: Oxford University Press, 1993).

40. "To wonder where the Moroccans are in *Casablanca* might seem beside the point to an American audience (though not to a Moroccan one). But that is precisely the question we must ask of the film." Edwards argues that this film is "the paradigmatic example of 'American Orientalism' " and that its release was a "key turning point in the cultural history of Western representations of the Maghreb." Edwards, *Morocco Bound*, pp. 70, 71.

41. Ibid., p. 88.

42. On authority as a productive modality of power, see Hannah Arendt, "What Is Authority?" in *Between Past and Future: Eight Exercises in Political Thought* (New York: Viking, 1968), pp. 91–141.

43. Eugenio Trias, "Thinking Religion: the Symbol and the Sacred," in Jacques Derrida and Gianni Vattimo (Eds.), *Religion* (Stanford: Stanford University Press, 1998), p. 96.

44. See Aimé Césaire, *Discourse on Colonialism*, trans. Joan Pinkham (New York: New York University Press, 2000), and Alice Conklin, A *"Mission to Civilize": The Republican Idea of Empire in France and West Africa, 1895–1930* (Stanford: Stanford University Press, 2000).

45. Timothy Worthington Marr, *Imagining Ishmael: Studies of Islamic Orientalism in America from the Puritans to Melville* (Ann Arbor, Mich.: UMI, 1998), p. 92. See also Timothy Marr, *The Cultural Roots of American Islamicism* (Cambridge: Cambridge University Press, 2006).

46. For a classic statement of the theory applied to communist China during the Cold War, see Karl Wittfogel, *Oriental Despotism: A Comparative Study of Total Power* (New Haven: Yale University Press, 1957).

47. Lockman, *Contending Visions*, p. 87. Halliday argues that "Oriental despotism," for all its recurrent fashion, can be historical sociology at its worst—neither historical,

176 · Notes to Chapter Three

in that it denies change, nor sociological, in that it abstracts the state from social context, and contemporary international connection." Halliday, *The Middle East in International Relations*, p. 288.

48. As Lockman argues, "the odious example of the Ottomans gave Montesquieu and others a safe way to criticize and resist what they saw as the despotic tendencies of European monarchs and to delineate, by means of a sharp contrast, their emerging vision of a new kind of rational and moral political order (*Contending Visions*, p. 48). See also Lucette Valensi, *The Birth of the Despot: Venice and the Sublime Porte*, trans. Arthur Denner (Ithaca: Cornell University Press, 1993).

49. Michael Hanchard, "Afro-Modernity: Temporality, Politics, and the African Diaspora," *Public Culture* 11, no. 1 (1999): 245–68.

50. Dipesh Chakrabarty, *Provincializing Europe: Postcolonial Thought and Historical Difference* (Princeton: Princeton University Press, 2000), p. 9.

51. Ibid.

52. Though not the subject of this chapter, there were local approximations of laicism in North African culture that predated European hegemony. Salem, for example, describes the *mutazalite* philosophers of the eleventh and twelfth centuries and classical poetry as having provided "non-religious views of life throughout the Islamic period." Paul Salem, "The Rise and Fall of Secularism in the Arab World," *Middle East Policy* 4, no. 3 (March 1996): 147.

53. In a fascinating account of "how a rewriting of the Algerian history of France took place at the moment of independence" (p. 11), Shepard traces the gap between French ideology, doctrine, and mythology of assimilation and actual conditions on the ground in French Algeria, arguing that "racism had an enormous and direct effect on the daily experience of Algerians with local civil status as well as on popular, intellectual, and official thinking about 'Muslim' Algerians." Todd Shepard, *The Invention of Decolonization: The Algerian War and the Remaking of France* (Ithaca: Cornell University Press, 2006), p. 34.

54. On the consolidation of British national identity as modern and enlightened in opposition to backward non-British societies, see Linda Colley, *Britons: Forging the Nation, 1707–1837* (New Haven: Yale University Press, 1992).

55. Shepard, *The Invention of Decolonization*, p. 33.

56. Ibid.

57. Timothy Mitchell, *Colonising Egypt* (Berkeley: University of California Press, 1991), p. 171.

58. Paul Silverstein, *Algeria in France: Transpolitics, Race, and Nation* (Bloomington: Indiana University Press, 2004), p. 44.

59. Ibid., p. 40.

60. Shepard, *Invention of Decolonization*, p. 271.

61. The continuation of this exclusionary mentality can be seen in French resistance to Muslim Algerian claims to French citizenship after the decolonization of Algeria. Ibid., ch. 9, "Rejecting the Muslims."

62. Silverstein, *Algeria in France*, p. 50.

63. Patricia M. E. Lorcin, *Imperial Identities: Stereotyping, Prejudice and Race in Colonial Algeria* (London: I. B. Tauris, 1995), p. 53.

64. Auguste Pomel, *Des races indigènes de l'Algérie et du role que leur reservent leurs aptitudes* (Oran: Veuve Dagorn, 1871), cited in Silverstein, *Algeria in France*, p. 50.

65. Silverstein, *Algeria in France*, p. 51. As Emile Larcher argued, "in the Mahometian civilization, religion and law are too intimately confused for the juridical condition of Muslims to be identical to that of Frenchmen or Europeans." Emile Larcher, *Traité élémentaire de legislation algérienne*, vol. 1 (Paris: Rousseau, 1903), cited in Silverstein, *Algeria in France*, p. 51.

66. On the Kabyle Myth, see Lorcin, *Imperial Identities*, and Silverstein, *Algeria in France*.

67. Silverstein, *Algeria in France*, pp. 53–58.

68. Eugène Guernier, cited in Silverstein, *Algeria in France*, p. 57.

69. Lorcin, *Imperial Identities*, p. 75.

70. Shepard describes the tensions between the two models guiding the French government's relationship with Algeria's inhabitants: assimilationism and coexistence. In the former model, "officials expected all male inhabitants of Algeria to become French citizens eventually. . . . French institutions would offer them access to a legal system, training, and education premised in universal principles and rationality. Irrationality and religious fanaticism, Muslim in particular, would crumble." He contrasts this with the coexistence model, which, though never officially adopted, was influential in practice in Algeria and "recognized that different groups existed . . . and that their relationship to the state and to the nation would necessarily be different." Shepard, *The Invention of Decolonization*, p. 22.

71. As Lorcin notes, "secularism as a force gathered strength throughout the [nineteenth] century." Lorcin, *Imperial Identities*, p. 245. See also Henri Pena-Ruiz, *Dieu et Marianne: Philosophie de la laïcite* (Paris: Presses Universitaires de France, 1999), and Jean Baudouin and Philippe Portier (Eds.), *La laïcité, une valeur d'aujourd'hui?: Contestations et renegotiations du modèle français* (Rennes: Presses Universitaires de Rennes, 2001).

72. On French nationalization of the metropole, see the classic work by Eugen Weber, *Peasants into Frenchmen: The Modernization of Rural France, 1870–1914* (Stanford: Stanford University Press, 1976), and Peter Sahlins, *Boundaries: The Making of France and Spain in the Pyrenees* (Berkeley: University of California Press, 1989).

73. Bauberot has argued that "the founding of secularism in France was rooted in the political victory of the anticlerical movement. . . . anticlericalism and the Third Republic were tied together for several reasons." Jean Bauberot, "Secularism and French Religious Liberty: A Sociological and Historical View," *Brigham Young University Law Review* 2 (2003): 451–64.

74. See Phyllis Stock-Morton, *Moral Education for a Secular Society: The Development of Morale Laïque in Nineteenth Century France* (Albany: State University of New York Press, 1988), and Laurence Loeffel, *La question du fondement de la morale laïque sous la IIIe République: 1870–1914* (Paris: Presses Universitaires de France, 2000).

75. As Robert notes, however, "the legal equality between religions is total and may be considered a constitutional principle drawn from secularism. However, the Law of 1905 actually only recognizes churches, or Christian institutions, and it is terribly complex and difficult to make Islamic communities fit the church mold." Jacques Robert, "Religious Liberty and French Secularism," *Brigham Young University Law Review* 2 (2003): 637–60.

76. Lorcin, *Imperial Identities*, p. 10.

77. Stock-Morton, *Moral Education*, p. 169.

178 • Notes to Chapter Three

78. Peter McPhee, *A Social History of France*, 2nd ed. (New York: Palgrave, 2004), p. 253.

79. Hendrik Spruyt, *Ending Empire: Contested Sovereignty and Territorial Partition* (Ithaca: Cornell University Press, 2005), p. 88.

80. McPhee, *Social History of France*, p. 255.

81. "Ferry was to institutionalize the concept of a secular morality as a part of the new system of universal primary education." Stock-Morton, *Moral Education*, p. 98.

82. McPhee, *Social History of France*, p. 255.

83. Ibid.

84. Lorcin, *Imperial Identities*, p. 247.

85. Pam Belluck, "Intolerance and an Attempt to Make Amends Unsettle a Chicago Suburb's Muslims," *New York Times*, August 10, 2000, p. A10. Parts of the following derive from Elizabeth Shakman Hurd, "Verso una politica postseculare: secolarismo e islamismo" (Toward a Postsecular Politics: Secularism and Political Islam), in Stefano Salzani (Ed.), *Teologie politiche islamiche. Casi e frammenti contemporanei* (Milan: Casa Editrice Marietti 1820, 2005), pp. 215–58.

86. On the historical significance of associating notions of true and false with religion, see Hurd, "Verso una politica postseculare: secolarismo e islamismo."

87. Belluck, "Intolerance and an Attempt to Make Amends." A Muslim-Christian dialogue association was eventually established in Palos Heights.

88. Examples can be found in Diana L. Eck, *A New Religious America: How a "Christian County" Has Become the World's Most Religiously Diverse Nation* (New York: HarperCollins, 2002).

89. Muslims were not, however, the only "religious other" in the early American imaginary. Morone, for instance, argues that "the Indians offered English colonists an irreducible, satanic other—perfect for defining the Christian community." Jim Morone, *Hellfire Nation: The Politics of Sin in American History* (New Haven: Yale University Press, 2003), p. 74.

90. For an expanded version of this argument that discusses the role of Western literary representations of Muslim women, the European colonization of Egypt, and Orientalism in American popular culture in contributing to the consolidation of Western modernity, see Elizabeth Shakman Hurd, "Appropriating Islam: The Islamic Other in the Consolidation of Western Modernity," *Critique: Critical Middle Eastern Studies* 12, no. 1 (Spring 2003): 25–41.

91. This phrase refers to nineteenth-century American representations of the inhabitants of the Barbary States—the North African regions of Algiers, Tunis, and Tripoli. Marr, *Imagining Ishmael*, p. 93.

92. Allison, *The Crescent Obscured*, p. xiv. Allison traces the ideological functions of the American war with Tripoli in the early nineteenth century, suggesting that it proved to Americans that they were both different from Europeans, who were content to pay tribute to the Barbary States, and from Muslims, who were seen as "ravaged by their rulers and torn apart by their impoverished and savage people." Ibid., p. xvi.

93. The missionaries were targeting principally Greek Orthodox Christians for conversion and expressed contempt for Turkish despotism, Jewish "unbelief," and the superstition of "nominal" Christians. Khalaf, "American Missions in the Levant."

94. Edward W. Hooker, ed., *Memoir of Mrs. Sarah L. Huntington Smith, Late of the Mission in Syria*, 3rd ed. (New York: American Tract Society, 1845), p. 173, cited in Marr, *Imagining Ishmael*, p. 76.

95. Ibid., p. 22.

96. Ibid., p. 24.

97. Luther, *Works*, V, 88, cited in Marr, *Imagining Ishmael*, pp. 28–29.

98. Ibid., p. 29.

99. "Any mention of natural calamities in the press, traveler's narratives, or any other form of intelligence that made its way from the east, were promoted as evidence of the imminent default of Islam." Ibid., p. 41.

100. Ibid., p. 43.

101. Ibid.

102. Ibid., p. 20, n. 27.

103. Khalaf, "American Missionaries in the Levant."

104. Marr, *Imagining Ishmael*, p. 43.

105. Ibid., p. 26.

106. Ibid., pp. 25–26. "Forcing diverse human communities into the procrustean bed of biblical metaphors, especially those describing them as locusts, scorpions, and other teratological beings, was a process of dehumanizing violence that sanctioned a religiously motivated prejudice. . . . these Christian thinkers demonstrated the degree to which the orientalism of eschatology produced ideological blinders which prevented the perception of human diversity" (p. 85).

107. Ibid., pp. 17–18.

108. Ibid., pp. 49–51.

109. Ibid., p. 39.

110. Ibid., p. 71. Strangely, as Marr observes, the missionaries relied upon biblical prophecy as their principal source of information about Islam *despite the fact* that Islam appeared many centuries after the Bible: "the major source for understanding Islam until this [twentieth] century, however, was not substantial comparative dialogue with Muslims and scholarly study of Islamic texts, but instead the investigation of what the Bible purportedly revealed about the existence of Islam and when and by what means its sway would be stilled. The fact that Islam had appeared centuries after the Bible itself did not concern these expositors. The Bible, as the textual source most available in their lives, had been sanctioned with the authority to explain the direction of human history." Marr, *Imagining Ishmael*, p. 23.

111. Alvan Bond, *Memoir of the Rev. Pliny Fisk* (Boston: Crocker and Brewster, 1828), 114, cited in Marr, *Imagining Ishmael*, p. 14, n. 9.

112. Ibid., p. 89.

113. Ibid., p. 87.

114. Ibid., p. 15.

115. The Islamic Orient figured "in early American foreign policy, literary production and cultural mythology as a site for the projection of democratic nationalism." Ibid., p. 87.

116. Allison, *The Crescent Obscured*, p. 46.

117. Marr, *Imagining Ishmael*, p. 88.

118. Allison, *The Crescent Obscured*, p. 35.

119. Marr, *Imagining Ishmael*, p. 91.

120. Ibid. See Charles de Secondat, Baron de Montesquieu, *The Spirit of the Laws* (Amherst, N.Y.: Prometheus Books, 2002), arguably the most influential work of Western political theory in the eighteenth century.

121. Marr, *Imagining Ishmael*, p. 3.

122. Allison, *The Crescent Obscured*, p. xvii.

123. Marr, *Imagining Ishmael*, p. 102.

124. "Orientalist conventions served as vehicles through which Americans were able to negotiate the difference of Islam on a cultural level as a means of counteracting its threat as a contending ethos. But such a process of compensatory co-optation not only diffused the challenge posed by Islam; it also enabled diverse Americans to share in the exoticism of oriental Islam by domesticating its alterity as a resource of significant power for framing their own cultural enterprises. This imaginative transformation enabled orientalist notions of Islamic belief and behavior to become integrated into the hybrid construction of American cultural identities early in the process of their formation." Ibid., pp. 2–3.

125. Another respondent noted that: "This country was founded on Christianity. If you read the Bill of Rights and the Constitution, those were written by Christians. The first settlers in this country were Christians. If you don't believe in God, fine, but don't try to make rules for the rest of us." Darrel Rowland, Joe Hallett, and Mark Niquette, ". . . under God, Divisible," *Columbus Dispatch*, May 7, 2006.

126. Marr, *Imagining Ishmael*, p. 92. See also Richard Falk, "False Universalism and the Geopolitics of Exclusion: The Case of Islam," *Third World Quarterly* 18, no. 1 (March 1997): 7–24.

CHAPTER FOUR
CONTESTED SECULARISMS IN TURKEY AND IRAN

1. Roxanne L. Euben, *Enemy in the Mirror: Islamic Fundamentalism and the Limits of Modern Rationalism* (Princeton: Princeton University Press, 1999), p. 44.

2. Anthony W. Marx, *Faith in Nation: Exclusionary Origins of Nationalism* (New York: Oxford University Press, 2003), p. ix.

3. Ann Laura Stoler, *Race and the Education of Desire: Foucault's History of Sexuality and the Colonial Order of Things* (Durham, N.C.: Duke University Press, 1995), p. 5.

4. Fred Halliday, "Turkey 1998: Secularism in Question," in *Nation and Religion in the Middle East* (Boulder: Lynne Rienner, 2000), p. 183. See also Jenny White, *Islamist Mobilization in Turkey: A Study in Vernacular Politics* (Seattle: University of Washington, 2002), p. 35.

5. Kemalism has been described as "the discourse of state power employed by the army" and as a Jacobinist "alternative religion." Yael Navaro-Yashin, *Faces of the State: Secularism and Public Life in Turkey* (Princeton, Princeton University Press, 2002), p. 202. See also Ihsan Yilmaz, "Secular Law and the Emergence of Unofficial Turkish Islamic Law," *Middle East Journal* 56, no. 1 (Winter 2002): 113–32.

6. Nilüfer Göle, "Authoritarian Secularism and Islamist Politics: The Case of Turkey," in Augustus Richard Norton (Ed.), *Civil Society in the Middle East* (New York: Brill, 1995), p. 22. Yavuz argues that "the raison d'être of the Kemalist establishment

is to keep the Islamic 'other' at bay, and this struggle is what unifies the Kemalist military-bureaucratic establishment." M. Hakan Yavuz, "Cleansing Islam from the Public Sphere," *Journal of International Affairs* 54, no. 1 (Fall 2000): 25.

7. Arthur Goldschmidt Jr., *A Concise History of the Middle East*, 7th ed. (Boulder: Westview, 2002), p. 219. Turks were unable to read Ottoman Turkish, whether it was used in classic works or in letters written by their own grandparents.

8. Yavuz, "Cleansing Islam from the Public Sphere," p. 24. Turkish women were granted the vote in 1934.

9. M. Hakan Yavuz, "Political Islam and the Welfare (*Refah*) Party in Turkey," *Comparative Politics* 30, no. 1 (October 1997): 65. See also Yavuz, *Islamic Political Identity in Turkey* (Oxford: Oxford University Press, 2003). After Atatürk's death in 1938, Turkey evolved away from single-party rule by the Republican People's Party (RPP) and in 1950 the Demokrat Party took power in a peaceful transition.

10. Yavuz, "Political Islam and the Welfare (*Refah*) Party in Turkey," p. 65.

11. Andrew Davison, "Turkey, a 'Secular' State? The Challenge of Description," *South Atlantic Quarterly* 102, nos. 2–3 (Spring–Summer 2003): 341. There is debate concerning the extent to which the Turkish state exercises hegemony over religion (the control account) versus the extent to which religious activities and institutions are separated from state activity (the separation account). Davison argues persuasively that there is tension between the separation and control dimensions at work in Turkish laicism and that elements of both accounts are operative. Davison, *Secularism and Revivalism in Turkey: A Hermeneutic Reconsideration* (New Haven: Yale University Press, 1998). On the control account, see Ümit Cizre Sakallioglu, "Parameters and Strategies of Islam — State Interaction in Republican Turkey," *International Journal of Middle East Studies* 28, no. 2 (1996): 231–51.

12. Nicholas Demerath III, *Crossing the Gods: World Religions and Worldly Politics* (New Brunswick, N.J.: Rutgers University Press, 2001), citing "one of my sources," p. 75.

13. Yilmaz, "Secular Law and the Emergence of Unofficial Turkish Islamic Law," p. 7.

14. Elizabeth Özdalga, *The Veiling Issue: Official Secularism and Popular Islam in Modern Turkey* (Surrey: Biddles Ltd. and King's Lynn, 1998), pp. 17–32. See also M. Hakan Yavuz and John L. Esposito (Eds.), *Turkish Islam and the Secular State: The Gulen Movement* (Syracuse: Syracuse University Press, 2003).

15. In this state-initiated modification of Kemalism, the Turkish state "tried to fuse Islam with the state ideology from top down," by selectively incorporating Islamists into the system. Yavuz, "Political Islam and the Welfare Party in Turkey," pp. 69–70.

16. RP received 4.4 percent of the votes in the March 1984 municipal elections, 7.7 percent in the November 1987 general elections, and 9.8 percent in the March 1989 municipal elections.

17. Electoral participation was 94 percent.

18. On the contributions of the radical wing to social theory, see Haldun Gülalp, "Globalizing Postmodernism: Islamist and Western Social Theory," *Economy and Society* 26, no. 3 (August 1997): 419–33.

19. Yavuz, "Political Islam and the Welfare Party in Turkey," pp. 79–80.

20. White, *Islamist Mobilization in Turkey*, p. 3.

21. Haldun Gülalp, "Globalization and Political Islam: The Social Bases of Turkey's Welfare Party," *International Journal of Middle East Studies* 33, no. 3 (August 2001): 444.

22. Göle, "Authoritarian Secularism," p. 39.

23. Ibid. Turkey's southeastern Kurdish region is composed of eleven provinces and produces 95 percent of the country's oil. The Kurds remain poor in part due to a war between Turkish security forces and PKK forces during the 1980s, which continues intermittently.

24. Ibid., p. 41.

25. Alev Çinar, "National History as a Contested Site," *Comparative Study of Society and History* 43, no. 2 (April 2001): 365.

26. As Atatürk famously stated, "I have no religion, and at times I wish all religions at the bottom of the sea." Cited in David Remnick, "The Experiment: Will Turkey be the Model for Islamic Democracy?" *New Yorker*, November 18, 2002, p. 51.

27. The NSC is comprised of the president, prime minister, foreign minister, defense minister, minister of internal affairs, and five top generals.

28. Yavuz, "Cleansing Islam from the Public Sphere," p. 38. RP also faced opposition from the leading Istanbul-based bourgeoisie and media cartel, which had been benefiting financially from the privatization of state companies. RP officials had opposed this process due to accusations of corruption. Ibid., p. 39.

29. Gülalp, "Globalization and Political Islam," pp. 433–34.

30. For the argument that AKP has successfully transformed Islamism in Turkey as well as the Kemalist state structure, see Ilhan Uzgel, "Turkey's Triple Transformations: The Self, Ideology, and the State under the Justice and Development Party," paper presented at the conference on "The Middle East and Central Asia: Authoritarianism and Democracy in the Age of Globalization" (University of Utah, Salt Lake City, September 9, 2005).

31. Jenny White, "Turkey's New 'Muslimhood': The End of 'Islamism'?" *Congress Monthly*, November–December 2003: 6–9.

32. Yavuz, *Islamic Political Identity in Turkey*, p. 254.

33. Koray Caliskan and Yuksel Taskin, "Turkey's Neo-Islamists Weigh War and Peace," *Middle East Report Online*, January 30, 2003 (http://www.merip.org/mero/mero013003.html).

34. Gülalp, "Globalizing Postmodernism," p. 431.

35. See chapter 5 on EU-Turkey relations. The majority opinion in this case was supported by judges from France, Turkey, Norway, and Albania. Judges dissenting from this opinion were from Austria, Cyprus, and Britain.

36. Human Rights Watch World Report 2002: Turkey (http://www.hrw.org/wr2k2/europe19.html, accessed April 17, 2006).

37. Press release issued by the Registrar of the European Court of Human Rights, "Judgment in the Case of Refah Partisi (The Welfare Party) Erbakan, Kazan and Tekdal v. Turkey," July 31, 2001 (http://www.echr.coe.int/Eng/Press/2001/July/RefahPartisi2001jude.htm, accessed April 17, 2006, emphasis added).

38. Göle, "Authoritarian Secularism," pp. 38–39. For an alternative perspective on Refah and the Fazilet Party, which succeeded it, emphasizing both parties' opportunist and authoritarian tendencies, see Haldun Gülalp, "The Poverty of Democracy in Turkey: The Refah Party Episode," *New Perspectives on Turkey* 21 (1999): 35–51.

39. See, for example, Thomas L. Friedman, "Who Lost Turkey?" *New York Times*, August 21, 1996.

40. Bernard Lewis, *The Emergence of Modern Turkey*, 3rd ed. (New York: Oxford University Press, 2002), p. 424.

41. Hakan Yavuz, "Islam and Europeanization in Turkish-Muslim Socio-Political Movements," in Peter J. Katzenstein and Timothy Byrnes (Eds.), *Religion in an Expanding Europe* (Cambridge: Cambridge University Press, 2006), p. 240.

42. Ibid., p. 241.

43. On the possibility that AKP is neither Islamist nor antisecular but is pursuing an alternative practice of secularism, see Ahmet T. Kuru, "Reinterpretation of Secularism in Turkey: The Case of the Justice and Development Party, in M. Hakan Yavuz (Ed.), *The Emergence of a New Turkey: Democracy and the AK Parti* (Salt Lake City: University of Utah Press, 2006), pp. 136–59.

44. Yavuz, "Islam and Europeanization in Turkish-Muslim Socio-Political Movements," pp. 244–45.

45. Alfred Stepan, "Religion, Democracy, and the 'Twin Tolerations,' " in Larry Diamond, Marc F. Plattner, and Philip J. Costopoulos (Eds.), *World Religions and Democracy* (Baltimore: Johns Hopkins University Press, 2005), p. 3.

46. Ibid., p. 44.

47. For a useful typology of the multiple groupings of Islamic politics on the Turkish theopolitical landscape, see Yavuz, "Islam and Europeanization in Turkish-Muslim Socio-Political Movements," pp. 240–47.

48. John L. Esposito, *The Islamic Threat: Myth or Reality?* 2nd ed. (New York: Oxford University Press, 1992), p. 103.

49. John L. Esposito, *The Islamic Threat: Myth or Reality?* 3rd ed. (New York: Oxford University Press, 1999), p. 115.

50. Frantz Fanon, *A Dying Colonialism* (London: Writers and Readers Press, 1967), p. 65, emphasis in original.

51. Cottam argues that in this case "the impact of American policy was substantial. It altered the direction of change away from those seeking to lead Iran toward liberal democracy and national assertiveness." Richard W. Cottam, *Iran and the United States: A Cold War Case Study* (Pittsburgh: University of Pittsburgh Press, 1988), p. 262.

52. Esposito, *The Islamic Threat* (3rd ed.), p. 108. On the 1953 coup, see Mark J. Gasiorowski and Malcolm Byrne (Eds.), *Mohammad Mosaddeq and the 1953 Coup in Iran* (Syracuse: Syracuse University Press, 2004); Stephen Kinzer, *All the Shah's Men: An American Coup and the Roots of Middle East Terror* (Hoboken, N.J.: John Wiley & Sons, 2003); James Goode, *The United States and Iran: In the Shadow of Musaddiq* (New York: Palgrave Macmillan, 1997); Mark J. Gasiorowski, "The 1953 Coup d'Etat in Iran," *International Journal of Middle East Studies* 19 (August 1987): 261–86; and David Painter, "The United States, Great Britain, and Mossadegh," *Pew Case Studies in International Affairs* 332 (Washington, D.C.: Institute for the Study of Diplomacy, 1993).

53. Fred Halliday, *Iran: Dictatorship and Development* (New York: Penguin Books, 1979), p. 252. On the international and inter-Arab politics of the Baghdad Pact, a controversial British-backed alliance also involving Turkey and Iraq, see Michael Barnett, *Dialogues in Arab Politics* (New York: Columbia University Press, 1998), pp. 108–

20. Barnett argues that "the pact represented a challenge not to the balance of power per se but to Arab nationalism and its contested norms by unleashing a debate among Arab states concerning what behavior was and was not proper for *Arab* states" (p. 118).

54. Ali Mirsepassi, *Intellectual Discourse and the Politics of Modernization: Negotiating Modernity in Iran* (Cambridge: Cambridge University Press, 2000), pp. 70–71.

55. Ibid., p. 76. "The ascent of political Islam owes much to the fragile foundations of secular politics and to the political vacuum that the Shah's regime effectively created in the 1960s and 1970s." Ibid., p. 73.

56. Esposito, *The Islamic Threat* (3rd ed.), p. 108.

57. Halliday, *Iran*, p. 253.

58. Intended as a response to U.S. involvement in Vietnam, the Nixon Doctrine declared that the U.S. would realize its Cold War foreign policy objectives by supporting regional allies rather than through direct intervention. Halliday, *Iran*, p. 249. He describes U.S.-Iranian relations during this era as "an unequal alliance, but one of converging interests" (p. 254).

59. Douglas Little, *American Orientalism: The United States and the Middle East since 1945* (Chapel Hill: University of North Carolina Press, 2002), p. 145.

60. Ibid.

61. Suzanne Maloney, "Identity and Change in Iran's Foreign Policy," in Shibley Telhami and Michael Barnett (Eds.), *Identity and Foreign Policy in the Middle East* (Ithaca: Cornell University, 2002), p. 96.

62. Ibid.

63. Esposito, *The Islamic Threat* (2nd ed.), p. 103; Halliday, *Iran*, p. 298.

64. Esposito, *The Islamic Threat* (3rd ed.), p. 107.

65. Halliday, *Iran*, p. 287.

66. "Mosques served as centers for dissent, political organization, agitation and sanctuary. The government could ban and limit political meetings and gatherings, but it could not close the mosques or ban prayer." Esposito, *The Islamic Threat* (2nd ed.), p. 110.

67. Gary A. Donaldson, *America at War since 1945: Politics and Diplomacy in Korea, Vietnam, and the Gulf War* (Westport, Conn.: Praeger Publishers, 1996), pp. 84–85.

68. Melani McAlister, *Epic Encounters: Culture, Media and U.S. Interests in the Middle East, 1945–2000* (Berkeley: University of California Press, 2001), p. 203.

69. Halliday, *Iran*, p. 64.

70. On this movement and for a fascinating account of the shah's progressive alienation of the *ulama*, see Nikki R. Keddie, *Modern Iran: Roots and Results of Revolution* (New Haven: Yale University Press, 2003), pp. 214–39.

71. Esposito, *The Islamic Threat* (3rd ed.), p. 109. Keddie, *Modern Iran*, pp. 226–28.

72. Halliday, *Iran*, p. 298.

73. Keddie, *Modern Iran*, p. 230.

74. Ervand Abrahamian, *Iran between Two Revolutions* (Princeton: Princeton University Press, 1982), pp. 500–501.

75. Numbers differ from source to source: Halliday writes that, "up to three thousand were killed" in the massacre. Halliday, *Iran*, p. 292. Abrahamian writes that "military authorities announced that the day's casualties totaled 87 dead and 205 wounded.

But the opposition declared that the dead numbered more than 4,000 and that as many as 500 had been killed in Jaleh Square alone." Abrahamian, *Iran between Two Revolutions*, p. 516.

76. Abrahamian, *Iran between Two Revolutions*, p. 516.

77. On the mixed messages to the shah from the Americans, particularly in the later stages of the revolution, see Said Amir Arjomand, *The Turban for the Crown: The Islamic Revolution in Iran* (New York: Oxford University Press, 1988), pp. 128–33, who argues that "from December 28, 1978, U.S. policy became a complete muddle and contradictory measures were taken by the U.S. government." See also James A. Bill, *The Eagle and the Lion: The Tragedy of American-Iranian Relations* (New Haven: Yale University Press, 1988), pp. 243–60, and Abrahamian, *Iran between Two Revolutions*, pp. 523–24.

78. Keddie, *Modern Iran*, p. 232.

79. Ibid., p. 233.

80. Cottam, *Iran and the United States*, p. 5.

81. Cited in Jonathan Rée, "The Treason of the Clerics," *Nation* 281, no. 5 (August 15, 2005): 33. Thanks to Talal Asad for this reference. On Foucault and religion, see Jeremy R. Carrette, *Foucault and Religion: Spiritual Corporality and Political Spirituality* (New York: Routledge, 2000), and Jeremy Carrette (Ed.), *Religion and Culture: Michel Foucault* (New York: Routledge, 1999). On Foucault's initially positive reactions to the revolution and the bitter rejection of his views in France by authorities such as Maxime Rodinson, see Janet Afary and Kevin B. Anderson, "The Seductions of Islamism: Revisiting Foucault and the Iranian Revolution," *New Politics* 10, no. 1 (Summer 2004): 113–22. For an English translation and analysis of Foucault's essays on Iran, see Afary and Anderson, *Foucault and the Iranian Revolution: Gender and the Seductions of Islamism* (Chicago: University of Chicago Press, 2005). For a trenchant critique of Afary and Anderson's conclusions, see Rée, "The Treason of the Clerics."

82. McAlister, *Epic Encounters*, p. 204.

83. Esposito, *The Islamic Threat* (3rd ed.), p. 102.

84. Hossein Bashiriyeh, "Transitional Situations, Changing Elite Configurations and Obstacles to Democratization in Iran," paper presented at Northwestern University (May 15, 2006). See also Hossein Bashiriyeh, *The State and Revolution in Iran, 1962–1982* (New York: St. Martin's Press, 1984).

85. Esposito, *The Islamic Threat* (3rd ed.), p. 115. On Khomeini's complex and ambiguous leadership style, see Daniel Brumberg, *Reinventing Khomeini: The Struggle for Reform in Iran* (Chicago: University of Chicago Press, 2001). He suggests that, "behind his charisma, and woven into its very fabric, was a contradiction between Khomeini's belief that the people should play a role in choosing their government, and his strong commitment to revolutionary action and clerical rule under the leadership of a quasi-infallible, charismatic Supreme Leader" (p. 3).

86. Edward Said, *Covering Islam: How the Media and the Experts Determine How We See the Rest of the World,* 2nd ed. (New York: Vintage Books, 1997), p. 100; see also Halliday, *Iran*, pp. 296–99.

87. Owen argues that for two years beginning in October 1981, when Ali Khamenei was elected president, "the clergy associated with the IRP crushed what was left of the opposition and established the type of theocratic government and politics which has

lasted to the present day." Roger Owen, *State, Power and Politics in the Making of the Modern Middle East*, 3rd ed (London: Routledge, 2004), p. 162.

88. Mirsepassi, *Intellectual Discourse*, pp. 65–66.

89. Ibid., p. 94.

90. Keddie, *Modern Iran*, p. 226.

91. "The explicit delegitimizing of local culture by an outside invader, who in turn insisted upon the singular universality of their own culture and practices, is especially relevant for our purposes because such a division led to the complete loss of the Shah's state power and the ruling class's legitimacy in pre-revolutionary Iran." Mirsepassi, *Intellectual Discourse*, p. 11.

92. Robert J. Allison, *The Crescent Obscured: The United States and the Muslim World, 1776–1815*, 2nd ed. (Chicago: University of Chicago Press, 2000), p. xiii.

93. Mark Juergensmeyer, *The New Cold War? Religious Nationalism Confronts the Secular State* (Berkeley: University of California Press, 1993), p. 19. This is similar to Foucault's response to the revolution.

94. Maloney, "Identity and Change in Iran's Foreign Policy," p. 98.

95. Esposito, *The Islamic Threat* (3rd ed.), p. 116.

96. Arjomand, *The Turban for the Crown*, pp. 89–174.

97. José Casanova, *Public Religions in the Modern World* (Chicago: University of Chicago Press, 1994), pp. 219–20. Iran experienced significant political liberalization during the 1990s under the leadership of Rafsanjani, with dissent and debate tolerated within certain parameters. Boroujerdi suggests that more recently Iran has experienced an intellectual flourishing: "far from engaging in esoteric and trivial polemics, the discussions now taking place in Iran are philosophically sophisticated, intellectually sound, socially relevant, and politically modern." Mehrzad Boroujerdi, *Iranian Intellectuals and the West: The Tormented Triumph of Nativism* (Syracuse: Syracuse University Press, 1996), p. 157. On recent challenges to the absolutism of the current regime, see also Jahangir Amuzegar, "Iran's Crumbling Revolution," *Foreign Affairs* 82, no. 1 (January–February 2003): 44–57.

98. Maloney, "Identity and Change in Iran's Foreign Policy," p. 101.

99. Esposito, *The Islamic Threat* (3rd ed.), p. 117.

100. Rée, "The Treason of the Clerics," p. 33.

101. As Euben argues, Islamic modernism is "not an uncomplicated embrace of the ideas and processes constitutive of Western modernism but is itself a hybrid." Roxanne L. Euben, "Contingent Borders, Syncretic Perspectives: Globalization, Political Theory, and Islamizing Knowledge," *International Studies Review* 4, no. 1 (2002): 29, n. 21.

102. Said, *Covering Islam*, p. 100.

103. Cottam, *Iran and the United States*, p. 208.

104. Keddie, *Modern Iran*, p. 232.

105. Rée, "The Treason of the Clerics," p. 34.

106. Mirsepassi, *Intellectual Discourse*, p. 168.

107. The reasons that the United States did not take this path are discussed in chapter 6.

108. Esposito, *The Islamic Threat* (3rd ed.), pp. 109–10. On Shariati, see also Ali Rahnema, *An Islamic Utopian: A Political Biography of Ali Shariati* (New York: I. B. Tauris, 1998).

109. Esposito, *The Islamic Threat* (3rd ed.), p. 110.

110. Ibid., p. 111.

111. Esposito, *The Islamic Threat* (2nd ed.), p. 108. On Shariati, see further Abdulaziz Sachedina, "Ali Shariati: Ideologue of the Iranian Revolution," in John L. Esposito (Ed.), *Voices of Resurgent Islam* (Oxford: Oxford University Press, 1983), pp. 191–214.

112. Mark LeVine and Armando Salvatore, "Socio-Religious Movements and the Transformation of 'Common Sense' into a Politics of 'Common Good,'" in Salvatore and LeVine (Eds.), *Religion, Social Practice, and Contested Hegemonies* (New York: Palgrave Macmillan, 2005), p. 45.

113. Thanks to Michael Loriaux for his suggestions on this section.

114. This term is from Davison, "Turkey, a 'Secular' State? The Challenge of Description," p. 333.

115. As Rée concludes, "whatever else you may think about them, the Iranian revolutionaries were as irreducible as Astérix, Obélix and Panoramix; and so too was the philosophical historian who did his best to listen to what they had to say." Rée, "The Treason of the Clerics," p. 34.

116. Robert W. Hefner, "Public Islam and the Problem of Democratization," *Sociology of Religion* 62, no. 4 (2001): 497.

117. Ibid., 497–98, citing James C. Scott, *Seeing Like a State: How Certain Schemes to Improve the Human Condition Have Failed* (New Haven: Yale University Press, 1998). Craig Calhoun develops a similar argument about the parallels between Islamic fundamentalism and the modern ideology of the French revolutionaries in *Nationalism* (Minneapolis: University of Minnesota, 1997), p. 115.

118. Göle, "Authoritarian Secularism," p. 39.

119. See Taha Parla and Andrew Davison, *Corporatist Ideology in Kemalist Turkey: Progress or Order?* (Syracuse: Syracuse University Press, 2004).

CHAPTER FIVE
THE EUROPEAN UNION AND TURKEY

1. Luis Lugo, Director, Pew Forum on Religion and Public Life, "Does 'Muslim' Turkey Belong in 'Christian' Europe?" (discussion, National Press Club, Washington, D.C., January 13, 2005).

2. On how "Europe" has been embedded in state and national identities, thereby contributing to the establishment of a security community, see Ole Wæver, "Insecurity, Security and Asecurity in the West European Non-war Community," in Emanuel Adler and Michael Barnett (Eds.), *Security Communities* (Cambridge: Cambridge University Press, 1998), pp. 69–160. He argues that "the regional identity 'Europe' clearly has become more important and today plays a key role *in* self conceptions. Its meaning is not settled once and for all, but of the concepts of state and nation that compete, most are thoroughly Europeanized" (p. 98).

3. As Rumelili argues, "the EU is implicated in an identity interaction with its Turkish 'other' that makes the European identity more insecure." Bahar Rumelili, "Constructing Identity and Relating to Difference: Understanding the EU's Mode of Differentiation," *Review of International Studies* 30 (2004): 45.

4. Nilüfer Göle, "Islam in Public: New Visibilities and New Imaginaries," *Public Culture* 14, no. 1 (2002): 183.

5. See Jocelyne Cesari and Sean McLoughlin (Eds.), *European Muslims and the Secular State* (Aldershot, Hampshire: Ashgate, 2005).

6. This argument appeared in Elizabeth Shakman Hurd, "Negotiating Europe: The Politics of Religion and the Prospects for Turkish Accession to the EU," *Review of International Studies* 32, no. 3 (July 2006): 401–18.

7. I am grateful to Karen Alter for this phrase.

8. David M. Wood and Birol A. Yesilada, *The Emerging European Union*, 3rd ed. (New York: Pearson Longman, 2004), p. 124, citing European Commission, *Commission Opinion on Turkey's Request for Accession to the Community*, Sec. (89) 2290 final (Brussels: Official Publications of the European Communities, December 18, 1989). For background on Turkey-EU relations, see Ali Çarkoglu and Barry Rubin (Eds.), *Turkey and the European Union: Domestic Politics, Economic Integration and International Dynamics* (London: Frank Cass: 2003), and Meltem Müftüler-Bac, *Turkey's Relations with a Changing Europe* (New York: St. Martin's Press, 1997).

9. Wood and Yesilada, *The Emerging European Union*, p. 124.

10. Ibid., p. 125.

11. Philip Gordon and Omer Taspinar, "Turkey's European Quest: The EU's Decision on Turkish Accession," *U.S.-Europe Analysis Series* (Center on the United States and Europe, Brookings Institution, September 2004).

12. Wood and Yesilada, *The Emerging European Union*, p. 125. Kösebalaban attributes this about-face on the part of the Europeans to the rise of social democratic governments in Europe, and particularly in Germany. Hasan Kösebalaban, "Turkey's EU Membership: A Clash of Security Cultures," *Middle East Policy* 9, No. 2 (June 2002): 136–37.

13. Gordon and Taspinar, "Turkey's European Quest," pp. 2–4. On these reforms, see also Michael Emerson, "Has Turkey Fulfilled the Copenhagen Political Criteria?" Centre for European Policy Studies, Brief No. 48 (April 2004).

14. Kösebalaban, "Turkey's EU Membership," p. 137.

15. David L. Phillips, "Turkey's Dreams of Accession," *Foreign Affairs* 83, no. 5 (September–October 2004): 94.

16. Gordon and Taspinar, "Turkey's European Quest," p. 4.

17. William Chislett, "Turkey's Membership in the European Union: A Rose or a Thorn?" Real Institute Elcano de Estudios Internacionales y Estratégicos (http://www.realinstitutoelcano.org/documentos/imprimir/101imp.asp, accessed June 16, 2004).

18. On this process, see Erkan Erdogdu, "Turkey and Europe: Undivided but Not United," *Middle East Review of International Affairs* 6, no. 2 (June 2002) (http://meria.idc.ac.il/journal/2002/issue2/jv6n2a4.html).

19. For survey results, see Kösebalaban, "Turkey's EU Membership," p. 138. The number of Turks supporting accession has been declining in recent surveys, however.

20. On disagreements within the European Parliament concerning Turkish accession, see Senem Aydin, "Views on Turkish Accession from the European Parliament," Center for European Policy Studies, *Turkey in Europe Monitor*, no. 4 (April 2004) (http://www.ceps.be/files/TurkeyM/TMonitor4.pdf), and Nathalie Tocci, "Turkey and the European Union: Preparing for the December 2004 European Council," Working

Paper, Mediterranean Programme Workshop, "Brainstorming: Developments in EU-Turkey Relations" (Robert Schuman Center for Advanced Studies, European University Institute, Florence, May 7, 2004).

21. Gordon and Taspinar, "Turkey's European Quest," p. 4. See also Daniel Dombey and Vincent Boland, "Brussels Says 'Yes' to Turkish Entry Talks," *Financial Times*, October 7, 2004, p. 2. *Eurobarometer* survey number 56 suggested that 34 percent of the EU 15 Public supports Turkish membership and 46 percent opposes it (20 percent had no opinion). Cited in Wood and Yesilada, *The Emerging European Union*, p. 123.

22. The argument is that the EU could not absorb Turkey's massive agricultural production into its subsidy program, which places limits on agricultural outputs to guard against overproduction.

23. See Ziya Önis, "Domestic Politics, International Norms and Challenges to the State: Turkey-EU Relations in the Post-Helsinki Era," *Turkish Studies* 4, no. 1 (Spring 2003): 9–34, and Önis, "Political Islam at the Crossroads: From Hegemony to Co-existence," *Contemporary Politics* 7 (December 2001): 281–98.

24. On the Greek Orthodox minority and obstacles to religious freedom in Turkey, see Elizabeth H. Prodromou, "Turkey between Secularism and Fundamentalism? The 'Muslimhood Model' and the Greek Orthodox Minority," *Brandywine Review of Faith and International Affairs* 3, no. 1 (Spring 2005): 11–22. On the Alevis, see David Shankland, *The Alevis in Turkey: The Emergence of a Secular Islamic Tradition* (New York: Routledge Curzon, 2003).

25. Douglas Frantz, "Military Bestrides Turkey's Path to the European Union," *New York Times*, January 14, 2001, p. 3. See also Eric Rouleau, "Turkey's Dream of Democracy," *Foreign Affairs* 79, no. 6 (November–December 2000): 100–114.

26. Frantz, "Military Bestrides Turkey's Path," p. 3.

27. BBC News, "Profile: Orhan Pamuk," December 16, 2005 (http://news.bbc.co.uk/2/hi/europe/4535476.stm, accessed May 1, 2006). The Turkish government is sensitive about representations of the 1915 killings of Armenians, insisting that the number of deaths is overstated and that they should be classified as war casualties rather than genocide. On this subject, see Taner Akçam, *A Shameful Act: The Armenian Genocide and the Question of Turkish Responsibility* (New York: Metropolitan Books, 2006).

28. BBC News, "Turk Writer's Insult Trial Halted," December 16, 2005 (http://news.bbc.co.uk/2/hi/europe/4533664.stm, accessed May 1, 2006).

29. See the debate surrounding the "non" vote in the French referendum of May 29, 2005, which rejected the European Constitution.

30. Of course, the definition of Europe is itself at stake in this debate. As Rumelili observes, "Europe is merely a geographical construct, with no natural or pre-given boundaries; the geographical parameters of Europe have not only shifted throughout the centuries but also within the short history of the European 'community' as well." Rumelili, "Constructing Identity and Relating to Difference," pp. 39–40.

31. Gordon and Taspinar, "Turkey's European Quest," p. 5. On the historical definition of Europe, see J.G.A. Pocock, "What Do We Mean by Europe?" *Wilson Quarterly* 21, no. 1 (Winter 1997). Pocock argues that contemporary Europe "is a set of arrangements designed to ensure that peoples will not again define themselves as states, and will surrender both the power to make war and the power to control the movements of market forces" (p. 29).

32. Gordon and Taspinar, "Turkey's European Quest," pp. 4–5.

33. Corrado Pirzio-Biroli, head of the cabinet of former EU commissioner Franz Fischler, "Does 'Muslim' Turkey Belong in 'Christian' Europe?" (discussion, National Press Club, Washington, D.C., January 13, 2005).

34. Interview with *Le Monde*, November 8, 2002. Echoing the original language of the Treaty of Rome, the Maastrict Treaty prescribes that "any European State may apply to become a Member of the Union." Article 0 under the Final Provisions (Title VII) of the Maastricht Treaty (7 February 1992).

35. Kösebalaban, "Turkey's EU Membership," p. 146, n. 18, citing Helmut Schmidt, *Die Selbstbehauptung Europas, Perspectiven für das 21. Jahrhundert* (Stuttgart: Deutsche Verlagsanstalt, 2000).

36. Cited in Michael S. Teitelbaum and Philip L. Martin, "Is Turkey Ready for Europe?" *Foreign Affairs* 82, no. 3 (May–June 2003): 98.

37. Cited in Bruno Waterfield, "Bolkestein: EU Faces Implosion Risk over Turkey," EUPolitix.com, September 7, 2004 (http://www.eupolitix.com/EN/News/200409/0c501627-c886-4fc1-95c2-e49c1945898a.htm, accessed May 16, 2005).

38. On this debate, see José Casanova, "Religion, European Secular Identities, and European Integration," in Peter Katzenstein and Timothy Byrnes (Eds.), *Religion in an Expanding Europe* (Cambridge: Cambridge University Press, 2006), pp. 65–92.

39. On the postcolonial cultural and historical context of the recent events in France, see Paul Silverstein and Chantal Tetreault, "Urban Violence in France," *Middle East Report Online*, November 2005 (http://www.merip.org/mero/interventions/silverstein_tetreault_interv.htm, accessed November 28, 2005), and on Muslims in Europe more generally, see the special issue on the subject of *Hagar: Studies in Culture, Polity and Identities* 6, no. 1 (2005).

40. Silverstein and Tetreault argue that "the rage expressed by young men from the *cités* does not spring from anti-imperialist Arab nationalism or some sort of anti-Western jihadism . . . but rather from lifetimes of rampant unemployment, school failure, police harassment and everyday discrimination that tends to treat the youths as the *racaille* of Sarkozy's insult—regardless of race, ethnicity or religion." See "Urban Violence in France."

41. As Lynch argues in her study of attitudes toward religious pluralism in theological discourses, there are subtle variations in and alternatives to the categories exclusivism and inclusivism. She describes four such attitudes: exclusivism (my belief is superior and the only truth); inclusivism (my belief is right but yours may contain partial truths); pluralism (truth is multiple, other beliefs are equal to my own); and syncretism (it is possible and inevitable to merge aspects of different belief systems). Applying this framework to my argument, Judeo-Christian secularist approaches to European identity would be categorized as exclusivist, while their laicist counterparts would be generally inclusivist, with an occasional sprinkling of pluralism and syncretism. Cecelia Lynch, "Dogma, Praxis, and Religious Perspectives on Multiculturalism," *Millennium: Journal of International Studies* 29, no. 3 (2000): 741–59.

42. E. Fuat Keyman and Ziya Onis, "Helsinki, Copenhagen and beyond: challenges to the New Europe and the Turkish state," in Mehmet Ugur and Nergis Canefe (Eds.), *Turkey and European Integration: Accession Prospects and Issues* (London: Routledge, 2004), pp. 188–89.

43. Charles Taylor, "Modern Social Imaginaries," *Public Culture* 14, no. 1 (2002): 106.

44. Alev Çinar, *Modernity, Islam, and Secularism in Turkey* (Minneapolis: University of Minnesota Press, 2005), p. 9. Secularist ideologies also can be situated in what Halliday has described as a "triple, explanatory context": socialization, or why and how particular ideas are transmitted and adjusted over time and by different groups of leaders; comparison, or looking at how ideas in one setting are similar to and/or differ from those in another set of circumstances; and historical context, or examining the social and historical sources and appeals of particular sets of beliefs. Fred Halliday, *The Middle East in International Relations: Power, Politics and Ideology* (New York: Cambridge University Press, 2005), pp. 227–28.

45. Charles Taylor, "Walls of Separation: A Metaphor Which Has Outlived Its Time," keynote address at the conference on "Theology, Faith and Politics" (Northwestern University, Evanston, Illinois, May 13, 2005).

46. See, for example, Bernard Lewis, *What Went Wrong? Western Impact and Middle Eastern Response* (Oxford: Oxford University Press, 2002). For a critique, see Adam Sabra, "What Is Wrong with 'What Went Wrong?'?" *Middle East Report Online*, August 2003 (http://www.merip.org/mero/interventions/sabra_interv.html, accessed May 16, 2005).

47. On the cultural boundaries of democracy, see Alfred Stepan, "The World's Religious Systems and Democracy: Crafting the 'Twin Tolerations,' " *Journal of Democracy* 11 (October 2000): 37–57.

48. "On rejetera la candidature turque à l'Union européene moins parce que l'Etat turc ne satisfait pas les exigences démocratiques, ce qui serait une bonne raison, que parce que la société turque n'est pas <européene>, c'est-à-dire ne partage pas le fonds de christianisme qui fonde sa laïcité meme." Olivier Roy, *Vers un Islam européen* (Paris: Editions Esprit, 1999), p. 10.

49. Samuel Huntington, *The Clash of Civilizations and the Remaking of World Order* (New York: Simon & Schuster, 1996), p. 158.

50. "Britons Back Christian Society," BBC News World Edition (http://news.bbc.co.uk/2/hi/uk_news/4434096.stm, accessed November 29, 2005).

51. Samuel Huntington, "The Clash of Civilizations," *Foreign Affairs* 72, no. 3 (1993): 42.

52. Nilüfer Göle, "Negotiating Europeanism and Republicanism: The Turkish Question in France," paper presented at "Cultures of Democracy" conference (Northwestern University, Evanston, Illinois, April 21, 2005).

53. Walter Russell Mead, "Secular Europe and Religious America: Implications for Transatlantic Relations" (discussion, Pew Forum on Religion and Public Life, Washington, D.C., April 21, 2005).

54. Göle, "Negotiating Europeanism and Republicanism: The Turkish Question in France."

55. Rumelili, "Constructing Identity and Relating to Difference," p. 44.

56. Ibid., p. 39.

57. Ibid.

58. David Martin, "Religion, Secularity, Secularism and European Integration," paper presented at a workshop on "Secularization and Religion" (Erfurt, Germany, July 17, 2003).

59. Daniel Nexon, "Religion, European Identity, and Political Contention in Historical Perspective," in Katzenstein and Byrnes, *Religion in an Expanding Europe,* p. 279.

60. Silverstein and Tetreault, "Urban Violence in France."

61. Talal Asad, "Responses," in David Scott and Charles Hirschkind (Eds.), *Powers of the Secular Modern: Talal Asad and His Interlocutors* (Stanford: Stanford University Press, 2006), p. 219.

62. Davison argues that secularism and laicism should not be conflated: "*secularism* and *laicism* are not two different words for the same institutional arrangement, but rather two distinct, complex, varied, contested, and dynamic possibilities in the range of nontheocratic politics." In Davison's reading, Turkey is laicist and not secularist because Kemalism did not seek to separate religion from the state and pursue a nonreligious state inasmuch as it used the state to control, regulate, and mix Islam and politics in a particular way. Andrew Davison, "Turkey, a 'Secular' State? The Challenge of Description," *South Atlantic Quarterly* 102, nos. 2–3 (Spring–Summer 2003): 333.

63. An example is the French debate in late 2003 and early 2004 over the findings of the Stasi Commission and the passage of legislation restricting religious expression in public spaces. See John R. Bowen, "Muslims and Citizens," *Boston Review,* February–March 2004, pp. 31–35.

64. Davison, "Turkey, a 'Secular' State?" pp. 344. See also Fred Halliday, "Turkey 1998: Secularism in Question," in *Nation and Religion in the Middle East* (Boulder: Lynne Rienner, 2000), p. 183.

65. Rumelili, "Constructing Identity and Relating to Difference," p. 44.

66. Ibid.

67. Ole Wæver, "Insecurity, Security and Asecurity," p. 100.

68. On commonalities and differences between European countries vis-à-vis the decline of individual and collective religious belief and expression, see Hugh McLeod and Werner Ustorf, *The Decline of Christendom in Western Europe: 1750–2000* (Cambridge: Cambridge University Press, 2003); Grace Davie, *Religion in Modern Europe: A Memory Mutates* (Oxford: Oxford University Press, 2000); René Rémond, *Religion and Society in Modern Europe* (Oxford: Blackwell, 1999); and Grace Davie, *Religion in Britain since 1945: Believing without Belonging* (Oxford: Blackwell, 1994).

69. See chapter 4. See also M. Hakan Yavuz, *Islamic Political Identity in Turkey* (New York: Oxford University Press, 2003), and Jenny White, *Islamic Mobilization in Turkey: A Study in Vernacular Politics* (Seattle: University of Washington Press, 2002).

70. For a controversial example of the argument that "much of Atatürk's legacy risks being lost" in contemporary Turkey, see Robert L. Pollack, "The Sick Man of Europe—Again," *Wall Street Journal,* February 16, 2005, p. A14.

71. Phillips, "Turkey's Dreams of Accession," p. 89. Philips adds that "although the U.S. government officially supports Erdogan, some Pentagon officials are uneasy about his Islamic orientation. They believe that the Turkish armed forces are far more reliable than the AKP in fighting terrorism" (p. 97).

72. Some Europeans have also expressed concern with the implications of the Kemalist model for democratization and, in particular, religious freedom in Turkey.

73. Kösebalaban, "Turkey's EU Membership," p. 138.

74. Erhard Franz, "Secularism and Islamism in Turkey,' in Kai Hafez (Ed.), *The Islamic World and the West: An Introduction to Political Cultures and International Relations* (Leiden: Brill, 2000), p. 173.

75. *Leyla Sahin v. Turkey*, European Court of Human Rights Grand Chamber, Application No. 4474/98, November 10, 2005. ECHR decisions may be accessed at http://www.echr.coe.int/echr.

76. Jill Marshall, "Freedom of Religious Expression and Gender Equality: *Sahin v Turkey*," *Modern Law Review* 69, no. 3 (2006): 453. There was a lone dissenting opinion from Judge Tulkens that according to Marshall represented "a more sophisticated analysis of secularism, equality and liberty" in comparison with the majority opinion (p. 454).

77. Paragraph 114, *Sahin* Grand Chamber judgment. Citing the Turkish Constitutional Court's Judgment of March 1989, the ECHR decision reads as follows: "the Constitutional Court stated that secularism, as the guarantor of democratic values, was the meeting point of liberty and equality. The principle prevented the State from manifesting a preference for a particular religion or belief; it thereby guided the State in its role of impartial arbiter, and necessarily entailed freedom of religion and conscience. It also served to protect the individual not only against arbitrary interference by the State but from external pressure from extremist movements. The Constitutional Court added that freedom to manifest one's religion could be restricted in order to defend those values and principles." Paragraph 113, *Sahin* Grand Chamber judgment.

78. Similar judgments were rendered in the cases of *Karaduman v. Turkey*, Application no. 16278/90, May 3, 1993, and *Dahlab v Switzerland*, Application no. 42393/98, February 15, 2001. See Marshall, "Freedom of Religious Expression," pp. 455–56.

79. Marshall, "Freedom of Religious Expression," p. 461.

80. "LOI n° 2004–228 du 15 mars 2004 encadrant, en application du principe de laïcité, le port de signes ou de tenues manifestant une appartenance religieuse dans les écoles, collèges et lycées publics. Text available at http://www.legifrance.gouv.fr/WAspad/Visu?cid=689656&indice=1&table=JORF&ligneDeb=1.

81. Halliday, *The Middle East in International Relations*, p. 7, n. 6.

82. http://europa.eu.int/comm/enlargement/docs/pdf/st20002_en05_TR_framedoc.pdf, accessed November 21, 2005.

83. Fabrizio Barbaso, "Turkey-EU Relations in the perspective of the December European Council" (Middle East Technical University, Ankara, May 25, 2004).

84. Göle, "Negotiating Europeanism."

85. It may be best that it remain so. As Wæver suggests, "maybe Europe is not even that much of a we, but a way, a how, where there is more and more of a European flavor to being French, German, and so on. . . . 'Europe' should be seen neither as a project replacing the nation/state nor as irrelevant. It is an additional layer of identification." Wæver, "Insecurity, Security, and Asecurity," p. 94.

86. Jenny White, "Turkey's New 'Muslimhood': The End of 'Islamism'?" *Congress Monthly*, November–December 2003, p. 9.

87. Yavuz, *Islamic Political Identity in Turkey*, p. 212.

88. Taylor, "Modern Social Imaginaries," p. 91. On the concept of multiple modernities, see Peter J. Katzenstein, "Multiple Modernities as Limits to Secular Europeanization?" in Katzenstein and Byrnes, *Religion in an Expanding Europe*, and S. N. Eisenstadt, "The Reconstruction of Religious Arenas in the Framework of

'Multiple Modernities,' " *Millennium: Journal of International Studies* 29, no. 3 (2000): 591–611.

89. Göle, "Islam in Public," p. 175.

90. Ibid., pp. 173, 183.

91. Çinar, *Modernity, Islam, and Secularism in Turkey*, p. 171.

92. Talip Küçükcan, "State, Islam, and Religious Liberty in Modern Turkey: Reconfiguration of Religion in the Public Sphere," *Brigham Young University Law Review* 2 (2003): 493.

93. Yavuz, *Islamic Political Identity in Turkey*, p. 267.

94. Çinar, *Modernity, Islam, and Secularism in Turkey*, p. 173.

95. Talal Asad, *Formations of the Secular: Christianity, Islam, Modernity* (Stanford: Stanford University Press, 2003), p. 180.

96. Peter van der Veer, "The Moral State," in Peter van der Veer and Hartmut Lehmann (Eds.), *Nation and Religion: Perspectives on Europe and Asia* (Princeton: Princeton University Press, 1999), p. 39.

97. For an alternative approach to the interface between the domestic and the international that explains the collapse of overseas empires in terms of institutional factors within the metropolitan countries, see Hendrik Spruyt, *Ending Empire: Contested Sovereignty and Territorial Partition* (Ithaca: Cornell University Press, 2005).

98. See Paul Kowert and Jeffrey Legro, "Norms, Identity, and Their Limits: A Theoretical Reprise," in Peter J. Katzenstein (Ed.), *The Culture of National Security: Norms and Identity in World Politics* (New York: Columbia University Press, 1996), p. 466.

99. This is exemplified in Huntington's statement that "modern Western man, being unable for the most part to assign a dominant and central place to religion in his own affairs, found himself unable to conceive that any other peoples in any other place could have done so, and was therefore impelled to devise other explanations of what seemed to him only superficial phenomena." Samuel Huntington, "The Return of Islam," *Commentary* 61, no. 1 (January 1976): 40.

CHAPTER SIX
THE UNITED STATES AND IRAN

1. "States Lights and Christmas Rights," *Time*, December 31, 1979, pp. 10–11, cited in Catherine V. Scott, "Bound for Glory: The Hostage Crisis as Captivity Narrative in Iran," *International Studies Quarterly* 44 (2000): 177.

2. Melani McAlister, *Epic Encounters: Culture, Media and U.S. Interests in the Middle East, 1945–2000* (Berkeley: University of California Press, 2001), p. 198.

3. See chapter 4. See also McAlister, "Iran, Islam and the Terrorist Threat, 1979–1989," in *Epic Encounters*, pp. 198–234. On the hostage crisis, see further David Farber, *Taken Hostage: The Iran Hostage Crisis and America's First Encounter with Radical Islam* (Princeton: Princeton University Press, 2004); David Harris, *The Crisis: The President, the Prophet, and the Shah—1979 and the Coming of Militant Islam* (New York: Little, Brown, 2004); and Stephen Kinzer, *All the Shah's Men: An American Coup and the Roots of Middle East Terror* (Hoboken, N.J.: John Wiley & Sons, 2003).

4. On competing explanations of the motivations of the hostage takers, see David Patrick Houghton, *U.S. Foreign Policy and the Hostage Crisis* (Cambridge: Cambridge University Press, 2001), especially ch. 3, "The Origins of the Crisis." Cottam argues that "the new regime had to move quickly, it felt, to preclude any attempt by the CIA and SAVAK to restore the old regime." Richard Cottam, *Iran and the United States: A Cold War Case Study* (Pittsburgh: University of Pittsburgh Press, 1988), p. 207.

5. "The embassy in Tehran opposed the decision [to grant the Shah's request to enter the United States for medical treatment] and warned of a possible takeover of the embassy by hostile forces." Cottam, *Iran and the United States*, p. 210.

6. Suzanne Maloney, "Identity and Change in Iran's Foreign Policy," in Shibley Telhami and Michael Barnett (Eds.), *Identity and Foreign Policy in the Middle East* (Ithaca: Cornell University, 2002), p. 105.

7. McAlister, *Epic Encounters*, p. 205.

8. William E. Connolly, *Pluralism* (Durham, N.C.: Duke University Press, 2005), p. 143.

9. Charles Kurzman, *The Unthinkable Revolution in Iran* (Cambridge, Mass.: Harvard University Press, 2004).

10. Talal Asad, "Responses," in David Scott and Charles Hirschkind (Eds.), *Powers of the Secular Modern: Talal Asad and His Interlocutors* (Stanford: Stanford University Press, 2006), p. 224.

11. Peter van der Veer, "The Moral State: Religion, Nation, and Empire in Victorian Britain and British India," in Peter van der Veer and Hartmut Lehmann (Eds.), *Nation and Religion: Perspectives on Europe and Asia* (Princeton: Princeton University Press, 1999), p. 20.

12. Anthony W. Marx, *Faith in Nation: Exclusionary Origins of Nationalism* (New York: Oxford University Press, 2003), pp. 25–26.

13. Ibid., p. 27.

14. Ibid., p. 29.

15. Stephen Saideman, "Thinking Theoretically about Identity and Foreign Policy," in Telhami and Barnett, *Identity and Foreign Policy in the Middle East*, p. 178.

16. Peter van der Veer and Hartmut Lehmann, introduction to *Nation and Religion*, p. 7.

17. Mlada Bukovansky, *Legitimacy and Power Politics: The American and French Revolutions in International Political Culture* (Princeton: Princeton University Press, 2002), p. 32.

18. Marx, *Faith in Nation*, p. 6.

19. Van der Veer and Lehmann, introduction to *Nation and Religion*, p. 7.

20. Mary Ann Heiss, "Real Men Don't Wear Pajamas: Anglo-American Cultural Perceptions of Mohammed Mossadeq and the Iranian Oil Nationalization Dispute," in Peter L. Hahn and Mary Ann Heiss (Eds.), *Empire and Revolution: The United States and the Third World since 1945* (Columbus: Ohio State University Press, 2001), p. 181.

21. Rodney Bruce Hall, *National Collective Identity: Social Constructs and International Systems* (New York: Columbia University Press, 1999), p. 5.

22. Ole Wæver, "Insecurity, Security and Asecurity in the West European Non-war Community," in Emanuel Adler and Michael Barnett (Eds.), *Security Communities* (Cambridge: Cambridge University Press, 1998), p. 105.

23. On this angle, see Boroujerdi's argument that some Iranian intellectuals have been critical of laicism for its association with Enlightenment presumptions including "the stripping of nature's divine essence, the advocacy of science and secular knowledge, and the privileging of mind and body over soul." Mehrzad Boroujerdi, "Iranian Islam and the Faustian Bargain of Western Modernity," *Journal of Peace Research* 34, no. 1 (1997): 2. On the creation of Iranian national identity and its relationship to Western thought in the context of contemporary Iranian intellectual history, see Boroujerdi's *Iranian Intellectuals and the West: The Tormented Triumph of Nativism* (Syracuse: Syracuse University Press, 1996). On the argument that violent antagonism toward the West, defined by a particular set of economic and political ideals including liberal democracy and capitalism, is not exclusive to non-Westerners but is an important part of the West's own heritage, see Ian Buruma and Avishai Margalit, *Occidentalism: The West in the Eyes of Its Enemies* (New York: Penguin Books, 2004).

24. On this subject, see Bahman Baktiari, "Dilemmas of Reform and Democracy in the Islamic Republic of Iran," in Robert Hefner (Ed.), *Remaking Muslim Politics: Pluralism, Contestation, Democratization* (Princeton: Princeton University Press, 2005), pp. 112–32; Setrag Manoukian, "Power, Religion, and the Effects of Publicness in 20th-Century Shiraz," in Armando Salvatore and Mark LeVine (Eds.), *Religion, Social Practice, and Contested Hegemonies* (New York: Palgrave Macmillan, 2005), pp. 57–83; Said Amir Arjomand, *The Turban for the Crown: The Islamic Revolution in Iran* (New York: Oxford University Press, 1988); Ali Mirsepassi, *Intellectual Discourse and the Politics of Modernization: Negotiating Modernity in Iran* (Cambridge: Cambridge University Press, 2000); Daniel Brumberg, *Reinventing Khomeini: The Struggle for Reform in Iran* (Chicago: University of Chicago Press, 2001); and Boroujerdi's *Iranian Intellectuals and the West*.

25. During the hostage crisis Frank Reynolds of ABC News referred to a "crescent of crisis, a cyclone hurling across a prairie." Edward Said, *Covering Islam: How the Media and the Experts Determine How We See the Rest of the World*, 2nd ed. (New York: Vintage Books, 1997), p. 84.

26. Some of the following material appears in Elizabeth Shakman Hurd, "The International Politics of Secularism: U.S. Foreign Policy and the Islamic Republic of Iran," *Alternatives: Global, Local, Political* 29, no. 2 (March–May 2004): 115–38.

27. John L. Esposito, *The Islamic Threat: Myth or Reality?* 3rd ed. (New York: Oxford University Press, 1999), p. 105.

28. Mirsepassi, *Intellectual Discourse and the Politics of Modernization*, p. 17.

29. John L. Esposito, *The Islamic Threat: Myth or Reality?* 2nd ed. (New York: Oxford University Press, 1992), p. 101.

30. Ervand Abrahamian's *Iran between Two Revolutions* (Princeton: Princeton University Press, 1982), Nikki Keddie's *Modern Iran: Roots and Results of Revolution* (New Haven: Yale University Press, 2003), and Arjomand's *The Turban for the Crown* are three landmark studies of the 1979 revolution. See also Misagh Parsa, *Social Origins of the Iranian Revolution* (Oxford: Columbia University Press, 1993); Roy Mottahedeh, *The Mantle of the Prophet: Religion and Politics in Iran* (New York: Pantheon Books, 1985); Hamid Dabashi, *Theology of Discontent: The Ideological Foundations of the Islamic Revolution in Iran* (New York: New York University Press, 1993); Fred Halliday, *Islam and the Myth of Confrontation: Religion and Politics in the Middle East* (London: I. B. Tauris, 1996), and Halliday, *Iran: Dictatorship and Development* (New York: Pen-

guin Books, 1979); Nikki Keddie, *Iran and the Muslim World: Resistance and Revolution* (London: Macmillan, 1995); Robin Wright, *The Last Great Revolution: Turmoil and Transformation* (New York: Knopf, 2000); Dariush Zahedi, *Iranian Revolution Then and Now: Indicators of Regime Instability* (Boulder: Westview Press, 2000); Mirsepassi, *Intellectual Discourse and the Politics of Modernization*; and Roger Owen, *State, Power and Politics in the Making of the Modern Middle East*, 3rd ed. (London: Routledge, 2004), chs. 5 and 6. Khomeini's main writings can be found in Hamid Algar (Trans.), *Islam and Revolution* (Berkeley: Mizan Press, 1981). On U.S.-Iranian relations, see William O. Beeman, *The "Great Satan" vs. the "Mad Mullahs": How the United States and Iran Demonize Each Other* (New York: Praeger, 2005); James A. Bill, *The Eagle and the Lion: The Tragedy of American-Iranian Relations* (New Haven: Yale University Press, 1988); and Gary Sick, *All Fall Down: America's Tragic Encounter with Iran* (New York: Random House, 1985).

31. McAlister, *Epic Encounters*, p. 199.

32. Ibid., p. 210.

33. Said, *Covering Islam*, p. 102. He argues that U.S. mainstream media coverage of the revolution coalesced around the following themes: Iranians are Shi'ites who long for martyrdom, are led by a nonrational Khomeini, hate America, are determined to destroy the satanic spies, and are unwilling to compromise (p. 104).

34. "'The secular' presents itself as the ground from which theological discourse was generated." Talal Asad, *Formations of the Secular: Christianity, Islam, Modernity* (Stanford: Stanford University Press, 2003), p. 192.

35. See William E. Connolly, *Why I Am Not a Secularist* (Minneapolis: University of Minnesota Press, 1999), p. 21.

36. Linda M. G. Zerilli, "Doing without Knowing: Feminism's Politics of the Ordinary," *Political Theory* 26, no. 4 (August 1998): 443.

37. John L. Esposito, "Islam and Secularism in the Twenty-First Century," in John L. Esposito and Azzam Tamimi (Eds.), *Islam and Secularism in the Middle East* (New York: New York University Press, 2000), p. 3.

38. Talal Asad, *Genealogies of Religion: Discipline and Reasons of Power in Christianity and Islam* (Baltimore: Johns Hopkins University Press, 1993), p. 269.

39. Cottam, *Iran and the United States*, pp. 5–6.

40. On November 18, 1979, Yassir Arafat negotiated the release of thirteen female and African American hostages who were not being held as suspected spies on the grounds that "neither of these groups was as central as white men to the dominant power structure of the United States." McAlister, *Epic Encounters*, p. 210. See also Charles W. Kegley Jr., "Hard Choices: The Carter Administration's Hostage Rescue Mission in Iran," *Pew Case Studies in International Affairs* 360 (Washington, D.C.: Institute for the Study of Diplomacy, Georgetown University, 1994).

41. McAlister, *Epic Encounters*, p. 210.

42. Cited in ibid., p. 210.

43. Saba Mahmood, *Politics of Piety: The Islamic Revival and the Feminist Subject* (Princeton: Princeton University Press, 2005), p. 32.

44. McAlister, *Epic Encounters*, p. 209.

45. Marx, *Faith in Nation*, p. 194.

46. Van der Veer, "The Moral State," p. 19.

47. Mark O'Keefe, "Has the United States Become Judeo-Christian-Islamic?" Newhouse News Service (http://www.newhouse.com/archive/okeefe051503.html, accessed May 21, 2003).

48. Will Lester, "AP Poll: Religion Key in American Lives," *Guardian Unlimited*, June 6, 2005 (http://www.guardian.co.uk/worldlatest/story/0,1280,-5056061,00.html, accessed June 9, 2005).

49. Eck counters this assumption with evidence of the religious diversification of the United States, while observing that some of the most strident Christian communities show little awareness of this diversification. Diana L. Eck, *A New Religious America: How a "Christian County" Has Become the World's Most Religiously Diverse Nation* (New York: HarperCollins, 2002), p. 4.

50. Hashemi refers to this as the "Islamic exceptionalist thesis" and maintains that it does not stand up to critical scrutiny. Nader Hashemi, "Change from Within," in Joshua Cohen and Deborah Chasman (Eds.), *Islam and the Challenge of Democracy* (Princeton: Princeton University Press, 2004), p. 51.

51. On the prestructuration of discourse, see Hayden White, *The Content of the Form* (Baltimore: Johns Hopkins University Press, 1989).

52. McAlister, *Epic Encounters*, p. 211.

53. Ibid.

54. Cottam, *Iran and the United States*, p. 13.

55. Said, *Covering Islam*, p. 84.

56. Van der Veer, "The Moral State," p. 39.

57. On this argument, see Mirsepassi, *Intellectual Discourse and the Politics of Modernization*, and Elizabeth Shakman Hurd, "The Political Authority of Secularism in International Relations," *European Journal of International Relations* 10, no. 2 (June 2004): 238.

58. On the history of American attempts to consolidate national identity in opposition to a range of internal and external others, see David Campbell, *Writing Security: United States Foreign Policy and the Politics of Identity* (Minneapolis: University of Minnesota Press, 1992); on this dynamic in the former Yugoslavia, see David Campbell, *National Deconstruction: Violence, Identity and Justice in Bosnia* (Minneapolis: University of Minnesota Press, 1998).

59. José Casanova, *Public Religions in the Modern World* (Chicago: University of Chicago Press, 1994), p. 20.

60. Marx, *Faith in Nation*, p. 21. On the productive relationship between "foreignness" and democratic theory and practice, see Bonnie Honig, *Democracy and the Foreigner* (Princeton: Princeton University Press, 2001).

61. Michael Dillon, "The Scandal of the Refugee: Some Reflections on the 'Inter' of International Relations and Continental Thought," in David Campbell and Michael J. Shapiro (Eds.), *Moral Spaces: Rethinking Ethics and World Politics* (Minneapolis: University of Minnesota, 1999), p. 104.

62. Bill, *The Eagle and the Lion*, p. 435.

63. Ibid.

64. Bernard Cohen, *The Political Process and Foreign Policy: The Making of the Japanese Peace Settlement* (Princeton: Princeton University Press, 1957), p. 29.

65. Saideman, "Thinking Theoretically," p. 195.

66. Bill, *The Eagle and the Lion*, pp. 436–37.

Chapter Seven
Political Islam

1. "We need to ask the fundamental question: is Islam compatible with laicism? But then, of which laicism are we speaking?" Olivier Roy, *Vers un Islam européen* (Paris: Editions Esprit, 1999), p. 11.

2. Talal Asad, *Genealogies of Religion: Discipline and Reasons of Power in Christianity and Islam* (Baltimore: Johns Hopkins University Press, 1993), pp. 28–29.

3. Timothy Mitchell, *Rule of Experts: Egypt, Techno-Politics, Modernity* (Berkeley: University of California Press, 2002), p. 7. On this subject, see Fernando Coronil, "Beyond Occidentalism: Toward Nonimperial Geohistorical Categories," *Cultural Anthropology* 11, no. 1 (1996): 58–87; David Scott, "Conversion and Demonism: Colonial Christian Discourse and Religion in Sri Lanka," *Comparative Studies in Society and History* 34, no. 2 (1992): 331–65; Elizabeth Hallam and Brian V. Street (Eds.), *Cultural Encounters: Representing "Otherness"* (New York: Routledge, 2000); Richard King, *Orientalism and Religion: Postcolonial Theory, India and "the Mystic East"* (London: Routledge, 1999); Martin Lewis and Karen Wigen, *The Myth of Continents: A Critique of Metageography* (Berkeley: University of California Press, 1997); and Tejaswini Niranjana, *Siting Translation: History, Post-Structuralism, and the Colonial Context* (Berkeley: University of California Press, 1992).

4. Talal Asad, "The Idea of an Anthropology of Islam," *Center for Contemporary Arab Studies Occasional Paper Series* (Washington, D.C.: Georgetown University, 1996), p. 11.

5. Charles Hirschkind, "What Is Political Islam?" *Middle East Report* 205 (December 1997): 14.

6. See, for example, Jonathan Fox and Shmuel Sandler, *Bringing Religion into International Relations* (New York: Palgrave, 2004). On religion and security, see Robert A. Seiple and Dennis R. Hoover, *Religion and Security: The New Nexus in International Relations* (New York: Rowman & Littlefield, 2004). On religion and conflict resolution, see R. Scott Appleby, *The Ambivalence of the Sacred: Religion, Violence, and Reconciliation* (Lanham, Md.: Rowman & Littlefield, 2000). On religion and intercivilizational dialogue, see Fred Dallmayr, *Dialogue among Civilizations: Some Exemplary Voices* (New York: Palgrave Macmillan, 2002).

7. Lynch argues that "the analysis of religious attitudes, ethics, and praxis by students of world politics more generally has been lacking. Even much contemporary 'critical' International Relations remains dominated by Enlightenment worldviews that cast religious belief, thought, and action in overly essentialist terms." Cecelia Lynch, "Dogma, Praxis, and Religious Perspectives on Multiculturalism," *Millennium: Journal of International Studies* 29, no. 3 (2000): 758.

8. See Stephen K. White, *Sustaining Affirmation: The Strengths of Weak Ontology in Political Theory* (Princeton: Princeton University Press, 2000), p. 3.

9. Saba Mahmood, *Politics of Piety: The Islamic Revival and the Feminist Subject* (Princeton: Princeton University Press, 2005), p. 33.

10. Guilain Denoeux, "The Forgotten Swamp: Navigating Political Islam," *Middle East Policy* 9, no. 2 (2002): 61.

11. Nazih N. Ayubi, *Political Islam: Religion and Politics in the Arab World* (New York: Routledge, 1992), p. ix. Zubaida divides the Islamist movement into "conserva-

tive Islam" (Saudi establishment); "radical Islam" (more violent appropriations of Islam associated with Sayyid Qutb and his followers); and "political Islam" (affiliated with nationalist and leftist projects advocating "ideas and programmes of socio-political transformation based on Islam"). Sami Zubaida, "Trajectories of Political Islam: Egypt, Iran and Turkey," in David Marquand and Ronald L. Nettler (Eds.), *Religion and Democracy* (Oxford: Blackwell, 2000), pp. 60–78.

12. Robert W. Hefner, "Introduction: Modernity and the Remaking of Muslim Politics," in Hefner (Ed.), *Remaking Muslim Politics: Pluralism, Contestation, Democratization* (Princeton: Princeton University Press, 2005), p. 18.

13. Armando Salvatore, *Political Islam and the Discourse of Modernity* (Reading, England: Ithaca Press, 1999), p. xxvi, n. 1.

14. Ibid., p. xx.

15. For a related argument regarding the alleged refusal of the Iranian hostage takers of 1979 to acknowledge the sanctity of the Western private sphere, see Melani McAlister, *Epic Encounters: Culture, Media and U.S. Interests in the Middle East, 1945–2000* (Berkeley: University of California Press, 2001), p. 220.

16. William E. Connolly, *Why I Am Not a Secularist* (Minneapolis: University of Minnesota Press, 1999), p. 22.

17. Roxanne L. Euben, *Enemy in the Mirror: Islamic Fundamentalism and the Limits of Modern Rationalism* (Princeton: Princeton University Press, 1999), p. xiv.

18. Raymond William Baker, *Islam without Fear: Egypt and the New Islamists* (Cambridge, Mass.: Harvard University Press, 2003), p. 4. See also Raymond Baker, "Building the World in a Global Age," in Armando Salvatore and Mark LeVine (Eds.), *Religion, Social Practice, and Contested Hegemonies* (New York: Palgrave Macmillan, 2005), pp. 109–31.

19. Baker, *Islam without Fear*, p. 4.

20. Fawaz Gerges, *America and Political Islam: Clash of Cultures or Clash of Interests?* (Cambridge: Cambridge University Press, 1999), p. 6. For a critique of Western approaches to political Islam, see Jason Burke, *On the Road to Kandahar: Travels through Conflict in the Islamic World* (Toronto: Bond Street Books, 2006).

21. Peter van der Veer and Hartmut Lehmann (Eds.), *Nation and Religion: Perspectives on Europe and Asia* (Princeton: Princeton University Press, 1999), p. 3, citing Bruce Lawrence, *Defenders of God: The Fundamentalist Revolt against the Modern Age* (San Francisco: Harper & Row, 1989).

22. Gertrude Himmelfarb, "The Illusions of Cosmopolitanism," in Martha C. Nussbaum, *For Love of Country?: Debating the Limits of Patriotism*, ed. Joshua Cohen (Boston: Beacon Press, 1996), p. 76.

23. Talal Asad, "Religion, Nation-State, Secularism," in van der Veer and Lehmann, *Nation and Religion*, p. 191.

24. Lynch, "Dogma, Praxis, and Religious Perspectives," pp. 741–59.

25. McAlister, *Epic Encounters*, p. 220.

26. Connolly, *Why I Am Not a Secularist*, p. 6.

27. Sheila Carapico, "Killing Live 8, Noisily: The G-8, Liberal Dissent and the London Bombings," *Middle East Report Online*, July 14, 2005 (http://www.merip.org/mero/mero071405.html).

28. Robert D. Lee, introduction to Mohammed Arkoun, *Rethinking Islam: Common Questions, Uncommon Answers*, trans. and ed. Robert D. Lee (Boulder: Westview Press, 1994), p. x.

29. Mohammed Ayoob, "Political Islam: Image and Reality," *World Policy Journal* 21, no. 3 (Fall 2004): 5.

30. Carapico, "Killing Live 8, Noisily."

31. Mark LeVine and Armando Salvatore, "Socio-Religious Movements and the Transformation of 'Common Sense' into a Politics of 'Common Good,' " in Salvatore and LeVine, *Religion, Social Practice, and Contested Hegemonies*, p. 51.

32. Olivier Roy, *L'échec de l'Islam politique* (Paris: Seuil, 1992).

33. Nilüfer Göle, "Islam in Public: New Visibilities and New Imaginaries," *Public Culture* 14, no. 1 (2002): 174.

34. An example is Mahmood who concludes that "in order to understand Islamism's enmeshment within, and challenges to, assumptions at the core of the secular-liberal imaginary, one must turn not to the usual spaces of political struggle (such as the state, the economy, and the law) but to arguments about what constitutes a proper way of living ethically in a world where such questions were thought to have become obsolete." Mahmood, *Politics of Piety*, p. 192.

35. Jonathan Fox, "Religion as an Overlooked Element of International Relations," *International Studies Review* 3, no. 3 (Fall 2001): 53–73.

36. McAlister argues in *Epic Encounters* (p. 232) that "the specific politics of women in the United States was presented as the gender order that emerged when there was no ideology present."

37. Connolly, *Why I Am Not a Secularist*, p. 23.

38. Norman Daniel, *Islam and the West: The Making of an Image* (Oxford: Oneworld, 2000, 1960), p. 327.

39. Gerges, *America and Political Islam*, p. 30.

40. Roger Owen, *State, Power and Politics in the Making of the Modern Middle East*, 3rd ed. (London: Routledge, 2004), p. 156. As Mahmood argues, "in this view, the project of restoring orthodox Islamic virtues crucially depends upon an oppositional stance toward what may be loosely defined as a modernist secular-liberal ethos— an ethos whose agents are often understood to be postcolonial Muslim regimes in cahoots with dominant Western powers." Mahmood, *Politics of Piety*, p. 24.

41. Graham Fuller, "The Future of Political Islam," *Foreign Affairs* 81, no. 2 (March–April 2002): 51.

42. Fred Halliday, *The Middle East in International Relations: Power, Politics and Ideology* (New York: Cambridge University Press, 2005), p. 122.

43. Bassam Tibi, "Post-Bipolar Order in Crisis: The Challenge of Politicised Islam," *Millennium: Journal of International Studies* 29, no. 3 (2000): 857.

44. John L. Esposito, *Political Islam: Revolution, Radicalism, or Reform?* (Boulder: Lynne Rienner Publishers, 1997), p. 2.

45. Hirschkind, "What Is Political Islam?" p. 12.

46. Ashis Nandy, "The Politics of Secularism and the Recovery of Religious Tolerance," in R.B.J. Walker and S. Mendlovitz (Eds.), *Contending Sovereignties: Redefining Political Community* (Boulder: Lynne Rienner, 1990), p. 140.

47. Mahmood uses the term in discussing the study of Muslim women and in particular "the assumptions triggered in the Western imagination [by this term] concerning
Islam's patriarchal and misogynist qualities." Mahmood, *Politics of Piety*, pp. 189–90.

48. Ibid., p. 189.

49. Ibid., p. 191.

50. Gilles Kepel, *The War for Muslim Minds: Islam and the West* (Cambridge,
Mass.: Belknap Press of Harvard University Press, 2004), p. 295.

51. Gerges, *America and Political Islam*, p. 231.

52. For a triumphalist account of the global potential of Western civilization, see
Rupert Emerson, *From Empire to Nation: The Rise to Self-Assertion of Asian and African Peoples* (Boston: Beacon Press, 1960). For a challenge, see Siba N. Grovogui,
*Sovereigns, Quasi-Sovereigns, and Africans: Race and Self-Determination in Interna-
tional Law* (Minneapolis: University of Minnesota Press, 1996).

53. See chapter 4. See also Taha Parla and Andrew Davison, *Corporatist Ideology
in Kemalist Turkey: Progress or Order?* (Syracuse: Syracuse University Press, 2004).

54. Gerges, *America and Political Islam*, p. 3. For an empirical challenge to the
alleged correlation between Islamic religious beliefs and autocracy, see the survey
findings in Ronald Inglehart (Ed.), *Islam, Gender, Culture, and Democracy: Findings
from the World Values Survey and the European Values Survey* (Willowdale, Ontario:
de Sitter Publications, 2003).

55. S.V.R. Nasr, "Democracy and Islamic Revivalism," *Political Science Quarterly*
110, no. 2 (Summer 1995): 262.

56. Asad, "Religion, Nation-State, Secularism," p. 191.

57. Mahmood, *Politics of Piety*, pp. 193–94.

58. Hirschkind, "What Is Political Islam?" p. 13. As King argues, "the very fact that
'the mystical' is seen as irrelevant to issues of social and political authority itself reflects
contemporary, secularized notions of and attitudes toward power. The separation of
the mystical from the political is itself a political decision!" Richard King, *Orientalism
and Religion: Postcolonial Theory, India and "the Mystic East"* (London: Routledge,
1999), p. 10 (emphasis in original).

59. On the argument that post- and anticolonial nationalism was never fully dominated by Western models of nationhood, see Chatterjee, who suggests that "the most
powerful as well as the most creative results of the nationalist imagination in Asia and
Africa are posited not on an identity but rather on a *difference* with the 'modular' forms
of the national society propagated by the modern West." Partha Chatterjee, *The Nation
and Its Fragments: Colonial and Postcolonial Histories* (Princeton: Princeton University Press, 1993), p. 5. See also Partha Chatterjee, *Nationalist Thought and the Colonial
World: A Derivative Discourse* (Minneapolis: University of Minnesota Press, 1993). For
the argument that Islamic modernism is a derivative discourse, see L. Carl Brown,
Religion and State: The Muslim Approach to Politics (New York: Columbia University
Press, 2000).

60. Anthony W. Marx, *Faith in Nation: Exclusionary Origins of Nationalism* (New
York: Oxford University Press, 2003), p. viii. Thanks to John Mearsheimer for recom-
mending this book.

61. Tibi, "Post-Bipolar Order in Crisis," p. 848.

62. Augustus Richard Norton, "Religious Resurgence and Political Mobilization
of the Shi'a in Lebanon," in Emile Sahliyeh (Ed.), *Religious Resurgence and Politics*

in the Contemporary World (Albany: State University of New York Press, 1990), pp. 231–32.

63. Hefner, "Muslim Democrats and Islamist Violence in Post-Soeharto Indonesia," in Hefner, *Remaking Muslim Politics*, p. 298.

64. Baker, *Islam without Fear*, p. 263.

65. Asad, "Religion, Nation-State, Secularism," p. 191.

66. Amartya Sen, "Humanity and Citizenship," in Nussbaum, *For Love of Country?* p. 118.

67. LeVine and Salvatore, "Socio-Religious Movements," pp. 47–48.

68. Talal Asad, *Formations of the Secular: Christianity, Islam, Modernity* (Stanford: Stanford University Press, 2003), p. 192.

69. Roosevelt to Spring Rice, July 1, 1907, in Morrison, *Letters of Theodore Roosevelt*, 5:698–99, cited in Douglas Little, *American Orientalism: The United States and the Middle East since 1945* (Chapel Hill: University of North Carolina Press, 2002), p. 15.

70. Cited in Martin Kramer, "Islam vs. Democracy," *Commentary* 95, no. 1 (January 1993): 37.

71. Cited in Laura Secor, "'Sands of Empire': Civilizations and Their Discontents," *New York Times Book Review*, June 26, 2005, p. 20. Merry argues that the United States is waging a civilizational war against Islam; on this argument, see Robert W. Merry, *Sands of Empire: Missionary Zeal, American Foreign Policy, and the Hazards of Global Ambition* (New York: Simon & Schuster, 2005), ch. 10 ("The World of Islam").

72. In a relatively nuanced example of this position, Buruma and Margulit argue that "the main difference between contemporary Islam and Protestantism is not that the former is more political, but that it insists on a greater moral regulation of the public sphere by religious authority." Ian Buruma and Avishai Margalit, *Occidentalism: The West in the Eyes of Its Enemies* (New York: Penguin Books, 2004), p. 128.

73. Mahmood, *Politics of Piety*, p. 199.

74. Bernard Lewis, "The Return of Islam," *Commentary* 61, no. 1 (January 1976): p. 40.

75. Sam Harris, *The End of Faith: Religion, Terror and the Future of Reason* (New York: W. W. Norton,, 2004), p. 110.

76. See Bernard Lewis, *What Went Wrong? Western Impact and Middle Eastern Response* (Oxford: Oxford University Press, 2002), and Lewis, "Islam and Liberal Democracy," *Atlantic Monthly* 271, no. 2 (February 1993): 89–98.

77. Benjamin Barber, *Jihad vs. McWorld: How Globalism and Tribalism Are Reshaping the World* (New York: Ballantine Books, 1996), p. 206.

78. Bernard Lewis, "The Roots of Muslim Rage," *Atlantic Monthly* 266, no. 3 (September 1990): 60.

79. Bernard Lewis, *Islam and the West*, (Oxford: Oxford University Press, 1994), pp. 135–36. See also Lewis, *The Political Language of Islam* (Chicago: University of Chicago Press, 1988). For a classic argument in defense of the incompatibility between Islam and modern politics, see Wilfred Cantwell Smith, *Islam in Modern History* (Princeton: Princeton University Press, 1957).

80. A. C. Grayling, "The New Crusade—for Understanding," *Financial Times, Weekend*, May 3–4, 2003, p. 5 (emphasis added), review of Richard Fletcher, *The Cross and the Crescent: Christianity and Islam from Muhammed to the Reformation* (London:

Penguin Press, 2003), and Andrew Wheatcroft, *Infidels: The Conflict between Christendom and Islam, 638–2002* (New York: Viking Press, 2003).

81. Barber, *Jihad vs. McWorld*, p. 205.

82. This explains, at least in part, the efforts of some North American evangelical Protestants to attempt to convert Muslims in Iraq to Christianity following the 2003 American invasion.

83. See, for instance, Daniel Pipes, "Same Difference: The Islamic Threat—Part I," *National Review*, 46, no. 7, November 1994, p. 63, and Daniel Pipes, "Political Islam Is a Threat to the West," in Paul H. Winters (Ed.), *Islam: Opposing Viewpoints* (San Diego: Greenhaven Press, 1995) pp. 190–96.

84. George W. Bush, cited in Matthew Davis, "Hamas Win Challenges US Policy," BBC News International, January 26, 2006 (http://news.bbc.co.uk/2/hi/middle_east/4652140.stm, accessed July 18, 2006).

85. Jim Hoagland, "Squaring Islam with Democracy," *Washington Post*, February 2, 2006, p. A21.

86. As Brumberg argues, "for a Khatami in Iran or an Abdurrahman Wahid in Indonesia, the challenge is not so much to produce a coherent synthesis of Islam and democracy, or pluralism and piety, as it is to find ways to make competing notions of political and religious community coexist." Daniel Brumberg, "Dissonant Politics in Iran and Indonesia," *Political Science Quarterly* 116, no. 3 (2001): 385.

87. Ayoob, "Political Islam: Image and Reality," p. 9.

88. Fred Halliday, *Islam and the Myth of Confrontation: Religion and Politics in the Middle East* (London: I. B. Tauris, 1996), p. 118.

89. Ira M. Lapidus, "The Separation of State and Religion in the Development of Early Islamic Society," *International Journal of Middle East Studies* 6 (1975): 363–85. "Despite the origins of Islam and its own teachings about the relationship between religious and political life, Islamic society has evolved in un-Islamic ways. In fact, religious and political life developed distinct spheres of experience with independent values, leaders and organizations. From the middle of the tenth century effective control of the Arab-Muslim empire had passed into the hands of generals, administrators, governors, and local provincial lords; the Caliphs had lost all effective political power. Governments in Islamic lands were henceforth secular regimes—sultanates—in theory authorized by the Caliphs, but actually legitimized by the need for public order. Henceforth, Muslim states were fully differentiated political bodies without any intrinsic religious character, though they were officially loyal to Islam and committed to its defense." Lapidus, "Separation of State and Religion," p. 364. Lapidus cites Sir Hamilton Gibb's argument that Muslim political thinkers were "aware of the separation of state and religion and recognized the emergence of an autonomous sphere of religious activity and organization" (ibid., p. 365). H.A.R. Gibb, "Constitutional Organization," in M. Khadduri and H. Liebesny (Eds.), *Law in the Middle East* (Washington, D.C.: Middle East Institute, 1955), pp. 3–27.

90. Ira M. Lapidus, "State and Religion in Islamic Societies," *Past and Present* 151 (1996): 24.

91. John L. Esposito, *The Islamic Threat: Myth or Reality?* 3rd ed. (New York: Oxford University Press, 1999), p. 106.

92. Muhammad Asad, *The Principles of State and Government in Islam* (Berkeley: University of California Press, 1961), p. 22. There have been many debates concerning

the proper interpretation of Islamic law vis-à-vis structures of governance. Tibi criticizes the attempt to use Islamic law as the basis for an Islamic state, arguing that in Islamic history the *shari'a* was never a constitution of the Islamic caliphate, which in fact was consistently an "absolute monarchy" and that there was a clear separation between *shari'a* and *siyasa* (rule). Tibi, "Post-Bipolar Order in Crisis," p. 852, citing Joseph Schacht, *An Introduction to Islamic Law* (Oxford: Clarendon Press, 1964), p. 54.

93. See Mehrzad Boroujerdi, "Iranian Islam and the Faustian Bargain of Western Modernity," *Journal of Peace Research* 34, no. 1 (1997): 1–5, and Bruce Lawrence, *Shattering the Myth: Islam beyond Violence* (Princeton: Princeton University Press, 1998).

94. Robert Hefner, "Public Islam and the Problem of Democratization," *Sociology of Religion* 62, no. 4 (2001): 509.

95. Hefner, "Muslim Democrats and Islamist Violence in Post-Soeharto Indonesia," p. 273.

96. Asad, "The Idea of an Anthropology of Islam," p. 7. As Asad argues, "An Islamic discursive tradition is simply a tradition of Muslim discourse that addresses itself to conceptions of the Islamic past and future, with reference to a particular Islamic practice in the present. Clearly, not everything Muslims say belongs to an Islamic discursive tradition. Nor is an Islamic tradition in this sense necessarily imitative of what was done in the past" (pp. 14–15).

97. Ayubi, *Political Islam*, p. 119. See also M. Hakan Yavuz, *Islamic Political Identity in Turkey* (Oxford: Oxford University Press, 2003).

98. Jenny White, *Islamist Mobilization in Turkey: A Study in Vernacular Politics* (Seattle: University of Washington Press, 2002), p. 6.

99. Dale F. Eickelman and James Piscatori, *Muslim Politics* (Princeton: Princeton University Press, 1996), p. 4.

100. Ibid., p. 5.

101. Ayubi, *Political Islam*, p. 230.

102. Daniel Brumberg, "Islamists and the Politics of Consensus," *Journal of Democracy* 13, no. 3 (July 2002): 111–12. Brumberg emphasizes that while Islam may be the dominant "language of politics" in many countries, social order is not determined exclusively by Islamic doctrine, tradition, or identity but also involves gender, ethnicity, professional status, economic opportunities, nonreligious political ties, family obligations, and a range of other factors.

103. Mahmood, *Politics of Piety*, p. 35.

104. Roxanne L. Euben, "Contingent Borders, Syncretic Perspectives: Globalization, Political Theory, and Islamizing Knowledge," *International Studies Review* 4, no. 1 (2002): 34.

105. Qutb was the author of *Milestones* and *In the Shade of the Koran*, among other works. Berman describes the latter as "vast, vividly written, wise, broad, indignant, sometimes demented, bristly with hatred, medieval, modern, tolerant, intolerant, paranoid, cruel, urgent, cranky, tranquil, grave, poetic, leaned and analytic . . . a work large and solid enough to create its own shade." Paul Berman, "The Philosopher of Islamic Terror," *New York Times Magazine*, March 23, 2003, pp. 24–29.

106. Ibid.

107. The Islamists and the Arab nationalists, though initially cooperative before and immediately following the 1952 Egyptian revolution that overthrew King Farouk, went

their separate ways not long afterward. The most radical nationalists sought to elevate the Arabs over other ethnic groups, while the Islamists sought to resurrect the caliphate in the form of a theocracy based in a strict interpretation of Islamic law. Not long after the revolution and following an assassination attempt alleged to be the work of the Muslim Brotherhood, Nasser began to repress the Islamists. Qutb spent most of the 1950s and 1960s imprisoned in difficult conditions.

108. Roxanne L. Euben, "Comparative Political Theory: An Islamic Fundamentalist Critique of Rationalism," *Journal of Politics* 59, no. 1 (1997): 31.

109. Ibid., p. 52. Juergensmeyer argues along similar lines that "many religious nationalists . . . do not have the rationalists' faith that reason alone is sufficient for finding the truth, nor do they feel that unbridled self-interest is an adequate moral base for political order." Mark Juergensmeyer, *The New Cold War? Religious Nationalism Confronts the Secular State* (Berkeley: University of California Press, 1993), p. 175.

110. Alexis de Tocqueville, *Democracy in America*, vol. 1, ed. J. P. Mayer (New York: Doubleday, 1969), p. 293.

111. Martha Nussbaum, "Patriotism and Cosmopolitanism," in Nussbaum, *For Love of Country?* p. 11.

112. Connolly, *Why I Am Not a Secularist*, p. 36.

113. Siba N. Grovogui, "Rituals of Power: Theory, Languages and Vernaculars of International Relations," *Alternatives* 23 (1998): 500–501.

114. Ayoob, "Political Islam," p. 10.

115. Michel Foucault, cited in Jonathan Rée, "The Treason of the Clerics," *Nation* 211, no. 5 (August 15, 2005): 31–34.

116. Roger Gaess, "Interview: Azzam Tamimi," *Middle East Policy* 13, no. 2 (Summer 2006): 27.

117. Marina S. Ottaway, "Promoting Democracy after Hamas' Victory," Carnegie Endowment for International Peace Working Paper Series, February 2, 2006 (http://www.carnegieendowment.org/publications/index.cfm?fa=view&id=17978&prog=zgp&proj=zdrl, accessed July 18, 2006).

118. Dipesh Chakrabarty, *Provincializing Europe: Postcolonial Thought and Historical Difference* (Princeton: Princeton University Press, 2000).

119. Ayoob, "Political Islam," p. 1.

CHAPTER EIGHT
RELIGIOUS RESURGENCE

1. Richard King, *Orientalism and Religion: Postcolonial Theory, India and "the Mystic East"* (London: Routledge, 1999), p. 14.

2. A survey of articles in leading journals of international relations found that during the period 1980–99 "only six or so out of a total of about sixteen hundred featured religion as an important influence." Daniel Philpott, "The Challenge of September 11 to Secularism in International Relations," *World Politics* 55 (October 2002): 69.

3. See Nikki R. Keddie, "The New Religious Politics: Where, When, and Why do 'Fundamentalisms' Appear?" *Comparative Studies of Society and History* 40, no. 4 (October 1998): 696–723.

4. On the resurgence, see Scott M. Thomas, "Taking Religious and Cultural Plural-ism Seriously: The Global Resurgence of Religion and the Transformation of Interna-tional Society," *Millennium: Journal of International Studies* 29, no. 3 (2000): 815–41, and Thomas, *The Global Resurgence of Religion and the Transformation of Interna-tional Relations* (New York: Palgrave Macmillan, 2005).

5. Thomas, *Global Resurgence*, p. 43.

6. For a statistical analysis documenting an increase in religious observance globally and an "existential risk" model of secularization, see Pippa Norris and Ronald Ingle-hart, *Sacred and Secular: Religion and Politics Worldwide* (New York: Cambridge Uni-versity Press, 2004). On transnational religious formations, see Susanne Hoeber Ru-dolph and James Piscatori (Eds.), *Transnational Religion and Fading States* (Boulder: Westview Press, 1997). On the American case, see Robert Wuthnow, *The Restructuring of American Religion* (Princeton: Princeton University Press, 1988); Roger Finke and Rodney Stark, *The Churching of America, 1776–1990: Winners and Losers in Our Reli-gious Economy* (Rutgers, N.J.: Rutgers University Press, 1992); and Christian Smith, *The Secular Revolution: Power, Interests and Conflict in the Secularization of American Public Life* (Berkeley: University of California Press, 2003). On the Indian case, see Rajeev Bhargava (Ed.), *Secularism and Its Critics*, 2nd ed. (Oxford: Oxford University Press, 2005); Peter van der Veer and Hartmut Lehmann (Eds.), *Nation and Religion: Perspectives on Europe and Asia* (Princeton: Princeton University Press, 1999); and Ashis Nandy, *Time Warps: Silent and Evasive Pasts in Indian Politics and Religion* (New Brunswick, N.J.: Rutgers University Press, 2002). On Latin America, see Christian Smith and Joshua Prokopy (Eds.), *Latin American Religion in Motion* (New York: Routledge, 1999); David Martin, *Tongues of Fire: The Explosion of Protestantism in Latin America* (Cambridge, Mass.: Blackwell, 1990); and on Catholicism in Latin America, see Anthony Gill, *Rendering unto Caesar: The Catholic Church and the State in Latin America* (Chicago: University of Chicago Press, 1993).

7. See Jeff Haynes, "Religion and International Relations: What Are the Issues?" *International Politics* 41 (2004): 451–62.

8. Anson Shupe, "The Stubborn Persistence of Religion in the Global Arena," in Emile Sahliyeh (Ed.), *Religious Resurgence and Politics in the Contemporary World* (Albany: State University of New York Press, 1990), p. 18.

9. Timothy Samuel Shah, Senior Fellow in Religion and International Affairs, Pew Forum on Religion and Public Life, Testimony before the House International Rela-tions Committee, United States House of Representatives, October 6, 2004 (http://wwwc.house.gov/international_relations/108/sha100604.htm, accessed December 14, 2004).

10. Peter L. Berger, "Reflections on the Sociology of Religion Today," *Sociology of Religion* 62, no. 4 (Winter 2001): 445.

11. Pavlos Hatzopoulos and Fabio Petito, "The Return from Exile: An Introduc-tion," in Petito and Hatzopoulos (Eds.), *Religion and International Relations: The Re-turn from Exile* (New York: Palgrave Macmillan, 2003), p. 3.

12. Alev Çinar, *Modernity, Islam, and Secularism in Turkey* (Minneapolis: Univer-sity of Minnesota Press, 2005), p. 9.

13. Thanks to Rabeah Sabri for introducing me to the Pakistan Awami Tehreek.

14. Haynes, "Religion and International Relations," p. 456. Haynes argues against the idea of resurgence and says that we are witnessing instead "the latest manifestation

of *cyclical* religious activity, made highly visible (and hence alarming) by advances in communications technology and availability" (ibid., p. 457; see also Haynes, "Religion, Secularization and Politics: A Postmodern Conspectus," *Third World Quarterly* 18, no. 4 [1997]: 715). My conceptual framework applies to and helps to explain this cyclical activity.

15. Thomas, *Global Resurgence of Religion*, p. 44.

16. José Casanova, *Public Religions in the Modern World* (Chicago: University of Chicago Press, 1994).

17. On the opposition between sacred and profane, see Mircea Eliade, *The Sacred and the Profane: The Nature of Religion*, trans. Willard R. Trask (New York: Harcourt, 1959).

18. See chapter 2 for a critique of the assumption that religion was privatized at Westphalia.

19. For an exception, see Falk's approach to religious resurgence as symptomatic of the "exhaustion of the creative capacity of the secular sensibility, especially as it is embodied in the political domain." Richard Falk, *The Declining World Order: America's Imperial Geopolitics* (New York: Routledge, 2004), p. 151.

20. Roxanne L. Euben, *Enemy in the Mirror: Islamic Fundamentalism and the Limits of Modern Rationalism* (Princeton: Princeton University Press, 1999), p. 7.

21. Casanova, *Public Religions*, p. 19.

22. Ibid., pp. 19–20.

23. Peter van der Veer and Hartmut Lehmann, introduction to *Nation and Religion*, p. 3.

24. Falk, *Declining World Order*, p. 140.

25. Haynes, "Religion, Secularization and Politics: a Postmodern Conspectus," p. 713.

26. Deborah J. Gerner and Philip A. Schrodt, "Middle Eastern Politics," in Deborah J. Gerner (Ed.), *Understanding the Contemporary Middle East* (Boulder: Lynne Rienner, 2000), p. 125 (emphasis added).

27. John Rawls, *Political Liberalism* (New York: Columbia University Press, 1993), p. 151.

28. Karl Marx, "On the Jewish Question," in Robert Tucker (Ed.), *The Marx-Engels Reader* (New York: W.W. Norton, 1978), p. 28.

29. J. F. Rinehart, "Religion in World Politics: Why the Resurgence?" *International Studies Review* 6 (2004): 271.

30. For an example of this argument, see Norris and Inglehart, *Sacred and Secular*.

31. Rinehart, "Religion in World Politics," p. 272.

32. For the argument that Christianity alone serves as the basis of modern forms of reason, logic, and progress, see Rodney Stark, *The Victory of Reason: How Christianity Led to Freedom, Capitalism and Western Success* (New York: Random House, 2005).

33. Ian Buruma, "An Islamic Democracy for Iraq?" *New York Times Magazine*, December 5, 2004, p. 46. Buruma traces this idea to the first European Christian democratic party (the Anti-Revolutionary Party) founded in 1879 by Abraham Kuyper, a Calvinist ex-pastor in the Netherlands.

34. Anthony D. Smith, "The 'Sacred' Dimension of Nationalism," *Millennium: Journal of International Studies* 29, no. 3 (2000): 792.

35. Bernard Lewis, *Islam and the West* (New York: Oxford University Press, 1993), p. 179.

36. Ted G. Jelen, *To Serve God and Mammon: Church-State Relations in American Politics* (Boulder: Westview Press, 2000), p. 90.

37. See Daniel Philpott, "The Religious Roots of Modern International Relations," *World Politics* 52 (2002): 206–45.

38. Stepan defines the twin tolerations as "the minimal boundaries of freedom of action that must somehow be crafted for political institutions vis-à-vis religious authorities, and for religious individuals and groups vis-à-vis political institutions." Alfred Stepan, "The World's Religious Systems and Democracy: Crafting the 'Twin Tolerations,'" *Journal of Democracy* 11 (October 2000): 37.

39. Daniel Philpott, "The Catholic Wave," *Journal of Democracy* 15, no. 2 (April 2004): 43, 36.

40. See chapter 2. See also Robert Bellah, *Beyond Belief: Essays on Religion in a Post-Traditional World* (Berkeley: University of California Press, 1991); Casanova, *Public Religions*; John Milbank, *Theology and Social Theory: Beyond Secular Reason* (Oxford: Blackwell, 1993); Hans Blumenberg, *The Legitimacy of the Modern Age*, trans. R. M. Wallace (Cambridge, Mass.: MIT Press, 1995); Connolly, *Why I Am Not a Secularist*; and van der Veer and Lehmann, *Nation and Religion*.

41. Stepan, "Religion, Democracy and the 'Twin Tolerations,'" p. 38.

42. Nader A. Hashemi, "Inching towards Democracy: Religion and Politics in the Muslim World," *Third World Quarterly* 24, no. 3 (2003): 563.

43. Stepan, "Religion, Democracy and the 'Twin Tolerations,'" p. 40.

44. Talal Asad, *Formations of the Secular: Christianity, Islam, Modernity* (Stanford: Stanford University Press, 2003), p. 36.

45. A. Claire Cutler, "Critical Reflections on the Westphalian Assumptions of International Law and Organization: A Crisis of Legitimacy," *Review of International Studies* 27, no. 2 (2001): 136.

46. Jean Bethke Elshtain, foreword to John D. Carlson and Erik C. Owens (Eds.), *The Sacred and the Sovereign: Religion and International Politics* (Washington, D.C.: Georgetown University Press, 2003), p. x.

47. Cutler, "Critical Reflections," pp. 133–50.

48. Ibid., p. 133.

49. Ibid.

50. Eric Helleiner, *States and the Reemergence of Global Finance: From Bretton Woods to the 1990s* (Ithaca: Cornell University Press, 1996); Susan Strange, *States and Markets* (London: Pinter, 1994); Jacques Derrida, "Faith and Knowledge: The Two Sources of 'Religion' at the Limits of Reason Alone," in Jacques Derrida and Gianni Vattimo (Eds.), *Religion* (Stanford: Stanford University Press, 1998), pp. 1–78; and King, *Orientalism and Religion*.

51. Armando Salvatore and Mark LeVine, "Reconstructing the Public Sphere in Muslim Majority Societies," in Armando Salvatore and Mark LeVine (Eds.), *Religion, Social Practice, and Contested Hegemonies* (New York: Palgrave Macmillan, 2005), p. 2.

52. Bonnie Honig, "Toward an Agonistic Feminism: Arendt and the Politics of Identity," in Judith Butler and Joan Scott (Eds.), *Feminists Theorize the Political* (New York: Routledge, 1992), p. 225.

53. Dipesh Chakrabarty, *Provincializing Europe: Postcolonial Thought and Historical Difference* (Princeton: Princeton University Press, 2000), p. 6.

54. See Alexander Wendt, *Social Theory of International Politics* (Cambridge: Cambridge University Press, 1999); Peter J. Katzenstein (Ed.), *The Culture of National Security: Norms and Identity in World Politics* (New York: Columbia University Press, 1996); Martha Finnemore, *National Interests in International Society* (Ithaca: Cornell University Press, 1996). For a critique of the constructivists' "thin conception of identity," see Steve Smith, "Wendt's World," *Review of International Studies* 26, no. 1 (2000): 151–64, and Thomas, *Global Resurgence of Religion*, pp. 93–96.

55. Carsten Bagge Laustsen and Ole Wæver, "In Defense of Religion: Sacred Referent Objects for Securitization," in Petito and Hatzopoulos, *Religion in International Relations*, p. 149.

CHAPTER NINE
CONCLUSION

1. William E. Connolly, *Identity\Difference: Democratic Negotiations of Political Paradox,* expanded ed. (Minneapolis: University of Minnesota, 2002), p. 211.

2. As Sachedina argues, secularism is in need of revision that guarantees "a public space for religion without succumbing to the claims of exclusivity." Abdulaziz Sachedina, *The Democratic Roots of Islamic Pluralism* (New York: Oxford University Press, 2001), p. 40.

3. Connolly, *Identity\Difference*, pp. x–xi.

4. William E. Connolly, *Why I Am Not a Secularist* (Minneapolis: University of Minnesota Press, 1999), p. 39.

5. Eleanor Brown, "Lieberman's Revival of the Religious Left," *New York Times*, August 30, 2000, p. A27.

6. Jonathan Turley, "We Wish You a Merry Lawsuit: Santa Brings Lots of Litigation on Religious Symbols," *Los Angeles Times*, December 16, 2002.

7. Ibid.

8. Peter van der Veer, "The Moral State: Religion, Nation, and Empire in Victorian Britain and British India," in Peter van der Veer and Hartmut Lehmann (Eds.), *Nation and Religion: Perspectives on Europe and Asia* (Princeton: Princeton University Press, 1999), p. 17.

9. See T. N. Madan, "Secularism in Its Place," *Journal of Asian Studies* 46, no. 4 (November 1987): 754.

10. Stephen D. Krasner, *Sovereignty: Organized Hypocrisy* (Princeton: Princeton University Press, 1999), p. 51.

11. "Social life is not simply a matter of systems of meaning. . . .These anthropological tendencies which accord a critical priority to systems of human meaning . . . leave unposed the question of how different forms of discourse come to be materially produced and maintained as authoritative systems." Talal Asad, "Anthropology and the Analysis of Ideology," *Man* 14, no. 4 (1979): 618–19.

12. Van der Veer and Lehmann, introduction to *Nation and Religion*, p. 3.

13. Barbara Metcalf, "Nationalism, Modernity, and Muslim Identity in India before 1947," in van der Veer and Lehmann, *Nation and Religion*, p. 138.

14. Van der Veer and Lehmann, introduction to *Nation and Religion*, p. 7.

15. Harry Harootunian, "Memory, Mourning, and National Morality: Yasukuni Shrine and the Reunion of State and Religion in Postwar Japan," in van der Veer and Lehmann, *Nation and Religion*, p. 148.

16. On the Indian case, see the work of Rajeev Bhargava, Ashis Nandy, T. N. Madan, and Partha Chatterjee.

17. Harootunian, "Memory, Mourning, and National Morality," p. 148.

18. Wilfred M. McClay, "The Soul of a Nation," *Public Interest* 155 (Spring 2004): 6.

19. Van der Veer, "The Moral State," p. 39.

20. Edward Said, *Covering Islam: How the Media and the Experts Determine How We See the Rest of the World*, 2nd ed. (New York: Random House, 1997), p. 102.

21. Connolly, *Identity\Difference*, p. 161.

22. Van der Veer and Lehmann, introduction to *Nation and Religion*, p. 10.

Select Bibliography

Abou El Fadl, Khaled. *Islam and the Challenge of Democracy*. Edited by Joshua Cohen and Deborah Chasman. Princeton: Princeton University Press, 2004.

Abrahamian, Ervand. *Iran between Two Revolutions*. Princeton: Princeton University Press, 1982.

Abrams, Elliot (Ed.). *The Influence of Faith: Religious Groups and U.S. Foreign Policy*. New York: Rowman & Littlefield, 2001.

Adler, Emanuel, and Michael Barnett (Eds.). *Security Communities*. Cambridge: Cambridge University Press, 1998.

Afary, Janet, and Kevin B. Anderson. *Foucault and the Iranian Revolution: Gender and the Seductions of Islamism*. Chicago: University of Chicago Press, 2005.

———. "The Seductions of Islamism: Revisiting Foucault and the Iranian Revolution." *New Politics* 10, no. 1 (Summer 2004): 113–22.

Ahmad, Mumtaz. "Political Islam: Can It Become a Loyal Opposition?" Forum, Middle East Policy Council, Washington, D.C., May 14, 1996.

Al-ʿAzm, Sadik Jalal. "Orientalism and Orientalism in Reverse." *Khamsin* 8 (1981): 5–26.

Algar, Hamid (Trans.). *Islam and Revolution*. Berkeley: Mizan Press, 1981.

Allison, Robert J. *The Crescent Obscured: The United States and the Muslim World, 1776–1815*. 2nd ed. Chicago: University of Chicago Press, 2000.

al-Masseri, Abdulwahab. "The Imperialist Epistemological Vision." *American Journal of Islamic Social Sciences* 11, no. 3 (1994): 403–15.

Amuzegar, Jahangir. "Iran's Crumbling Revolution." *Foreign Affairs* 82, no. 1 (January–February 2003): 44–57.

Anderson, Benedict. *Imagined Communities*. London: Verso, 1983.

Appleby, R. Scott. *The Ambivalence of the Sacred: Religion, Violence, and Reconciliation*. Lanham, Md.: Rowman & Littlefield, 2000.

Arendt, Hannah. *The Human Condition*. Chicago: University of Chicago Press, 1958.

———. *On Revolution*. New York: Viking, 1963.

———. "What Is Authority?" In *Between Past and Future: Eight Exercises in Political Thought*, pp. 91–142. New York: Viking, 1968.

Arjomand, Said Amir. *The Turban for the Crown: The Islamic Revolution in Iran*. New York: Oxford University Press, 1988.

Arkoun, Mohammed. *Rethinking Islam: Common Questions, Uncommon Answers*. Edited by and translated by Robert D. Lee. Boulder: Westview Press, 1994.

Asad, Muhammad. *The Principles of State and Government in Islam*. Berkeley: University of California Press, 1961.

Asad, Talal. "Anthropology and the Analysis of Ideology." *Man* 14, no. 4 (1979): 607–27.

———. *Formations of the Secular: Christianity, Islam, Modernity*. Stanford: Stanford University Press, 2003.

Asad, Talal. *Genealogies of Religion: Discipline and Reasons of Power in Christianity and Islam.* Baltimore: Johns Hopkins University Press, 1993.

———. "The Idea of an Anthropology of Islam." *Center for Contemporary Arab Studies Occasional Paper Series.* Washington, D.C.: Georgetown University, 1996.

———. "Muslims and European Identity: Can Europe Represent Islam?" In Elizabeth Hallam and Brian V. Street (Eds.), *Cultural Encounters: Representing "Otherness,"* pp. 11–27. New York: Routledge, 2000.

Aydin, Senem. "Views on Turkish Accession from the European Parliament." *Turkey in Europe.* Center for European Policy Studies. *Turkey in Europe Monitor,* no. 4 (April 2004). http://www.ceps.be/files/TurkeyM/TMonitor4.pdf.

Ayoob, Mohammed. "Political Islam: Image and Reality." *World Policy Journal* 21, no. 3 (Fall 2004): 1–14.

Ayubi, Nazih N. *Political Islam: Religion and Politics in the Arab World.* New York: Routledge, 1992.

———. "Rethinking the Public/Private Dichotomy: Radical Islam and Civil Society in the Middle East." *Contention* 4, no. 2 (Winter 1995): 79–105.

BBC News. "Profile: Orhan Pamuk." December 16, 2005. http://news.bbc.co.uk/2/hi/europe/453476.stm, accessed May 1, 2006.

———. "Turk Writer's Insult Trial Halted." December 16, 2005. http://news.bbc.co.uk/2/hi/europe/4533664.stm, accessed May 1, 2006.

Baker, Raymond William. *Islam without Fear: Egypt and the New Islamists.* Cambridge, Mass.: Harvard University Press, 2003.

Barbaso, Fabrizio. "Turkey-EU Relations in the Perspective of the December European Council." Middle East Technical University, Ankara, May 25, 2004.

Barber, Benjamin. *Jihad vs. McWorld: How Globalism and Tribalism Are Reshaping the World.* New York: Ballantine Books, 1996.

Barnett, Michael. *Dialogues in Arab Politics: Negotiations in Regional Order.* New York: Columbia University Press, 1998.

Barnett, Michael, and Raymond Duvall. "Power in International Politics." *International Organization* 59 (Winter 2005): 39–75.

Bashiriyeh, Hossein. *The State and Revolution in Iran, 1962–1982.* New York: St. Martin's Press, 1984.

———. "Transitional Situations, Changing Elite Configurations and Obstacles to Democratization in Iran." Paper presented at Northwestern University, Evanston, Illinois, May 15, 2006.

Bauberot, Jean. "Secularism and French Religious Liberty: A Sociological and Historical View." *Brigham Young University Law Review* 2 (2003): 451–64.

Baudouin, Jean, and Philippe Portier (Eds.). *La laïcité, une valeur d'aujourd'hui?: Contestations et renegotiations du modèle français.* Rennes: Presses Universitaires de Rennes, 2001.

Baylis, John, and Steve Smith (Eds.). *The Globalization of World Politics: An Introduction to International Relations.* 3rd ed. Oxford: Oxford University Press, 2005.

Beeman, William O. *The "Great Satan" vs. the "Mad Mullahs": How the United States and Iran Demonize Each Other.* New York: Praeger, 2005.

Bellah, Robert Neelly. *Beyond Belief: Essays on Religion in a Post-Traditional World.* Berkeley: University of California Press, 1991.

Belluck, Pam. "Intolerance and an Attempt to Make Amends Unsettle a Chicago Suburb's Muslims." *New York Times*, August 10, 2000, p. A10.

Bennett, Jane. *The Enchantment of Modern Life: Attachments, Crossings, and Ethics.* Princeton: Princeton University Press, 2001.

Berger, Peter L. (Ed.). *The Desecularization of the World: Resurgent Religion and World Politics.* Grand Rapids, Mich.: Ethics and Public Policy Center and Wm. B. Eerdmans, 1999.

————. *The Heretical Imperative: Contemporary Possibilities of Religious Affirmation.* Garden City, N.Y.: Anchor, 1979.

————. "Reflections on the Sociology of Religion Today." *Sociology of Religion* 62, no. 4 (Winter 2001): 443–54.

————. *The Sacred Canopy: Elements of a Sociological Theory of Religion.* New York: Doubleday, 1967.

————. *The Social Reality of Religion.* London: Allen Lane, 1973.

Berger, Peter L., and Thomas Luckman. *The Social Construction of Reality.* New York: Doubleday, 1966.

Berman, Paul. "The Philosopher of Islamic Terror." *New York Times Magazine*, March 23, 2003, pp. 24–29.

Bhabha, Homi K. *The Location of Culture.* London: Routledge, 2002.

Bhargava, Rajeev (Ed.). *Secularism and Its Critics.* Oxford: Oxford University Press, 1998.

Biersteker, Thomas, and Cynthia Weber (Eds.). *State Sovereignty as a Social Construct* Cambridge: Cambridge University Press, 1996.

Bill, James A. *The Eagle and the Lion: The Tragedy of American-Iranian Relations.* New Haven: Yale University Press, 1988.

Blumenberg, Hans. *The Legitimacy of the Modern Age.* Translated by Robert M. Wallace. Cambridge, Mass.: MIT Press, 1995.

Bond, Alvan. *Memoir of the Rev. Pliny Fisk.* Boston: Crocker and Brewster, 1828.

Boroujerdi, Mehrzad. *Iranian Intellectuals and the West: The Tormented Triumph of Nativism.* Syracuse: Syracuse University Press, 1996.

————. "Iranian Islam and the Faustian Bargain of Western Modernity." *Journal of Peace Research* 34, no. 1 (1997): 1–5.

Bowen, John R. "Muslims and Citizens." *Boston Review*, February–March 2004, pp. 31–35.

Brooks, David. "Kicking the Secularist Habit: A Six-Step Program." *Atlantic Monthly* 291, no. 2 (March 2003): 27–28.

Brouwer, Steve, Paul Gifford, and Susan Rose. *Exporting the American Gospel: Global Christian Fundamentalism.* New York: Routledge, 1996.

Brown, Eleanor. "Lieberman's Revival of the Religious Left." *New York Times*, August 30, 2000, p. A27.

Brown, L. Carl. *Religion and State: The Muslim Approach to Politics.* New York: Columbia University Press, 2000.

Bruce, Steve (Ed.). *Religion and Modernization: Sociologists and Historians Debate the Secularization Thesis.* New York: Oxford University Press, 2001.

Brumberg, Daniel. "Dissonant Politics in Iran and Indonesia." *Political Science Quarterly* 116, no. 3 (2001): 381–411.

Brumberg, Daniel. "Islamists and the Politics of Consensus." *Journal of Democracy* 13, no. 3 (2002): 109–15.

———. *Reinventing Khomeini: The Struggle for Reform in Iran*. Chicago: University of Chicago Press, 2001.

Bueno de Mesquita, Bruce. *The War Trap*. New Haven: Yale University Press, 1981.

Bueno de Mesquita, Bruce, and David Lalman. *War and Reason: Domestic and International Imperatives*. New Haven: Yale University Press, 1992.

Bukovansky, Mlada. *Legitimacy and Power Politics: The American and French Revolutions in International Political Culture*. Princeton: Princeton University Press, 2002.

Bulliet, Richard W. *The Case for Islamo-Christian Civilization*. New York: Columbia University Press, 2004.

Burke, Jason. *On the Road to Kandahar: Travels through Conflict in the Islamic World*. Toronto: Bond Street Books, 2006.

Buruma, Ian. "An Islamic Democracy for Iraq?" *New York Times Magazine*, December 5, 2004, pp. 42–49.

Buruma, Ian, and Avishai Margalit. *Occidentalism: The West in the Eyes of Its Enemies*. New York: Penguin Books, 2004.

Bush, George W. "Remarks at the 20th Anniversary of the National Endowment for Democracy." United States Chamber of Commerce, Washington, D.C., November 6, 2003.

Butler, Judith, and Joan W. Scott (Eds.). *Feminists Theorize the Political*. New York: Routledge, 1992.

Calhoun, Craig (Ed.). *Habermas and the Public Sphere*. Cambridge, Mass.: MIT Press, 1991.

———. *Nationalism*. Minneapolis: University of Minnesota Press, 1997.

Caliskan, Koray, and Yuksel Taskin. "Litmus Test: Turkey's Neo-Islamists Weigh War and Peace." *Middle East Report Online*, January 30, 2003. http://www.merip.org/mero/mero013003.html.

Campbell, David. *National Deconstruction: Violence, Identity and Justice in Bosnia*. Minneapolis: University of Minnesota Press, 1998.

———. *Writing Security: United States Foreign Policy and the Politics of Identity*. Minneapolis: University of Minnesota Press, 1992.

Campbell, David, and Michael J. Shapiro (Eds.). *Moral Spaces: Rethinking Ethics and World Politics*. Minneapolis: University of Minnesota Press, 1999.

Carapico, Sheila. "Killing Live 8, Noisily: The G-8, Liberal Dissent and the London Bombings." *Middle East Report Online*, July 14, 2005. http://www.merip.org/mero/mero071405.html.

Carkoglu, Ali, and Barry Rubin (Eds.). *Turkey and the European Union: Domestic Politics, Economic Integration and International Dynamics*. London: Frank Cass, 2003.

Carlson, John D., and Erik C. Owens (Eds.). *The Sacred and the Sovereign: Religion and International Politics*. Washington, D.C.: Georgetown University Press, 2003.

Carrette, Jeremy R. *Foucault and Religion: Spiritual Corporality and Political Spirituality*. New York: Routledge, 2000.

——— (Ed.). *Religion and Culture: Michel Foucault*. New York: Routledge, 1999.

Carter, Stephen L. *The Culture of Disbelief: How American Law and Politics Trivialize Religious Devotion*. New York: Doubleday, 1993.

Casanova, José. *Public Religions in the Modern World*. Chicago: University of Chicago Press, 1994.

———. "Secularization Revisited: A Reply to Talal Asad." Paper presented at a workshop on "Secularization and Religion," Erfurt, Germany, July 2003.

Cavanaugh, William T. "A Fire Strong Enough to Consume the House: The Wars of Religion and the Rise of the State." *Modern Theology* 11, no. 4 (October 1995): 397–420.

Césaire, Aimé. *Discourse on Colonialism*. Translated by Joan Pinkham. New York: New York University Press, 2000.

Cesari, Jocelyne. "Islam in Europe: Modernity and Globalization Revisited." Lecture, University of Wisconsin-Madison, May 3, 2001.

Cesari, Jocelyne, and Sean McLoughlin (Eds.). *European Muslims and the Secular State*. Aldershot, Hampshire: Ashgate, 2005.

Chakrabarty, Dipesh. *Provincializing Europe: Postcolonial Thought and Historical Difference*. Princeton: Princeton University Press, 2000.

Chan, Stephen. "Too Neat and Under-Thought a World Order: Huntington and Civilizations." *Millennium: Journal of International Studies* 26, no. 1 (1997): 137–40.

Chatterjee, Partha. *The Nation and Its Fragments: Colonial and Postcolonial Histories*. Princeton: Princeton University Press, 1993.

———. *Nationalist Thought and the Colonial World: A Derivative Discourse*. Minneapolis: University of Minnesota Press, 1993.

Chaves, Mark. "Secularization as Declining Religious Authority." *Social Forces* 72 (1994): 749–74.

Chislett, William. "Turkey's Membership in the European Union: A Rose or a Thorn?" Real Institute Elcano de Estudios Internacionales y Estratégicos. http://www.realinstitutoelcano.org/documentos/imprimir/101imp.asp, accessed June 16, 2004.

Çinar, Alev. *Modernity, Islam, and Secularism in Turkey*, Minneapolis: University of Minnesota Press, 2005.

———. "National History as a Contested Site." *Comparative Study of Society and History* 43, no. 2 (April 2001): 364–91.

Cohen, Bernard. *The Political Process and Foreign Policy: The Making of the Japanese Peace Settlement*. Princeton: Princeton University Press, 1957.

Cohen, Joshua. and Deborah Chasman (Eds.). *Islam and the Challenge of Democracy*. Princeton: Princeton University Press, 2004.

Cohen, Roger. "For 'New Danes,' Differences Create a Divide." *New York Times*, December 18, 2000, pp. A1, A10.

Colley, Linda. *Britons: Forging the Nation, 1707–1837*. New Haven: Yale University Press, 1992.

Conklin, Alice. A *"Mission to Civilize": The Republican Idea of Empire in France and West Africa, 1895–1930*. Stanford: Stanford University Press, 2000.

Connolly, William E. *The Ethos of Pluralization*. Minneapolis: University of Minnesota Press, 1995.

———. *Identity\Difference: Democratic Negotiations of Political Paradox*. Expanded ed. Minneapolis: University of Minnesota, 2002.

———. "The New Cult of Civilizational Superiority." *Theory and Event* 2, no. 4 (1999). http://muse.jhu.journals/theory_and_event/v002/2.4connolly.html, accessed December 21, 2006.

Connolly, William E. *Pluralism*. Durham, N.C.: Duke University Press, 2005.

———. *Political Theory and Modernity*. Ithaca: Cornell University Press, 1993.

———. *Why I Am Not a Secularist*. Minneapolis: University of Minnesota Press, 1999.

Cooper, John, Ronald L. Nettler, and Mohamed Mahmoud (Eds.). *Islam and Modernity: Muslim Intellectuals Respond*. London: I. B. Tauris, 2000.

Coronil, Fernando. "Beyond Occidentalism: Toward Nonimperial Geohistorical Categories." *Cultural Anthropology* 11, no. 1 (1996): 58–87.

Cottam, Richard W. *Iran and the United States: A Cold War Case Study*. Pittsburgh: University of Pittsburgh Press, 1988.

Cox, Harvey. *The Secular City*. New York: Macmillan, 1965.

Cutler, A. Claire. "Critical Reflections on the Westphalian Assumptions of International Law and Organization: A Crisis of Legitimacy." *Review of International Studies* 27, no. 2 (2001): 133–50.

Dallmayr, Fred. *Dialogue among Civilizations: Some Exemplary Voices*. New York: Palgrave Macmillan, 2002.

Damasio, Antonio. *Descartes' Error: Emotion, Reason, and the Human Brain*. New York: G. P. Putnam, 1994.

———. *Looking for Spinoza: Joy, Sorrow, and the Feeling Brain*. New York: Harcourt, 2003.

Daniel, Norman. *Islam and the West: The Making of an Image*. New York: Columbia University Press, 1989.

Davaney, Sheila. *Pragmatic Historicism: A Theology for the Twenty-First Century*. Albany: State University of New York Press, 2000.

Davie, Grace. *Religion in Britain since 1945: Believing without Belonging*. Oxford: Blackwell, 1994.

———. *Religion in Modern Europe: A Memory Mutates*. Oxford: Oxford University Press, 2000.

Davis, Matthew. "Hamas Win Challenges US Policy." BBC News International, January 26, 2006. http://news.bbc.co.uk/2/hi/middle_east/4652140.stm, accessed August 18, 2006.

Davison, Andrew. *Secularism and Revivalism in Turkey: A Hermeneutic Reconsideration*. New Haven: Yale University Press, 1998.

———. "Turkey, a 'Secular' State? The Challenge of Description." *South Atlantic Quarterly* 102, nos. 2–3 (Spring–Summer 2003): 333–50.

Deleuze, Gilles. *Difference and Repetition*. Translated by Paul Patton. New York: Columbia University Press, 1994.

Deleuze, Gilles, and Félix Guattari, *What Is Philosophy?* New York: Columbia University Press, 1994.

Demerath, Nicholas III. *Crossing the Gods: World Religions and Worldly Politics*. New Brunswick, N.J.: Rutgers University Press, 2001.

Denoeux, Guilain. "The Forgotten Swamp: Navigating Political Islam." *Middle East Policy* 9, no. 2 (2002): 56–81.

Derrida, Jacques, and Gianni Vattimo (Eds.), *Religion*. Stanford: Stanford University Press, 1998.

Diamond, Larry, Marc F. Plattner, and Philip J. Costopoulos (Eds.), *World Religions and Democracy*. Baltimore: Johns Hopkins University Press, 2005.

Dombey, Daniel, and Vincent Boland. "Brussels Says 'Yes' to Turkish Entry Talks." *Financial Times*, October 7, 2004, p. 2.

Donaldson, Gary A. *America at War since 1945: Politics and Diplomacy in Korea, Vietnam, and the Gulf War*. Westport, Conn.: Praeger, 1996.

Doty, Roxanne Lynn. *Imperial Encounters: The Politics of Representation in North-South Relations*. Minneapolis: University of Minnesota Press, 1996.

Dreyfus, Hubert L., and Paul Rabinow. *Michel Foucault: Beyond Structuralism and Hermeneutics*. Chicago: University of Chicago Press, 1983.

Eberle, Christopher J. *Religious Conviction in Liberal Politics*. Cambridge: Cambridge University Press, 2002.

Eck, Diana L. *A New Religious America: How a "Christian County" Has Become the World's Most Religiously Diverse Nation*. New York: HarperCollins, 2002.

Edwards, Brian. *Morocco Bound: Disorienting America's Maghreb, from Casablanca to the Marrakech Express*. Durham, D.C.: Duke University Press, 2005.

Edwards, Holly, et al. *Noble Dreams, Wicked Pleasures: Orientalism in America, 1870–1930*. Princeton: Princeton University Press and Sterling and Francine Clark Art Institute, 2000.

Eickelman, Dale F., and James Piscatori. *Muslim Politics*. Princeton: Princeton University Press, 1996.

Eisenstadt, S. N. "The Reconstruction of Religious Arenas in the Framework of 'Multiple Modernities.' " *Millennium: Journal of International Studies* 29, no. 3 (2000): 591–611.

Eliade, Mircea. *The Sacred and the Profane: The Nature of Religion*. Translated by Willard R. Trask. New York: Harcourt, 1959.

Emerson, Michael. "Has Turkey Fulfilled the Copenhagen Political Criteria?" Centre for European Policy Studies, Brief No. 48, April 2004, pp. 1–5. http://www.shop .ceps.be.

Emerson, Rupert. *From Empire to Nation: The Rise to Self-Assertion of Asian and African Peoples*. Boston: Beacon Press, 1960.

Erdoğdu, Erkan. "Turkey and Europe: Undivided but Not United." *Middle East Review of International Affairs* 6, no. 2 (June 2002). http://meria.idc.ac.il/journal/2002/issue2/jv6n2a4.html.

Esposito, John. *The Islamic Threat: Myth or Reality?* 2nd ed. New York: Oxford University Press, 1992.

———. *The Islamic Threat: Myth or Reality?* 3rd ed. New York: Oxford University Press, 1999.

———. *Political Islam: Revolution, Radicalism, or Reform?* Boulder: Lynne Rienner, 1997.

Esposito, John, and Azzam Tamini (Eds.). *Islam and Secularism in the Middle East*. New York: New York University Press, 2000.

Euben, Roxanne L. "Comparative Political Theory: An Islamic Fundamentalist Critique of Rationalism." *Journal of Politics* 59, no. 1 (1997): 28–55.

———. "Contingent Borders, Syncretic Perspectives: Globalization, Political Theory, and Islamizing Knowledge." *International Studies Review* 4, no. 1 (2002): 23–48.

———. *Enemy in the Mirror: Islamic Fundamentalism and the Limits of Modern Rationalism*. Princeton: Princeton University Press, 1999.

European Commission. *Commission Opinion on Turkey's Request for Accession to the Community*, Sec. (89) 2290 final. Brussels: Official Publications of the European Communities, December 18, 1989.

European Court of Human Rights. "Judgment in the Case of Refah Partisi (The Welfare Party) Erbakan, Kazan and Tekdal v. Turkey." Press release issued by the Registrar of the Court, July 31, 2001. http://www.echr.coe.int/Eng/Press/2001/July/RefahPartisi2001jude.htm, accessed 4/17/2006.

Falk, Richard. *The Declining World Order: America's Imperial Geopolitics*. New York: Routledge, 2004.

———. "False Universalism and the Geopolitics of Exclusion: The Case of Islam." *Third World Quarterly* 18, no. 1 (March 1997): 7–24.

———. *Religion and Humane Global Governance*. New York: Palgrave, 2001.

———. "Religion and Politics: Verging on the Postmodern." *Alternatives* 13, no. 3 (1988): 379–94.

Fanon, Frantz. *A Dying Colonialism*. London: Writers and Readers Press, 1967.

Ferguson, James. *The Anti-Politics Machine: "Development," Depoliticization, and Bureaucratic Power in Lesotho*. 4th ed. Minneapolis: University of Minnesota, 1997.

Finke, Roger, and Rodney Stark. *The Churching of America, 1776–1990: Winners and Losers in our Religious Economy*. Rutgers, N.J.: Rutgers University Press, 1992.

Finnemore, Martha. *National Interests in International Society*. Ithaca: Cornell University Press, 1996.

Fletcher, Richard. *The Cross and the Crescent: Christianity and Islam from Muhammed to the Reformation*. London: Penguin Press, 2003.

Ford, Peter. "What Place for God in Europe?" *Christian Science Monitor*, February 22, 2005. www.csmonitor.com/2005/0222/p01s04-woeu.html.

Foucault, Michel. *The Archaeology of Knowledge*. New York: Pantheon, 1972.

———. *The Order of Things: An Archaeology of the Human Sciences*. New York: Random House, 1994.

Fox, Jonathan. *Ethnoreligious Conflict in the Late 20th Century: A General Theory*. Lanham, Md.: Lexington Books, 2002.

———. "Religion as an Overlooked Element of International Relations." *International Studies Review* 3, no. 3 (Fall 2001): 53–73.

Fox, Jonathan, and Shmuel Sandler. *Bringing Religion into International Relations*. New York: Palgrave, 2004.

Frantz, Douglas. "Military Bestrides Turkey's Path to the European Union." *New York Times*, January 14, 2001, p. 3.

Franz, Erhard. "Secularism and Islamism in Turkey." In Kai Hafez (Ed.), *The Islamic World and the West: An Introduction to Political Cultures and International Relations*, pp. 161–75. Leiden: Brill, 2000.

Friedman, Thomas L. "Who Lost Turkey?' *New York Times*, August 21, 1996.

Fukuyama, Francis. "The End of History?' *National Interest* 16 (1989): 3–18.

Fuller, Graham. "The Future of Political Islam." *Foreign Affairs* 81, no. 2 (March–April 2002): 48–60.

Gaess, Roger. "Interview: Azzam Tamimi." *Middle East Policy* 13, no. 2 (Summer 2006): 23–29.

Gasiorowski, Mark J. "The 1953 Coup d'Etat in Iran." *International Journal of Middle East Studies* 19 (August 1987): 261–86.

Gasiorowski, Mark J., and Malcolm Byrne (Eds.). *Mohammad Mosaddeq and the 1953 Coup in Iran*. Syracuse: Syracuse University Press, 2004.

Gaskin, John (Ed.). *The Epicurean Philosophers*. London: J. M. Dent, 1995.

Gedicks, Frederick Mark. "The Religious, the Secular, and the Antithetical." *Capital University Law Review* 20, no. 1 (1991): 113–45.

Gerges, Fawaz. *America and Political Islam: Clash of Cultures or Clash of Interests?* Cambridge: Cambridge University Press, 1999.

Gerner, Deborah J. (Ed.). *Understanding the Contemporary Middle East*. Boulder: Lynne Rienner, 2000.

Gill, Anthony. *Rendering unto Caesar: The Catholic Church and the State in Latin America*. Chicago: University of Chicago Press, 1993.

Gills, B. K. "Historical Materialism and International Relations Theory." *Millennium* 16 (1987): 265–72.

Goldschmidt, Arthur, Jr. *A Concise History of the Middle East*. 7th ed. Boulder: Westview, 2002.

Goldstein, Judith, and Robert O. Keohane (Eds.). *Ideas and Foreign Policy: Beliefs, Institutions and Political Change*. Ithaca: Cornell University Press, 1993.

Göle, Nilüfer. "Islam in Public: New Visibilities and New Imaginaries." *Public Culture* 14, no. 1 (2002): 173–90.

———. "Negotiating Europeanism and Republicanism: The Turkish Question in France." Paper presented at the "Cultures of Democracy" conference, Northwestern University, Evanston, Illinois, April 21, 2005.

Goode, James. *The United States and Iran: In the Shadow of Musaddiq*. New York: Palgrave Macmillan, 1997.

Gordon, Philip, and Omer Taspinar. "Turkey's European Quest: The EU's Decision on Turkish Accession." U.S.-Europe Analysis Series. Center on the United States and Europe, Brookings Institution, September 2004.

Grayling, A. C. "The New Crusade–for Understanding." *Financial Times Weekend*, May 3–4, 2003, p. 5.

Greeley, Andrew. *Ecstasy: A Way of Knowing*. Englewood Cliffs, N.J.: Prentice-Hall, 1974.

Grell, Ole Peter, and Roy Porter (Eds.). *Toleration in Enlightenment Europe*. Cambridge: Cambridge University Press, 1999.

Grovogui, Siba N. "Rituals of Power: Theory, Languages and Vernaculars of International Relations." *Alternatives* 23 (1998): 499–530.

———. *Sovereigns, Quasi Sovereigns, and Africans: Race and Self-Determination in International Law*. Minneapolis: University of Minnesota Press, 1996.

Gülalp, Haldun. "Globalization and Political Islam: The Social Bases of Turkey's Welfare Party." *International Journal of Middle East Studies* 33, no. 3 (August 2001): 433–48.

———. "Globalizing Postmodernism: Islamist and Western Social Theory." *Economy and Society* 26, no. 3 (August 1997): 419–33.

———. "The Poverty of Democracy in Turkey: The Refah Party Episode." *New Perspectives on Turkey* 21 (1999): 35–51.

Habermas, Jürgen. *Postmetaphysical Thinking*. Translated by William M. Hohengarten. Cambridge, Mass.: MIT Press, 1992.

Habermas, Jürgen. *Structural Transformation of the Public* Sphere. Cambridge, Mass.: MIT Press, 1989.

Hahn, Peter L., and Mary Ann Heiss (Eds.). *Empire and Revolution: The United States and the Third World since 1945*. Columbus: Ohio State University Press, 2001.

Hall, Rodney Bruce. *National Collective Identity: Social Constructs and International Systems*. New York: Columbia University Press, 1999.

Hallam, Elizabeth, and Brian V. Street (Eds.), *Cultural Encounters: Representing "Otherness."* London: Routledge, 2000.

Halliday, Fred. *Iran: Dictatorship and Development*. New York: Penguin Books, 1979.

———. *Islam and the Myth of Confrontation: Religion and Politics in the Middle East*. London: I. B. Tauris, 1996.

———. *The Middle East in International Relations: Power, Politics and Ideology*. New York: Cambridge University Press, 2005.

———. *Nation and Religion in the Middle East*. Boulder: Lynne Rienner, 2000.

Hamilton, Malcolm B. *The Sociology of Religion: Theoretical and Comparative Perspectives*. London: Routledge, 1995.

Hammond, Phillip (Ed.). *The Sacred in a Secular Age*. Berkeley: University of California Press, 1985.

Hampshire, Stuart. *Freedom of Mind, and Other Essays*. Princeton: Princeton University Press, 1971.

Hanchard, Michael. "Afro-Modernity: Temporality, Politics, and the African Diaspora." *Public Culture* 11, no. 1 (1999): 245–68.

Harris, Sam. *The End of Faith: Religion, Terror and the Future of Reason*. New York: W. W. Norton, 2004.

Hashemi, Nader A. "Inching towards Democracy: Religion and Politics in the Muslim World." *Third World Quarterly* 24, no. 3 (2003): 563–78.

Haynes, Jeff. "Religion and International Relations: What Are the Issues?" *International Politics* 41 (2004): 451–62.

———. "Religion, Secularization and Politics: A Postmodern Conspectus." *Third World Quarterly* 18, no. 4 (1997): 709–28.

Hefner, Robert. "Public Islam and the Problem of Democratization." *Sociology of Religion* 62, no. 4 (2001): 491–514.

——— (Ed.). *Remaking Muslim Politics: Pluralism, Contestation, Democratization*. Princeton: Princeton University Press, 2005.

Held, David. *Democracy and the Global Order: From the Modern State to Cosmopolitan Governance*. Stanford: Stanford University Press, 1996.

Helleiner, Eric. *States and the Reemergence of Global Finance: From Bretton Woods to the 1990s*. Ithaca: Cornell University Press, 1996.

Hirschkind, Charles. "What Is Political Islam?' *Middle East Report* 205 (December 1997): 12–14.

Hoagland, Jim. "Squaring Islam with Democracy." *Washington Post*, February 2, 2006, p. A21.

Höfert, Almut, and Armando Salvatore (Eds.). *Between Europe and Islam: Shaping Modernity in a Transcultural Space*. New York: Peter Lang, 2000.

Honig, Bonnie. *Democracy and the Foreigner*. Princeton: Princeton University Press, 2001.

————. *Political Theory and the Displacement of Politics*. Ithaca: Cornell University Press, 1993.

Hooker, Edward W. (Ed.). *Memoir of Mrs. Sarah L. Huntington Smith, Late of the Mission in Syria*. 3rd ed. New York: American Tract Society, 1845.

Houghton, David Patrick. *U.S. Foreign Policy and the Hostage Crisis*. Cambridge: Cambridge University Press, 2001.

Human Rights Watch World Report 2002: Turkey. http://www.hrw.org/wr2k2/europe19.html, accessed April 17, 2006.

Hunt, Michael. *Ideology and U.S. Foreign Policy*. New Haven: Yale University Press, 1987.

Huntington, Samuel P. "The Clash of Civilizations." *Foreign Affairs* 72, no. 3 (1993): 22–49.

————. *The Clash of Civilizations and the Remaking of World Order*. New York: Simon & Schuster, 1996.

————— (Ed.). *The Clash of Civilizations: The Debate*. New York: Foreign Affairs, 1996.

————. "The Return of Islam." *Commentary* 61, no. 1 (January 1976): 39–52.

Hurd, Elizabeth Shakman. "Appropriating Islam: The Islamic Other in the Consolidation of Western Modernity." *Critique: Critical Middle Eastern Studies* 12, no.1 (Spring 2003): 25–41.

————. "Chain Reactions: U.S. and Britain Got What They Wanted in Iran in 1953, but Where Did It Lead?' *Chicago Tribune*, March 9, 2003.

————. "The International Politics of Secularism: U.S. Foreign Policy and the Islamic Republic of Iran." *Alternatives: Global, Local, Political* 29, no. 2 (March–May 2004): 115–38.

————. "Negotiating Europe: The Politics of Religion and the Prospects for Turkish Accession to the EU." *Review of International Studies* 32, no. 3 (July 2006): 401–18.

————. "The Political Authority of Secularism in International Relations." *European Journal of International Relations* 10, no. 2 (June 2004): 235–62.

Hurd, Ian. *After Anarchy: Legitimacy and Power in the United Nations Security Council*. Princeton: Princeton University Press, 2007.

Hurrell, Andrew. "Kant and the Kantian Paradigm in International Relations." *Review of International Studies* 16 (1990): 183–205.

Inden, Ronald B. *Imagining India*. Bloomington: Indiana University Press, 2001.

Inglehart, Ronald (Ed.). *Islam, Gender, Culture, and Democracy: Findings from the World Values Survey and the European Values Survey*. Willowdale, Ontario: de Sitter Publications, 2003.

Israel, Jonathan. *Radical Enlightenment: Philosophy and the Making of Modernity, 1650–1750*. Cambridge: Cambridge University Press, 2001.

Jackson, Patrick Thaddeus. " 'Civilization' on Trial." *Millennium: Journal of International Studies* 28, no. 1 (1999): 141–54.

Jacobsohn, Gary J. *The Wheel of Law: India's Secularism in Comparative Constitutional Context*. Princeton: Princeton University Press, 2005.

Jacobson, Matthew Frye. *Barbarian Virtues: The United States Encounters Foreign Peoples at Home and Abroad, 1876–1917*. New York, Hill & Wang, 2001.

James, William. *A Pluralistic Universe*. Lincoln: University of Nebraska Press, 1996.

Jelen, Ted G. *To Serve God and Mammon: Church-State Relations in American Politics*. Boulder: Westview Press, 2000.

Juergensmeyer, Mark. *The New Cold War? Religious Nationalism Confronts the Secular State*. Berkeley: University of California Press, 1993.

———. *Terror in the Mind of God: The Global Rise of Religious Violence*. Berkeley: University of California Press, 2001.

Kahf, Mohja. *Western Representations of the Muslim Woman: From Termagant to Odalisque*. Austin: University of Texas Press, 1999.

Kant, Immanuel. *The Conflict of the Faculties*. Translated by Mary J. Gregor. Lincoln: University of Nebraska Press, 1979.

———. *Perpetual Peace, and Other Essays on Politics, History, and Morals*. Translated by Ted Humphrey. Indianapolis: Hackett, 1983.

Katzenstein, Peter J. (Ed.). *The Culture of National Security: Norms and Identity in World Politics*. New York: Columbia University Press, 1996.

Katzenstein, Peter J., and Timothy Byrnes (Eds.). *Religion in an Expanding Europe*. Cambridge: Cambridge University Press, 2006.

Kaufman, Gordon. *God the Problem*. Cambridge, Mass.: Harvard University Press, 1972.

Keddie, Nikki R. *Iran and the Muslim World: Resistance and Revolution*. London: Macmillan, 1995.

———. *Modern Iran: Roots and Results of Revolution*. New Haven: Yale University Press, 2003.

———. "The New Religious Politics: Where, When, and Why Do 'Fundamentalisms' Appear?" *Comparative Studies of Society and History* 40, no. 4 (October 1998): 696–723.

———. "Secularism and the State: Towards Clarity and Global Comparison." *New Left Review* 226 (November–December 1997): 21–40.

Kegley, Charles W., Jr. "Hard Choices: The Carter Administration's Hostage Rescue Mission in Iran." *Pew Case Studies in International Affairs* 360. Washington, D.C.: Institute for the Study of Diplomacy, Georgetown University, 1994.

Keohane, Robert O. (Ed.). *Neorealism and Its Critics*. New York: Columbia University Press, 1986.

Kepel, Gilles. *The War for Muslim Minds: Islam and the West*. Cambridge, Mass.: Belknap Press of Harvard University Press, 2004.

Key, V. O. *Public Opinion and American Democracy*. New York: Alfred A. Knopf, 1961.

Khadduri, Majid, and Herbert J. Liebesny (Eds.). *Law in the Middle East: Origin and Development of Islamic Law*. Washington, D.C.: Middle East Institute, 1984.

Khalaf, Samir. "American Missionaries in the Levant: Precursors to Soft Power and High Culture." Paper presented at the "Globalizing American Studies" conference, Northwestern University, Evanston, Illinois, May 5, 2006.

King, Richard. *Orientalism and Religion: Postcolonial Theory, India and "the Mystic East."* London: Routledge, 1999.

Kinzer, Stephen. *All the Shah's Men: An American Coup and the Roots of Middle East Terror*. Hoboken, N.J.: John Wiley & Sons, 2003.

Kösebalaban, Hasan. "Turkey's EU Membership: A Clash of Security Cultures." *Middle East Policy* 9, no. 2 (June 2002): 130–46.

Kramer, Martin. "Islam vs. Democracy." *Commentary* 95, no.1 (January 1993): 35–42.

Krasner, Stephen D. "Sovereignty." *Foreign Policy* 122 (January–February 2001): 20–29.

———. *Sovereignty: Organized Hypocrisy*. Princeton: Princeton University Press, 1999.

Kratochwil, Friedrich V. *Rules, Norms, and Decisions: On the Conditions of Practical and Legal Reasoning in International Relations and Domestic Affairs*. Cambridge: Cambridge University Press, 1989.

Küçükcan, Talip. "State, Islam, and Religious Liberty in Modern Turkey: Reconfiguration of Religion in the Public Sphere." *Brigham Young University Law Review* 2 (2003): 475–506.

Kurzman, Charles. *The Unthinkable Revolution in Iran*. Cambridge, Mass.: Harvard University Press, 2004.

Lapid, Yosef, and Friedrich Kratochwil (Eds.). *The Return of Culture and Identity in IR Theory*. Boulder: Lynne Rienner, 1996.

Lapidus, Ira M. "The Separation of State and Religion in the Development of Early Islamic Society." *International Journal of Middle East Studies* 6 (1975): 363–85.

———. "State and Religion in Islamic Societies." *Past and Present* 151 (1996): 3–27.

Larcher, Emile. *Traité élémentaire de legislation algérienne*. Vol. 1. Paris: Rousseau, 1903.

Lawrence, Bruce. *Defenders of God: The Fundamentalist Revolt against the Modern Age*. San Francisco: Harper & Row, 1989.

———. *Shattering the Myth: Islam beyond Violence*. Princeton: Princeton University Press, 1998.

Layachi, Azzedine. *The United States and North Africa: A Cognitive Approach to Foreign Policy*. New York: Praeger, 1990.

Lerner, Daniel. *The Passing of Traditional Society: Modernizing the Middle East*. New York: Macmillan, 1958.

Lester, Will. "AP Poll: Religion Key in American Lives. " *Guardian Unlimited*, June 6, 2005. http://www.guardian.co.uk/worldlatest/story/0,1280,-5056061,00.html, accessed June 9, 2005.

Lewis, Bernard. *The Emergence of Modern Turkey*. 3rd ed. New York: Oxford University Press, 2002.

———. "Freedom and Justice in the Modern Middle East." *Foreign Affairs* 84, no. 3 (May–June 2005): 36–51.

———. "Islam and Liberal Democracy." *Atlantic Monthly* 271, no. 2 (February 1993): 89–98.

———. *Islam and the West*. Oxford: Oxford University Press, 1994.

———. "Islam and the West: A Conversation with Bernard Lewis." Pew Forum on Religion and Public Life, Luis Lugo, moderator. Washington, D.C., April 27, 2006. http://pewforum.org/events/index.php?EventID=107, accessed May 25, 2006.

———. "The Return of Islam. " *Commentary* 61, no. 1 (January 1976): 39–49.

———. "The Roots of Muslim Rage." *Atlantic Monthly* 266, no. 3 (September 1990): 47–60.

———. *What Went Wrong? Western Impact and Middle Eastern Response*. Oxford: Oxford University Press, 2002.

Lewis, Martin, and Karen Wigen. *The Myth of Continents: A Critique of Metageography*. Berkeley: University of California Press, 1997.

Linker, Damon. *The Theocons: Secular America under Siege*. New York: Doubleday, 2006.

———. "Without a Doubt: A Catholic Priest, a Pious President, and the Christianizing of America." *New Republic*, April 3, 2006, pp. 25–33.

Little, Douglas. *American Orientalism: The United States and the Middle East since 1945*. Chapel Hill: University of North Carolina Press, 2002.

Lockman, Zachary. *Contending Visions of the Middle East: The History and Politics of Orientalism*. Cambridge: Cambridge University Press, 2004.

Loeffel, Laurence. *La question du fondement de la morale laïque sous la IIIe République: 1870–1914*. Paris: Presses Universitaires de France, 2000.

Lorcin, Patricia M. E. *Imperial Identities: Stereotyping, Prejudice and Race in Colonial Algeria*. London: I. B. Tauris, 1995.

Löwith, Karl. *Meaning in History*. Chicago: University of Chicago Press, 1949.

Lugo, Luis. "Does 'Muslim' Turkey Belong in 'Christian' Europe?" National Press Club, Washington, D.C., January 13, 2005.

Lynch, Cecelia. "Dogma, Praxis, and Religious Perspectives on Multiculturalism." *Millennium: Journal of International Studies* 29, no. 3 (2000): 741–59.

Lynch, Marc. *State Interests and Public Spheres: The International Politics of Jordan's Identity*. New York: Columbia University Press, 1999.

MacIntyre, Alasdair. *After Virtue: A Study in Moral Theory*. Notre Dame: University of Notre Dame Press, 1984.

———. *Whose Justice? Whose Rationality?* London: Duckworth, 1988.

Madan, T. N. "Secularism in Its Place." *Journal of Asian Studies* 46, no. 4 (November 1987): 747–59.

Mahmood, Saba. *Politics of Piety: The Islamic Revival and the Feminist Subject*. Princeton: Princeton University Press, 2005.

Maier, Charles S. (Ed.). *Changing Boundaries of the Political: Essays on the Evolving Balance between the State and Society, Public and Private in Europe*. Cambridge: Cambridge University Press, 1987.

Marquand, David, and Ronald L. Nettler (Eds.). *Religion and Democracy*. Oxford: Blackwell, 2000.

Marr, Timothy Worthington. *The Cultural Roots of American Islamicism*. Cambridge: Cambridge University Press, 2006.

———. *Imagining Ishmael: Studies of Islamic Orientalism in America from the Puritans to Melville*. Ann Arbor, Mich.: UMI, 1998.

Marshall, Jill. "Freedom of Religious Expression and Gender Equality: *Sahin v. Turkey*." *Modern Law Review* 69, no. 3 (2006): 452–61.

Martin, David. *A General Theory of Secularization*. Oxford: Blackwell, 1978.

———. "Religion, Secularity, Secularism and European Integration." Paper presented at a workshop on "Secularization and Religion," Erfurt, Germany, July 17, 2003.

———. *Tongues of Fire: The Explosion of Protestantism in Latin America*. Cambridge, Mass: Blackwell, 1990.

Marx, Anthony W. *Faith in Nation: Exclusionary Origins of Nationalism*. New York: Oxford University Press, 2003.

Massumi, Brian. "The Autonomy of Affect." *Cultural Critique* 31 (Autumn, 1995): 83–109.

McAlister, Melani. *Epic Encounters: Culture, Media and U.S. Interests in the Middle East, 1945–2000*. Berkeley: University of California Press, 2001.

McClay, Wilfred M. "The Soul of a Nation." *Public Interest* 155 (Spring 2004): 4–19.

McGreevy, John T. *Catholicism and American Freedom: A History*. New York: W. W. Norton, 2003.

McLeod, Hugh, and Werner Ustorf. *The Decline of Christendom in Western Europe: 1750–2000*. Cambridge: Cambridge University Press, 2003.

McPhee, Peter. *A Social History of France*. 2nd ed. New York: Palgrave, 2004.

Mead, Walter Russell. "Secular Europe and Religious America: Implications for Transatlantic Relations." Discussion, Pew Forum on Religion and Public Life, Washington, D.C., April 21, 2005.

Menocal, Maria Rosa. *The Arabic Role in Medieval Literature: A Forgotten Heritage*. Philadelphia: University of Pennsylvania Press, 1987.

Merry, Robert W. *Sands of Empire: Missionary Zeal, American Foreign Policy, and the Hazards of Global Ambition*. New York: Simon & Schuster, 2005.

Milbank, John. *Theology and Social Theory: Beyond Secular Reason*. Oxford: Blackwell, 1993.

Mirsepassi, Ali. *Intellectual Discourse and the Politics of Modernization: Negotiating Modernity in Iran*. Cambridge: Cambridge University Press, 2000.

Mitchell, Timothy. *Colonising Egypt*. Berkeley: University of California Press, 1991.

———. *Rule of Experts: Egypt, Techno-Politics, Modernity*. Berkeley: University of California Press, 2002.

Montesquieu, Charles de Secondat, Baron de. *The Spirit of the Laws*. Amherst, N.Y.: Prometheus Books, 2002.

Morgenthau, Hans J. *Politics among Nations: The Struggle for Power and Peace*. Abridged ed. New York: McGraw-Hill, 1993.

Morone, James A. *Hellfire Nation: The Politics of Sin in American History*. New Haven: Yale University Press, 2003.

Mottahedeh, Roy. *The Mantle of the Prophet: Religion and Politics in Iran*. New York, Pantheon Books, 1985.

Müftüler-Bac, Meltem. *Turkey's Relations with a Changing Europe*. New York: St. Martin's Press, 1997.

Murray, John Courtney, S.J. *We Hold These Truths: Catholic Reflections on the American Proposition*. New York: Rowman & Littlefield, 2005.

Nandy, Ashis. *Time Warps: Silent and Evasive Pasts in Indian Politics and Religion*. New Brunswick, N.J.: Rutgers University Press, 2002.

Nasr, S.V.R. "Democracy and Islamic Revivalism." *Political Science Quarterly* 110, no. 2 (Summer 1995): 261–85.

Navaro-Yashin, Yael. *Faces of the State: Secularism and Public Life in Turkey*. Princeton: Princeton University Press, 2002.

Neuhaus, Richard John. *Catholic Matters: Confusion, Controversy and the Splendor of Truth*. New York: Basic Books, 2006.

———. *The Catholic Moment: The Paradox of the Church in the Postmodern World*. New York: HarperCollins, 1990.

———. *The Naked Public Square*. Grand Rapids, Mich.: Eerdmans, 1984.

Neumann, Iver B. *Uses of the Other: "The East" in European Identity Formation*. Minneapolis: University of Minnesota Press, 1998.

Neumann, Iver B., and Ole Wæver (Eds.). *The Future of International Relations: Masters in the Making?* New York: Routledge, 1997.

Neumann, Iver B., and Jennifer M. Welsh. "The Other in European Self-Definition: An Addendum to the Literature on International Society." *Review of International Studies* 17 (1991): 327–48.

Nieves, Evelyn. "Judges Ban Pledge of Allegiance from Schools, Citing 'Under God.' " *New York Times*, June 27, 2002, p. A1.

Niranjana, Tejaswini. *Siting Translation: History, Post-Structuralism, and the Colonial Context.* Berkeley: University of California Press, 1992.

Norris, Pippa, and Ronald Inglehart. *Sacred and Secular: Religion and Politics Worldwide.* New York: Cambridge University Press, 2004.

Norton, Augustus Richard (Ed.). *Civil Society in the Middle East.* New York: Brill, 1995.

Nussbaum, Martha C. *For Love of Country?: Debating the Limits of Patriotism.* Edited by Joshua Cohen. Boston: Beacon Press, 1996.

Nye, Joseph S., Jr. *Bound to Lead: The Changing Nature of American Power.* New York: Basic Books, 1990.

————. *The Paradox of American Power: Why the World's Only Superpower Can't Go It Alone.* Oxford: Oxford University Press, 2002.

————. "Soft Power: The Means to Success in World Politics." Carnegie Council Books for Breakfast, New York, April 13, 2004. Transcript available at http://www.cceia.org/viewMedia.php/prmTemplateID/8/prmID/4466, accessed May 8, 2006).

O'Keefe, Mark. "Has the United States become Judeo-Christian-Islamic?" *Newhouse News Service.* http://www.newhouse.com/archive/okeefe051503.html, accessed May 21, 2003).

Önis, Ziya. "Domestic Politics, International Norms and Challenges to the State: Turkey-EU Relations in the Post-Helsinki Era." *Turkish Studies* 4, no. 1 (Spring 2003): 9–34.

————. "Political Islam at the Crossroads: From Hegemony to Co-existence." *Contemporary Politics* 7 (December 2001): 281–98.

Ottaway, Marina S. "Promoting Democracy after Hamas' Victory." Carnegie Endowment for International Peace Working Paper Series, February 2, 2006. http://www.carnegieendowment.org/publications/index.cfm?fa=view&id=17978&prog=zgp&proj=zdrl, accessed July 18, 2006.

Owen, J. Judd. *Religion and the Demise of Liberal Rationalism: The Foundational Crisis of the Separation of Church and State.* Chicago: University of Chicago Press, 2001.

Owen, Roger. *State, Power and Politics in the Making of the Modern Middle East.* 3rd ed. London: Routledge, 2004.

Özdalga, Elizabeth. *The Veiling Issue: Official Secularism and Popular Islam in Modern Turkey.* Nordic Institute of Asian Studies Report Series, No. 33. Surrey: Biddles Ltd. and King's Lynn, 1998.

Özkırımlı, Ümut. *Theories of Nationalism: A Critical Introduction.* New York: Palgrave, 2000.

Pagden, Anthony. *Lords of all the World: Ideologies of Empire in Spain, Britain and France, c. 1500–c. 1800.* New Haven: Yale University Press, 1995.

Page, Benjamin I., and Marshall M. Bouton. *The Foreign Policy Disconnect: What Americans Want from Our Leaders but Don't Get*. Chicago: University of Chicago Press, 2006.

Painter, David. "The United States, Great Britain, and Mossadegh." *Pew Case Studies in International Affairs* 332. Washington, D.C.: Institute for the Study of Diplomacy, 1993.

Parla, Taha, and Andrew Davison. *Corporatist Ideology in Kemalist Turkey: Progress or Order?* Syracuse: Syracuse University Press, 2004.

Parsa, Misagh. *Social Origins of the Iranian Revolution*. Oxford: Columbia University Press, 1993.

Patton, Paul (Ed.). *Deleuze: A Critical Reader*. Oxford: Blackwell, 1996.

Payne, Richard J. *The Clash with Distant Cultures: Values, Interests and Force in American Foreign Policy*. Albany: State University of New York Press, 1995.

Pelikan, Jaroslav. *Credo: Historical and Theological Guide to Creeds and Confessions of Faith in the Christian Tradition*. New Haven: Yale University Press, 2005.

———. Radio Interview with Krista Tippett. *Speaking of Faith*, May 21, 2006. Transcript available at http://speakingoffaith.publicradio.org/programs/pelikan/transcript.shtml, accessed May 24, 2006.

Pena-Ruiz, Henri. *Dieu et Marianne: Philosophie de la laïcite*. Paris: Presses Universitaires de France, 1999.

Petito, Fabio, and Pavlos Hatzopoulos (Eds.) *Religion and International Relations: The Return from Exile*. New York: Palgrave Macmillan, 2003.

Pew Forum on Religion and Public Life and the Pew Christian Scholars Program conference on "Theology, Morality, and Public Life." University of Chicago Divinity School, February 25–27, 2003.

Phillips, David L. "Turkey's Dreams of Accession." *Foreign Affairs* 83, no. 5 (September–October 2004): 86–97.

Philpott, Daniel. "The Catholic Wave." *Journal of Democracy* 15, no. 2 (April 2004): 32–46.

———. "The Challenge of September 11 to Secularism in International Relations." *World Politics* 55 (October 2002): 66–95.

———. "The Religious Roots of Modern International Relations." *World Politics* 52 (2000): 206–45.

———. *Revolutions in Sovereignty: How Ideas Shaped Modern International Relations*. Princeton: Princeton University Press, 2001.

Pipes, Daniel. "Same Difference: The Islamic Threat–Part I." *National Review* 46, no. 7 (November 7, 1994): 61–65.

Pirzio-Biroli, Corrado. "Does 'Muslim' Turkey Belong in 'Christian' Europe?" National Press Club, Washington, D.C., January 13, 2005.

Plantinga, Alvin. *Warranted Christian Belief*. New York: Oxford University Press, 2000.

Pocock, J.G.A. "What Do We Mean by Europe?' *Wilson Quarterly* 21, no. 1 (Winter 1997): 12–30.

Pollack, Robert L. "The Sick Man of Europe–Again." *Wall Street Journal*, February 16, 2005, p. A14.

Pomel, Auguste. *Des races indigènes de l'Algérie et du role que leur reservent leurs aptitudes*. Oran: Veuve Dagorn, 1871.

Porpora, Douglas V. "Methodological Atheism, Methodological Agnosticism and Religious Experience." *Journal for the Theory of Social Behaviour* 36, no. 1 (March 2006): 57–75.

Price, Richard, and Christian Reus-Smit. "Dangerous Liaisons? Critical International Relations Theory and Constructivism." *European Journal of International Relations* 4, no. 3 (September 1998): 259–94.

Prodromou, Elizabeth H. "Turkey between Secularism and Fundamentalism?: The 'Muslimhood Model' and the Greek Orthodox Minority." *Brandywine Review of Faith and International Affairs* 3, no. 1 (Spring 2005): 11–22.

Rahnema, Ali. *An Islamic Utopian: A Political Biography of Ali Shariati*. New York: I. B. Tauris, 1998.

Rawls, John. *Political Liberalism*. New York: Columbia University Press, 1993.

Rée, Jonathan. "The Treason of the Clerics." *Nation* 211, no. 2 (August 15, 2005): 31–34.

Remnick, David. "The Experiment: Will Turkey Be the Model for Islamic Democracy?" *New Yorker*, November 18, 2002. http://www.newyorker.com/fact/content/?021118fa_fact, accessed December 21, 2006.

Rémond, René. *Religion and Society in Modern Europe*. Oxford: Blackwell, 1999.

Rich, Paul. "European Identity and the Myth of Islam: A Reassessment." *Review of International Studies* 25 (1999): 435–51.

Rinehart, J. F. "Religion in World Politics: Why the Resurgence?" *International Studies Review* 6 (2004): 271–74.

Robert, Jacques. "*Religious Liberty and French Secularism.*" *Brigham Young University Law Review* 2 (2003): 637–60.

Rosenberg, Justin. *The Empire of Civil Society*. London: Verso, 1994.

Rosenblum, Nancy (Ed.). *Obligations of Citizenship and Demands of Faith: Religious Accommodation in Pluralist Democracies*. Princeton: Princeton University Press, 2000.

Rouleau, Eric. "Turkey's Dream of Democracy." *Foreign Affairs* 79, no. 6 (November–December 2000): 100–114.

Rowland, Darrel, Joe Hallett, and Mark Niquette. " . . . under God, Divisible." *Columbus Dispatch*, May 7, 2006.

Roy, Olivier. *L'échec de l'Islam politique*. Paris: Seuil, 1992.

———. *Vers un Islam européen*. Paris: Editions Esprit, 1999.

Rubin, Barry. "Religion and International Affairs." *Washington Quarterly* 13, no. 2 (1990): 51–64.

Rudolph, Susanne Hoeber, and James Piscatori (Eds.). *Transnational Religion and Fading States*. Boulder: Westview Press, 1997.

Rumelili, Bahar. "Constructing Identity and Relating to Difference: Understanding the EU's Mode of Differentiation." *Review of International Studies* 30 (2004): 27–47.

Sabra, Adam. "What Is Wrong with 'What Went Wrong'?" *Middle East Report Online*, August 2003. http://www.merip.org/mero/interventions/sabra_interv.html, accessed May 16, 2005.

Sachedina, Abdulaziz. *The Democratic Roots of Islamic Pluralism*. New York: Oxford University Press, 2001.

Sahlins, Peter. *Boundaries: The Making of France and Spain in the Pyrenees.* Berkeley: University of California Press, 1989.

Sahliyeh, Emile (Ed.). *Religious Resurgence and Politics in the Contemporary World.* Albany: State University of New York Press, 1990.

Said, Edward W. *Covering Islam: How the Media and the Experts Determine How We See the Rest of the World.* 2nd ed. New York: Vintage Books, 1997.

———. *Orientalism.* New York: Random House, 1987.

Sakallioglu, Ümit Cizre. "Parameters and Strategies of Islam–State Interaction in Republican Turkey." *International Journal of Middle East Studies* 28, no. 2 (1996): 231–51.

Salem, Paul. "The Rise and Fall of Secularism in the Arab World." *Middle East Policy* 4, no. 3 (March 1996): 147–60.

Salvatore, Armando. *Political Islam and the Discourse of Modernity.* Reading, England: Ithaca Press, 1999.

Salvatore, Armando, and Mark LeVine (Eds.). *Religion, Social Practice, and Contested Hegemonies.* New York: Palgrave Macmillan, 2005.

Salzani, Stefano (Ed.). *Teologie politiche islamiche. Casi e frammenti contemporanei.* Milan: Casa Editrice Marietti 1820, 2005.

Sardar, Ziauddin. *Islamic Futures: The Shape of Ideas to Come.* London: Mansell, 1985.

Schacht, Joseph. *An Introduction to Islamic Law.* Oxford: Clarendon Press, 1964.

Schlag, Pierre. "The Problem of the Subject." *Texas Law Review* 69 (1991): 1627–1743.

Schmidt, Helmut. *Die Selbstbehauptung Europas, Perspectiven für das 21. Jahrhundert.* Stuttgart: Deutsche Verlagsanstalt, 2000.

Schmitt, Carl. *Political Theology: Four Chapters on the Concept of Sovereignty.* Translated by George Schwab. Cambridge, Mass.: MIT Press, 1985.

Scott, Catherine V. "Bound for Glory: The Hostage Crisis as Captivity Narrative in Iran." *International Studies Quarterly* 44 (2000): 177–88.

Scott, David. "Conversion and Demonism: Colonial Christian Discourse and Religion in Sri Lanka." *Comparative Studies in Society and History* 34, no. 2 (1992): 333.

Scott, David, and Charles Hirschkind (Eds.). *Powers of the Secular Modern: Talal Asad and His Interlocutors.* Stanford: Stanford University Press, 2006.

Scott, James C. *Seeing Like a State: How Certain Schemes to Improve the Human Condition Have Failed.* New Haven: Yale University Press, 1998.

Secor, Laura. " 'Sands of Empire': Civilizations and Their Discontents." *New York Times Book Review,* June 26, 2005, p. 20.

Seiple, Robert A., and Dennis R. Hoover. *Religion and Security: The New Nexus in International Relations.* New York: Rowman & Littlefield, 2004.

Shah, Timothy Samuel. Testimony Before the House International Relations Committee, United States House of Representatives, October 6, 2004. http://wwwc.house.gov/international_relations/108/sha100604.htm, accessed December 14, 2004.

Shankland, David. *The Alevis in Turkey: The Emergence of a Secular Islamic Tradition.* New York: Routledge Curzon, 2003.

Shapiro, Michael. "Samuel Huntington's Moral Geography." *Theory and Event* 2, no.4 (1999). http://muse.jhu.edu.turing.library.northwestern.edu/journals/theory_andevent/v002/2.4shapiro.html, accessed December 21, 2006.

Shapiro, Michael, and Hayward R. Alker (Eds.). *Challenging Boundaries: Global Flows, Territorial Identities*. Minneapolis: University of Minnesota Press, 1996.

Shepard, Todd. *The Invention of Decolonization: The Algerian War and the Remaking of France*. Ithaca: Cornell University Press, 2006.

Shotter, John. *The Cultural Politics of Everyday Life*. Toronto: University of Toronto Press, 1993.

Sick, Gary. *All Fall Down: America's Tragic Encounter with Iran*. New York: Random House, 1985.

Silverstein, Paul. *Algeria in France: Transpolitics, Race, and Nation*. Bloomington: Indiana University Press, 2004.

Silverstein, Paul, and Chantal Tetreault. "Urban Violence in France." *Middle East Report Online*, November 2005. http://www.merip.org/mero/interventions/silverstein_tetreault_interv.htm, accessed November 28, 2005.

Skinner, Quentin. *The Foundations of Modern Political Thought*. Vol. 2. Cambridge: Cambridge University Press, 1978.

Smith, Anthony D. "The 'Sacred' Dimension of Nationalism." *Millennium: Journal of International Studies* 29, no. 3 (2000): 791–814.

Smith, Christian. *The Secular Revolution: Power, Interests and Conflict in the Secularization of American Public Life*. Berkeley: University of California Press, 2003.

Smith, Christian, and Joshua Prokopy (Eds.). *Latin American Religion in Motion*. New York: Routledge, 1999.

Smith, Steve. "Wendt's World." *Review of International Studies* 26, no. 1 (2000): 151–64.

Smith, Wilfred Cantwell. *Islam in Modern History*. Princeton: Princeton University Press, 1957.

Sontag, Susan (Ed.). *Antonin Artaud: Selected Writings*. Berkeley: University of California Press, 1988.

Spinoza, Benedict de. *Ethics*. Translated by Edwin Curley. New York: Penguin, 2005.

Spruyt, Hendrik. *Ending Empire: Contested Sovereignty and Territorial Partition*. Ithaca: Cornell University Press, 2005.

———. *The Sovereign State and Its Competitors*. Princeton: Princeton University Press, 1994.

Stark, Rodney. "Secularization, R.I.P." *Sociology of Religion* 60, no. 3 (Fall 1999): 249–73.

———. *The Victory of Reason: How Christianity Led to Freedom, Capitalism and Western Success*. New York: Random House, 2005.

Stepan, Alfred. "The World's Religious Systems and Democracy: Crafting the 'Twin Tolerations.'" *Journal of Democracy* 11 (October 2000): 37–57.

Stephanson, Anders. *Manifest Destiny: American Expansion and the Empire of Right*. 5th ed. New York: Hill & Wang, 2000.

Stock-Morton, Phyllis. *Moral Education for a Secular Society: The Development of Morale Laïque in Nineteenth Century France*. Albany: State University of New York Press, 1988.

Stoler, Ann Laura. *Race and the Education of Desire: Foucault's History of Sexuality and the Colonial Order of Things*. Durham, N.C.: Duke University Press, 1995.

Strange, Susan. *States and Markets*. London: Pinter, 1994.

Strauss, Leo. *Liberalism, Ancient and Modern*. Chicago: University of Chicago Press, 1968.

Sylvester, Christine. *Feminist Theory and International Relations in a Post-Modern Era*. Cambridge: Cambridge University Press, 1994.

Tamimi, Azzam, and John L. Esposito (Eds.). *Islam and Secularism in the Middle East*. New York: New York University Press, 2000.

Taylor, Charles. "Modern Social Imaginaries." *Public Culture* 14, no. 1 (2002) 91–124.

———. *Modern Social Imaginaries*. Durham, N.C.: Duke University Press, 2004.

———. *Varieties of Religion Today*. Cambridge, Mass.: Harvard University Press, 2002.

———. "Walls of Separation: A Metaphor Which Has Outlived Its Time." Keynote address, conference on "Theology, Faith and Politics." Northwestern University, Evanston, Illinois, May 13, 2005.

Teitelbaum, Michael S., and Philip L. Martin. "Is Turkey Ready for Europe?" *Foreign Affairs* 82, no.3 (May–June 2003): 97–111.

Telhami, Shibley, and Michael Barnett (Eds.) *Identity and Foreign Policy in the Middle East*. Ithaca: Cornell University Press, 2002.

Teschke, Benno. *The Myth of 1648: Class, Geopolitics and the Making of Modern International Relations*. London: Verso, 2003.

Thomas, Scott M. "Faith, History and Martin Wight: The Role of Religion in the Historical Sociology of the English School of International Relations." *International Affairs* 77, no. 4 (2001): 905–29.

———. *The Global Resurgence of Religion and the Transformation of International Relations: The Struggle for the Soul of the Twenty-First Century*. New York: Palgrave Macmillan, 2005.

———. "Taking Religious and Cultural Pluralism Seriously: The Global Resurgence of Religion and the Transformation of International Society." *Millennium: Journal of International Studies* 29, no. 3 (2000): 815–41.

Tibi, Bassam. "Post-Bipolar Order in Crisis: The Challenge of Politicised Islam." *Millennium: Journal of International Studies* 29, no. 3 (2000): 843–60.

Tocci, Nathalie. "Turkey and the European Union: Preparing for the December 2004 European Council." Working Paper, Mediterranean Programme Workshop, "Brainstorming: Developments in EU-Turkey Relations." Robert Schuman Center for Advanced Studies, European University Institute, Florence, May 7, 2004.

Tocqueville, Alexis de. *Democracy in America*. Translated by George Lawrence. New York: Harper & Row, 1969.

Tschannen, Olivier. "The Secularization Paradigm: A Systematization." *Journal for the Scientific Study of Religion* 30 (1991): 395–415.

Tucker, Robert (Ed.). *The Marx-Engels Reader*. New York: W. W. Norton, 1978.

Turley, Jonathan. "We Wish You a Merry Lawsuit: Santa Brings Lots of Litigation on Religious Symbols." *Los Angeles Times*, December 16, 2002.

Ugur, Mehmet, and Nergis Canefe (Eds.). *Turkey and European Integration: Accession Prospects and Issues*. London: Routledge, 2004.

Uzgel, Ilhan. "Turkey's Triple Transformations: The Self, Ideology, and the State under the Justice and Development Party." Paper presented at the conference on "The Middle East and Central Asia: Authoritarianism and Democracy in the Age of Globalization," University of Utah, Salt Lake City, September 9, 2005.

Valensi, Lucette. *The Birth of the Despot: Venice and the Sublime Porte*. Translated by Arthur Denner. Ithaca: Cornell University Press, 1993.

van der Veer, Peter, and Hartmut Lehmann (Eds.). *Nation and Religion: Perspectives on Europe and Asia*. Princeton: Princeton University Press, 1999.

van Leeuwen, Arend Theodor. *Christianity in World History: The Meeting of the Faiths of East and West*. Translated by H. H. Hoskins. New York: Scribner's, 1964.

Vatter, Miguel. "Strauss and Schmitt as Readers of Hobbes and Spinoza: On the Relation between Political Theology and Liberalism." *New Centennial Review* 4 (Winter 2004): 161–214.

Walker, R.B.J., and Saul H. Mendlovitz (Eds.). *Contending Sovereignties: Redefining Political Community*. Boulder: Lynne Rienner Publishers, 1990.

Waltz, Kenneth N. *Man, the State and War*. New York: Columbia University Press, 1954.

Waterfield, Bruno. "Bolkestein: EU faces implosion risk over Turkey." EUPolitix.com, September 7, 2004. http://www.eupolitix.com/EN/News/200409/0c501627-c886-4fc1-95c2-e49c1945898a.htm, accessed May 16, 2005.

Weber, Eugen. *Peasants into Frenchmen: The Modernization of Rural France, 1870–1914*. Stanford: Stanford University Press, 1976.

Weber, Max. *The Sociology of Religion*. Translated by Ephraim Fischoff. Boston: Beacon Press, 1993.

Wendt, Alexander. *Social Theory of International Politics*. Cambridge: Cambridge University Press, 1999.

Wheatcroft, Andrew. *Infidels: The Conflict between Christendom and Islam, 638–2002*. New York: Viking Press, 2003.

White, Hayden. *The Content of the Form*. Baltimore: Johns Hopkins University Press, 1989.

White, Jenny. *Islamist Mobilization in Turkey: A Study in Vernacular Politics*. Seattle: University of Washington Press, 2002.

———. "Turkey's New 'Muslimhood': The End of 'Islamism'?" *Congress Monthly*, November–December 2003, pp. 6–9.

White, Stephen K. *Sustaining Affirmation: The Strengths of Weak Ontology in Political Theory*. Princeton: Princeton University Press, 2000.

Williams, Michael. "Hobbes and International Relations: A Reconsideration." *International Organization* 50, no. 2 (Spring 1996): 213–37.

Wilson, Bryan. *Religion in Sociological Perspective*. Oxford: Oxford University Press, 1982.

Winters, Paul A. (Ed.). *Islam: Opposing Viewpoints*. San Diego: Greenhaven Press, 1995.

Wittfogel, Karl. *Oriental Despotism: A Comparative Study of Total Power*. New Haven: Yale University Press, 1957.

Wolff, Diane. "Encounter with Islam." *Orlando Sentinel*, February 13, 2005.

Wolterstorff, Nicholas. " 'For the Authorities Are God's Servants': Is a Theological Account of Political Authority Viable?" Comments on paper presented at the Pew Forum on Religion and Public Life and the Pew Christian Scholars Program conference on "Theology, Morality, and Public Life." University of Chicago Divinity School, February 25–27, 2003.

Wood, David M., and Birol A. Yesilada. *The Emerging European Union*. 3rd ed. New York: Pearson Longman, 2004.

Wright, Robin. *The Last Great Revolution: Turmoil and Transformation*. New York: Knopf, 2000.

Wuthnow, Robert. *The Restructuring of American Religion*. Princeton: Princeton University Press, 1988.

Yamane, David. "Secularization on Trial: In Defense of a Neosecularization Paradigm." *Journal for the Scientific Study of Religion* 36, no. 1 (March, 1997): 109–22.

Yavuz, M. Hakan. "Cleansing Islam from the Public Sphere." *Journal of International Affairs* 54, no. 1 (Fall 2000): 21–42.

——— (Ed.). *The Emergence of a New Turkey: Democracy and the AK Parti*. Salt Lake City: University of Utah Press, 2006.

———. *Islamic Political Identity in Turkey*. New York: Oxford University Press, 2003.

———. "Political Islam and the Welfare (*Refah*) Party in Turkey." *Comparative Politics* 30, no. 1 (October 1997): 63–82.

Yavuz, M. Hakan, and John L. Esposito (Eds.). *Turkish Islam and the Secular State: The Gulen Movement*. Syracuse: Syracuse University Press, 2003.

Yilmaz, Ihsan. "Secular Law and the Emergence of Unofficial Turkish Islamic Law." *Middle East Journal* 56, no. 1 (Winter 2002): 113–32.

Young, T. C. (Ed.). *Near Eastern Culture and Society*. Princeton: Princeton University Press, 1951.

Zahedi, Dariush. *Iranian Revolution Then and Now: Indicators of Regime Instability*. Boulder: Westview Press, 2000.

Zerilli, Linda M. G. "Doing without Knowing: Feminism's Politics of the Ordinary." *Political Theory* 26, no. 4 (August 1998): 435–58.

Index

Abrahamian, Ervand, 75, 184n75
Adiver, Advan, 166n56
Akçam, Taner, 189n27
Afary, Janet and Kevin B. Anderson, 185n81.
    See also Foucault, Michel
Afghanistan, 106, 120; *mujahideen* of, 106;
    and Taliban, 11, 120
agent-structure debate, 20
agnosticism, methodological, 18
atheism: methodological, 18; radical as form
    of faith, 19
agonal democracy. *See* democracy
Al-Qaeda, 11, 120, 135
Al Salam Mosque Foundation, 58
Algeria, 55, 72–73, 125; Armed Islamic
    Group (GIA) of, 120; and French colonial-
    ism, 55–57; and War of 1954–62, 55
Allison, Robert, 60, 62, 63, 77, 178n92
'*almaniyah* (secularism or laicism), 15
America. *See* United States
Anderson, Benedict, 52, 158n63, 159n83
Anglo-Iranian Oil Company, 73. *See also* Iran
Appleby, Scott, 37, 163n4
Arendt, Hannah, 45, 175n42
Arjomand, Said Amir, 78, 185n77
Arkoun, Mohammed, 120
Armed Islamic Group (GIA). *See* Algeria
Artaud, Antonin, 162n124
Asad, Talal, 2, 21, 23, 24, 52, 93, 104, 144,
    197n34; and atheism, 19; and authoritative
    discourse, 159n84, 210n11; and definitions
    of sacred, 142; and Europe, 99–100; and Is-
    lamism, 123, 125; and laicism, 30, 33; and
    modernity, 109; and politics of representa-
    tion, 51; and tradition 156n26, 205n96
assumptions of study, 16–20; bicameral ap-
    proach to, 17–20, 160n99
Atatürk, 7, 65, 66, 95, 182n26
atheism, 34; radical, 19
Augustine, Saint, 39
authoritative discourse, 51, 100, 104, 114;
    definition of, 159n184; secularism as, 16,
    45, 49, 91

authority: emergence of postsecular forms of,
    3; genealogy of secularist forms of, 50; and
    international relations theory, 144; and
    Judeo-Christian secularism, 38; laicism as
    form of, 121; secularism as form of, 1, 3, 4,
    12, 31, 148; in relation to Westphalia, 3,
    31; sovereign, 31; theistic account of, 38.
    See also authoritative discourse
Awami Tehreek. *See* Pakistan
Ayoob, Mohammed, 128, 133
Ayubi, Nazih N., 117, 129

Baghdad Pact, 73, 183n53
Baker, Raymond William, 118, 124
Bani-Sadr, Abolhassan, 77, 78
Barber, Benjamin, 126, 127
Barnett, Michael, 2, 45, 183n53
Barnett, Michael, and Raymond Duvall, 1,
    17, 20
Bashiriyeh, Hossein, 76
Bauberot, Jean, 177n73
Bazargan, Mehdi, 77, 78, 80, 102
belief systems: collective, 14; purposive, 14,
    158n65
Bellah, Robert, 41, 170n141
Bennet, Jane, 20, 162n134
Berbers, 56. *See also* France
Berger, Peter, L., 6, 18, 19, 20, 134–35,
    161nn113 and 114
Berger, Peter L. and Thomas Luckman,
    158n61
Berman, Paul, 130, 205n105
Bhabha, Homi, 49
Bill, James, 114–15
Boroujerdi, Mehrzad, 185n97, 196n23
Britain, 55, 73, 104; and colonialism, 55; and
    Egypt, 55; and invasion of Iran, 73; mod-
    ern nationalism in, 104; national identity
    construction of, 176n54; —, in relation to
    Judeo-Christian secularism, 92
Brown, L. Carl, 124, 202n59
Brumberg, Daniel, 185n85, 204n86, 205n102
Bukovansky, Mlada, 8, 14, 32, 45, 105
Bulliet, Richard W., 172n2